INTRODUCTION to
Crisis *and*
Trauma
COUNSELING

edited by
Thelma Duffey and **Shane Haberstroh**

AMERICAN COUNSELING
ASSOCIATION

2461 Eisenhower Avenue, Suite 300 • Alexandria, VA 22314
www.counseling.org

INTRODUCTION to
Crisis and
Trauma
COUNSELING

American Counseling Association
2461 Eisenhower Avenue, Suite 300 • Alexandria, VA 22314

Associate Publisher • Carolyn C. Baker

Digital and Print Development Editor • Nancy Driver

Senior Production Manager • Bonny E. Gaston

Copy Editor • Tyler Krupa

Cover and text design by Bonny E. Gaston

Library of Congress Cataloging-in-Publication Data
Names: Duffey, Thelma, editor. | Haberstroh, Shane, editor.
Title: Introduction to crisis and trauma counseling / edited by Thelma Duffey and Shane Haberstroh.
Description: Alexandria : American Counseling Association, 2020. | Includes bibliographical references and index.
Identifiers: LCCN 2019054174 | ISBN 9781556203770 (paperback)
Subjects: LCSH: Counseling psychology. | Counselor and client. | Crisis intervention (Mental health services)
Classification: LCC BF636.6 .I5797 2020 | DDC 158.3—dc23
LC record available at https://lccn.loc.gov/2019054174

DEDICATION

This book is dedicated to the children and staff at
Sandy Hook Elementary School and their families,
and to the Sutherland Springs community and surrounding areas.

To the Jeremy Richman family and the Mathew Molak family, and to
the counselors and mental health professionals
who walk alongside them.

TABLE OF CONTENTS

PREFACE

Life brings its blessings and its tragedies, and in the midst of it all, growth-fostering, healing relationships can leave an indelible mark on our psyches and in our lives. The literature is replete with data that now show the intrinsic value of supportive therapeutic relationships and the ways in which they can inspire growth and promote healing following devastating losses. As an introductory text to crisis and trauma counseling, we present an integration of cutting-edge, evidence-based theoretical constructs and models used in crisis and trauma work by counselors—such as cognitive behavioral therapy, behavioral therapy, neurofeedback, and mindfulness-based practices—and we underscore the fundamental role that relationship plays in therapeutic healing.

Throughout the course of our more than 15-year collaboration, we (Thelma and Shane) continue to discuss challenges and opportunities related to counseling and the complexities that people face in living life. As referenced in Chapter 11, we have partnered in responding to numerous community traumas and challenges, and we have worked with hundreds of people who have shared their healing journeys with us. We have also researched and published various works and imagined the content and tenor of a book that focused on a counselor's work with crisis and trauma. When we were afforded the opportunity to write this introductory text on crisis and trauma counseling, we had a vision for what we hoped to offer our readers. We also invited the visions of colleagues who generously shared their expertise and experiences related to their practices in crisis and trauma counseling. As you read this text, know that you have a community of scholars and practitioners who share in this most important work with you.

Now, we invite you to think for a moment to a time when you may have desperately wanted to help a client or another person, but in spite of your best efforts, you were unsuccessful. Consider the dynamics that interfered with your ability to truly connect in a way that your client could trust. Perhaps it was hard for your client to trust that she or he could be helped or that you would know *how* to help. Perhaps, the latter may have even been the case. It could also be that your client feared being truly genuine and honest with you, afraid that your judgment would be ultimately painful. Perhaps your client's painful experiences with previous authority figures made it difficult to imagine a different outcome with you. Alternatively, oppressive societal messages could induce shame and mistrust within your client that could make authentic disclosure understandably challenging.

One of the goals of this text is to think about our clients by considering their current and historical social contexts and by exploring nuanced and progressive views of relational dynamics to help navigate the process of healing. We also provide a relational roadmap for how to truly see and be with your clients in ways that take into account the challenges that all relationships, including therapeutic ones, invariably bring. We explore the role that power, privilege, culture, and context play in navigating a growth-fostering therapeutic process in crisis and trauma work.

This book is intended for counselors and mental health professionals interested in learning evidence-based, cutting-edge theories and practices in crisis and trauma counseling, and we introduce a relational framework attuned to offering dignity and respectful care. Relational-cultural theory (RCT) affords dignity and provides theory-grounded guidance to conceptualize the complexities inherent in healing counseling relationships. We also introduce and describe the wide range of modalities used in trauma-specific counseling and trauma-informed care. We believe that readers familiar with RCT will resonate with the growth-fostering principles involved in therapeutic work as applied to crisis and trauma counseling. In addition to evidence-based models frequently used in crisis and trauma work, readers unfamiliar with RCT will be introduced to a progressive counseling theory that informs and complements the numerous evidence-based practices and models included in this text.

Manualized practices offer potential structures for *what* many counselors *do* in crisis and trauma counseling. For example, cognitive processing therapy (Resick, Monson, & Chard, 2014) and trauma-focused cognitive-behavioral therapy (TF-CBT; Cohen, Mannarino, & Deblinger, 2006) outline processes to explore maladaptive trauma-related cognitions and provide steps to desensitize people to the acute distress and avoidance of traumatic memories (Resick et al., 2014). As we outline the informed research base and structure offered by evidence-based treatments, we invite you to share in our commitment to provide relational and creative counseling *with* people living in the immediacy or aftermath of crises and traumas.

A major emphasis in this text explores *how* and *who* we are with people in distress. Chapters 1 and 2 provide a rich framework for conceptualizing the dynamics and processes in relationships that bring life-sustaining connections, authentic experiencing, and shared power. The established literature in counseling and trauma research emphasizes the centrality of the bonds and shared creativity formed in the counseling space. In this introductory preface and throughout the text, we articulate how we see the extant research into the counseling relationship, creativity in counseling, and relational neuroscience support, and we validate the tenets of RCT proposed more than 40 years ago (Miller, 1976).

The Counseling Relationship

Meta-analytic research into counseling outcomes has revealed that when counselors (a) establish and maintain connections with a wide variety of clients, (b) work with people collaboratively and responsively toward mutual goals, and

(c) infuse evidence-based and theoretical constructs naturally and authentically, they most benefit their clients (Wampold, 2015). In fact, Wampold's (2015) research clearly shows that counselors who focus solely on manualized treatments and prescriptive approaches are minimally effective at best. By contrast, Wampold has articulated a contextual model of counseling in which people experience a real relationship in counseling, work toward mutually defined goals, and experience hope that counseling will work for them. These relational principles overwhelmingly predict counseling outcomes and are foundational for crisis and trauma work.

Mutual Empathy

In reviewing how contemporary researchers articulate empathy in counseling, we found that they reiterate what RCT scholars define as mutual empathy (Jordan, 2018). As cited in Wampold (2015, p. 271), Gelso (2014) defined the therapeutic relationship as "the personal relationship between therapist and patient marked by the extent to which each is genuine with the other and perceives/experiences the other in ways that befit the other." Likewise, Bessel van der Kolk (2014) has contended that social reciprocity builds the kind of relational contexts where people can feel safe, connected, and less alone in their suffering. Our social reciprocity (van der Kolk, 2014) and engagement in real counseling relationships (Wampold, 2015) closely reflect what RCT scholars call mutual empathy. Jordan (2018, p. 7) has explained mutual empathy as "I empathize with you, with your experience and pain, and I am letting you see that your pain has affected me, and you matter to me." We navigate this mutuality following principles of relational ethics, and we describe the nuances of ethical connection and mutual empathy in Chapters 1 and 2. When working with people in crisis, or those who have experienced trauma, the mutuality we share and the real connections we support and nourish can begin to invite the potential for hope on the basis of authentic and affirming experiences in the counseling process.

Integrating Creative and Relational Practice With Trauma-Informed Care

Creativity is a key feature in many evidence-based and manualized treatments for trauma. On the TF-CBT training site, the Medical University of South Carolina (n.d.) states that "TF-CBT is best delivered by creative, resourceful therapists who have developed close therapeutic alliances with their clients" (para. 7). Many other prominent cognitive-focused, evidence-based treatments highlight the role of creativity as an effective practice, including cognitive therapy (Beck, 2012), cognitive processing therapy (Resick et al., 2014), and the Cognitive Behavioral Intervention for Trauma in Schools intervention (Jaycox, Langley, & Hoover, 2018). Although manuals and protocols can provide structure and protocols, a counselor's and client's shared creativity fuel the process of counseling (Duffey, Haberstroh, & Trepal, 2016). Finally, expressive and creative approaches—such as movement, music, yoga, dance, play, and art—allow for creative expression of pain that transcends words. Whole body approaches (Porges, 2011) that ignite our inner rhythms through expressive mediums can integrate sensory and fragmented memories, calling on the strength of community when shared in groups (van der Kolk, 2014).

Context, Culture, and Society

Throughout this text, and specifically in Chapter 3, the authors explore how societal messages, cultural norms, and historical and cultural traumas create expectations that can support healing or isolate people from resources and connections that can provide hope. Historical collective traumatic experiences pervade generations of people who suffered abuses of power, disenfranchisement, and rejection of their humanity. Our perceptions and true experiences of powerlessness and injustice resonate throughout cultures and across generations (Yehuda & Lehrner, 2018). These contextual and historical traumas can be seen in physiological markers of health, experiences of well-being, and neurological functioning. Trauma, when experienced collectively, leaves an imprint on society. Fortunately, counselors can provide healing contexts to attenuate these legacies; they can also engage in constructive social action to advocate for and enact compassionate and culturally responsive social change (Hartling & Lindner, 2017).

Relational Neurobiology and Trauma

Our brains evolved to connect and thrive in social contexts where we give and receive care, understanding, and compassionate feedback. In Chapter 4, we provide an overview of the relational brain, and we explore how trauma can disrupt and override our natural responses to stress and create distance in interpersonal relationships (Banks, 2011; Banks & Hirschman, 2015). These disconnections are especially profound when people suffered abuse within their close relationships or in contexts where they expected interpersonal and physical safety (Banks, 2011; Banks & Hirschman, 2015). van der Kolk (2014) explored how our brains and our bodies can harbor the residual memories and emotional impact of trauma; he also contended that connections with others and creative mind-body interventions can bring life, and perhaps feelings of joy, back into a physiology fragmented by traumatic experiences. Many prominent researchers and practitioners have contended that the human brain is neuroplastic and that brain health thrives from bonding and growth-fostering connections throughout the life span (Banks, 2011; Banks & Hirschman, 2015; Porges, 2011, Shapiro, 2018; Siegel, 2015; van der Kolk, 2014). These scholars have articulated therapeutic models that integrate the body and brain in the healing process. Chapter 4 provides an overview of these connections and how these relationships can stimulate growth psychologically and neurobiologically (Banks & Hirschman, 2015).

Approaches and Models Specific to Crisis and Trauma Counseling

As we build on the relational, social, contextual, and neurobiological factors that help us understand and respond to the many forms of traumatic stress, we introduce prominent models and approaches that counselors follow when providing trauma-informed care. We see these approaches as practical and evidence-based pathways for healing that rest on a solid relational foundation. Chapter 5 highlights and explores the many decisional and relational factors involved in providing immediate and responsive care for clients experiencing acute distress. Chapter 6 provides examples and models for working with clients who suffer from the residual effects of traumatic stress, including posttraumatic stress disorder and acute stress disorder. Finally, Chapter 7 reviews factors and approaches involved when working with people experiencing suicidal ideations and plans. As you read through these various approaches and models that outline processes and decision trees found in crisis and posttrauma work, we hope that you conceptualize these models with a deep appreciation for the voluminous evidence supporting the primacy of the counseling relationship.

Developmental and Contextual Considerations in Crisis and Trauma Counseling

As you read Chapters 8–15, we ask you to consider the various losses and tragedies experienced by people, and how counselors offer their hope, resources, training, and presence to partner with them through turbulent times. These chapters offer an overview of the many faces of crises and trauma that occur throughout the life span and within distinct social contexts. For example, we explore a wide range of traumatic experiences—including sexual assault, sexual abuse, child abuse, elder abuse, and other violent acts—in Chapter 8.

In Chapter 9, we honor the many life crises associated with work, parenting, family life, and educational setbacks that can at times compound life stress and wear down people's resilience, especially when they may feel isolated and alone (Jordan, 2018). Likewise, Chapter 10 speaks to various stressors, crises, and traumatic experiences commonly seen in families, such as divorce, infidelity, incest, child abuse, medical emergencies, and substance abuse. Chapter 11 reviews the various community crises that can occur—such as natural disasters, mass shootings, and community violence—and the means by which counselors can respond. Chapter 12 offers counseling considerations when working with veterans, and Chapter 13 offers K–12 information for counselors in the schools. You will also find common crises and traumatic experiences seen on college and university campuses in Chapter 14, as well as ways in which counselors can support students and others in these settings. Finally, in Chapter 15, we offer traditional and progressive perspectives on resilience and the ways in which resilience can be strengthened through relationships and the honoring of all people's dignity.

Compassion and Care for Counselors

As is so often the case for counselors when working with others, we experienced our own losses, transitions, and community traumas and disasters during the writing and editing of this book. Our community neighbor, Sutherland Springs, Texas, experienced a mass shooting at the local Baptist church that destroyed entire families and affected community members far and wide. I (Shane) underwent a significant career and life transition via a major geographic move that not only affected my family and me but also those with whom I had shared life for 15 years. Finally, in the midst of this writing and the significant life-changing events Shane described, I (Thelma) experienced the most painful and significant loss of my life to date—the sudden loss of my precious mother. Crises come in many forms, and sometimes they come in clusters. As we are sure many of you can attest to, finding ways to care for ourselves and our well-being, with the compassion we hope to offer others, is critical to our personal welfare and continued work as counselors. We strongly articulate this message in Chapter 1 and reinforce it throughout the text.

Closing Thoughts

Our vision for this text was to present a most humane perspective on crisis and trauma experiences and to introduce cutting-edge, evidence-based resources and modalities for this work. We hope this text prepares you to conceptualize that experiences of crises and trauma can be interwoven in our lives in many ways. For example, a person may be in the throes of a loss when another turbulent life crisis or trauma arises, compounding the impact. We conclude by reiterating the great need for counselors to be prepared and trained in the complex understandings of crisis and trauma work. Moreover, we trust that this introductory text will provide you with a substantive foundation from which you can continue your growth and expand your potential for this most important counselor-client partnership.

References

Banks, A. (2011). Developing the capacity to connect. *Zygon, 46*(1), 168–182.

Banks, A., & Hirschman, L. (2015). *Four ways to click.* New York, NY: Penguin Random House.

Beck, A. T. (2012, November 7). *Tips for cognitive behavior therapists.* Retrieved from https://beckinstitute.org/tips-for-cognitive-behavior-therapists/

Cohen, J. A., Mannarino, A. P., & Deblinger, E. (2006). *Treating trauma and traumatic grief in children and adolescents* (2nd ed.). New York, NY: Guilford Press.

Duffey, T., Haberstroh, S., & Trepal, H. (2016). Creative approaches in counseling and psychotherapy. In D. Capuzzi & M. D. Stauffer (Eds.), *Counseling and psychotherapy: Theories and interventions* (pp. 445–468). Alexandria, VA: American Counseling Association.

Hartling, L. M., & Lindner, E. G. (2017). Toward a globally informed psychology of humiliation: Comment on McCauley (2017). *American Psychologist, 72,* 705–706. https://doi.org/10.1037/amp0000188

Jaycox, L. H., Langley, A. K., & Hoover, S. (2018). *Cognitive Behavioral Intervention for Trauma in Schools (CBITS)* (2nd ed.). Santa Monica, CA: RAND Corporation.

Jordan, J. V. (2018). *Relational–cultural therapy* (2nd ed.). Washington, DC: American Psychological Association.

Medical University of South Carolina. (n.d.). *Trauma-focused cognitive behavioral therapy (TF-CBT).* Retrieved from https://medicine.musc.edu/departments/psychiatry/divisions-and-programs/divisions/ncvc/programs/project-best/tf-cbt

Miller, J. B. (1976). *Toward a new psychology of women.* Boston, MA: Beacon Press.

Porges, S. W. (2011). *The polyvagal theory: Neurophysiological foundations of emotions, attachment, communication, and self-regulation.* New York, NY: Norton.

Resick, P. A., Monson, C. M., & Chard, K. M. (2014). *Cognitive processing therapy: Veteran/military version: Therapist and patient materials manual.* Washington, DC: Department of Veterans Affairs.

Shapiro, F. (2018). *Eye movement desensitization and reprocessing (EMDR) therapy: Basic principles, protocols, and procedures* (3rd ed.). New York, NY: Guilford Press.

Siegel, D. J. (2015). *The developing mind: How relationships and the brain interact to shape who we are.* New York, NY: Guilford Press.

van der Kolk, B. (2014). *The body keeps the score: Brain, mind, and body in the healing of trauma.* New York, NY: Viking.

Wampold, B. E. (2015). How important are the common factors in psychotherapy? An update. *World Psychiatry, 14,* 270–277. https://doi.org/10.1002/wps.20238

Yehuda, R., & Lehrner, A. (2018). Intergenerational transmission of trauma effects: Putative role of epigenetic mechanisms. *World Psychiatry, 17,* 243–257. https://doi.org/10.1002/wps.20568

ABOUT THE EDITORS

Thelma Duffey, PhD, is professor and chair in the Department of Counseling at the University of Texas at San Antonio (UTSA) and is past president of the American Counseling Association (ACA). An ACA fellow, she is currently serving as ACA treasurer. Professor Duffey was the founding president of the Association for Creativity in Counseling (ACC), a division within the ACA, and she is editor for the *Journal of Creativity in Mental Health.* Professor Duffey has received numerous leadership and research awards from professional organizations, including the Association for Counselor Education and Supervision, the Southern Association for Counselor Education and Supervision, the ACA, the Texas Counseling Association, the Texas Association for Counselor Education and Supervision, and the Association for Assessment and Research in Counseling. The ACC established an award in her name. Professor Duffey has more than 60 peer-reviewed publications and three edited and coedited books: *Creative Interventions in Grief and Loss Therapy: When the Music Stops, a Dream Dies; A Counselor's Guide to Working With Men;* and *Child and Adolescent Counseling Case Studies: Developmental, Systemic, Multicultural, and Relational Contexts.* Her research interests include relational-cultural theory, developmental relational counseling, creativity in counseling, and grief and loss counseling. Professor Duffey provided support and consultation in Newtown, Connecticut, following the shootings at Sandy Hook Elementary School and co-led efforts to provide crisis and trauma services to Sutherland Springs and neighboring communities. Professor Duffey codirects the Academy for Crisis and Trauma Counseling within the Department of Counseling. During her tenure as ACA president, Professor Duffey led a national antibullying and interpersonal violence initiative, and she currently leads efforts within the UTSA Department of Counseling to support the works of the David's Legacy Foundation.

Shane Haberstroh, EdD, is associate professor of counseling in the Department of Educational Psychology at Northern Arizona University (NAU). Before his appointment at NAU, he served as associate professor, assistant department chair, and doctoral program chair at the University of Texas at San Antonio (UTSA). His research focuses on technology in counseling; creativity in counseling; developmental relational counseling; and the losses and recovery processes related to addiction, crises, and traumatic events. Professor Haberstroh is associate editor for the *Journal of Creativity in Mental Health* and has more than 35 published journal articles and book chapters. He is coeditor of *Child and Adolescent Counseling Case Studies: Developmental, Systemic, Multicultural, and Relational Contexts.* Professor Haberstroh is past president of the Association for Creativity in Counseling (ACC) and serves as the ACC's treasurer. He is the recipient of numerous awards, including several awards from the ACC and the AARC/CORE (Association for Assessment and Research in Counseling/ *Counseling Outcome Research and Evaluation*) Outstanding Outcome Research Award. He served on the American Counseling Association (ACA) 20/20: A Vision for the Future of Counseling from 2005 to 2013 and served as the ACC's representative to the ACA Governing Council from 2013 to 2019. Dr. Haberstroh participated in efforts to support the Newtown, Connecticut, community following the Sandy Hook Elementary School shootings. Recently, he worked with colleagues at the UTSA to establish counseling services for the communities affected by the Sutherland Springs shooting. Before working as a faculty member, he worked for 6 years at the Department of Neuropsychiatry, Texas Tech University Health Sciences Center. As a counselor and the associate director of substance abuse services, he led initiatives to integrate substance abuse and mental health treatment in outpatient and inpatient settings.

ABOUT THE CONTRIBUTORS

Deborah Bergmann, MS, works at HopeWise Integrative Mental Health, a private practice specializing in chronic pain, chronic illness, and trauma. Ms. Bergmann also has experience working in primary care behavioral health. She has an undergraduate degree in molecular biology from Yale University and a master's degree in clinical mental health counseling.

Deb Del Vecchio-Scully, LPC, is a licensed professional and nationally certified counselor. She holds American Mental Health Counselors Association diplomat status as a clinical mental health specialist in trauma counseling. She is nationally known as a stress and trauma expert, having worked with survivors of the 9/11 terrorist attacks as well as adults and children affected by the Sandy Hook Elementary School shooting and the Stoneman Douglas school shooting in Parkland. Ms. Del Vecchio-Scully previously served as Clinical Recovery Leader and Trauma Specialist of the Newtown Recovery and Resiliency Team. She is a special advisor to Professionals United for Parkland.

Madelyn Duffey, MA, received a bachelor of arts degree from the University of Colorado at Boulder and a master of arts degree in Southern Studies from the University of Mississippi. Ms. Duffey, a member of Chi Sigma Iota International Honor Society, is a graduate student in the Clinical Mental Health Counseling program at the University of Texas at San Antonio and a student representative on the steering committee for the College of Education and Human Development Center for Student Success.

Katherine A. Feather, PhD, is a licensed professional counselor and an assistant clinical professor in the Department of Educational Psychology at Northern Arizona University. Dr. Feather is experienced in working with people with disabilities—specifically, children diagnosed with autism spectrum disorder (ASD) and adults adjusting to their visual disability. Her research interests include ASD and establishing competencies for the counseling profession, counselors' preparedness to work with people with disabilities, school-to-career transition of students with disabilities, and psychosocial adjustment and family adaptation to a disability.

J. Claire Gregory is a PhD student in the Counselor Education and Supervision program at the University of Texas at San Antonio (UTSA). Ms. Gregory danced professionally with Ballet San Antonio for 7 seasons before working at a non–12 step, mindfulness-based inpatient program as a licensed professional counselor for 2 years. Ms. Gregory's interests include increasing wellness for professional dancers, research creativity in counseling, and neurofeedback. Ms. Gregory is the president of the Neurofeedback Society of UTSA and was selected as a 2019–2020 Emerging Leader for the Association for Creativity in Counseling.

Tonya R. Hammer, PhD, is an associate professor at the Oklahoma State University–Tulsa. She is the director of the Relational-Cultural Theory and Body Image and Disordered Eating Research labs. Dr. Hammer has numerous publications grounded in relational-cultural theory and is a past president of the Association for Lesbian, Gay, Bisexual and Transgender Issues in Counseling.

Linda Hartling, PhD, is director for the Human Dignity and Humiliation Studies and former associate director of the Jean Baker Miller Training Institute at the Stone Center, Wellesley College. Dr. Hartling is the editor for the *Journal of Human Dignity and Humiliation Studies*, coeditor of *The Complexity of Connection: Writings from the Jean Baker Miller Training Institute at the Stone Center*, and author of the Humiliation Inventory. She holds a doctoral degree in clinical-community psychology and has published articles on resilience, substance abuse prevention, shame and humiliation, relational practice in the workplace, and relational-cultural theory. Dr. Hartling is the recipient of the 2010 Research Award presented by the Association for Creativity in Counseling (a division of the American Counseling Association) and has received the Human Dignity Lifetime Award.

Barbara Herlihy, PhD, is a professor in practice in the Department of Counseling at the University of Texas at San Antonio. Currently a counselor educator, she has worked as a counselor in schools, community agencies, and private practice. She has a passion for social justice and transcultural counseling and is the author or coauthor of three current books as well as numerous articles and book chapters on counseling ethics and feminist therapy.

Nathaniel Ivers, PhD, is chair in the Department of Counseling at Wake Forest University and is a licensed professional counselor in North Carolina and Texas. Dr. Ivers has provided counseling and supervision in nonprofit agencies, hospital settings, and college counseling centers. His research interests are related to multicultural counseling competence, bilingual counseling, and the mental health needs of Latinx communities.

Brenda Jones, PhD, has a professional career that spans over 42 years, with 9 years of public school teaching experience, 23 years of professional school counseling experience, and 10 years of serving as a clinical assistant professor. Dr. Jones is a licensed and certified school counselor, a nationally certified counselor, and a licensed professional counselor. Her work has appeared in several professional publications, and she is a frequent presenter at local, state, and national conferences. Professor Jones has received several professional awards during her tenure in academia.

Mark Jones, PhD, is an adjunct professor and the director of the Neurofeedback Training Program at the University of Texas at San Antonio. Dr. Jones has a doctorate in pastoral care and is a licensed professional counselor (LPC), a licensed marriage and family therapist (LMFT), a board-approved LPC and LMFT supervisor, and a trained spiritual director. He is also board certified in neurofeedback and quantitative electroencephalography. He is the author of several books and articles on psychological and spiritual approaches to life and therapy.

Judith V. Jordan, PhD, is the founding director of the International Center for Growth in Connection. She is a founding scholar of relational-cultural theory and holds an appointment as assistant professor in psychiatry at the Harvard Medical School. Dr. Jordan is the recipient of the American Psychological Association's Distinguished Psychologist Award (given to one psychologist each year for outstanding contribution to the field of psychotherapy and psychology.) She is the author of *Relational-Cultural Therapy*; coauthor of *Women's Growth in Connection*; and editor of numerous other books, chapters, and articles.

Meredith Klipple is a PhD candidate at the University of Texas at San Antonio (UTSA) and is a licensed professional counselor intern at the UTSA Academy for Crisis and Trauma Counseling. Ms. Klipple uses relational-cultural theory as the framework for her clinical practice, supervision, and teaching, and her professional experience primarily involves trauma and crisis work.

Evelin Lindner, PhD, is a licensed psychologist, medical doctor, and holder of two PhD degrees: one in psychological medicine and the other in social psychology. She is the founding president of Human Dignity and Humiliation Studies, a global community of concerned academics and practitioners who wish to promote dignity around the world. This work has been nominated for the Nobel Peace Prize in 2015, 2016, and 2017.

Derrick A. Paladino, PhD, is a professor of counseling at Rollins College and has received the Cornell Distinguished Faculty Award. He is a licensed mental health counselor in Florida and holds a nationally certified counselor certification. His areas of expertise are crisis assessment and intervention, multiracial identity, and college counseling and student development theory. In addition to his experience in the field of college crisis counseling, he has served as a Red Cross Disaster Mental Health volunteer. He currently teaches crisis counseling and has presented and written about this topic.

Erin Kern Popejoy, PhD, is an assistant professor at the University of Arkansas with research lines focused on grief and trauma—particularly with military populations—and creativity in counseling and counselor education. She is published in several counseling-related journals and is a frequent presenter at local, state, and national conferences.

Allison Marsh Pow, PhD, is a clinical assistant professor and director of the Nicholas A. Vacc Counseling and Consulting Clinic at the University of North Carolina at Greensboro (UNCG). Dr. Pow received her PhD in counselor education and supervision at UNCG, and she has practiced as a licensed professional counselor for more than 10 years. Her research interests include trauma, crisis, attachment, as well as mentorship and supervision in counseling. Professor Pow's teaching experience includes work at the doctoral, master's, undergraduate, and community college levels.

Vincent Schroder, PhD, holds a doctor of psychology in clinical psychology degree from the American School of Professional Psychology and a master's degree in counselor education from the University of Central Florida. His scholarly interests include emotional trauma, spiritual transformation, modern attachment theory, affective neuroscience, regulation theory, polyvagal theory, and Somatic meditation.

Hope Schuermann, PhD, is a faculty member at the University of Florida in the Counselor Education program. Her clinical work has focused around trauma, specifically natural disaster recovery and child abuse recovery. Professor Schuermann's publications and research focus on trauma and on counselor education pedagogy and supervision.

Elias Zambrano, PhD, is a professor in practice in the Department of Counseling at the University of Texas at San Antonio (UTSA). Dr. Zambrano has more than 40 years of experience as a school counselor and school counseling program administrator. As a district director of counseling services, he was invested in securing the counselor skills and organizational structures needed to provide effective and timely responses to critical incidences in schools. He continues to advocate and lead in these efforts. Dr. Zambrano is currently the codirector for the Academy of Crisis and Trauma Counseling at UTSA.

ACKNOWLEDGMENTS

We feel deeply indebted to the many people whose support and assistance have helped to make this book possible. We are immensely grateful to the American Counseling Association. You afforded us with this rich opportunity to create a textbook that speaks to our passion. We extend our deep appreciation to our authors for generously sharing their most valuable experiences and knowledge with our readers. To the students who provided assistance throughout this work, we are most grateful! Jessica Claire Gregory, Gretchen McClain, Ashley Morgan, and Meredith Klipple, please know how much we so appreciate you! Deb Del Vecchio-Scully, your invitation to support the community of Newtown began what has come to be a life-changing trajectory. Thank you for partnering with us on this healing journey. Jeremy Richman, you introduced us to the concept of brain health in your inspiring keynote speech at the American Counseling Association conference in Montreal. Your kindness, courage, and relentless dedication to creating a world of compassion and safety through the Avielle Foundation will live on through those you touched. We promise this. Matthew and Maurine Molak, your visionary work with the David's Legacy Foundation to create safe places in schools and online is changing the lives of children every day.

And to Judy Jordan, your inspirational leadership in codeveloping relational-cultural theory (RCT) is something for which we are immensely grateful. RCT provides a home base for countless counselors and mental health professionals, and your chapter on counseling relationships is integral to our message of hope and healing. Linda Hartling and Evelin Lindner, it is an immense honor to include your most gracious contributions in this text. In a time when hurt and injury are rampant across the globe, we are grateful for your message of global inclusion and compassion as well as your life-changing work with the Human Dignity and Humiliation Studies.

To our clients, students, colleagues, and friends, we thank you for helping create a space where connection and goodness prevail. And to our families, it is because of your support, inspiration, and love that we do the work we do. You inspire, motivate, and support us, and for that we are deeply grateful.

CHAPTER 1

Introduction to Crisis and Trauma Counseling

Thelma Duffey and Shane Haberstroh

There are critical incidences and traumatic events that occur daily in the lives of unsuspecting people. Every day, women, men, and children are in the midst of living their lives when, much to their horror, crises arise in their homes, schools, workplaces, and communities. Illnesses, accidents, job layoffs, and sudden deaths occur, seemingly out of nowhere, and people are plunged into crisis. Far too often, communities and the larger world experience critical events and tragedies of significant proportions. When these calamities occur, the media instantaneously broadcasts images of mass murders, war, and acts of terrorism and violence. These tragedies create unimaginable images in the psyches of contemporary society.

Introduction to Key Terms and Philosophies

Crisis

By definition, a *crisis* is often an immediate, unpredictable event that occurs in people's lives—such as receiving a threatening medical diagnosis, experiencing a miscarriage, or undergoing a divorce—that can overwhelm the ways that they naturally cope. People can experience crises individually or as part of a group, community, or other connected system (James & Gilliland, 2013; Myer & Moore, 2006). Crisis experiences often compromise people's feelings of safety and can induce feelings of fear, sadness, and even a sense of devastation. Crises can also interfere with a person's ability to function in the world by negatively affecting several life domains, such as work, family, and social connections. Crises can aggravate existing emotional injuries, further obstructing a person's ability to respond to the incident. This aggravation can lead to a person's sense of hypervigilance following a painful and unexpected violation of trust and safety. This violation can increase the intensity of a person's feelings, resulting in a deepened experience of anger, anxiety, guilt, and grief. Furthermore, the "intensity, duration, and suddenness" (James & Gilliland, 2013, p. 8) of an experience may result in a person's experience of trauma.

Trauma

Trauma involves an emotional, mental, and physical response to a powerfully negative experience or series of situations in which people perceived that they or a loved one experienced serious psychological, physical, or emotional harm (Substance Abuse and Mental Health Services Administration [SAMHSA], 2014). Trauma can result from an event or a series of events that subsequently causes intense physical and psychological stress reactions (SAMHSA, 2014). These experiences can include violence, sexual assault, abuse, neglect, disaster, terrorism, and war. Chronic abuse, abandonment, a tragic loss of a loved one, or war experiences, for example, can all result in trauma that can be both enduring and complex. In those cases in which *complex trauma* exists, a person experiences serious stressors that "(a) are repetitive or prolonged, (b) involve harm or abandonment by caregivers or other ostensibly responsible adults, and (c) occur at developmentally vulnerable times" (Ford & Courtois, 2009, p. 13).

These stressors can also involve complex interpersonal traumatic experiences such as betrayal, loss, rejection, and relational violence. People suffer trauma individually and within their communities. These tragedies, and the trauma that ensues, may upend the emotional, physical, and relational landscapes of communities, resulting in generational trauma—at times altering the fabric of that community for years to come (Dupré, Dawe, & Barling, 2014). In fact, history has shown how traumas and crises have helped shape the values of nations, diverse cultural groups, and generations throughout the years (Martz, 2010). As a result, these societal, cultural, and familial messages often guide an individual's response to crises and trauma and can either derail or facilitate healing (Duffey, 2005; Hartling & Lindner, 2016). Every day, professional counselors assist people as they navigate life crises and the immediate and acute aspects of traumatic events and loss (McAdams & Keener, 2008).

Conceptualizing Crisis and Trauma

One of the purposes of this text is to practically identify the many faces of crisis, the ways in which crises can occur, and the relational processes that counselors can use when working through crises and traumatic injuries. We also explore important distinctions between crises and trauma because, although these terms are at times used interchangeably, there are clear differences that distinguish one from the other. Recognizing and understanding these differences is important to the work of counseling.

For example, although most people experience crises in their lives (e.g., relationship loss, acute illness, job loss, academic disappointments), not every crisis is followed by trauma. In other words, crises, in and of themselves, do not constitute a trauma, and they do not always lead to traumatic responses. In contrast, trauma can be seen as a profound and often overwhelming response to a critical loss or injury, such as accidents, deaths, and acts of violence.

Although crises tend to resolve over time, people undergoing trauma may continually experience flashbacks and other debilitating symptoms, such as nightmares, as well as physical, emotional, spiritual, and social concerns. Trauma can also result in a pattern of acute anxiety, depression, and posttraumatic stress. Like many loss situations, traumatic injuries can affect a person's personal relationships; behavioral, sleep, and nutritional patterns; and ability to function in life. Empathic, informed, relational, and skilled professional counseling can support people undergoing periods of crises and experiences of trauma.

Trauma-Informed Care (TIC)

TIC is a model used by counselors and institutions to place trauma assessment, treatment, and recovery as a primary goal for counseling. SAMHSA, an agency within the U.S. Department of Health and Human Services, discussed how TIC involves using every person within an organization—from the president or chief executive officer of a company to the maintenance person, and everyone in between—in the service of health and healing. All parties involved recognize the role of trauma in a person's life and understand that people use diverse coping mechanisms to deal with trauma. TIC also involves working with the whole being of a person, taking trauma history into account and considering the person's coping mechanisms. TIC recognizes that trauma can affect a person's interpersonal functioning, including interaction with others, work performance, and sleep patterns (SAMHSA, 2014).

This model considers the way that trauma can influence a person's daily responses to events, potentially including isolation, anxiety, substance misuse, and over- or undereating that can increase health risks (SAMHSA, 2014). A person's functioning and emotional, physical, social, and spiritual health can be affected. SAMHSA described how a person's mind and body can be stuck in a state of threat when experiencing trauma because the brain is unable to filter information temporally and contextually. This condition can result in an impaired sense of self and disconnection, not only from one's body but also from others. Disconnection can lead to a person's distressing reactions to a traumatic event, including intrusive memories, images, thoughts, and dreams as well as a sense of feeling numb and dissociated. When faced with cues or triggers that mirror the trauma event, a person may react as if the trauma is happening in that moment. This experience can be perpetually devastating. As a result, a counselor's compassion, responsiveness, and resourcefulness can bring needed support and relief.

The Relational Foundation for Crisis and Trauma Counseling

Numerous theories related to crisis and trauma counseling support counselors in this important work, and we offer a description and applications of the more prevailing theories in the following chapters. We also discuss outstanding resources in subsequent chapters, such as the American Red Cross, the American Counseling Association (ACA), and the National Child Traumatic Stress Network. In this chapter, however, we introduce the works of the Jean Baker Miller Training Institute and the Human Dignity and Humiliation Studies (HumanDHS); moreover, we identify these works and SAMHSA's TIC model as foundational to this text.

This book is structured to provide counselors and mental health professionals with current essential information and examples of practical application to crisis and trauma counseling. Relationally framed, we emphasize (a) the power of the connections counselors form with people in crisis and as they work through traumatic experiences; (b) an intentional focus on safeguarding a person's dignity throughout the work; (c) the relational, societal, political, and cultural contexts that affect a person's experience of crisis and trauma; (d) the various contexts in which crises and trauma arise; and (e) the diverse means by which counselors can intervene and support people who face them.

We invited scholars and practitioners experienced in working with crisis and trauma situations to contribute to this book, and together, we draw on our practices and research as we discuss the many dynamics of crisis and trauma and strategies to promote hope and healing. With the exception of publicly documented crises addressed in this text, the case examples we use throughout the book are compilations of actual client stories, de-identified to protect confidentiality. Our goal is to provide you with guiding theories and interventions for working with crisis and trauma situations while underscoring the role of humane connection as a most salient feature of crisis and trauma counseling.

Relationship is at the core of counseling, as indicated in its definition (Kaplan, Tarvydas, & Gladding, 2014), and research speaks to the primary role of relationship in therapeutic success (Norcross & Wampold, 2018). It is therefore essential that counselors explore the means by which healing and compassionate relationships are formed, which is particularly salient when working with people following traumatic losses. We offer leading theoretical constructs focused on crisis and trauma counseling and integrate guiding relational principles throughout this text. Judith V. Jordan—renowned scholar and cofounder of the Jean Baker Miller Training Institute, which is home to relational-cultural theory (RCT)—also provides a detailed description of the role of connection in Chapter 2. We begin our discussion with a brief overview of RCT.

RCT

Counseling theories provide frameworks to understand the human experience. At the most fundamental level, our theoretical perspectives guide the questions we ask, the way we relate to our clients, and how we conceptualize the counseling process. RCT is based on the early works of Jean Baker Miller, who recognized that traditional psychological theories largely ignored the emotional needs of women and marginalized groups (Jordan, 2018; Miller, 1976). Miller (1976) discussed how these clinical models emphasized separation from others as key to human development (Hartling & Sparks, 2008; Jordan, 2017). In response, she documented what she saw as the undervalued, yet indisputable, relational strengths of women in her book, *Toward a New Psychology of Women* (Miller, 1976).

Her work with other RCT founding scholars at the Stone Center at Wellesley College evolved into a theory that identified the importance of authentic, mutual connection as particularly relevant to the experiences of marginalized groups. Since then, scholars have explored the unique challenges facing many men societally and have described RCT in application to counseling men (Duffey & Haberstroh, 2014). RCT's focus on (a) the importance of growth through connection, (b) the societal and cultural influences that affect people's responses to life and to one another, (c) the role of power and privilege, and (d) the means by which these factors affect a person's response to trauma and resilience make it a progressive theory relevant to working with men, women, and children.

Relational Principles

Relational Neuroscience

RCT's theoretical principles, particularly as they relate to trauma work, are supported by neuroscientific findings showing that human beings are "wired for connection" (Banks & Hirschman, 2015). Dr. Amy Banks, director of Advanced Training at the Jean Baker Miller Institute at Wellesley Centers for Women, has referred to this principle as *relational neuroscience.* Relational neuroscience addresses the impact of interpersonal exchanges on the brain and identifies the impact of trauma on a person's neurobiological structure and changing brain chemistry. This change can affect the ways that people who experience trauma interact with others.

For some people who have already suffered compounded losses after trauma, recognition of brain change and its potential impact on relationships can be discouraging. Fortunately, research has indicated that people's brains have the capacity to regenerate and heal. Scientists refer to this occurrence as the brain's neuroplasticity (Banks & Hirschman, 2015). An awareness that growth-fostering connection with others (Jordan, 2018) and relational counseling experiences can promote brain health and influence neuroplasticity (Banks & Hirschman, 2015; Jordan, 2018) brings hope to people with trauma experiences and direction to their counselors. These concepts are addressed in Chapter 4.

Growth in Connection

According to RCT, the nature of a person's relationships deeply influences one's psychological development across the life span (Miller, 2008). Furthermore, mutually rewarding social connections facilitate emotional growth and a desire for continued connection (Banks, 2006, 2011, 2016; Lenz, 2016). The concept of *growth in connection* diverges from traditional psychological approaches that purport independence from others as a cornerstone to growth. In a sense, RCT reinforces the idea that people need one another, and it introduces a model that proposes how people indeed grow in relationship. This paradigm is particularly salient given that the United States, as a culture, commonly privileges stoicism and rugged individualism and often views presenting pain or expressing need as weakness (O'Malley, Arbesman, Steiger, Fowler, & Christakis, 2012).

Authenticity
In contrast, RCT recognizes the courage and strength involved in authenticity, and it identifies *authenticity*—the ability to represent oneself fully in relationship—as central to growth (Jordan, 2018). We believe that RCT's reframing, and a counselor's conceptualization of the client through this lens, provides a source of direction, hopefulness, and relief for people in crisis.

Context

Professional counselors and mental health clinicians using relationally competent principles consider the life circumstances and contextual factors that affect their clients. Context helps counselors look at all sides of a situation, and it brings perspective to behaviors, attitudes, and feelings that could otherwise be pathologized. For example, far too many women with trauma histories are disproportionately misdiagnosed with borderline personality disorder (BPD; Cloitre, Garvet, Weiss, Carlson, & Bryant, 2014; Lewis & Grenyer, 2009). We have worked with several women who held tightly to this BPD diagnosis after receiving it from former mental health professionals. Some of these women may experience "unstable relationships with others, efforts to avoid real or imagined abandonment, identity disturbances, [and other symptomology]" (American Psychiatric Association, 2013, p. 663), which are characteristically seen in BPD. In many of these cases, however, these women also have a history of exploitation, abuse, domination, and other misuses of power. These histories bring context to their diagnoses, and counselors can conceptualize their situations using a trauma-informed (SAMHSA, 2014) and relational lens.

Although diagnoses of BPD can be appropriate, there are several cases in which posttraumatic stress disorder (PTSD) is a more appropriate and realistic diagnosis (Cloitre et al., 2014; Lewis & Grenyer, 2009). For example, there is context to the way these women respond to situations, and their relationships, and focusing on these contexts may help them begin to understand their responses from a perspective that Jordan, Kaplan, Miller, Stiver, and Surrey (1991) described as an "internalized deficiency model of women" (p. 26). In these cases, women who internalize these deficiencies have difficulty noticing their own strengths and values, and "they end up believing the way they think and feel is unimportant" (Jordan et al., 1991, p. 27). This dynamic can set a woman up to carry a distorted sense of her own value.

Reconceptualizing client concerns from a strength-based, relational lens provides clients with an opportunity to face their crises or revisit their traumatic histories with self-compassion and a perspective that can support posttraumatic growth (Jordan, 2017; Kress, Haiyasoso, Zoldan, & Trepal, 2018), making the contextual aspect of RCT especially relevant to crisis and trauma counseling. See Sidebar 1.1 for more information on RCT.

Power

RCT examines the difference between *power-with* and *power-over.* Power-with reflects a shared power, whereas power-over involves exploitation, control, or dismissiveness. These dynamics can be played out within supervisory and personal relationships as well as in exploitive business dealings.

Central Relational Paradox

RCT shows that in spite of people's yearning for connection, they sometimes engage in protective, but disconnecting, strategies that prevent their desired con-

Sidebar 1.1 • Relational-Cultural Theory

Relational-cultural theory posits that people need healthy and meaningful connections in their lives for growth. Research now shows how the brain is actually wired to desire connection with others and can even grow from healthy connections. With this in mind, how do you instill this hope with your clients?

nections. People may hide how they feel or think to maintain some semblance of life-giving relationship.

Strategy for Disconnection and Strategy for Survival

Given the protective nature of these disconnections, RCT conceptualizes these strategies for disconnection as also being strategies for survival. When people undergo chronic disconnection and worry that further attempts to connect will be met with more rejection or loss, they may behave in ways that keep them out of connection, even though connection is what they truly desire. They may act this way because they see themselves as essentially unfit for connection, or they fear being seen as unfit. In these cases, they may hide aspects of themselves that they consider defective, which results in forsaking their true nature to sustain a relationship or connection. Tragically, these efforts can result in continued disconnection and isolation.

Condemned Isolation

When loss through disconnection becomes chronic, or when people are alone in their experiences without support, they may experience what RCT refers to as *condemned isolation*, which RCT contends is the "greatest form of human suffering" (Jordan, 2008, 2017; Miller, 1976; Pompeo-Fargnoli, 2017, p. 65).

Relational Resilience

In contrast, when genuine relational connections are available and people are able to process their experiences in an environment of safety and respect, they are better able to experience what RCT refers to as *relational resilience* (Jordan, Walker, & Hartling, 2004, p. 32). Linda Hartling, former director of the Jean Baker Miller Training Institute and current director of HumanDHS, and Evelin Lindner, the founding president of HumanDHS (Hartling & Lindner, 2016), coauthor Chapter 15, which focuses on this important topic. Resilience is experienced in relation to others; therefore, RCT counselors acknowledge connection and mutuality as invaluable resources in their work with individuals experiencing crisis and trauma (Banks, 2006, 2016; Kress et al., 2018).

Relational Ethics

RCT counselors live out their steadfast commitment to the well-being of the client, which is at the heart of RCT, by practicing relational ethics. Relational ethics is a relatively new perspective that is less widely known than the mainstream approach called principle ethics, which is rule based and rooted in certain "absolute" moral principles. In principle ethics, counselors are taught to ask themselves "what should I do?" when faced with an ethical issue, whereas relational ethicists ask themselves "who should I be?" in this relationship with this client. In relational ethics, the focus is on the actor rather than the action (Remley & Herlihy, 2020).

Principle ethics privileges an ethical decision-making process that is linear, paternalistic, dispassionate, universal, and abstract. By contrast, relational ethics values a process that is holistic, mutual, intuitive, compassionate, personal, and contextual. Rather than searching for answers using a step-by-step, decision-making model, relational ethics instructs counselors to be comfortable with the contextual nuances of ethical decision making and to engage clients in this process (Birrell & Bruns, 2016). Finally, rather than taking a mental and emotional step back as the authority to determine and remedy ethical issues, relational ethics teaches counselors to remain fully present in the moment with their clients, engaging them in the process.

This is not to say that counselors applying relational ethics do not follow a logical mind-set or minimize professional standards. On the contrary, counselors following a relational ethical model respect both logic and mutuality when navigating ethical dilemmas. This approach is in contrast to models that promote searching for a universal principle that can be applied to a generalized "other" (Benhabib, 1987). In some respects, relational ethics makes greater demands on counselors because they cannot find answers by simply applying a model or consulting a code (Birrell & Bruns, 2016). However, this approach helps counselors to better grasp the client's inner world and create a power-with dynamic that strengthens connection and fosters healing.

Counselor Compassion, Responsiveness, and Resourcefulness in Crisis and Trauma Counseling

Think for a minute to a time when you experienced an event that was outside of your control—an experience that may have felt like a punch to the stomach or an unexpected turn of events that some would consider debilitating. Imagine there was a counselor present. Now consider what that counselor could say or do that would, at least in part, create some sense of safety in that moment. You might imagine being comforted, heard, validated, and supported by your counselor. You might also imagine feeling connected with your counselor as you access and brainstorm your shared resources and strengths. Perhaps you can imagine feeling truly cared for and understood as you sort through the shock and loss of this experience. What could the counselor say or do that would communicate an understanding of your pain? What could the counselor do to communicate care and compassion?

Although people vary in the ways they express and receive compassion during times of injury or distress, they all need it. Counselor compassion, responsiveness, and resourcefulness are all vital to any experience with clients undergoing crises and traumatic experiences. Recognizing their impact is an integral part of serving clients in crisis and trauma situations.

Compassion

The Dalai Lama XIV was quoted as saying, "If you want others to be happy, practice compassion. If you want to be happy, practice compassion" (Dalai Lama & Cutler, 2009, p. 18). Compassion is an experience that can move the hearts of those who feel it and those who receive it. Gilbert and Choden (2013) described a counselor's compassion as being particularly relevant, defining it as "a way to develop the kindness, support, and encouragement to promote the courage we need—to take the actions we need—to promote the flourishing and well-being of ourselves and others" (p. 98). This process involves connecting with another's experience, feeling it, and wishing to make a difference in the experience.

Neff (2011) also offered a conceptual framework for understanding compassion. Much like the experience of RCT's mutual empathy, in which the counselor is able to communicate to a client a sense of truly being moved and affected by the client's experience (Jordan et al., 2004), Neff described the first step in experiencing compassion for others as *noticing the suffering*. Do we notice someone's pain? Are we truly attuned to the other person's experience? We cannot overlook the experience of a person whose experience is far different from ours and also believe we feel compassion. Without connecting in that way, we cannot connect with how difficult it may be to stand in that person's shoes (Neff, 2011). Neff used the word "compassion" to describe the experience of "suffering with." Through this connection, we feel a sense of warmth, caring, and the yearning to support the suffering person (Neff, 2011). In other words, we recognize and connect with the person's inherent humanity as well as our own advocacy and sense of making a difference.

Responsiveness and Anticipatory Empathy

Judith V. Jordan highlighted the importance of counselors' responsiveness in her discussions on anticipatory empathy. Jordan (2017) described responsiveness as involving a mutual interplay in which counselors use their emotional response to promote the well-being and growth of clients. For example, as counselors, we reflect on and anticipate how our responses may affect our clients. We notice, care, and solicit feedback from clients on how our actions affect them. Feedback is central to a framework delineated within developmental relational counseling, a model that provides a graphic illustration or roadmap for counselors to identify and consider their connection to their compassion and clarity, as well as their awareness of self and others, through feedback (Duffey & Haberstroh, 2012).

On a practical level, what are the ways in which counselors can respond to clients in crisis? For one, counselors working in crisis and trauma counseling recognize the devastation of loss as experienced in their clients' lives and work with clients accordingly. For example, in the immediate aftermath of a trauma or crisis, counselors attend to a person's loss of control, desire for safety, and basic needs (Zaleski, Johnson, & Klein, 2016). Counselors working with clients facing critical events focus on issues such as creating safety, assessing needs, providing human connection during a perilous time, and connecting clients with resources.

These responses differ in some ways from treatment for PTSD and other long-term mental health care needs, also discussed throughout the book. For example, counselors engaged in long-term trauma work, such as treating PTSD, also consider the impact of trauma on the brain and offer resources and interventions grounded in relational neuroscience and principles (Banks, 2011, 2016). Trauma work may also focus on helping clients reevaluate their beliefs about the trauma and, through genuine relating and mutual empathy (Banks, 2016), cope with feelings they expected to diminish over time (Mackinnon & Derickson, 2013).

Crisis and trauma work, being systemic in nature, involves not only considering the needs of the client, family, or larger community, but also the readiness and the timely appropriateness of the counselor's presence and intervention. Counselors, by profession, often feel a desire to intervene and offer support when a need exists. Many times, this support is helpful, and the compassionate response is welcome. However, counselors must be attuned to the desires of the communities and respect the resources within the communities as capable and well equipped.

We (Thelma and Shane) considered these factors when we supported the work in Newtown, Connecticut. These factors were also important for us to remember when we were asked to participate in the counseling recovery services during the aftermath of the mass shootings in Sutherland Springs, Texas. In both cases, we offered support when needed and responded to requests as communicated. It is important that counselors should not assume that a community is ready for, or receptive to, outside support. Rather, counselors can stay abreast of the reported needs of the community, connect with the local resources (such as the American Red Cross or other community agencies) and coordinate any efforts that involve travel to communities in crisis. See Sidebar 1.2 for more information on community trauma.

Although manualized practices exist and are reported in this text, the authenticity, responsiveness, and creativity that counselors cultivate attune them to the losses in their clients' world. This attunement supports a counselor's work with clients facing crises and trauma, recognizing that, for some, their world has shattered (Duffey, 2005; Duffey & Haberstroh, 2014).

Counselor Wellness in Crisis and Trauma Counseling

Counseling as a profession requires both authenticity and empathy, with a goal being to promote healing and growth. Research has consistently demonstrated that the quality of the therapeutic relationship is more predictive of counseling outcomes than any other factor (Ardito & Rabellino, 2011; Lambert & Barley, 2001; Norcross & Wampold, 2018). Because counselors, as relatable and trustworthy people, are an essential component of effective counseling, it is vital that they nourish their own wellness. Wellness, from a counseling perspective, involves integrating the body, mind, and spirit of a person while connecting with the larger community (Myers, Sweeney, & Witmer, 2000). In other words, when counselors invest in their own wellness, health, and care, they increase the potential for connection with their clients and become more attentive and creative in their work. Clients experiencing trauma and seeking counseling need and deserve their counselors' full and available resources. They need and deserve a genuine connection with their counselors, making self-care an important counselor responsibility.

As counselors, we can better prepare for trauma and crisis counseling by recognizing our own needs and prioritizing wellness and self-care in our own lives. Self-care can be as simple as walking outside on a sunny day to take in some vitamin D rays while feeling the warmth of the sun on our faces. Perhaps, self-care can involve talking on the phone with a loved one or someone with whom we can laugh and share. Recognizing what brings us joy is an important job for a counselor—taking part in activities that do so are vital.

Research has indicated that higher levels of wellness relate to higher levels of job satisfaction when counseling clients with trauma (Foreman, 2018). Counsel-

Sidebar 1.2 • Community Trauma

A community trauma may affect how members of the community see the world and how they respond with each other. What type of community trauma can you think of that has changed a group's outlook on life?

ors' intentional focus on wellness, their access to supportive trauma-informed systems, and a grounded awareness of their thoughts, feelings, and visceral reactions may serve to buffer them from being overwhelmed, avoidant, and rejecting of detailed and horrific accounts shared by clients. Counselors and clients alike can experience secondary or vicarious trauma when hearing about the terrible and heart-wrenching events shared by others. Vicarious trauma can leave counselors with an altered view of themselves and can cause them to reevaluate whether they see the world as a safe place (Foreman, 2018).

When, as counselors, we experience vicarious trauma and do not practice self-care, we run the risk of developing impairments and decrease our opportunities to productively connect with our clients or lead the lives we intend. The *ACA Code of Ethics* (ACA, 2014) speaks to these issues and requires us to monitor our clinical effectiveness and to reflect on our level of functioning in our work with clients. If we do not engage in these reflections, we may cause harm to our relationship with our clients and their progress, and we may also become negatively affected by the traumatic stories they bring (Foreman, 2018).

Research on counselor wellness is growing in the literature, and it is important that counselors continue to understand ways to create better balance in their lives. The indivisible self model, which is an evidence-based wellness model in which counselors are used as participants (Myers & Sweeney, 2008), has produced interesting findings. Research has indicated that counselors-in-training have higher levels of wellness when they participate in a wellness class as part of their academic training (Myers & Sweeney, 2008). By using resources such as the indivisible self model, counselors can identify where they stand in their own wellness development (Myers & Sweeney, 2008). Given the avocation of counseling as a career, and the research that demonstrates that counselors involved in career-sustaining behaviors of balancing professional and personal life thrive (Lawson & Myers, 2011), self-care becomes an increasingly important priority. When we, as counselors, spend time with loved ones and exercise self-awareness, we are better able to navigate the challenges of trauma counseling and experience higher levels of wellness (Lawson & Myers, 2011).

Technology and Chronic Media Exposure During Times of Crisis and Trauma

On September 11, 2001, I (Thelma) awoke to a crisis situation that connected me to a gut-wrenching primal pain I will never forget. My son, Rob, was studying at New York University as a freshman, minutes from the World Trade Center, and his father, Mike, was in Washington, DC. News commentators were frantically describing the terrorist attacks on the World Trade Center and then the Pentagon. I was at home in Texas, and with thousands of miles between us, I was besieged by media accounts of such graphic proportions that I could barely contain myself.

Thankfully, I heard from Mike early in the day, but we did not know our son's fate for most of the day. With profound gratitude, I can report that my son survived that experience intact. Knowing we would be frantic, Rob hurriedly sent an email message that morning, letting his father and me know that he was okay. However, until we received the message, and for hours that felt like a lifetime, images of the Twin Towers captured by the media personally terrorized me and those around me. Days later, I met a new client whose close friend died in the Twin Tower bombings. As she described the televised images she saw of the streets in New York, and as she relayed how horrified and grief stricken she was by the graphic and intrusive images of people attempting to escape, I recalled the graphic depictions that had haunted my own thoughts just days before.

In the current era, technology connects people with information instantaneously. When the news is critical or tragic, the media can be the means by which people first hear devastating news that can rock their worlds and change their lives forever. Even people who are not directly affected by the reported events can experience vicarious trauma in the blink of any eye (Comstock & Platania, 2017). Although people are often cautioned to minimize exposure to these events, cell phones and social media make avoiding exposure to tragic events or mass violence challenging. Keep in mind that research has shown that limiting exposure to electronic media can help to reduce vicarious trauma in adults and children (Hamblen, 2016; Wang et al., 2006). However, technology often plays a central role in people's lives. It is deeply important that counselors recognize the impact of this exposure on their clients and themselves.

Furthermore, understanding the recommendations of groups, such as ACA (2014), surrounding use of technology during critical incidences and traumatic events is critical. These recommendations include attending to physical and emotional needs, seeking support when needed, monitoring media exposure, and engaging in familiar and historically successful activities or coping strategies while remembering what it is that provides comfort and makes life meaningful. Finally, we encourage all counselors to seek help if the experience becomes unmanageable (Dailey, n.d.). Remember that a safe and trustworthy therapeutic relationship, coupled with interventions and approaches geared toward healing and resiliency, can provide comfort and hope in the midst of chaos and trauma.

Case Example and Applications for Hope and Healing

The community in which we live is now grief stricken by the suicide of a beloved, bright-eyed, and brilliant young man of 16, "David," who was victim to the brutal and traumatic bullying behaviors of his peers. Despite his family's attempts to intervene and protect David through every means possible, David could not escape the pain of social exclusion and humiliation, taunting, and ridicule. First perpetuated on the school grounds, and later in cyberspace following his transfer to another school, these experiences proved too traumatic for David to bear.

Consider the crisis to a family in knowing that one of their children is hurt in this way. Bullying and acts of interpersonal violence create crisis situations and traumatic injuries that can result in a ripple effect of pain and devastation for those directly inflicted, for those who love them, and for the communities in which they live. Trauma is not only experienced within the family but also within the community and, via technology, within communities worldwide.

David's loss was unimaginable for both his family and the community that loved him. His story touched the lives of people far and wide. In fact, when I (Thelma) served as president of ACA, I selected antibullying and interpersonal violence as a presidential initiative. In the midst of that work, I heard of David's passing. Horrified by this tragic loss, I took his story across the nation, and hundreds of counselors participated in these antibullying efforts. Moreover, as a result of his family's efforts and those of community members and legislators, a new law exists (Senate Bill 179, formerly known as David's Law, 2017) within the state of Texas designed to protect children in schools against bullying.

In addition to the law, David's family and volunteers travel statewide to present information to teachers, students, administrators, and parents, with a goal of protecting children from this devastating injury. David's parents valiantly share their experience, offer guidance and information on antibullying and character-building resources, and use their loss as a catalyst to save other children from the pain their child could not escape.

David's parents are not alone. Humbled and propelled by their strength and perseverance, members of the community, our faculty and students at the University of Texas at San Antonio, and countless others join them in the challenge of securing safety for all children. The challenge is formidable—too often, injuries and injustices as well as critical events and traumas catapult people's lives. However, we are heartened in knowing that we can come together to contribute in our own ways, encouraging a climate of compassion and empathy while honoring and promoting David's legacy of hope, healing, and love.

Factors, Approaches, and Interventions That Foster Healing and Resiliency

Individuals often attend individual counseling with hopes of successfully navigating critical or traumatic events. Other times, couples or families seek counseling during times of conflict, loss, or tragedy. Finally, there are times when tragedies strike an entire community or communities, and counselors are recruited to offer support and crisis intervention. When counselors are open to creating a space for clients that allows connection and mutuality, they humanize the client's experience in such a way that the client can feel empowered and even hopeful. Throughout the course of this book, we review approaches and interventions used in crisis and trauma counseling and consider factors that support client healing and resiliency.

Future Directions and Emerging Research

There are several emerging approaches counselors may encounter when working with clients who live with PTSD. Technological, virtual, brief, and mind-body focused treatments address the complex factors that predict PTSD and posttraumatic growth. As the horizon of counseling options expand, both counselors and clients have access to more tools, pathways for growth, and approaches that may resonate with individuals' personal trauma stories and hopes for healing. As new approaches emerge, and the evidence becomes established related to their efficacy, counselors remain mindful of the healing power of relationships to create safety, energize hope, and respect and honor the pain that may haunt clients. Through collaboration and shared decision making, counselors and clients can consider how emergent therapies may be useful.

Technological Advances: Neurofeedback and Virtual Reality (VR)

Harnessing the power of technology and advanced computer processing, neurofeedback and VR provide novel avenues to work directly with the brain. Neurofeedback is a tool that supports clients through visual processing and modulating brain functioning (Thibault, Lifshitz, & Raz, 2016). The goal of neurofeedback is to reduce the autonomic reactions to stressful memories, flashbacks, and emotional pain that may seem uncontrollable at times.

Neurofeedback

Neurofeedback is a technology-facilitated process in which clinicians target specific brain regions by using protocols to help clients gain mastery over their brain waves via feedback (Thibault et al., 2016). Qualified counselors who use neurofeedback in practice receive extensive training in neuroanatomy, trauma-focused treatment protocols, the proper application of electrodes on the scalp, and interpretation of the data that informs the treatment process. Neurofeedback studies have produced positive outcomes for clients, even with varied methodologies (Panisch & Hai, 2018). Panisch and Hai (2018) conducted a systematic review of neurofeedback and PTSD and reported that neurofeedback holds promise for reducing PTSD symptoms.

After clients begin their neurofeedback training, they engage in an audiovisual experience in which their brain begins to learn or relearn brain wave patterns that lead to decreased stress, increased frontal lobe activity, and integration of their thoughts and feelings through physical activation and processing. During this process, the counselor modifies the feedback to slowly modulate their clients' brain waves according to established protocols. The client experiences images or sounds that alert them when their brain deviates from the treatment parameters. People learn through feedback when their brain is under duress, and they also learn to experience optimal brain wave functioning.

VR

Another emerging technology in trauma work involves the use of VR to create environments where clients can gain mastery over stressful events in real time (Powers & Rothbaum, 2019). Initial studies have shown that the VR setting can be a powerful sensory experience in which clients interact in stressful situations with therapeutic support and monitoring. VR environments can create more vivid experiences than memory alone and can help facilitate exposure therapies (Powers & Rothbaum, 2019). As with neurofeedback, counselors and clients should feel comfortable and technically proficient using this technology as a medium to explore traumatic events and recovery. See Sidebar 1.3 for more information on technology usage.

Sidebar 1.3 • Technology Usage

Technology can be a useful tool for counselors to connect with people from all over the world. However, disturbing information can reach us as it occurs and in environments where we are not prepared to receive this content. Have you ever experienced a time when you were on your phone or social media and learned about an incident when you felt unprepared? Where were you, and how did this affect you?

Mind-Body Approaches

In a review of the numerous complementary and alternative interventions for the treatment of PTSD, the mind-body approaches received the most research support (Metcalf et al., 2016). These interventions included acupuncture, emotional freedom technique, mantra-based meditation, and yoga. Each of these methods seems to access the integration of the mind and body in a way that promotes healing. However, because the studies showed limited effectiveness, more research is needed that focuses on alternative and complementary modalities as first line or conjoint therapies in trauma counseling.

Brief and Targeted Approaches

In many current talk-focused treatments for PTSD, clinicians retell and imagine traumatic events in great detail and explore cognitive distortions while using techniques to moderate the emotional and visceral impact of the traumatic memories (Najavits, 2015). These approaches focus on encouraging both clients and counselors to lean into the potential avoidance that characterizes PTSD. Counselors and clients walk through the terror together and reconstruct new meanings of the trauma. Although research has shown that these approaches are effective, many people do not complete the required number of sessions (Najavits, 2015). Others may choose to avoid the process altogether because they are asked to relive terrorizing moments and profound losses.

Two emerging briefer interventions titled accelerated response therapy (ART; Kip et al., 2015) and written exposure therapy (WET; Sloan, Marx, Lee, & Resick, 2018), may address some of the shortcomings associated with traditional practices. ART and WET distill select therapeutic activities from existing practices and take far fewer sessions to complete. For example, ART uses aspects of eye movement desensitization and reprocessing, cognitive behavioral, and gestalt therapies in a structured, time-limited format. Likewise, WET spans five sessions and focuses on writing about the trauma event while following prompts to process the impact of the event on the client's life. Much fewer participants dropped out of the WET study compared with existing interventions, and the initial results demonstrated that participants experienced benefits from this modality (Sloan et al., 2018).

All of the emerging research and counseling practices described in this section are based on efforts from counselors, clients, and researchers to provide ongoing opportunities for healing. As new techniques, programs, and interventions gain research support, counselors and clients can creatively tailor a counseling process that meets clients' hopes for successful counseling outcomes. We contend that future directions in crisis and trauma work will continue to focus on integrating systems at all levels—from political and institutional structures to neurobiological, relational, spiritual, and emotional realities.

Resources

Crisis and trauma work is challenging on all levels and becomes increasingly complex when violence affects a community or when a person's loss is complicated by mixed feelings and circumstances (Westmarland & Alderson, 2013). In addition, although all traumatic situations can create the kind of havoc that leaves people reeling, the nature of a person's relationships can affect the tenor and intensity of the pain that follows. Accessing internal and external resources is paramount for a person in crisis or experiencing trauma. Clearly, crisis and trauma work is multifaceted and fluid. This kind of work challenges counselors to be present with their own loss, as they engage in and hear devastating stories and circumstances from their clients' lives, while fostering a counseling relationship grounded in safety and hope.

Therefore, because it is important that, as counselors, we remain equipped with personal clarity, professional acumen, and a relational framework, it is also vital that we connect with those resources that provide self-care and that enhance our own sense of wellness and productivity. We focus on what inspires our sense of self-compassion, compassion for others, and authenticity. In this text, we offer a comprehensive exploration of crisis and trauma counseling using a relational lens and a professional counseling worldview.

References

American Counseling Association. (2014). *ACA code of ethics.* Alexandria, VA: Author.

American Psychiatric Association. (2013). *Diagnostic and statistical manual of mental disorders* (5th ed.). Arlington, VA: Author.

Ardito R. B., & Rabellino, D. (2011). Therapeutic alliance and outcome of psychotherapy: Historical excursus, measurements, and prospects for research. *Frontiers in Psychology, 2,* 270. https://doi.org/10.3389/fpsyg.2011.00270

Banks, A. (2006). Relational therapy for trauma. *Journal of Trauma Practice, 5,* 25–47. https://doi.org/10.1300/J189v05n01_03

Banks, A. (2011). Developing the capacity to connect. *Zygon, 46,* 168–182. https://doi.org/10.1111/j.1467-9744.2010.01164.x

Banks, A. (2016). *Wired to connect.* New York, NY: Tarcher/Penguin.

Banks, A., & Hirschman, L. A. (2015). *Wired to connect: The surprising link between brain science and strong, healthy relationships.* New York, NY: Penguin Random House.

Benhabib, S. (1987). The generalised and the concrete other. In E. F. Kiray & D. R. Meyers (Eds.), *Women and moral theory* (pp. 154–177). Totowa, NJ: Rowman & Littlefield.

Birrell, P., & Bruns, C. (2016). Ethics and relationship: From risk management to relational engagement. *Journal of Counseling & Development, 94,* 391–397. https://doi.org/10.1002/jcad.12097

Cloitre, M., Garvet, D. W., Weiss, B., Carlson, E. B., & Bryant R. A. (2014). Distinguishing PTSD, complex PTSD, and borderline personality disorder: A latent class analysis. *European Journal of Psychotraumatology, 5*(1). https://doi.org/10.3402/ejpt.v5.25097

Comstock, C., & Platania, J. (2017). The role of media-induced secondary traumatic stress on perceptions of distress. *American International Journal of Social Science, 6,* 1–10.

Dailey, S. F. (n.d.). *Coping in the aftermath of a shooting.* Retrieved from https://www.counseling.org/knowledge-center/coping-in-the-aftermath-of-a-shooting

Dalai Lama & Cutler, H. (2009). *The art of happiness* (10th ed.). New York, NY: Penguin Group.

David's Law, S. 179, TX Penal Code §42.07 (2017). Retrieved from https://www.esc20.net/page/open/47320/0/David_s_Law_Overview.pdf

Duffey, T. (2005). A musical chronology and the emerging life song. *Journal of Creativity in Mental Health, 1,* 140–147. https://doi.org/10.1300/J456v01n01_09

Duffey, T., & Haberstroh, S. (2012). Developmental relational counseling: A model for self-understanding in relation to others. *Journal of Creativity in Mental Health, 7,* 262–271. https://doi.org/10.1080/15401383.2012.711709

Duffey, T., & Haberstroh, S. (2014). Developmental relational counseling: Applications for counseling men. *Journal of Counseling & Development, 92,* 104–113. https://doi.org/10.1002/j.1556-6676.2014.00136.x

Dupré, K., Dawe, K., & Barling, J. (2014). Harm to those who serve: Effects of direct and vicarious customer-initiated workplace aggression. *Journal of Interpersonal Violence, 29,* 2355–2377. https://doi.org/10.1177/0886260513518841

Ford, J. D., & Courtois, C. A. (2009). Defining and understanding complex trauma and complex traumatic stress disorders. In C. A. Courtois & J. D. Ford (Eds.), *Treating complex traumatic stress disorders: An evidence-based guide* (pp. 13–30). New York, NY: Guilford Press.

Foreman, T. (2018). Wellness, exposure to trauma, and vicarious traumatization: A pilot study. *Journal of Mental Health Counseling, 40,* 142–155. https://doi.org/10.17744/mehc.40.2.04

Gilbert, P., & Choden. (2013). *Mindful compassion: Using the power of mindfulness and compassion to transform our lives.* London, England: Robinson Publishing.

Hamblen, J. (2016, February 23). *Media coverage of traumatic events: Research on effects.* Retrieved from https://www.ptsd.va.gov/professional/treat/type/media_coverage_trauma.asp

Hartling, L., & Lindner, E. (2016). Healing humiliation: From reaction to creative action. *Journal of Counseling & Development, 94,* 383–390. https://doi.org/10.1002/jcad.12096

Hartling, L., & Sparks, E. (2008). Relational-cultural practice: Working in a nonrelational world. *Women and Therapy, 31,* 165–188. https://doi.org/10.1080/02703140802146332

James, R. K., & Gilliland, B. E. (2013). *Crisis intervention strategies* (7th ed.). Belmont, CA: Brooks/Cole.

Jordan, J. V. (2008). Recent developments in relational-cultural theory. *Women and Therapy, 31,* 1–4. https://doi.org/10.1080/02703140802145540

Jordan, J. V. (2017). Relational-cultural theory: The power of connection to transform our lives. *Journal of Humanistic Counseling, 56,* 228–243. https://doi.org/10.1002/johc.12055

Jordan, J. V. (2018). *Relational–cultural therapy* (2nd ed.). Washington, DC: American Psychological Association.

Jordan, J. V., Kaplan, A. G., Miller, J. B., Stiver, I. P., & Surrey, J. L. (1991). *Women's growth in connection: Writings from the Stone Center.* New York, NY: Guilford Press.

Jordan, J. V., Walker, M., & Hartling, L. M. (Eds.). (2004). *The complexity of connection: Writings from the Stone Center's Jean Baker Miller Training Institute.* New York, NY: Guilford Press.

Kaplan, D., Tarvydas, V., & Gladding, S. (2014). 20/20: A vision for the future of counseling: The new consensus definition of counseling. *Journal of Counseling & Development, 92,* 366–372. https://doi.org/10.1002/j.1556-6676.2014.00164.x

Kip, K. E., Hernandez, D. F., Shuman, A., Witt, A., Diamond, D. M., Davis, S., . . . Rosenzweig, L. (2015). Comparison of accelerated resolution therapy (ART) for treatment of symptoms of PTSD and sexual trauma between civilian and military adults. *Military Medicine, 180,* 964–971. https://doi.org/10.7205/MILMED-D-14-00307

Kress, V. E., Haiyasoso, M., Zoldan, J. A., & Trepal, H. (2018). The use of relational-cultural theory in counseling clients who have traumatic stress disorders. *Journal of Counseling & Development, 96*, 106–114. https://doi.org/10.1002/jcad.12182

Lambert, M. J., & Barley, D. E. (2001). Research summary on the therapeutic relationship and psychotherapy outcome. *Psychotherapy: Theory, Research, Practice, Training, 38*, 357–361. https://doi.org/10.1037/0033-3204.38.4.357

Lawson, G., & Myers, J. E. (2011). Wellness, professional quality of life, and career-sustaining behaviors: What keeps us well? *Journal of Counseling & Development, 89*, 163–171. https://doi.org/10.1002/j.1556-6678.2011.tb00074.x

Lenz, A. (2016). Relational-cultural theory: Fostering the growth of a paradigm through empirical research. *Journal of Counseling & Development, 94*, 415–428. https://doi.org/10.1002/jcad.12100

Lewis, K. L., & Grenyer, B. F. (2009). Borderline personality or complex posttraumatic stress disorder? An update on the controversy. *Harvard Review of Psychiatry, 17*, 322–328. https://doi.org/10.3109/10673220903271848

Mackinnon, D., & Derickson, K. (2013). From resilience to resourcefulness: A critique of resilience policy and activism. *Progress in Human Geography, 37*, 253–270. https://doi.org/10.1177/0309132512454775

Martz, E. (Ed.). (2010). *Trauma rehabilitation after war and conflict.* New York, NY: Springer.

McAdams, C. R., & Keener, H. J. (2008). Preparation, action, recovery: A conceptual framework for counselor preparation and response in client crises. *Journal of Counseling & Development, 86*, 388–398. https://doi.org/10.1002/j.1556-6678.2008.tb00526.x

Metcalf, O., Varker, T., Forbes, D., Phelps, A., Dell, L., DiBattista, A., . . . O'Donnell, M. (2016). Efficacy of fifteen emerging interventions for the treatment of posttraumatic stress disorder: A systematic review. *Journal of Traumatic Stress, 29*, 88–92. https://doi.org/10.1002/jts.22070

Miller, J. B. (1976). *Toward a new psychology of women.* Boston, MA: Beacon Press.

Miller, J. B. (2008). VI. Connections, disconnections, and violations. *Feminism and Psychology, 18*, 368–380. https://doi.org/10.1177/0959353508092090

Myer, R., & Moore, H. (2006). Crisis in context theory: An ecological model. *Journal of Counseling & Development, 84*, 139–147. https://doi.org/10.1002/j.1556-6678.2006.tb00389.x

Myers, J. E., & Sweeney, T. J. (2008). Wellness counseling: The evidence base for practice. *Journal of Counseling & Development, 86*, 482–493. https://doi.org/10.1002/j.1556-6678.2008.tb00536.x

Myers, J. E., Sweeney, T. J., & Witmer, J. M. (2000). The wheel of wellness counseling for wellness: A holistic model for treatment planning. *Journal of Counseling & Development, 78*, 251–266. https://doi.org/10.1002/j.1556-6676.2000.tb01906.x

Najavits, L. M. (2015). The problem of dropout from "gold standard" PTSD therapies. *F1000Prime Reports, 7*, 43. https://doi.org/10.12703/P7-43

Neff, K. D. (2011). Self-compassion, self-esteem, and well-being. *Social and Personality Psychology Compass, 5*, 1–12. https://doi.org/10.1111/j.1751-9004.2010.00330.x

Norcross, J., & Wampold, B. (2018). A new therapy for each patient: Evidence-based relationships and responsiveness. *Journal of Clinical Psychology, 74*, 1889–1906.

O'Malley, A. J., Arbesman, S., Steiger, D. M., Fowler, J. H., & Christakis N. A. (2012). Egocentric social network structure, health, and pro-social behaviors in a national panel study of Americans. *PLoS ONE, 7*(5), e36250. https://doi.org/10.1371/journal.pone.0036250

Panisch, L., & Hai, A. H. (2018). The effectiveness of using neurofeedback in the treatment of post-traumatic stress disorder: A systematic review. *Trauma, Violence, and Abuse,* 1524838018781103. https://doi.org/10.1177/1524838018781103

Pompeo-Fargnoli, A. M. (2017). Women and relationships: Introduction to relational cultural theory. In J. Schwarz (Ed.), *Counseling women across the life span: Empowerment, advocacy, and intervention* (pp. 57–78). New York, NY: Springer.

Powers, M., & Rothbaum, B. (2019). Recent advances in virtual reality therapy for anxiety and related disorders: Introduction to the special issue. *Journal of Anxiety Disorders, 61,* 1–2. https://doi.org/10.1016/j.janxdis.2018.08.007

Remley, T. P., & Herlihy, B. (2020). *Ethical, legal, and professional issues in counseling.* Hoboken, NJ: Pearson Education.

Sloan, D. M., Marx, B. P., Lee, D. J., & Resick, P. A. (2018). A brief exposure-based treatment vs cognitive processing therapy for posttraumatic stress disorder: A randomized noninferiority clinical trial. *JAMA Psychiatry, 75,* 233–239. https://doi.org/10.1001/jamapsychiatry.2017.4249

Substance Abuse and Mental Health Services Administration. (2014). *TIP 57: Trauma-informed care in behavioral health services.* Retrieved from https://store.samhsa.gov/product/TIP-57-Trauma-Informed-Care-in-Behavioral-Health-Services/SMA14-4816

Thibault, R., Lifshitz, M., & Raz, A. (2016). The self-regulating brain and neurofeedback: Experimental science and clinical promise. *Cortex, 74,* 247–261. https://doi.org/10.1016/j.cortex.2015.10.024

Wang, Y., Nomura, Y., Pat-Horenczyk, R., Doppelt, O., Abramovitz, R., Brom, D., & Chemtob, C. (2006). Association of direct exposure to terrorism, media exposure to terrorism, and other trauma with emotional and behavioral problems in preschool children. *Annals of the New York Academy of Sciences, 1094,* 363–368. https://doi.org/10.1196/annals.1376.051

Westmarland, N., & Alderson, S. (2013). The health, mental health, and well-being benefits of rape crisis counseling. *Journal of Interpersonal Violence, 28,* 3265–3282. https://doi.org/10.1177/0886260513496899

Zaleski, K. L., Johnson, D. K., & Klein, J. T. (2016). Grounding Judith Herman's trauma theory within interpersonal neuroscience and evidence-based practice modalities for trauma treatment. *Smith College Studies in Social Work, 86,* 377–393. https://doi.org/10.1080/00377317.2016.1222110

Resources for Crisis and Trauma Counseling

American Counseling Association (ACA)

ACA provides fact sheets and resources for counselors working with trauma and disaster mental health.

https://www.counseling.org/knowledge-center/mental-health-resources/trauma-disaster#disaster

American Red Cross

The American Red Cross provides online and in-person disaster response and disaster mental health trainings.

https://www.redcross.org/take-a-class/disaster-training

Cognitive Behavioral Intervention for Trauma in Schools (CBITS)

CBITS provides free online training to implement the CBITS program in school settings.

https://cbitsprogram.org/

Columbia Lighthouse Project

The Columbia Lighthouse Project provides free online training related to the administration and interpretation of the Columbia Suicide Severity Rating Scale.

http://cssrs.columbia.edu/

Human Dignity and Humiliation Studies (HumanDHS)

HumanDHS is a global network of people who commit to stimulate systemic change—globally and locally—to open space for dignity, mutual respect, and esteem to take root and grow.

http://www.humiliationstudies.org/

Medical University of South Carolina

The Medical University of South Carolina provides free online training in cognitive processing therapy.

https://cpt.musc.edu/

National Center for PTSD (Posttraumatic Stress Disorder)

Led by the U.S. Department of Veterans Affairs, this site offers resources and online trainings for working with adults experiencing PTSD.

https://www.ptsd.va.gov/

National Center for School Crisis and Bereavement (NCSCB)

The NCSCB provides training and free technical assistance to help schools during crises.

https://www.schoolcrisiscenter.org/

National Child Traumatic Stress Network (NCTSN)

The NCTSN provides online trainings covering a variety of topics for treating trauma experienced by youth. NCTSN also offers online psychological first aid training.

https://learn.nctsn.org/course/index.php?categoryid=3

Readiness and Emergency Management for Schools (REMS)

REMS provides in-person and online trainings to address crises and violence in all school settings (K–12 and higher education). REMS also provides templates and recommendations for developing school safety plans.

https://rems.ed.gov/

Stopbullying.gov

The stopbullying.gov website provides online training and resources to address bullying prevention and intervention.

https://www.stopbullying.gov/

Substance Abuse and Mental Health Services Administration (SAMHSA)

SAMHSA provides numerous resources focused on trauma-informed care in behavioral health, PTSD, and suicide prevention.

TIP 57: Trauma-Informed Care in Behavioral Health Services:

https://store.samhsa.gov/product/TIP-57-Trauma-Informed-Care-in-Behavioral-Health-Services/SMA14-4816

Suicide and PTSD Prevention Screening and Triage Tools

SAMHSA and the Health Resources and Services Administration (HRSA) offer free evidence-based screening tools and resources.

https://www.integration.samhsa.gov/clinical-practice/screening-tools#suicide

Suicide Prevention Resource Center (SPRC)

The SPRC provides online trainings and resources focused on suicide prevention.

https://www.sprc.org/

Multiple-Choice Questions

1. Relationally framed crisis and trauma counseling would agree with emphasizing
   a. The power of connection with clients during crisis and trauma.
   b. Techniques for clients to practice.
   c. Intensive inpatient treatment for recovery.
   d. Pushing the client to process though events quickly.

2. One main goal of this book is to
   a. Discount previous neurobiology research about neuroplasticity.
   b. Provide the reader with assessments.
   c. Provide the reader with guiding theories and interventions.
   d. None of the above

3. Who authored the book *Toward a New Psychology of Women*?
   a. Judith Jordan
   b. Mark Smith
   c. Linda Hartling
   d. Jean Baker Miller

4. Relational-cultural theory (RCT) promotes
   a. Authenticity and mutual empathy.
   b. Only cultural influences.
   c. Techniques.
   d. Providing various homework assignments for clients.

5. According to RCT, what can mutually rewarding social connections provide?
   a. Only emotional growth
   b. Humor and fun
   c. Disconnections from other relationships
   d. Emotional growth and a desire for more connection

6. RCT also explores cultural influences. Which statement would RCT agree with about culture?
   a. Cultural influences affect people's responses to one another and life.
   b. Culture does not have a vital impact on development.
   c. Culture is an element that never comes into the counseling session.
   d. None of the above

7. Relational neuroscience posits that
   a. Trauma will damage areas of the brain forever.
   b. Neurons can never reconnect and grow.
   c. Trauma changes the brain, but healthy social connections can promote brain health.
   d. Trauma changes the brain, and there is little a counselor can do to help.

8. If clients are hiding parts of themselves in session and worry about suffering increased rejection, they may be experiencing
   a. Central relational paradox.
   b. A disorder.
   c. Autonomy.
   d. None of the above

9. Which agency in the U.S. Department of Health and Human Services discusses the trauma-informed care (TIC) model?
   a. CAAP
   b. SAMHSA
   c. SAAMH
   d. NIHA

10. Compassion is most related to which RCT concept?
    a. Mutual empathy
    b. Central relational paradox
    c. Chronic disconnection
    d. Relational images

11. The _____ model may help counselors-in-training develop their compassion and self-awareness.
    a. CBT
    b. REBT
    c. Developmental relational counseling (DRC)
    d. Fundamental

12. According to Myers and Sweeney (2008), counselors may experience higher level of wellness if they participate in a wellness class.
    a. False
    b. False, because this will only add another class to the student's schedule
    c. True
    d. True, if all the students have the same self-care plan

13. Which statement about neurofeedback is true?
    a. Neurofeedback puts little shocks into the brain.
    b. Neurofeedback helps people regulate their brain activity.
    c. Neurofeedback is not safe for children.
    d. Neurofeedback is not a good tool for reducing trauma symptoms.

14. New approaches for trauma include interventions that use acupuncture, yoga, and meditation. These are known as
    a. Behavioral therapy.
    b. Mystical approaches.
    c. Mind-body approaches.
    d. None of the above

15. If people experience a crisis, they will also experience trauma.
    a. True, because crisis and trauma are the same thing
    b. True, if the crisis happened when they were older adults
    c. False, because some people can experience crisis and not trauma
    d. None of the above

Essay Questions

1. Crisis and trauma counseling is not a new topic. Research is expanding by incorporating relational theories (e.g., relational-cultural theory [RCT]) and emerging research on neuroplasticity. How have these topics changed counselors' viewpoints on crisis and trauma?

2. In the case example of David, he experienced bullying and felt the pain of social exclusion. Following his death, his family took action and worked to create an antibullying law in Texas known as David's Law. If you knew a child or adolescent was being bullied or cyberbullied, what type of action might you take, given your role?

3. According to this book, there are new and emerging approaches for helping people who have experienced crisis and trauma. If you had unlimited resources, how would you propose researching crisis and trauma from an RCT lens?

4. According to the Substance Abuse and Mental Health Services Administration (2014), trauma experiences can lead to a wide array of symptoms, including isolation, substance abuse, and anxiety. Considering this information, how often do you feel like trauma plays a part in misdiagnosis?

5. As Chapter 1 states, this book will focus on relational aspects of crisis and trauma. What are the key principles you learned from this focus?

CHAPTER 2

The Counseling Relationship

Judith V. Jordan and Thelma Duffey

Creative and innovative approaches to counseling practice are well documented in the counseling and mental health literature. Progressive trends in creative and innovative counseling practice give promise to the various methods that support clients experiencing loss, crisis, and traumatic events. This textbook includes several interventions that support healing for people dealing with crises and traumatic events and contains compelling examples of creative and innovative counseling resources. At the same time, recent research also suggests that interventions void of a strong therapeutic relationship lack the power that relationships can bring. Together, creativity and growth-fostering therapeutic relationships provide meaningful opportunities for counselors and clients to be resourceful and to form the kind of connections that support healing.

In this chapter, we discuss creativity as a construct within counseling practice and highlight the role that the therapeutic relationship plays in promoting health and healing, particularly within a crisis and trauma context (Duffey, Haberstroh, & Trepal, 2016). We use relational-cultural theory (RCT) as a lens to view the foundation of relationship and the unfolding of relationship within a therapeutic context. We also use relational ethics as a framework for conceptualizing the needs of clients undergoing traumatic losses and the means by which counselors can support clients as they navigate these stressful and devastating times.

As discussed in Chapter 1, RCT is a progressive theory focused on growth through relationships. Developed in the 1970s by an informal and collaborative group of female psychologists and a psychiatrist—including the first author of this chapter, Judith V. Jordan—this model provides a roadmap for people to work through relational challenges and connect with others while considering the myriad dynamics that support and impede growth. Unlike other models of mental health that look at ways in which a person can grow and thrive by focusing on the "self," this group views the self differently. With a perspective that identifies connection and relationship at the core of development, the self, according to this model, is viewed in relation to others.

RCT (a) offers a framework for conceptualizing how relationships develop, (b) normalizes the role of disconnections in relationship, (c) describes the often-traumatic consequences of chronic disconnection, and (d) views resilience as relationally driven rather than as an indication of singular accomplishment (Jordan, 2018). In addition, RCT considers the role of culture and context when conceptualizing a person's circumstances and brings focus to the role of power and privilege when considering the life circumstances of people navigating distressing situations. Multicultural and ethical considerations are at the core of RCT, and applying these considerations to crisis and trauma work is essential.

This focus on relationship was reinforced by a group of counseling professionals who came together in what is now known as "20/20: A Vision for the Future of Counseling" to discuss and determine important considerations within the profession (Kaplan, Tarvydas, & Gladding, 2014). In a process that spanned numerous years, this group tackled some of the dominant issues facing the field of counseling. One important outcome of the process included developing the official definition of counseling as "a professional relationship that empowers diverse individuals, families, and groups to accomplish mental health, wellness, education, and career goals" (Kaplan et al., 2014, p. 368). Research supports this definition by clarifying the important role of relationship in therapeutic success (Norcross & Wampold, 2011). Given our understanding of the role of relationship in counseling and within our lives, we see identifying theories that guide relationship development, particularly when applied to the personal and powerful work of crisis and trauma counseling, as particularly salient. We use RCT as a framework for conceptualizing this work.

Fundamental RCT Philosophy

As we discussed in Chapter 1, RCT purports that all people have a basic need for relationship, and when these relationships are growth fostering, they thrive. In fact, RCT identifies "five good things" (Miller & Stiver, 1997) as integral to growth. For example, people feel clarity, zest, a sense of worth, productivity, and a desire for more connection when they are experiencing a good relational connection (Miller & Stiver, 1997). RCT also discusses the role of mutual empathy, which is integral to RCT and is illustrated later in this chapter via the case of Gina. Mutual empathy is distinct from the "one-way empathy" often discussed in mental health literature (Jordan, 2018). RCT describes *mutual empathy* as an experience in which a person recognizes his or her impact on the listener—an experience in which the listener acknowledges being "moved" by, and because of, the sharer's experience. This awareness of impact—of mattering and significance—has a profound effect on the person sharing the experience. RCT would say that both people are changed by the experience, and growth and connection occur in that context. See Sidebar 2.1 for information on the five good things in relationships.

Sidebar 2.1 • Five Good Things

Reflecting on relational-cultural theory and the concept of maintaining healthy relationships in your life, how would you describe your key relationships? Are they growth-fostering relationships that reflect the "five good things"? Do your clients have growth-fostering relationships in their lives or with you?

Connection and Disconnection

Most people yearn for connection and a sense of empathic understanding with one another. However, disconnections are ubiquitous in life. People misunderstand each other, get preoccupied, and try to change others to fit their idea of how they should be. People fail one another in many ways. Acute disconnections occur when one person does not understand the other or does not care about the other's feelings. If the person who feels shut out from connection has less power, and the more powerful person is not responsive or does not show that the other matters, and if the less powerful person cannot represent her experience to the more powerful person and be responded to empathically, she learns to keep certain aspects of herself out of relationship over time.

Chronic disconnections can lead to a person's sense of being cut off and excluded—outside the human community and isolated. Neuroscience teaches us that the pain of exclusion affects us in the same way, and through the same pathways, as physical pain (Lieberman & Eisenberger, 2009). Relationships are so essential to people's survival that they register in the body and the brain in the same way as physical injury, lack of water, or loss of oxygen. In that respect, relationships are not luxuries for human existence. They are absolutely essential. Recent neuroscience demonstrates this finding beyond question: People need connections like they need air and water, and they are hardwired to suffer when they are isolated or excluded (Banks, 2015).

Traumatic Disconnections

Whereas many disconnections occur within the range of anticipated everyday experience (occasional misunderstandings and oversights), some disconnections are traumatic and distort people's reality. Traumatic disconnections arise when a person experiences physical, sexual, verbal, or emotional abuse. These experiences happen in the lives of children every day and in families with substance abuse and domestic violence dynamics. These situations are complex, exacerbated by power and control factors and larger systemic issues.

As shown in Chapter 1, RCT posits that in spite of people's yearning for connection, they sometimes engage in protective, but disconnecting, strategies that keep them out of their desired connections. For example, a person may hide important feelings or thoughts to maintain some semblance of life-giving relationship. People hide their truths, pretend they are fine (when they are not), and behave in ways that are not congruent with who they are and how they feel. RCT refers to these behaviors as *strategies of disconnection*. However, engaging in these behaviors makes sense when it does not feel safe to behave otherwise. RCT also refers to these as *strategies for survival.*

These survival strategies and relationships are far from life sustaining. In fact, they demand an altered and twisted version of the person's real experience. As Jean Baker Miller noted, people will twist themselves to fit into the only relationship that is available (e.g., the child has to let go of certain truths to stay in the appearance of connection with a nonempathic parent; Stiver, Rosen, Surrey, & Miller, 2008). However, the connection becomes less and less authentic. In these cases, and over time, people often suffer from what Miller (2008) called "condemned isolation" and a sense of being beyond the pale—flawed in some essential way and thus responsible for the disconnection. When people are in less powerful positions, they may be challenged to see things as they are and blame themselves for actions that are not theirs. If this course continues, it could lead to a pervasive sense of shame, vulnerability, despair, and immobilization. See Sidebar 2.2 for information on maintaining connection.

Relational Images

RCT speaks to the relational images or ideas that people create about who they are and how others respond or will respond to them on the basis of their experiences. When children are responded to with love and acceptance, these images are more positive, and they grow to expect good things in their relationships. However, when childhood experiences are negative or punitive, these are also generalized inappropriately to new relationships. These images play a large role in how people interact with others.

For example, a person who suffered neglect or abuse might think, "when I stand up for myself, I will get kicked out," which leads him or her to withdraw or submit and to fail to represent him- or herself more fully in relationship. In another example, people who suffered neglect or abuse, and who find themselves in a position of power as adults, may use power in ways that hurt others, their relationships, and ultimately themselves. Rather than using their strength to connect and build relationships, they compete and overpower others, ultimately creating the chasm they want to avoid. At a personal level, these relational images keep people stuck, unable to discern the shifts in their lives and the possibilities for different relationships. On a broader cultural level, people experience what Patricia Hill Collins (1990) and RCT have referred to as *controlling images,* or ideas about who and how we are as people. These images are communicated from the culture and influence people to carry limiting understandings of their own experience.

Children who grew up believing they were not "college material" because members of their culture were not expected to go to college may have to overcome feeling inferior or inadequate intellectually and academically. These controlling

Sidebar 2.2 • Maintaining Connection

Course work consumes attention and time, and being aware of disconnections is important. Knowing how disconnections happen in life, how would you help someone pursue reconnection with others?

images socialize people to see themselves in certain, and often inaccurate, limiting ways. In essence, the culture creates these controlling images and disempowers and marginalizes groups of devalued people (Collins, 1990; Windsor, Dunlap, & Golub, 2011).

It is heartening to know that although traumatic disconnections lead people into isolation and a sense of being responsible, or at fault, for relational failures, these relational images can be altered. In cases in which a person can make sense of hurtful disconnections and see these as resulting from the limitations of other powerful individuals in past experiences, this awareness creates a sense of possibility. Given that most abusive situations create a sense of shame for the person who is experiencing the trauma or abuse, making sense of these experiences has the potential to influence a person's self-perception. Shame often creates a need to pull away from others, mistakenly believing that the other person could not possibly respond with empathy and understanding. Alternatively, if people find themselves in a place of power, and connect with their sense of shame, they may belittle others or hurt people whom they see as more vulnerable.

People perform this behavior when they have learned in earlier nonresponsive and unempathetic relationships that they cannot expect to be treated in respectful ways—in ways that showed they matter. After a while, they may feel relationally incompetent, unseen, and "wrong" in some global way. Retreating into shame connects people with that sense of being wrong, that somehow their being is wrong. Moving into aggression can lead them toward protecting their sense of self at the expense of others and their relationships. Either direction can lead a person to feelings of loneliness and despair.

Finding a Way Through Relational Trauma

RCT provides a clear way through the anguish of relational trauma. For example, most abuse of children occurs in settings where there is a powerful other who the child was led to believe was a "safe" person. Tragically, this person proved unresponsive, unempathetic, and violating. For clients with experiences of posttraumatic stress disorder (PTSD) and early childhood trauma, the early counseling setting can be reminiscent of the conditions surrounding their abuse, and it can, thus, trigger them. Alone, invited into vulnerability, behind closed doors with a person who holds considerable power, clients might begin to be triggered into a place of terror and closing down.

When empathic failures occur in counseling, as they invariably do, the client may experience a sense of alarm and fear of sliding into a dangerous sense of being misunderstood and retraumatized. Whereas the counselor may only feel a small tremor of disconnection, the client may move into full-blown dissociation and isolation. Often, these abrupt movements into disconnection for trauma survivors also occur when they have moved into increasing vulnerability (i.e., letting go of some of the protective strategies of disconnection, which served as protective functions for some time). An empathic failure on the part of the counselor can lead to this leap into overwhelming disconnection.

Similarly, movement into a more trusting and vulnerable connection may also trigger an abrupt and dramatic flight into traumatic disconnection. Closeness can feel frightening and potentially hurtful to a person who may not know how to trust it. Furthermore, the surrender of some protective strategies for survival may leave the person feeling too vulnerable and unsafe. These sudden shifts may be unsettling for the counselor; or worse, the counselor may feel like he is being experienced as a perpetrator, when, in fact, he has the best intentions and has tried carefully to create trust and responsiveness. When these disconnects are understood as protective strategies on the path to greater overall connection, the counselor can honor the usefulness of these disconnects and respect the client's need to temporarily gain greater distance and control her sense of safety. Being with the client; keeping the context of the client's history in mind; recognizing the courage it takes to be in counseling; and honestly connecting with your own good intentions, limitations, and the realities of the interaction while communicating the client's sense of mattering are all important factors that support the therapeutic relationship and success.

The Research Evidence for the Power of the Counseling Relationship

In a longitudinal study that amassed a series of meta-analyses and a panel of helping-professional experts, Norcross and Wampold (2011) documented evidence of the power that a healing counseling relationship can bring and discussed how the counseling relationship contributed in unique and significant ways to therapeutic outcome. This research also indicated that even well-known, evidence-based practices are not considered to be effective without a productive and trusting counseling relationship (Norcross & Wampold, 2011). The research identified key aspects that demonstrate effective client-reported outcomes, including sustaining alliances, cohesion, taking in client feedback, and empathy (Norcross & Wampold, 2011). Moreover, this research indicated that receptivity to client feedback was integral to supporting relationship and promoting counseling success (Norcross & Wampold, 2011).

Amy Banks—psychiatrist, author of *Four Ways to Click* (2015), and senior research fellow at the Jean Baker Miller Training Institute—has added to the research on the power of the counseling relationship in unique ways. Using the concepts of relational neuroscience, neuroplasticity, and RCT, Banks (2015) has focused on human connectedness and the ways in which people grow in connection with one another. Acknowledging that the dominant U.S. culture values separation and autonomy and uses these as measuring tools for growth and development, Banks discussed how RCT offers an alternative model of relationship now supported in the research literature.

New studies in neuroscience have reported that healthy connections with others actually strengthen neural pathways in the brain and, over time, increase the capacity for relationships (Banks, 2015). In other words, the brain's neuroplasticity enables people to rewire their connection to others at any age (Banks, 2015). Moreover, empathy, cohesion, and connection are integral to therapeutic connection and positively affect brain change (Banks, 2015). The counseling relationship, then, becomes an immensely powerful, and potentially life-changing, aspect of the counseling process.

Expanding the Concepts of RCT: Competence Building in Disconnection

Given that disconnections invariably occur in life, relational skill building is vital to repairing these ruptures. Relational competence involves a person's having the capacity to listen to others, listen to oneself, represent personal experiences authentically, and allow for a shared vulnerability that can transform experiences (Duffey & Somody, 2011). When people are able to rework their acute disconnections, meaning that they are able to find their way through them respectfully with one another, they have the potential to gain greater connection, trust, and authenticity. However, when a person is unable to do so, they develop patterns of chronic disconnection that can lead to isolation, and a sense of being cut off, outside the human community. When people are isolated, they feel disempowered and experience heightened anxiety and depression. Therefore, if people can learn to rework acute disconnections, they have an opportunity to grow and to thrive. If, however, acute disconnections settle in and become distorting and constricting *chronic disconnections,* people suffer another level of trauma to their system, and their experience of excruciating relational pain is deepened (Jordan, 2018).

Relating and Connecting During Trauma Work

Gina is a client who grew up in an abusive and terrifying home. When she tried to let her mother know that she was being sexually abused by her stepfather, her mother chided her for having an overactive imagination and for making up such stories to get attention. Gina felt ashamed, alone, and at risk. She was hospitalized for her first suicide attempt at age 14. She had seen many therapists before meeting with me (Judy) when she was again hospitalized for suicidal ideation. She had never discussed the abuse in any of her previous therapies, and her mother—who had never believed her—never mentioned to her daughter's clinical team the possibility of past abuse. Gina was skeptical that I would be of any more use to her than previous treaters.

When a person is treated without empathy and is humiliated, physically injured, or misunderstood, and when the person who inflicts this pain shows no concern for the feelings or well-being of the less powerful person, chronic disconnection and fear-based relating set in. The less powerful person must twist herself to fit into a relationship that does not support her growth. When trauma occurs, the person uses strategies of disconnection (also called strategies of survival) to be less vulnerable. The pattern of being triggered by empathic failures can lead to a bumpy ride in the counseling sessions. Even more difficult for the counselor is when there is progress and movement toward more connection, and suddenly the client feels exposed, raw, and unprotected; the client may close down in terror or burst forth with rage. Often, counselors report feeling "off balance" or "deskilled." If the counselor can allow the shifts and hold an image of the overall movement toward greater connection and safety, this practice goes a long way to shifting old, maladaptive relational images and overly generalized expectations.

We can understand Gina's experience by recognizing that interpersonal trauma breaks connections. It leads to shame, isolation, and silencing. A person's sense of mattering to others, of being lovable, is destroyed. Someone suffering with PTSD, like Gina, cannot believe that she would be empathically responded to by others. In fact, she could feel a profound sense of unworthiness. Moreover, because a person in this position cannot imagine another's empathic caring, she would isolate further and show little of her inner experience of vulnerability. The healing response that would be so desperately needed would feel unattainable. This outcome occurs because shame cuts people off from others, and they begin to believe something along the lines of, "If you really knew me, you wouldn't care about me."

A person's capacity to be authentic decreases with each attempt to censor and show only those personal aspects they believed to be acceptable. As people hide and pretend to be other than who they are, their conviction of their innate and pervasive "badness" expands. Abused and used by others, their need for good connection increases, but the risk of being hurt, invalidated, and rejected now feels too great. See Sidebar 2.3 for more information on Gina's case.

Relational Responsiveness During Times of Crisis

What people need is healing relationship. However, when people experience trauma, it can push them toward isolation and hiding. Then, when they receive positive responses, they can invalidate them by fearing that if the counselor could see *all* of them (including the shameful parts), she would never care about or want to do counseling with them. What people fear in that withdrawal is the vulnerability necessary to engage in real, growth-fostering relationships.

RCT offers a way of understanding this dance of connection and disconnection. It allows the counselor to step back and see the larger pattern of movement toward greater and safer connection. The client needs real and genuine responses from the counselor. Therapeutic authenticity and anticipatory empathy support the growth of mutual empathy—that is, the kind of empathy that communicates impact and that ultimately supports the growth of all involved.

The concept of mutual empathy can be confusing, particularly when mutuality is misinterpreted as reciprocity or equality, which is not so. Rather, from an RCT perspective, we grow as people when we feel empathy for others and from others—when we feel connected and not alone. In these cases, we feel worthy of trust and connection. Therefore, in cases in which a counselor is working with a client in trauma, and for empathy to contribute to healing, the client must see, know, and feel that she has had an impact on the counselor.

When the client notices that she has "touched" the counselor, she feels that she matters. She feels her own impact. She feels that the counselor really cares. Expressing this impact can involve a certain amount of vulnerability on the counselor's part. However, as Jean Baker Miller observed, if in a relationship both people are not growing, neither person is growing. RCT describes how we grow through our authenticity and how authentic growth is mutual. If, however, the counselor has been taught to be neutral and practice "blank screen" counseling, he or she may struggle with how real to be. This struggle can affect a client's experience of counseling and, certainly, the therapeutic relationship.

You may wonder what the parameters are for this level of authenticity, and relational ethics speaks to this issue (Birrell & Bruns, 2016). When practicing rela-

Sidebar 2.3 • Gina's Case

> Think about the case of Gina. The counselor expressed that she was moved by Gina's experience, which helped Gina know she mattered. How does empathy and compassion facilitate connection and growth?

tional ethics, which we described in Chapter 1, counselors should be comfortable with the unknown or uncertainty of the counseling process (Birrell & Bruns, 2016) and be mindful of the flow of mutuality. This method can enable counselors to offer their full presence in their sessions and to attend to the experiences of both the client and counselor. A counselor can then be truly authentic, participate in *ethical listening*—that is, the practice of using information gleaned in a discussion for the benefit of the other person and not for oneself (Birrell & Bruns, 2016)—and attend to the inherent power dynamics. Counselors can apply the concept of relational ethics by including the client in the decision-making process, empowering them to feel heard and effective in their counseling process.

Another avenue for empowering clients could be the counselor's self-disclosure. The idea behind such disclosure is not for counselors to relay their own experiences or to shift the focus of the work onto themselves. Rather, it is to *genuinely* (guided by their understanding of what might be healing) respond to clients and thus enhance the well-being of the client (Birrell & Bruns, 2016). One of the hopes in counseling is to lessen the client's sense of isolation, and part of that work involves (a) the counselor guiding the client in making sense of old relational images and (b) finding images that challenge the certainty with which these old, restrictive images are held. RCT refers to these as discrepant *relational images* (Jordan, 2018). The counselor's responsiveness provides important data for the client, which eventually allows the client to believe in the possibility of growth-fostering and safe relationships.

Although forming a connection is an important goal of counseling, the counselor needs to be deeply respectful of the wisdom of the client's original movement into strategies of disconnection and survival (i.e., those behaviors we discussed earlier in the chapter wherein people engage in behaviors that, although meant for survival, can result in disconnection from others). Avoiding others, hiding important aspects of themselves, and saying they are fine (when they are not) are some examples of how these strategies can emerge.

The counselor's work is to stay present and to try not to repeat traumatic disconnections. RCT offers a different outcome, a discrepant experience that begins to erode the certainty with which negative relational images are held and, thus, affect current experience. The counselor must follow the lead of the client in pacing—moving toward greater connection while also allowing movement away from connection. This process can be challenging, with rapid descent into terrifying disconnection. It can also be a hopeful form of grasping for small reassurances that, indeed, relationships can be anchored in mutual empathy and care. Some have described the process of seeking connection and descending into disconnection as akin to being on a roller coaster. No doubt, it takes work for counselors to be personally responsive and therapeutically transparent without getting tangled and reactive. Meditational and awareness practices can be helpful for counselors in learning how to traverse along this edge of vulnerability and safety. Holding the perspective of overall movement toward connection for clients assists in developing a kind of trustworthy presence that does not promise the rainbow (or a rose garden) but does allow the development of hope.

Relational Creativity

People undergoing crisis situations and traumatic events experience losses of such gravity that their lives are inextricably changed. Accidents, illnesses, acts of terror, and sudden deaths can be felt with such impact and can trigger feelings of intense loneliness, disconnection, and panic. It is during those times that even words of comfort can feel empty. We all experience grave losses in different ways, and such factors as the nature of the loss, our relationship to the loss, our internal resources, and the resources around us affect our survival.

The Association for Creativity in Counseling is a division within the American Counseling Association focused on using internal and external creative resources as well as the shared creativity of the counselor and client in counseling practice (Duffey, 2005; Duffey, Haberstroh, & Trepal, 2016). *Creativity in counseling* (CIC), as a model, is defined as "a shared counseling process involving growth-promoting shifts that occur from an intentional focus on the therapeutic relationship and the inherent human creative capacity to affect change" (Duffey, Haberstroh, & Trepal, 2016, p. 448).

According to CIC, creativity is as integral to counseling practice as the therapeutic relationship. The relationship helps us feel connected and know we matter in the midst of such chaos, and it sustains us as we try to understand, come to terms with, and adapt to unanticipated life changes. Our shared creativity fosters compassion and creates space for the process to unfold. Even in those moments when we cannot begin to connect with the concept of creativity, our creative forces are at work.

Joanna came to counseling following the death of her only son, months before he was to graduate from college. Losing her beloved boy was the greatest crisis ever experienced by her family. Amidst the chaos and consolations that came in its aftermath, to hear her tell it, all she could do was put one foot in front of the other and remember to carry a bottle of water with her because "water is good for you."

Joanna was in shock following the accident and for many months afterward. She sought counseling because she did not know what else to do and wanted to do something. On the first visit, she entered the office, sat on the couch, gave a faint smile, and sighed. There began what came to be one of my (Thelma's) most powerful experiences in counseling, and Joanna became one of my greatest teachers.

Joanna grieved her son and her life every day. She also allowed herself the space, without judgment, to just be. She spent considerable time alone, which was helpful to her, at the same time that she found solace in some close relationships. She attended counseling every week for months and would bring in heart-shaped artifacts that she would find along her path. Sometimes she would see a heart-shaped carving in a door and would take a picture of the door. These served as signs, or reminders, to her that there is much more to life than we know. Joanna's faith sustained her, and it was in faith that she most connected with her creativity.

Working with people in grief, or those undergoing crisis and loss, is deeply humbling. As counselors, we do not have the magic words that can make things better. We do not have the most brilliant interventions that can change the course of a person's life after loss. What we do have, however, is the human connection and compassion that can foster a sense of hope and the training that can help us be present and connected with the unimaginable pain that people suffer. Moreover, it is in relationship that we can find the creative strength to move forward.

There are times when our traumatic experiences can leave us feeling immobilized. We may find ourselves thinking and feeling in debilitating ways. In Joanna's case, her creativity, faith, and relationships helped her move past these obstacles. Not all people are so fortunate. Others succumb to their grief, sadness, and loss, and they do not find their way home. These are tragic realities. As counselors, we bring our authenticity, training, and hope to our work and relationships, and we co-create a space where our clients can, to the best of their capacities, connect with their own.

Empathy and Responsiveness as Creativity

RCT is not technique driven, yet it does offer guidelines for working with trauma, and it helps both counselor and client make sense of what are often confusing dynamics. For example, RCT proposes the need for responsiveness rather than re-activity (Jordan & Hartling, 2002). Being responsive is not akin to complete spontaneity, or what RCT refers to as *amygdala authenticity,* on the part of the counselor (Jordan, 2018). This method is not what RCT suggests. Borrowing from the brain health literature, we know that amygdala reactivity will inevitably occur at times on the part of the counselor, but it is to be worked with, not let loose (Kindsvatter, Russotti, & Tansey, 2019). Thus, the counselor engages respectfully and honors both the client's yearning for connection and the need for protective strategies of disconnection.

Empathic Failures

There are times when empathic failures will occur. In these times, it is important that the counselor let the client know that she earnestly wants to understand the client better and suggests they take a look at the disconnection that occurred. There are also times the counselor simply notices the client's need to pull away and does not comment, prod, or analyze it. Sometimes the counselor simply "stays with" the client at an emotional distance that feels safe to the client. If necessary, calming or grounding approaches might be suggested to help the client with her reactivity. When safety is reestablished, the counselor might decide to make a gentle inquiry about the process, or she might decide to simply allow the comfort level in the room to settle in and engage around less-charged topics.

There are times when counselors are off track or do not follow the client's lead. In these cases, counselors can apologize and acknowledge the situation. More important than the counselor's need to feel effective or like a "good helper" is the need for the client to see that she is being listened to and taken seriously and that her healing supersedes all else. In addition, counselors need to practice steady presence and be on the lookout for their emergence of ego, investment in being right, or retreat into theory. To the extent that the counselor is invested in building or maintaining an image of "the good counselor" or "empathic listener," he or she will not be available for real relationship.

Reworking Disconnections

When, however, the counselor is present in healing moments, the brain's parasympathetic and sympathetic systems rebalance (Banks, 2015). "Good vagal tone" (Porges, 2011), which allows a person to find comfort and growth in relationships, is reestablished. The pain of exclusion is lessened as the client feels joined-with (Banks, 2015). In RCT therapy, the underlying neural patterns that are the result of trauma and chronic disconnection begin to shift. Together, with persistence and gentleness, the counselor and client address the inevitable empathic failures that occur in treatment. The client begins to experience the possibility of participating in a responsive, loving, and compassionate relationship. This movement toward growth-fostering connection creates healing and well-being. Some may say that this is so simple, yet this work is deeply challenging! Therapeutic use of responsiveness helps clients learn how they affect others and how they are affected. This information helps open up new relational opportunities.

Crises in Relational Connectedness and Relational Resilience

When considering the traumatic experiences that clients bring to counseling, we see RCT as being especially suited for work with clients suffering from PTSD. The broken connections with others, the disrupted awareness of one's own experience, and the unpredictable autonomic nervous system all conspire to leave the client feeling alone, without hope or a sense of possibility. Gradations of affect develop when one is not being emotionally hijacked and thrown into crisis mode at each twist of disappointment or misunderstanding.

Relational resilience, the capacity to use relationships to realign and move toward growth through empathic responsiveness, is one of the keys to recovery (Jordan, 2018). In these contexts, people reestablish the healthy neuronal pathways that are present at birth, guiding them to turn to others when they are in pain, sadness, fear, alarm, or isolation. These pathways are broken and eroded in trauma, leaving people vulnerable to emotional tsunamis and destructive withdrawal from potentially growth-fostering relationships. To regain the possibility that others will be there, for and with us, and when we suffer, ensures our human capacity to be creative and loving.

In this respect, we grow, not simply in receiving healing attention but also in participating in the growth of others. RCT tells us that good relationships lead to the desire for more connection. Rather than a homeostatic process of "taking in," "getting," settling into cozy or established nesting relationships, as we grow personally, there are ripples of change that move into our communities that contribute to the common good.

RCT is a model about personal development, but it is also a model that suggests we are not single, separated beings responsible only for our own happiness or well-being. We are connected via empathy and compassion. We are wired to be responsive and empathic. We are wired to eschew isolation, to recognize it as a life-threatening force. Moreover, RCT posits that we thrive in connection, not in separation. Although we all have a "sense of self," we are biologically and neurologically connected. We *are* deeply interdependent beings.

In fact, RCT recognizes that connection, not separate-self-assertion, ensures survival. Although the U.S. culture privileges independence, competition, and standing on one's own two feet, our neurobiology leads us to experience resonance with others within a web of interdependence. We live a destructive paradox: The culture celebrates the separate self and teaches us to stand strong alone, but our intrinsically connecting nature leads us to need others and to find safety in building growth-fostering relationships.

People face a stress-filled dilemma: They are hardwired for connection, but their culture privileges independence, autonomy, and building a strong separate self

(Jordan, 2018). Neurobiologically equipped for connection and interdependence, people are stressed simply by virtue of living in a world that valorizes competition and separation. Unrealistic expectations of the success of the lone hero can leave people feeling like failures. Trauma dynamics make these challenges all the more destructive. Alone, in pain, and shamed, the natural sources of healing feel inaccessible. Hope becomes dim. In that context, RCT can bring in the possibility of good connection and provide experiences of mutual empathy and healing. These experiences, then, can be carried out into the larger world. Clients may think, "perhaps the empathy I experience here, with this increasingly safe person, is something I can find and generate in other relationships."

Case Example and Applications for Hope and Healing

Gina had little hope that her pain would be heard, let alone healed. She was locked in secrecy and a sense of unlovability. Each step toward connection brought a tidal wave of fear. Each evidence of untrustworthiness settled in with her already existing conviction that no one was safe or capable of caring for her. She experienced my (Judith's) failures in counseling as massive and dangerous. However, she was also a smart and capable young woman. In the hospital setting where our work occurred, we were surrounded by senior staff and former supervisors of mine.

As Gina thrashed about with her deep despair and fear, she started to call some of my former supervisors (some of whom had also treated her in previous hospitalizations) to tell them of my latest empathic failure—some were doozies! These esteemed colleagues of mine would then approach me in the hospital cafeteria to inquire whether I had indeed said "such and such." I would flush, mumble, "yes, I had" (Gina was spot on with my failures and vulnerabilities). I was filled with shame about being such a "loser therapist"—her words, but close to becoming my description of myself during this time too. Using my own survival strategy, I stopped going to the cafeteria to avoid my esteemed, but critical, past supervisors. I was simply embarrassed about my many failures and sad about the hurt inflicted on her. I felt isolated and confused as she felt stronger and clearer.

As I slowly came to understand, Gina had developed a wise way to feel "safe enough" to take the small risks involved in giving up old strategies of disconnection. This relationship, for her, triggered images of her childhood abuse: behind closed doors, with a powerful other who presented as trustworthy and invited her into more vulnerability. It was simply too reminiscent of the original abuse at the hands of her stepfather. Therefore, she developed a method to bring this counseling relationship out from behind closed doors, making it public.

Gina demanded accountability from me, and she put me on notice. If I messed up, which to her suggested I had become dangerous, others would hear about this mistake and step in to protect her. I, a young therapist at the time, felt the burden of this behavior. Although I could have offloaded the whole matter onto her "pathology," I had to stay with the truth of her responses; at the same time, I had to help her find ways to express her anger and disappointment that would ultimately get her what she needed. I had to be responsive, tolerant of my own shame and sense of ineffectuality, and maintain my overarching appreciation of the relationship we were building, often so painfully. Initially, I did not understand how wise her action was; she made a private relationship public, and each time any kind of transgression or failure occurred, she made sure others heard about it.

Many of the people she complained to about me did approach me to ask about the accuracy of these complaints. Although I sometimes still felt like she "was making too much of it," I had to keep stepping into her shoes and her neurobiology. I had to stay empathic with her pain, even when I was the culprit creating the pain. Warning signs arising from empathic failures quickly mushroomed for her into deeply distressing indications of imminent danger. The gradations of failure simply did not exist when Gina was in a triggered state. The modulation of the vagus nerve, the capacity to measure the scope of the failure, and the ability of the neocortex to sift through the incoming data and come to a balanced sense of what was going on were unavailable to her triggered neurobiology. To make matters worse, I often tipped into reactivity. My work involved maintaining respect for her efforts to cope and acknowledging the part I played at times in letting her down.

I had to manage my own shame in being such an imperfect helper. It took time for me to grasp what a brilliant strategy she had created. She was determined to make this therapeutic relationship safe enough to take the risks she needed to take to heal. This process involved slowly letting go of the protective strategies of disconnection but reemploying these strategies when necessary. Gradually, there was movement into safety, movement into safe-enough vulnerability.

At times, our focus was on helping Gina get grounded and managing an overly reactive autonomic system. We used meditation, relaxation, and other means to help her deal with "over-the-top" distress. When triggered, she was in major disconnection, and pushing for connection would have only escalated her anxiety. At these times, the counselor is not trying to make sense of things with the client but rather wants to bring about a more regulated presence so the work of connecting can resume as the dysregulation subsides.

As our work progressed, Gina let me know how angry or upset she was when I misunderstood or gave what to her was an inauthentic response (and it likely was). Rather than automatically getting caught up with a destabilized neurobiology and out-of-control fear, she could, with the memory of our connection, modulate her own distress. I was able, in word and presence, to let her know that I was affected by the realization that I had hurt her. Sometimes, I felt deeply sad, sometimes inept, and sometimes irritable. Once, when she was describing going from one hiding place to the next as she could hear her stepfather cajoling her to get to bed, I found tears welling up. I felt such pain for the panicked child. She noticed, "You crying?" I nodded. "It matters to you?" she continued. "You matter to me. So painful to see you, that little girl, trying so hard to be safe and so terribly scared. I wish someone could have been there to protect you." A long pause: "Yeah, me too." She kept looking at me. She could see the caring in that moment. She quieted. Later, she would remember that moment as "our moment of trust." It was mutual empathy at work: She could see my empathy with her, and she could see, know, and feel that she mattered to me, that she moved me, and that her pain caused me pain.

Factors, Approaches, and Interventions That Foster Healing and Resilience

Although traditional psychodynamic theory warns that this kind of therapeutic authenticity will lead to a distortion of the counseling relationship, in which the client feels she has to take care of the counselor, such shifts are not common. Gina felt cared for, like she mattered to me. She was able to see my empathy for her. She felt joined—less alone.

As we described in Chapter 1, condemned isolation, a term first used by Jean Baker Miller, speaks to the sense of being cast out, beyond the pale, isolated from others, and unable to act on one's own agency to alter the situation: alone, immobilized, self-blaming, and overwhelmed. Gina's sense of condemned isolation began to soften. This process is at the heart of posttraumatic experience (Jordan, 2018). RCT therapy encourages, and literally builds, courage to take small, safe steps toward connection—toward an increasing sense of efficacy, self-empathy, and a deep experience of radical hope. The client thinks, "Perhaps my experience can change, be different; I can be welcomed into the community from which I now feel so alienated. People can get to know me and want to understand and trust me with their vulnerability."

This experience can feel like a tectonic shift: from feeling alone, unloved, and without a future that can embrace transformation to a sense of connection and possibility. Our despair is tempered with a more accurate reading of our relational resources. We drop the pathological certainty of our outdated, negative relational images that keep us locked in old patterns. We begin to question the overgeneralization of these constricting images and provide support as vulnerability ebbs and flows. Validation and meaning making are an important part of what the relationship offers. We also know that mutual engagement, in which both parties expand and develop feelings and thoughts, tones the vagal nerve and thus allows us to increasingly rediscover comfort and healing through relationships (Jordan, 2018). As research attests, it is the relationship itself that provides the primary resource for healing (Duffey, Haberstroh, Ciepcielinski, & Gonzales, 2016; Norcross & Wampold, 2011; Oakley et al., 2013).

The use of RCT in counseling and therapy has spread. Many of the more traditional psychodynamic and cognitive approaches (Beck, 2011; Ellis, 2003) have cast aside or modified a monolithic intrapsychic emphasis to increasingly honor the power of relationship to heal (Jordan, 2018). RCT has also been used to study mentoring (Alvarez & Lazzari, 2016; Spencer, 2006), organizational problems, marginalization, eating disorders, management consultation, antiracism efforts, forensic work, educational applications, and parenting. Popular self-help messages have elaborated on the core relational-cultural concepts (Brown, 2011). The language of connection-disconnection, strength in vulnerability, courage, and the power of shame has gained currency in the last 10 years.

The importance of connection has found its way into these popular renditions (Brown, 2011). Our critique of power dynamics, and speaking to the need for broad social transformation, however, distinguishes RCT from the many approaches that maintain a focus on the individual, or possibly, the nuclear family. RCT requires a penetrating analysis of the dynamics of racism, sexism, heterosexism, and classism to question existing social structures that contribute to extensive pain for so many. RCT looks at marginalization as a process of exclusion and abuse of power.

Modern neuroscience has corroborated almost every single tenet of RCT 35 years after these ideas were first put forth (Craddock & Banks, 2015). RCT attempts to better understand human nature and human needs. However, RCT also advocates for change: personal and societal. If we as counselors or educators fully embrace our role as change agents, we must extend our understanding and action to the larger social structures. We have a responsibility to actively seek to effect change in the looming structures that limit human possibility. We must live by an ethic of mutual benefit and empathy. Our children are depending on our ability to develop radical empathy—empathy across difference.

To accomplish these goals, we will need to practice anticipatory empathy, feeling our way into the future, looking and listening for beneficial connection, and reworking damaging disconnections when possible. What will be needed to support future generations in reaching their potential? And what will be needed to ensure that we treat our precious planet with empathy and respect? Easy answers are not forthcoming, which can leave us feeling lost and uneasy. However, in our connections, we can ignite hope. Hope resides in turning from an ethic of separation to more neurobiologically sound engagement in building growth-fostering relationships. Safety resides in building bridges, not walls, and in developing better relational skills, not bigger weapons. Well-being ensues when we honor good connection and when we surrender what Einstein called the "illusion of separation" (Bilan, 2015).

Future Directions and Emerging Research

We discuss future directions and emerging research as they relate to therapeutic relationships in Chapter 1 and the role of people's neurobiology in supporting these relationships in Chapter 4. We also discuss relational resilience and its impact on relationships in Chapter 15. As we can see, the groundwork has been set for exciting research and developments in the area of fostering mutually empathic relationships in counseling. When considering the needs of people in the throes of crises and trauma, this advancement could not be more salient.

Finding ways that counselors can best contribute to growth-fostering connections with clients and support clients navigating times of loss continue to be important next steps in our profession's development. Crises and traumatic events have the potential to trigger an excruciating sense of loss and disconnection—of displacement and despair. At the same time, the connections we form can be a lifeline of sorts, and the quality of these connections can serve as a source of promise and a conduit for hope.

References

Alvarez, A., & Lazzari, M. (2016). Feminist mentoring and relational cultural theory: A case example and implications. *Affilia, 31*(1), 41–54. https://doi.org/10.1177/0886109915612512

Banks, A. (2015). *Four ways to click: Rewire your brain for stronger, more rewarding relationships.* New York, NY: Penguin Group.

Beck, J. (2011). *Cognitive behavioral therapy: Basics and beyond* (2nd ed.). New York, NY: Guilford Press.

Bilan, A. (2015, October 12). *Ponder this break down . . .* Retrieved from https://positivehead.com/ponder-this/2015/10/12/our-separation-is-an-optical-illusion-of-consciousness/

Birrell, P., & Bruns, C. (2016). Ethics and relationship: From risk management to relational engagement. *Journal of Counseling & Development, 94,* 391–397. https://doi.org/10.1002/jcad.12097

Brown, B. (2011, January 3). *The power of vulnerability* [Video file]. Retrieved from https://www.youtube.com/watch?v=iCvmsMzlF7o

Collins, P. H. (1990). *Black feminist thought: Knowledge, consciousness, and the politics of empowerment.* Boston, MA: Unwin Hyman.

Craddock, K., & Banks, A. (2015). *Stopping the pain of social exclusion.* Retrieved from https://www.wcwonline.org/News-Events-Extra-Information/full-article-stopping-the-pain-of-social-exclusion-full-blog-article

Duffey, T. (2005). The relational impact of addiction across the lifespan. In D. Comstock (Ed.), *Diversity and development: Critical contexts that shape our lives and relationships* (pp. 299–318). Belmont, CA: Brooks/Cole.

Duffey, T., Haberstroh, S., Ciepcielinski, E., & Gonzales, C. (2016). Relational-cultural theory and supervision: Evaluating developmental relational counseling. *Journal of Counseling & Development, 94,* 405–414. https://doi.org/10.1002/jcad.12099

Duffey, T., Haberstroh, S., & Trepal, H. (2016). Creative approaches in counseling and psychotherapy. In D. Capuzzi & M. D. Stauffer (Eds.), *Counseling and psychotherapy: Theories and interventions* (pp. 445–468). Alexandria, VA: American Counseling Association.

Duffey, T., & Somody, C. (2011). The role of relational-cultural theory in mental health counseling. *Journal of Mental Health Counseling, 33,* 223–242. https://doi.org/10.17744/mehc.33.3.c10410226u275647

Ellis, A. (2003). The relationship of rational emotive behavior therapy (REBT) to social psychology. *Journal of Rational-Emotive and Cognitive-Behavior Therapy, 21,* 5–20. https://doi.org/10.1023/A:1024177000887

Jordan, J. V. (2018). *Relational–cultural therapy* (2nd ed.). Washington, DC: American Psychological Association.

Jordan, J. V., & Hartling, L. M. (2002). New developments in relational-cultural theory. In M. Ballou & L. S. Brown (Eds.), *Rethinking mental health and disorder: Feminist perspectives* (pp. 48–70). New York, NY: Guilford Press.

Kaplan, D., Tarvydas, V., & Gladding, S. (2014). 20/20: A vision for the future of counseling: The new consensus definition of counseling. *Journal of Counseling & Development, 92,* 366–372. https://doi.org/10.1002/j.1556-6676.2014.00164.x

Kindsvatter, A., Russotti, J., & Tansey, M. (2019). The development of the fear response circuitry of the brain: A neurodevelopmental case for family counseling. *The Family Journal, 27,* 167–174. https://doi.org/10.1177/1066480719834874

Lieberman, M., & Eisenberger, N. (2009, February 13). Pains and pleasures of social life. *Science, 323,* 890–891. https://doi.org/10.1126/science.1170008

Miller, J. B. (2008). VI. Connections, disconnections, and violations. *Feminism and Psychology, 18,* 368–380. https://doi.org/10.1177/0959353508092090

Miller, J .B., & Stiver, I. P. (1997). *The healing connection: How women form relationships in therapy and in life.* Boston, MA: Beacon Press.

Norcross, J. C., & Wampold, B. E. (2011). Evidence-based therapy relationships: Research conclusions and clinical practices. *Psychotherapy, 48,* 98–102. https://doi.org/10.1037/a0022161

Oakley, M. A., Addison, S. C., Piran, N., Johnston, G. J., Damianakis, M., Curry, J., . . . Weigeldt, A. (2013). Outcome study of brief relational-cultural therapy in a women's mental health center. *Psychotherapy Research, 23,* 137–151. https://doi.org/10.1080/10503307.2012.745956

Porges, S. W. (2011). *The polyvagal theory: Neurophysiological foundations of emotions, attachment, communication, and self-regulation.* New York, NY: Norton.

Spencer, R. (2006). Understanding the mentoring process between adolescents and adults. *Youth and Society, 37*, 287–315. https://doi.org/10.1177/0743558405278263

Stiver, I. P., Rosen, W., Surrey, J., & Miller, J. B. (2008). Creative moments in relational-cultural therapy. *Women and Therapy, 31*(2–4), 7–29. https://doi.org/10.1080/02703140802145631

Windsor, L., Dunlap, E., & Golub, A. (2011). Challenging controlling images, oppression, poverty, and other structural constraints: Survival strategies among African-American women in distressed households. *Journal of African American Studies, 15,* 290–306. https://doi.org/10.1007/s12111-010-9151-0

Multiple-Choice Questions

1. Relational-cultural theory (RCT) would agree the most with which statement?
   a. Counseling is not a creative process.
   b. RCT has five important techniques to use with clients.
   c. Disconnections happen and are a normal part of life.
   d. Showing too much empathy with a client is not a good idea.

2. RCT was developed by
   a. Only male counselors and social workers.
   b. One really intelligent woman.
   c. A group of female psychologists.
   d. A group of female psychologists and a psychiatrist.

3. Research supports which of the following as the most important factor for positive client outcomes?
   a. The counselor's primary theory
   b. The therapeutic relationship
   c. The counselor's training
   d. The goals of the session

4. What are RCT's "five good things" for experiencing a good relational connection?
   a. Clarity, zest, sense of worth, productivity, desire for more connection
   b. Clarity, fun, empathy, sympathy, zest
   c. Communication, enjoyment, active listening, responsiveness, zest
   d. Relational connection, disconnection, growth, communication, empathy

5. According to RCT, disconnections in life are
   a. Avoidable and should never happen.
   b. Inevitable.
   c. Happening far too often, and counselors must change this.
   d. Only possible when rapport is not present.

6. According to RCT, culture is most likely to influence
   a. Controlling images.
   b. College outcomes.
   c. Addiction.
   d. Family issues.

7. Brain development research shows that after we are a certain age, our brains cannot change.
   a. True
   b. False
   c. True until we reach the age of 65
   d. True until we reach the age of 25

8. Research shows that physical pain affects us in the same way as emotional pain.
   a. True
   b. False
   c. Can be true for some people
   d. Can be true for people over the age of 40

9. Relational ethics would agree with the idea of
   a. Adhering strictly to ethical codes.
   b. Ignoring all ethical codes and only relying on the relational connection.
   c. Being mindful of the flow of mutuality.
   d. Refrain from using empathy when ethical issues arise.

10. If an empathic failure occurs, the counselor should
    a. Refer the client to another counselor.
    b. Reestablish a sense of safety before analyzing the failure.
    c. Instantly examine the situation with the client in each case.
    d. Immediately place this information in their notes.

11. As counselors, our ability to be authentic decreases as
    a. We censor ourselves.
    b. We get older.
    c. We learn more about brain health.
    d. None of the above

12. According to the chapter, self-disclosure can
    a. Always harm the client.
    b. Empower clients and help them feel less alone.
    c. Only be used my seasoned counselors.
    d. Always be the right tool to use.

13. Creativity in counseling (CIC) posits that creativity is
    a. Great to use if a client feels safe.
    b. Not the right tool for some people.
    c. Integral to the counseling process.
    d. Both a and b

14. Research attests to which tenet as a primary source of healing?
    a. Theory used by counselor
    b. Advanced counseling techniques
    c. The counseling relationship
    d. None of the above

15. RCT asks for a penetrating analysis of the dynamics of sexism and racism.
    a. True, of certain geographic locations
    b. True
    c. False
    d. False in the United States

Essay Questions

1. Relational-cultural theory (RCT) posits that relational connection is vital for a strong therapeutic relationship. Also, creativity in counseling (CIC) encourages creativity for building these strong relationships. How would you incorporate relational creativity into your sessions or into your personal life?

2. Given that Western culture often values autonomy at the expense of connection, how would you and your client cultivate a power-with relationship in your collaborative work?

3. Think about the case of Gina. Can you recall a time when you were "reactive" with someone? How did that feel to you, and how did this affect the connection? Furthermore, how did you process this experience in reflection?

4. Think about the case of Joanna. According to the chapter, counselors do not have magic words or tricks to use when someone is experiencing intense grief. We do, however, have the power of human connection. Does this connection excite you or scare you? If it scares you, why?

5. The authors of the chapter humbly talk about some disconnections during their sessions. Do you feel that, as a counselor or student, you must be perfect? Where does that message stem from?

CHAPTER 3

Crisis and Trauma Counseling
in Social and Cultural Contexts

Shane Haberstroh, Thelma Duffey, and Tonya R. Hammer

Most crises and traumatic events happen in social contexts. Natural disasters and wars ravage communities, interpersonal violence permeates the fabric of families and relationships, and workplace violence and harassment exploit professional status and power. Genocides, forced migration, and war result in horrendous losses across the global community. For many people, belonging to a certain group can mean a potential death sentence. Moreover, economic, racial, ethnic, gender, and sexuality majority power-over hierarchies can limit access to much needed resources, social support, and opportunities for healing (Jordan, 2018), affecting millions of people. Finally, subtle and nuanced disenfranchisement and rejection by others online and in person can leave people who seem different feeling abandoned, lonely, and defeated.

In this chapter, we explore conceptual models to help you appreciate the complex social, cultural, and relational worlds that crises upend. Effective counseling relationships begin from our commitment to developing our personal awareness (Substance Abuse and Mental Health Services Administration [SAMHSA], 2014a). Jordan's (2018) five good things speak to the energy, clarity, action, and nurturance of worth that can cultivate resilience as we walk with diverse people through some of the darkest days of their lives. We may find that this kind of counseling work changes us, broadening our perspectives about the painful sociocultural realities many people bear while humbling us as we witness human courage and compassion in the direst of circumstances.

Ecological-Social Conceptualizations

Like a stone thrown in a pond, crises can ripple through a person's life, their family, and the local and broader communities where they live (SAMHSA, 2014b).

Depending on the severity of an event, someone could be facing the loss of their neighborhood, death of loved ones, a shattered sense of safety, and the means to meet their basic needs. When a community is overcome by a disaster, the compounded losses eradicate familiar routines, relationships, and basic structure of people's lives. At other times, losses, violence, and crisis situations pervade the inner workings of close relationships, driving wedges of misery into the heart of the connections people need to thrive (Jordan, 2018; Siegel, 2012; van der Kolk, 2014). From this perspective, traumas ripple out from within intimate relationships to affect neighborhoods and communities at large. In a reciprocal manner, the broader systems influence normative and cultural expressions within smaller groups. When calamities cascade like a wave of destruction through a group, almost every relationship reels from the destabilizing consequences. These effects compound for people who also live in abusive or dehumanizing contexts when they confront a devastating community-level trauma.

Applying the ecological-social model (see Figure 3.1) to crisis and trauma work involves conceptualizing traumatic events among many interwoven social systems that reciprocally influence one another (SAMHSA, 2014b). From this perspective, people relate to each other in intimate relationships, family constellations, local communities and organizations, and within the broader societal strata. Cultural influences are crosscutting and inform all levels of interaction. These relationships also exist within a period of *human history* that embodies the collective messages about trauma, crisis, abuse, and neglect. For example, in 1964, Snell, Rosenwald, and Robey reviewed 37 cases of domestic violence and concluded that an intoxicated husband will beat his wife to (a) soothe his fears about his ineffectual masculinity and (b) gratify his wife's masochistic needs, while (c) alleviating her "guilt arising from the intense hostility expressed in her controlling, castrating behavior" (p. 111). *Time* magazine echoed this message of the therapeutic benefits and stabilizing effects of domestic violence. Imagine how a woman of that time, who suffered repeated physical brutality, would make sense of the bloodied beatings she survived. What might the others close to her say? Would she even think to reach out for help? How would the neighbors and police respond? It is clear that social, familial, and collective norms can invalidate a person's suffering and normalize violence and exploitation.

Overview of Cultural Influences

The U.N. Educational, Scientific and Cultural Organization (2001) defined *culture* as "the set of distinctive spiritual, material, intellectual and emotional features of society or a social group [that encompasses not only] art and literature, but lifestyles, ways of living together, value systems, traditions and beliefs" (p. 3). Approaching diversity from a global perspective, Hofstede (2011) identified several domains that varied among cultures. In crisis situations, these domains shape cultural and social responses from community members as well as framing how helpers engage. Each of these terms lies on a spectrum, and cultural belief systems will vary on each of these domains.

The *individualism-collectivism* spectrum focuses on how people relate within their communities. Cultures and groups that value individualism primarily focus on caring for themselves and those in their family, and they may tangentially help

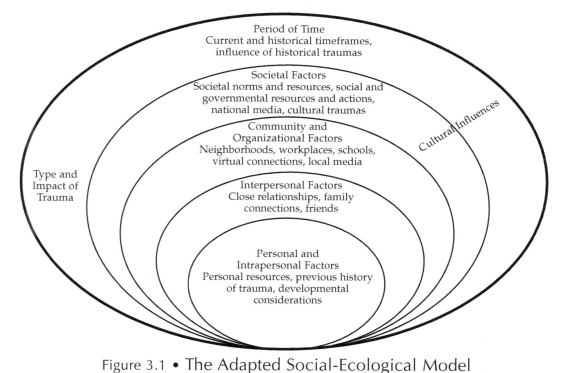

Figure 3.1 • The Adapted Social-Ecological Model

Note. Adapted from Substance Abuse and Mental Health Services Administration (SAMHSA, 2014b, p. 15). *Trauma-Informed Care in Behavioral Health Services. Treatment Improvement Protocol (TIP) Series 57.* U.S. Department of Health and Human Services (HHS) Publication No. (SMA) 13-4801. Rockville, MD: SAMHSA. All materials appearing in this volume except those taken directly from copyrighted sources are in the public domain and may be reproduced or copied without permission from SAMHSA or the authors. .

others. Societies founded on collective ideals feel tightly bonded to each other and share a strong sense of ingroup and outgroup membership. Imagine volunteering in a disaster response effort for a community that values collectivism. Understanding this nuanced cultural feature can help you work with people to prioritize needs and response efforts aimed at reconnecting members, joining shared recovery efforts, and probably recognizing you are seen as an outsider with some power who may not be trusted immediately (Hofstede, 2011).

The second dimension in this model relates to power in hierarchies and social structures. The *power-distance* continuum refers to how much people believe that power is distributed unevenly, how much latitude people have to disagree with those in power, and the extent of shared decision-making processes. In societies where people adhere to hierarchical power structures, the nature of a crisis strikes at the heart of hierarchical order. They may look to responsive services to restore order and may see benefit from direct advice and solutions (Hofstede, 2011).

Uncertainty-avoidance explores how people respond to ambiguity, tolerate differences within their community, and support rules and a belief in absolutes. From this perspective, a gay man living in a heteronormative community that does not tolerate different sexual orientations may be deprioritized during a community crisis. This bias may become apparent should he need to share shelter space with intolerant community members. Other cultural dimensions focus on indulgence and restraint as well as short- or long-term orientations (Hofstede, 2011). Short term–oriented societies value traditions, whereas long term–focused collectives look to the future.

Cultural groups vary considerably in these domains, creating clashes among people. As we work with diverse people, assessing a person's or community's experience within social contexts can help us identify relevant approaches and foci. Equally important, we should assess our own cultural and social perspectives on these domains.

Standards for Culturally and Contextually Competent Counseling

The Association for Multicultural Counseling and Development and Counselors for Social Justice developed competencies to guide counselors who work with diverse peoples and marginalized groups. These counselor competencies include developing our attitudes, knowledge, and skills when working with people different from you (Arredondo et al., 1996; Ratts & Greenleaf, 2018). Counselors invest in learning about many different cultural approaches to healing, incorporate local customs, respect indigenous and religious practices, and learn the unique ways a person or community responds to trauma and crises. Simply put, a counselor's words and actions have meaning, and a well-meaning but unaware and insensitive counselor can broach any number of cultural and community mores, bringing more pain and desperation to critical situations. An ancient proverb cited by Alvarado and Cavazos (2008) reflects this need for awareness and cultural competence:

> One day during the monsoon season, there was a big storm and it rained for a long time. The rushing waters washed everything downstream. While the monkey was firmly holding on to a branch of a tree with all his might, the fish was swimming vigorously against the current. "My friend is in trouble," thought the monkey, "I need to help him." Without thinking twice, he reached down and pulled his friend out of the water. (p. 57)

The U.S. Department of Health and Human Services, Office of Minority Health (2010b) published the National Standards for Culturally and Linguistically Appropriate Services in Health and Health Care. These standards focused on (a) developing awareness and acceptance of diverse people, (b) increasing awareness of cultural values, (c) deepening understanding and strategies to manage the "dynamics of difference," (d) developing knowledge of various cultures, and (e) learning approaches to adapt in different cultural contexts.

Cultural Awareness

Given the many crisis situations and contexts in which we work, it is essential that we develop awareness of our own cultural and contextual background, learn about cultural concepts and traditions, and approach crisis and trauma counseling with respect and humility (Nader, Dubrow, & Stamm, 2013). In many disaster response situations, we may be an outsider, working in shelters, perhaps in another part of the country or the world. Cultural and social mismatches can lead marginalized people to feel disempowered, especially when counselors lack cultural awareness and skills (U.S. Department of Health and Human Services, Office of Minority

Health, 2010b). Therefore, the first step in developing cultural competence is to gain a basic sense of the cultural and contextual factors that shape our worldview, recognizing that our cultural contexts are often overlapping and varied.

SAMHSA (2014a) defined *cultural competence* as "recognizing that each of us, by virtue of our culture, has at least some ethnocentric views that are provided by that culture and shaped by our individual interpretation of it" (p. 9). The U.S. Department of Health and Human Services, Office of Minority Health (2010a) has provided free online training focused on developing cultural competencies for disaster preparedness and crisis response.

According to one U.S. Department of Health and Human Services, Office of Minority Health (2010b) self-assessment measure, people who are culturally *unaware* easily believe stereotypes about different cultures, may unknowingly violate equity laws, and have difficulty seeing biased behaviors in themselves and others. Usually, people who are unaware gain awareness through feedback from others. As we discuss later in this chapter, these individuals may be prone to committing all forms of microaggressions (Sue, 2010). Counselors who maintain a *traditional* mind-set about culture recognize their own biases but engage in subtle discriminatory practices, may make demeaning jokes, and may create toxicity in professional and personal settings. Counselors identified as *neutral* generally strive to be self-aware but do not intervene in discriminatory behaviors by others. Others may see their silence as complicity. *Change agents* see their own biases, recognize prejudice in others, and intervene when they see discrimination and abuse of power to help systems and others value the intrinsic worth of diverse individuals. Finally, *rebels* are highly attuned to discriminatory practices. Their heightened sense of advocacy may lead others to not take them seriously, and in the worst cases, rebels can engage in reverse discrimination. As you read these categories, think about situations in your life where you may have rebelled, been a bystander, realized your stark unawareness, or stepped in and made changes that mattered to people with less power than you.

Knowledge of Cultural Differences: Reponses to Crises and Traumas

Cultural variables play a vital role in key aspects of trauma reactions and recovery strategies (SAMHSA, 2014b). Certain cultural groups are at risk to experience more traumatic events than others, and specific traumatic events may occur more frequently within certain communities. For example, White people experienced more sexual assaults than African American individuals, who, in turn, faced increased levels of physical violence and assault (SAMHSA, 2014b). Political violence, wars, and environmental factors contribute to certain groups falling victim to institutionalized violence and strife (SAMHSA, 2014b). Finally, cultural lenses and within-culture relationships provide meaning making about traumas and guide recovery practices. Thus, our use of language and societal labels and appreciation of differences within cultures and within clients can help set the stage for productive counseling.

Labels, Language, and Examples of Sociocultural Aspects of Trauma

For many people, external labels of their ethnicity, race, gender, and sexuality may not match with their identity and the identifiers used within their communities.

Although the U.S. Census and other agencies provide broad definitions of demographic factors, people will vary considerably with how they identify themselves. We provide some general examples of differing cultural features of several of the main racial and ethnic groups and LGBTQ+ (lesbian, gay, bisexual, transgender, queer or questioning) concerns related to trauma and recovery. Please be aware that these are general observations of diverse and often marginalized groups categorized by SAMHSA (2014a). We encourage you to avoid imposing labels and broad cultural assumptions on others as rigid expectations. Instead, know that this information could be relevant for your clients to differing degrees. See Sidebar 3.1 for more information on the importance of cultural and social awareness.

American Indian and Alaskan Native Populations

In the United States, 573 tribal nations span territories across 36 states (National Congress of American Indians, 2015). Although tribes may share some commonalities, there are many distinct customs and practices unique to each of them (National Congress of American Indians, 2015). When I (Shane) started working in northern Arizona, I began learning about the tribal communities in the area and quickly realized my ignorance of the nuanced dynamics of tribal cultures. A colleague shared a story about a student who refused to go back to school after a death in the building. A culturally unaware counselor might have referred the client to disciplinary procedures or a psychological evaluation. What worked for this student was to invite a medicine man from his tribe to perform a spiritual cleansing ritual.

Working with tribal communities involves a recognition of the deep interrelationships among nature, community, and the spiritual world. The "healing forest" model (Coyhis & Simonelli, 2005) of mental health speaks to the idea that when someone removes a tree from a sick forest, it cannot be replanted back into the same sick forest and thrive. Communal bonds and whole community recovery efforts may make the most sense when working with individuals from tribal nations. Moreover, when working in crisis situations in native communities, it is imperative to work closely with tribal elders and leaders and to gain approval for any approaches and programs (SAMHSA, 2014a). The soul wound (Duran, Firehammer, & Gonzalez, 2008; Gone, 2013) that many people from tribal communities experience is a direct result of the historical trauma embedded in indigenous cultural narratives.

African American and Black Populations

Although people and agencies use the terms "Black" and "African American" alike, there are some potentially conceptual differences between these terms. The term Black may be more inclusive for people not of African descent; however, some may prefer African American regardless of their lineage. As we describe cultural and historical traumas, members of Black communities experience high

Sidebar 3.1 • Cultural and Social Awareness

Every client develops in his or her own community, and it is important for a counselor to consider a client's context. Also, it is vital for you as counselor to identity your own cultural and social perspectives. If you have greater awareness of your own cultural and social contexts, you may have a better understanding of your client's world.

levels of institutional discrimination, disproportionate mislabeling of behaviors and mental health concerns as criminality, and overrepresentation in incarceration rates. Themes of equality in counseling relationships, community advocacy and change, and church and family bonds are important elements to consider when planning for and responding to crisis events (Bell-Tolliver, Burgess, & Brock, 2009; Boyd-Franklin & Karger, 2012).

Asian Populations

People of Asian descent come from a wide range of regions and cultural backgrounds. Issues of shame and humiliation may be present, especially when people perceive themselves as being insufficient or believe they may offend others (SAMHSA, 2014a). In Japan, this fear is known as *Taijin kyofusho* (SAMHSA, 2014a). Crisis situations strike at the heart of this fear, because they render people inadequate and place them into contexts beyond their immediate capacity to control. The resulting shame or humiliation may make it difficult for Asian people to reach out for help, and they may continue to suffer in silence for fear of revealing their shortcomings publicly.

Hispanic Populations

Some people may identify themselves as Hispanic, whereas others may prefer other identities, such as Latino, Latina, or Latinx (SAMHSA, 2014a). With the idea that labels are social constructions, your warmth, empathy, and efforts to connect with people of Hispanic descent speaks to the cultural concept of *personalismo*, which is a valued cultural process (SAMHSA, 2014a). Detached professionalism may not serve you well in these communities. Mutuality and respect for family structures and engagement in community advocacy can set the stage for trust in sessions and community work.

LGBTQ+ Populations

LGBTQ+ refers to the varied sexual and gendered sexual identities of the human experience (Singh & Gonzales, 2014). According to McCormick, Scheyd, and Terrazas (2018), LGBTQ+ youth experience much higher rates of trauma than their gender-conforming and straight peers. The Human Rights Campaign (2018) reported that LGBTQ+ individuals face high rates of hate crimes and sexual assaults. According to Federal Bureau of Investigation hate crime statistics, violence against sexual minority individuals rose 5% from 2016 to 2017 (Human Rights Campaign, 2018). Suicide rates are much higher for sexual minorities (Human Rights Campaign, 2018). Effective services for LGBTQ+ individuals begin with assessing your own biases, fears, and reactions to sexuality and sexual identity as well as your work to affirm your clients. We invite you to review the competencies for counseling lesbian, gay, bisexual, queer, questioning, intersex, and ally (LGBQQIA) individuals (Association for Lesbian, Gay, Bisexual, and Transgender Issues in Counseling [ALGBTIC] LGBQQIA Competencies Taskforce, 2013) and transgender clients (ALGBTIC, 2010) at https://algbtic.org/.

Culturally Centered Empowerment and Advocacy

Working as a culturally aware counselor and as a change agent is a lifelong journey. Chapters 1 and 2 of this text provide a detailed relational-cultural framework for conceptualizing crisis and trauma work with clients and highlight relational-cultural theory (RCT) as a context for conceptualizing how people (a) grow, (b) connect with one another, (c) find their way through relational ruptures to reconnection, and (d) foster resilience through authenticity and mutuality (Jordan, 2018). RCT considers the role of context, culture, gender, power, and privilege as well as how these factors influence a person's trajectory through loss (Duffey & Somody, 2011). We believe these concepts are especially relevant when considering the social and cultural factors involved in crisis and trauma work.

In Chapter 11, we also discuss community approaches to trauma and disaster recovery. When you work in community settings, you may interact with people from various cultural groups, from various social economic statuses, and within the mores and norms that exist within that community. In our work with communities who experienced massive traumas, we (Shane and Thelma) learned to carefully attend to the themes and words used by members of communities to explain their experiences and potential pathways for healing. Whether you work one-on-one or in larger communal settings, you most likely will begin as an outsider (U.S. Department of Health and Human Services, Office of Minority Health, 2010a). Armed with research and theory, we often have our own ideas of what people need to heal. Although counselors bring along valuable insights, we approach crisis situations with cultural humility.

Cultural Humility and Culturally Centered Care

Knowledge of different cultures and specialized competencies requires research, practice, and adaptability. In a crisis situation or new setting, you may not have the time or sources to investigate nuanced cultural factors. Conversely, approaching clients with a bevy of cultural factoids without humility may damage the counseling relationship (Hook, Davis, Owen, Worthington, & Utsey, 2016). In contrast, a culturally humble counselor does not assume competence but rather approaches the counseling encounter with openness to what is most culturally relevant for their client, and this practice enhances and supports the relationship (Hook et al., 2016; Jordan, 2018).

According to Waters and Asbill (2013), a worldview grounded in cultural humility serves as a foundational state of being in which you work from a set of principles that guide culturally grounded care. Waters and Asbill further conceptualized cultural humility as a lifelong process whereby counselors grow from interactions with diverse people, remaining open to learning and integrating new concepts into practice. Moreover, like in RCT, counselors actively strive to address power imbalances and join with groups who advocate for equity and change. The movement toward culturally centered care (Holden et al., 2014) echoed these sentiments.

Relational Foundations for Crisis and Trauma Work: Contextual Considerations

No one is immune to loss, yet people often avoid really listening to the suffering of others (Neimeyer, Klass, & Dennis, 2014) or may be blind to the pain of people who experience a different social location (McIntosh, 1989, 1992). Imagine accessing your courage and sharing your most shameful and frightening experiences of loss or cruelty, and your counselor pulls back or minimizes your story, feelings, or experiences. You could be left to question what is true and real, and perhaps even your worth. Most important, you learned that in the *context* of that conversation, the topics you shared and your pain were now off limits, even to those trained to help. See Sidebar 3.2 for more information on counselor withdrawal.

Clients who experienced horrendous abuse, witnessed death, feel suicidal, or watched a loved one suffer may share gruesome and heart-wrenching details. As you work with people who experienced terrifying life events, or people who lived with multiple episodes of abuse, rejection, and abandonment, your presence and the connection you have with them as they share gruesome and harrowing stories is an essential counseling skill. Exploring the circumstances of someone's abuse or trauma with interest, genuineness, and a sense of shared humanity can create a new social context for your clients. When you engage in culturally humble growth fostering relationships (Jordan, 2018), each of you will be affected and changed.

It is evident that people who abuse and commit violence exploit their power, seek to control others, and dismiss the pain and fear of others while ignoring their own sense of accountability. During times of crisis and trauma, power and privilege are at play before, during, and after these events. Abuses of power and privilege often lead to incidences of trauma, such as incest and abuse. It is the power-over dynamic (Jordan, 2018) that facilitates an environment where sexual abuse and harassment of others may be legitimized or authorized.

More nuanced forms of disenfranchisement and microaggressions also emerge. Sue (2010) described varying levels of microaggressions in counseling practice that Hook et al. (2016) suggested lead to increased dropout rates and ruptures in the counseling relationship. In their study of 2,212 racial and ethnic minority individuals, Hook et al. noted that 81% of participants experienced at least one of the following microaggressions. According to Sue, *microassaults* are intentional denigrating acts committed against marginalized people. An example would be shelter workers intentionally giving extra food to someone of their own race while demonstrably limiting food to others. In a more subtle manner, *microinsults* emerge from a counselor's lack of awareness and can disempower and humiliate others. Finally, *microinvalidations* can result when people dismiss and minimize the experiences of other people. For example, someone who says they "only see people, not the color of their skin" invalidates experiences of racism.

Power intersects with privilege, which is a system of unearned advantage gained through another's disadvantage (McIntosh, 1989, 1992). These factors are at play in major cultural and historical traumas. Those with power and privilege may also work to bring about changes within society to reshape perspectives and to confront social and institutional injustices that foster abuses. However, as Jordan (2018) noted, in individualistic, competitive cultures, power is guarded and resources

Sidebar 3.2 • Counselor Withdrawal

The counseling relationship is a unique social context in which people can hopefully share the details of their abuse and traumas. When a counselor pulls away or avoids difficult conversations, clients experience one more empathic failure, and they can withdraw into isolation.

are restricted from people within marginalized communities. Thus, a radical shift in the understanding and application of social power would move from an individualistic hoarding of power to mutuality and equity, with the understanding that the separate self is a metaphor that emerged from a psychology of masculine privilege. The abuse of power and greed for more power can lead to catastrophic collective destruction.

Collective Traumatic Experiences Explored

Wars, natural disasters, and other collective losses leave indelible changes on the patterns of human interaction within many groups. *Collective trauma* refers to the broad effects that calamitous forces inflict on social groups of any size (Hirschberger, 2018). The group size can be as diffuse and diverse as a nation or group of nations. *Cultural traumas* embody atrocities committed against a particular cultural group that dramatically shape the collective identity of that group. *Historical traumas* refer to traumatic events experienced by marginalized groups throughout history, with the effects persisting through generations. *Intergenerational trauma* speaks to the effects of trauma passed through family lineages.

The events of 9/11 forever shaped national and cultural dialogues about terrorism, patriotism, and religion (Holman & Silver, 2011). The many wars and armed conflicts throughout history represent a myriad of collective, cultural, and historical traumas. For example, World War II can be seen as a collective trauma that included the historical trauma of the Holocaust, which, in turn, led to lasting intergenerational effects for families of Holocaust survivors (Yehuda & Lehrner, 2018). Understanding how these historical and macrolevel traumas play out will help you consider the broader social influences in your clients' lives.

Numerous groups endure oppression and traumas rooted in cultural exploitation and historical abuses by dominant groups (J. Alexander, Eyerman, Giesen, Smelser, & Sztompka, 2004; Mohatt, Thompson, Thai, & Tebes, 2014). According to Birrell and Freyd (2006), many individuals experience an imposed power-under dynamic, which foments pain and social-cultural trauma born from oppression and social exclusion. Although these traumatic injustices invade the everyday life of so many people, counselors may not attend to these dynamics because of fear and lack of knowledge or because a counselor's privilege blinds them to the chronic suffering of others (McIntosh, 1989, 1992). We all exist as cultural beings, with unique and varied experiences, and we enter into crisis and trauma work aware of the intrapersonal and cultural narratives guiding our work. Historical and current cultural traumas are profound tragedies that shape worldviews, transform societies, and scar cultures.

Cultural Traumas

J. Alexander et al. (2004) defined cultural trauma as a process "when members of a collective feel they have been subjected to a horrendous event that leaves indelible marks on their group consciousness, marking their memories forever and changing their future identity in fundamental and irrevocable ways" (p. 1). SAMHSA (2014b) further articulated that culturally traumatic events and periods of time are remembered, culturally destructive, and associated with suffering and painful feelings. Collective memories of group trauma shape how people see themselves in the context of current social structures and can fuel advocacy efforts or lead to cultural meaning making in the face of persistent traumatic and discriminatory practices.

In recent history, many groups faced cultural traumas born from specific incidents exacerbated by systematic political, economic, and social injustices. These events represent collective and cultural traumas because these groups were profoundly affected on the basis of their culture, religion, sexual orientation, or nationality (J. Alexander et al., 2004). These traumas also highlighted the oppressive functions of ongoing social and bureaucratic biases (Onwuachi-Willig, 2016). We explore several recent examples that dominated the news cycle over the past several years with a keen awareness that so many more instances of cultural trauma happen on a routine basis.

Shootings of Black People and Routine Injustice
The killing of Trayvon Martin and subsequent acquittal of George Zimmerman ignited conversations about the injustices committed against Black people. From this tragic death, Alicia Garza, Patrisse Cullors, and Opal Tometi organized what is now known as Black Lives Matter (Black Lives Matter, n.d.) to address the gross inequities of systemic and state-directed violence and to affirm the inherent worth and the resilience of Black people. Further focusing on the role of systematic trauma and expected community trauma, Onwuachi-Willig (2016) expanded on J. Alexander et al.'s (2004) definition to include the concept of routine traumas rooted in "systematic oppression and discrimination" (p. 347). This conceptualization highlighted how systematic injustices compound the violence and dehumanization that many African American people experience when community members are slain and the perpetrators exonerated. The despair that hardens when systems of justice fail to protect marginalized groups while protecting the privileged retraumatizes communities through narratives of expected injustice. When institutions routinely abuse power, there is no resolution, peace, or justice, and these factors keep the wounds of loss jagged and open. Only the mobilization of social justice efforts and affirmation of human dignity can bring about change.

Forced Migration, Human Smuggling, and Human Trafficking
Alan Kurdi was 3 years old when his body washed up on the shores of Greece after his family fled from the Syrian war in a ramshackle raft (Ojebode, 2017). Images of his still body lying face down in the sand, waves rolling over his sneakers and bright red shirt permeated the media. Alan was one of the more than 2.5 million children running from the violent conflict in Syria (Schweiger, 2016).

Policies (Krogstad & Gonzalez-Barrera, 2019) related to separating migrant children from their parents at the southern border of the United States prompted leading mental health organizations to advocate for the mental health of children separated from their loved ones. In letters written to the president of the United States, professional mental health organizations reiterated the trauma of forced separations and delineated how these practices can lead to serious and debilitating psychosocial and physical problems later in life.

These journeys of people fleeing violence and war create a black-market economy focused on smuggling people across borders, some of whom end up trafficked into slavery, prostitution, or other exploitive contexts (U.N. Office on Drugs and Crime [UNDOC], 2018). UNDOC differentiates smuggling and trafficking on the basis of consent, exploitation, and transnationality. People may consent to be smuggled across national borders as a method of transportation. By contrast, people who are trafficked do not consent to their capture; may not travel between nations; and may be victims of forced prostitution, sexual exploitation, and mutilation of their bodies and death through organ harvesting. However, many people who consent to being smuggled across borders become victims of human trafficking (UNDOC, 2018).

Hurricanes Katrina and Maria

These calamities affect many marginalized populations because of delays in response and reduction of funds from the Federal Emergency Management Agency (U.S. House of Representatives Select Bipartisan Committee to Investigate the Preparation for Response to Hurricane Katrina, 2006). Communities faced high death tolls, delayed infrastructure restoration, and an erosion of public trust. This outcome led to long-term impacts for those affected and created barriers to relationships within the community (LaJoie, Sprang, & McKinney, 2010). The inadequate response for Hurricane Maria was also tragic. Puerto Ricans are U.S. citizens, yet a recent poll found that only 54% of respondents believed this to be the case (Morning Consult, 2017). With a large percentage of people believing that the people of Puerto Rico are foreigners, it may be easy to relegate these citizens to the status of "other," ignoring their plight and need for equitable recovery resources.

The #MeToo Movement

The #MeToo movement, founded in 2006, brought the epidemic of sexual assault against women and others to prominence in 2018 when the hashtag #MeToo went viral (Me Too, n.d.). Focused on addressing the systematic perpetuation of sexual violence, this movement brought increased national awareness to the silencing of people who survive sexual assaults and violence. However, this movement speaks to the often unspoken collective and traumatic sexual violence that affects the lives of many people, and this awareness has brought about international discussions about disempowerment and advocacy.

Pulse Nightclub

In the early hours of June 6th, 2016, 50 people died, and another 53 were seriously wounded at the hands of a person who funneled his hatred for the LGBTQ+ community and radicalized religious beliefs into one of the most violent domestic terror attacks in the United States. Eddie Justice was one of the people murdered at the club. His texts, sent over a 25-minute span to his mother, capture his final moments (B. K. Alexander & Weems, 2017): "Mommy I love you. In club they shooting. Trapp in bathroom. call them mommy. Now I'm tell I'm [in] bathroom. He's coming, I'm gonna die. He has us he's in here with us" (p. 486).

His last words of love and pleas for help portray the terror and loss that shattered so many families gripped by this senseless act of violence. Ferguson (2018) contended that although political leaders and many in the media condemned the shooting as inspired by the Islamic State of Iraq and Syria (ISIS), it was in fact an act rooted in "everyday poisons of homophobia, racism, colonialism, and xenophobia" (p. 37). A counselor who recognizes that people belonging to the LGBTQ+ community, and those who support it, face routine discrimination and threats to their safety and well-being can help create a space of safety through recognizing their daily persecutions.

Racially, Religiously, and Ethnically Motivated Church Shootings

Religious communities and places of worship provide significant sources of support and refuge for those experiencing traumatic events and community-wide disasters, and they also provide spiritual comfort and needed resources. When people are murdered in their place of worship, sanctuaries of peace and hope become tarnished with hate and violence. As in the case of the hate crime murders committed in the Emmanuel African Methodist Episcopal Church in 2015, parishioners were targeted because of being Black and because the church was a longstanding beacon for civil rights. While in jail, Dylann Roof, who committed these murders, wrote in his journal that "I would like to make it crystal clear, I do not regret what I did. I am not sorry. I have not shed a tear for the innocent people I killed" (Berman, 2017).

Other recent prominent church-based, hate-motivated shootings include violence perpetrated at the Christchurch Mosque (New Zealand) in 2018, the Antioch Church (Tennessee) in 2017, and the Tree of Life Synagogue (Pittsburgh) in 2018 (Associated Press, 2018). These acts of terror against people in places of worship bring racial and religious hate to the forefront of cultural and national conversations. They also illustrate the capacity to love, heal, and act courageously in the face of certain death and during recovery processes as many of these churches and parishioners continue to share their message of forgiveness, hope, and spiritual growth.

Cultural traumas exist as atrocities embedded in the present time, often persisting through ongoing dehumanization and invalidation. Over time, they will become historical narratives that shape societal and cultural views. Clearly, appreciating the historical roots of trauma helps counselors understand how people may make meaning of current devastation and loss.

Historical Traumas

History is replete with examples of horrors inflicted on various groups that can seem bewildering in their sheer magnitude and terror. Mohatt et al. (2014) defined historical trauma as trauma that (a) is experienced collectively among individuals who share a common identity, (b) spans generations, and (c) is remembered through images and stories that may transmit intergenerationally as negative health and psychological effects. Researchers found links between historical trauma and adverse effects on current levels of psychological and physical health (Yehuda & Lehrner, 2018).

Our chapter cannot represent the abject terror, unimaginable violence, and spiritual wounds inflicted on loving families and innocent children. Each number in the statistics we review was a person like you in many ways. A person with all the complex mix of hopes, fears, dreams, friendships, family dynamics, loves, losses, and mistakes that make us human. This person may have witnessed children executed, siblings dying of malnutrition, friends killed, a loved one murdered, and brutal exploitation of humanity. Take a moment here to witness and honor these people with compassion and mourning as you reflect on the genocides and mass atrocities that shaped many communities.

Slavery

According to the Trans-Atlantic Slave Trade Database (https://archive.slavevoyages.org/), approximately 12.5 million African people were exported as chattel to destinations in the new world. Millions died in the journey. After arriving in the United States, more than three hundred thousand human beings experienced systematic dehumanization, living as property in atrocious conditions. Following the end of slavery, African American people endured ongoing oppression and the persistent threat of murder by lynching. In 1918, Mary Turner's husband was killed after being accused of shooting an abusive plantation owner. Steadfast in her belief of her husband's innocence, she advocated against his killing and threatened to bring whatever legal action she could to his murderers. Her love and advocacy were met with brutality:

> On May 19th, a mob of several hundred brought her to Folsom Bridge which separates Brooks and Lowndes counties in Georgia. The mob tied her ankles, hung her upside down from a tree, doused her in gasoline and motor oil and set her on fire. (National Association for the Advancement of Colored People, n.d., para. 13)

The U.S. Congress only recently outlawed lynching after more than 200 failed attempts to pass this legislation (Dreier, 2019). Senator Cory Booker authored the bill, citing the atrocity of lynching and the injustice that the vast majority of those who committed these murders never faced any consequences. These legislative efforts speak to the fact that a majority (63%) of Americans perceive that the history of slavery continues to affect the position of Black people in America. Of note, Black and White people were divided on this issue, with 58% of White individuals acknowledging the impact of this historical trauma, and 84% of Black people recognizing the ongoing deleterious social effects of slavery.

The Holocaust

The German government murdered nearly 6 million Jewish people during the Holocaust (U.S. Holocaust Memorial Museum [USHMM], n.d.). They also killed nearly a quarter million young children, infants, and toddlers with disabilities during their euthanasia program (USHMM, n.d.). The Nazi regime also slaughtered hundreds of thousands of other marginalized groups they deemed as less than ideal (USHMM, n.d.). The USHMM website includes a section titled, "Behind Every Name a Story," and we invite you to read these stories of people who endured these horrors. Jakob Blankitny, only one of 42 Jewish people who survived from his village of more than 4,000, wrote the following in regard to his time in the concentration camps:

> We were beaten and abused constantly, especially if someone unfortunately fell or moved in place because of the hard beatings. These beatings were executed at that immediate instant; making the vile SS soldiers fill with laughter to see in our faces, the horror to which we were subjected. (USHMM, n.d., para. 11)

The effects of the Holocaust are wide ranging and remind all of us that all societies have the potential to institute sustained cruelty and systematic dehumanization of people (Yehuda & Lehrner, 2018).

Subjugation, Forced Relocation, and Massacres of Indigenous and Native American People

Native American people endured horrific abuses and suffer from the historical and ongoing effects of colonialism. Duran, Duran, Yellow Horse Brave Heart, and Yellow Horse-Davis (1998) wrote that "for American Indians, the United

States is the perpetrator of their holocaust" (p. 345). The Trail of Tears began with native people being forced from their homes and land under the threat of violence. The passage was deadly. Wahnenaui, a Cherokee woman, wrote her first-hand account:

> Perish or remove! It might be—remove and perish! [A] long journey through the Wilderness—could the little ones endure? [A]nd how about the sick? [T]he old people and infirm, could they possibly endure the long tedious journey; Should they leave? This had been the home of their Ancestors from time out of mind. Everything they held dear on earth was here, must they leave? (Mintz & McNeil, 2018, para. 2)

Duran et al. (2008) reiterated the importance of recognizing the soul wound that remains present in native cultures as a result of oppression and colonialism. As we recognize the powerful forces of historical and cultural traumas that affect so many people in their lives, new and emerging contexts intersect with these powerful social forces.

Applying Sociocultural, Relational, and Contextual Concepts in Practice

To summarize, although the details, circumstances, and types of traumatic events can vary considerably among people, we can apply the information provided in this chapter as touchstones to guide our work with diverse people and communities. Consider the following:

1. Continually *develop* your own cultural and personal awareness through training and investment in people and communities different from you and also integrate feedback from trusted colleagues and supervisors.
2. *Recognize* your power and privilege and use this to empower people and communities with less power and resources.
3. *Recognize* that different traumatic events may carry different and nuanced meanings for people. Interpersonal traumas and natural disasters can devastate families, but the familial, social, and cultural messages and social norms related to these events differ considerably.
4. Explore and *discover* as much information as possible related to the community and cultural factors present within your client's social networks. Co-create *culturally and community-centered* programs when possible. For example, when we (Thelma and Shane) worked with the Sutherland Springs community, we met with community members to hear about their perspectives to collaborate on the best approaches to support the community.
5. *Appreciate* the social and cultural contexts of trauma. Many people live with the experiences of historical and cultural traumas that frame and exacerbate current distress.
6. *Recognize* and respect how people identify themselves within their social and cultural worlds.
7. *Engage* in mutually empathic ways, showing your compassion and humanness.
8. Stay *connected* with the people and groups that nourish your well-being and development.

Case Example and Applications for Hope and Healing

The Martinez family was living in Florida when a hurricane destroyed their home. Marcos and his partner, Juan, rely on Marcos's income while Juan pursues his education. The business where Marcos was working was destroyed in the hurricane, and his paycheck was their family's primary source of income. Juan has withdrawn from classes and has obtained a part-time job, and Marcos has found a temporary job making half of his salary. They have two children, ages 9 and 10, adopted in the past 2 years. Both currently attend a local elementary school, damaged in the hurricane. Marcos's family disowned him when he came out as gay, but Juan's family is supportive. However, Juan's family is not financially able to assist them in this crisis. Since the hurricane, which occurred 6 months ago, some relationship issues have developed between Juan and Marcos, and their 10-year-old has started acting out in class.

Envisioning Yourself as Marcos

We ask you to place yourself in this family's position for a moment. Imagine you are living in a city devastated by natural disaster. Your home and place of business are ravaged by a hurricane, and the family you have fought so hard to create is left homeless. In fact, there is no part of your family's daily life or physical history left unscathed. Like Marcos, you are the sole breadwinner in the family, and your place of business is destroyed. You must seek out work in whatever way you can, and the best you can do—given the great needs for resources within your community—is to take on a part-time job. Your relationship, which you went to great lengths to legitimize, is now threatened. You have survived so much together, yet it is hard to maintain the mutual support you so enjoy. The fourth- and fifth-grade children you recently embraced into your family are seeing their lives upended once again. There were reasons why at 9 and 10 years old your children needed a new home and family, and the hurricane crisis not only threatened their security but it may have also triggered disturbing feelings from their former losses.

We invite you to stay with this image. Your keepsakes, photographs, and all things tangible that connect you with your history are all gone. Favorite furnishings, decorative objects, books, and belongings were washed away. Your spouse's education, a truly treasured goal, must be put on hold. Your relationship is stressed as you try to navigate rebuilding your lives, dealing with the logistics of living and trying to create a sense of safety and continuity. You cannot afford the cost of counseling, and you seek out services offered within the community. You place your name on a waiting list and hope that whoever you are assigned to can help.

Consider walking in the counselor's office, and what that might be like. There is so much in your heart and on your mind, and you do not know where to begin. You want to do the right thing, but it seems that everything you do does not seem to be enough. You and your family are becoming increasingly disconnected from one another in spite of how hard you try.

Growing up, you went through hard times, but the love and support of family and extended family would see you through them. Now, you are disconnected from your family of origin, and although your feelings may be mixed, you miss them. It has been several years since you spoke, and reaching out now seems impossible. In fact, the one thing that helped you get through the loss of your family was trusting the love of your partner and believing you could see each other through anything. However, now the strife you feel together feels immobilizing, and you are at a loss on how to nurture it and your children. What do you hope to find in a counselor? What social and cultural factors are in play that support or interfere with your recovery?

Envisioning Yourself as the Counselor

After you have taken the time to place yourself in Marcos Martinez's place, and you are able to connect with the various dynamics that Marcos and his family are navigating, we ask that you step back again and metaphorically switch gears. Imagine you are the counselor, and the Martinez family has sought your help. Marcos and Juan are in your office, and the children will be seeing a family counselor too. You will be working together in support of this family. What cultural, contextual, systemic, and logistical factors would you need to consider in this work? Hope and healing can feel truly elusive for families who undergo such losses, yet as counselors, it is our goal to help our clients move through crises as best they can, together and with one another—and we see the therapeutic relationship as integral to our work.

A Relational-Cultural Response

Each of the models reflected in this chapter consider context and culture as integral factors when conceptualizing crisis and trauma counseling. Herein we use RCT as a model to briefly conceptualize a counselor's work with the Martinez family. Using RCT as a framework, a counselor would look at the impact of the crisis on the family relationships by considering familial, societal, cultural, and societal factors. For example, Marcos and Juan are gay and married. They do not have Marcos's family's blessing and are, in fact, estranged. It may be that Juan and Marcos underwent considerable efforts to formalize their union, and there may be incidences of discrimination and prejudice in the process. Although this is not something the counselor would assume, the counselor would listen for the possibility and seek to empower both Marcos and Juan through the relationship. In addition, an RCT counselor would consider that the family adopted two children who, at a young age, have lived through numerous life transitions and losses and are undergoing a significant loss and transition now. How might these lead to disconnections and ruptures at home and at school?

Recognizing the vulnerability of family members, counselors using a RCT framework are aware that people in crisis need relationships they can trust, and they would strive to create authentic and empowering connections with and among them. Counselors would recognize that the crisis context could create expectations within the Martinez family that would be based on previous experiences. For example, Marcos is alienated from his family and unsupported by them, and he may have difficulty believing that his family will be supported by others now. RCT conceptualizes these beliefs as relational images (Jordan, 2018).

Furthermore, a counselor applying RCT would empower the Martinez family by using "power-with" the family (Jordan, 2018) in support of its needs. There are any number of empathic failures that counselors may make, and responding in ways that help clients feel understood and seen could help them see their impact. Moreover, when disconnections arise, the counselor would refrain from assuming a power-over role, which, by the nature of the position, counselors can assume. The counselor would help Marcos and Juan navigate any such family disconnections similarly. Recognizing basic survival needs and the healing power of connection and relationship, counselors working with the Martinez family could walk alongside them on this journey from hope to healing.

Future Directions and Emerging Research

Online Social Worlds—Virtual Contexts

Virtual interconnectivity provides communal opportunities for healing and vital associations with people sharing mutual concerns. Online platforms also spread social and relational toxicity (Anderson & Jiang, 2018). Anderson and Jiang (2018) referenced a recent Pew Research Center survey that examined social media use for teens and found that adolescents recognized these features in online interactions. Most of the teens reported that they felt more connected (81%) to their friends, could reach out to peers in times of need (68%), and appreciated the exposure to diverse people (69%). However, most expressed concerns about online abuse, cyberbullying, and interpersonal strife.

Cyberbullying, Trolling, and Online Social Toxicity

Social media platforms often serve as megaphones for predatory abuse and cyberbullying. A majority (59%) of adolescents experienced others calling them offensive names, spreading false rumors about them, sending them explicit images, stalking and harassing them, physically threatening them, and broadcasting privately shared explicit photographs (Anderson & Jiang, 2018). These abuses lead to dire consequences for many youth (John et al., 2018). The public humiliation and permanent digital documentation of online abuse amplifies social brutality. Targets of abuse see others applaud their tormentors with comment likes and cheerful emoticons. They live with the stark awareness that no one stands up for them, and they can revisit these painful and humiliating moments over and over again (John et al., 2018). The anonymity of online interactions adds to the viciousness of cyberattacks and the feelings of powerlessness to combat unseen tormentors.

Online Support and Advocacy

Many groups and online relationships also serve as means for communication, support, information, and targeted interventions to help people in crisis (Anderson & Jiang, 2018). Numerous websites connect people coping with crises, stressors, suicidal thoughts, and disasters. Others provide education and moderated social support for people as they cope with stresses and traumatic events. For example, the National Suicide Hotline, the National Child Traumatic Stress Network, and the Red Cross are examples of sites that provide information online to help those in crisis and during the aftermath.

Ecological and Climate Conditions—Geographic Contexts

The nature of a changing climate means that natural disasters are on the rise, extreme weather events grow more threatening, food and water supplies may dwindle in some areas, and infrastructures may become increasingly threatened (Union of Concerned Scientists [UCS], n.d.). In fact, the UCS predicts a major climate crisis by the year 2040. This will mean that many people will be displaced as a result of climate changes. The United Nations addressed this topic in 2018 and stated, "climate, environmental degradation and natural disasters increasingly interact with the drivers of refugee movements" (U.N. Refugee Agency, 2018, para. 2). Clearly, the impact of climate change and the resultant population displacements and human suffering will affect global communities. These ruinous events especially affect underprivileged societies and groups who may have limited resources to cope with these calamities (U.N. Refugee Agency, 2018). See Sidebar 3.3 for the importance of knowledge of historical narratives.

We live in contexts in which many of our interactions during stressful events can make sense to a compassionate listener. Although people may have personal histories and risk factors that influence their response to trauma and resilience, the connections people have with their multilayered social worlds can bring gifts of healing, whereas the disconnections can burden them with additional pain and isolation. Cultural and social expectations and access to resources vary among people. Thus, counselors approach crisis and trauma counseling with humility and an appreciation, openness, and active investment in forging connections and learning about their clients' meaning making within their contextual and cultural worldviews.

References

Alexander, B. K., & Weems, M. E. (2017). June 12, 2016: Terrorism and hate in Orlando, America—Poetic and performative responses. *Qualitative Inquiry, 23*, 483–487. https://doi.org/10.1177/1077800417718282

Alexander, J., Eyerman, R., Giesen, B., Smelser, N. J., & Sztompka, P. (2004). *Cultural trauma and collective identity.* Berkeley: University of California Press.

A list of some US house of worship shootings since 2012. (2018, October 27). *The Associated Press.* Retrieved from https://apnews.com/0b2a73fdcf944d19aaafa620bb1d94c0

Alvarado, V. I., & Cavazos, L. J. (2008) Allegories and symbols in counseling. *Journal of Creativity in Mental Health, 2*(3), 51–59. https://doi.org/10.1300/J456v02n03_05

Anderson, M., & Jiang, J. (2018, November 28). *Teens' social media habits and experiences.* Pew Research Center. Retrieved from https://www.pewinternet.org/2018/11/28/teens-social-media-habits-and-experiences/

Sidebar 3.3 • Knowledge of Historical Narratives

Counselors who appreciate the historical narratives of collective groups can help their clients make meaning of their loss. Counselors do not need to be experts on all the historical narratives, but they can research their clients' background. However, the best tool a counselor has is to create a space of authentic connection and understanding. Clients want to share their life stories, and we do not assume to be an expert about their lives; instead, we encourage them to share their own unique experiences and perspectives.

Arredondo, P., Toporek, R., Brown, S. P., Jones, J., Locke, D. C., Sanchez, J., & Stadler, H. (1996). Operationalization of the multicultural counseling competencies. *Journal of Multicultural Counseling and Development, 24,* 42–78. https://doi.org/10.1002/j.2162-1912.1996.tb00288.x

Association for Lesbian, Gay, Bisexual, and Transgender Issues in Counseling. (2010). American Counseling Association: Competencies for counseling with transgender clients. *Journal of LGBT Issues in Counseling, 4*(3), 135–159.

Association for Lesbian, Gay, Bisexual, and Transgender Issues in Counseling LGBQQIA Competencies Taskforce. (2013). Association for Lesbian, Gay, Bisexual, and Transgender Issues in Counseling (ALGBTIC) competencies for counseling with lesbian, gay, bisexual, queer, questioning, intersex, and ally individuals. *Journal of LGBT Issues in Counseling, 7*(1), 2–43.

Bell-Tolliver, L., Burgess, R., & Brock, L. J. (2009). African American therapists working with African American families: An exploration of the strengths perspective in treatment. *Journal of Marital and Family Therapy, 35,* 293–307.

Berman, M. (2017, March 31). Dylann Roof will plead guilty to murder for Charleston church massacre, avoiding second death-penalty trial. *The Washington Post.* Retrieved from https://www.washingtonpost.com/news/post-nation/wp/2017/03/31/dylann-roof-will-plead-guilty-to-murder-for-charleston-church-massacre-avoiding-second-death-penalty-trial/

Birrell, P. J., & Freyd, J. J. (2006). Betrayal trauma: Relational models of harm and healing. *Journal of Trauma Practice, 5*(1), 49–63. https://doi.org/10.1300/J189v05n01_04

Black Lives Matter. (n.d.). *Herstory.* Retrieved from https://blacklivesmatter.com/about/herstory/

Boyd-Franklin, N., & Karger, M. (2012). Intersections of race, class, and poverty. In F. Walsh (Ed.), *Normal family processes: Growing diversity and complexity* (4th ed., pp. 273–296). New York, NY: Guilford Press.

Coyhis, D., & Simonelli, R. (2005). Rebuilding Native American communities. *Child Welfare, 84,* 323–336.

Dreier, P. (2019, January 3). After a century of delays, the Senate finally votes to outlaw lynching. *The Nation.* Retrieved from https://www.thenation.com/article/senate-lynching-congress-racism/

Duffey, T., & Somody, C. (2011). The role of relational-cultural theory in mental health counseling. *Journal of Mental Health Counseling, 33,* 223–242. https://doi.org/10.17744/mehc.33.3.c10410226u275647

Duran, E., Duran, B., Yellow Horse Brave Heart, & Yellow Horse-Davis. (1998). Healing the American Indian soul wound. In Y. Danieli (Ed.), *International handbook of multigenerational legacies of trauma* (pp. 341–354). Boston, MA: Springer.

Duran, E., Firehammer, J., & Gonzalez, J. (2008). Liberation psychology as the path toward healing cultural soul wounds. *Journal of Counseling & Development, 86,* 288–295. https://doi.org/10.1002/j.1556-6678.2008.tb00511.x

Ferguson, R. A. (2018). The Pulse nightclub and the state of our world. *GLQ: A Journal of Lesbian and Gay Studies, 24*(1), 36–38.

Gone, J. (2013). Redressing First Nations historical trauma: Theorizing mechanisms for indigenous culture as mental health treatment. *Transcultural Psychiatry, 50,* 683–706. https://doi.org/10.1177/1363461513487669

Hirschberger G. (2018). Collective trauma and the social construction of meaning. *Frontiers in Psychology, 9*, 1–14. https://doi.org/10.3389/fpsyg.2018.01441

Hofstede, G. (2011). Dimensionalizing cultures: The Hofstede model in context. *Online Readings in Psychology and Culture, 2*(1). https://doi.org/10.9707/2307-0919.1014

Holden, K., McGregor, B., Thandi, P., Fresh, E., Sheats, K., Belton, A., . . . Satcher, D. (2014). Toward culturally centered integrative care for addressing mental health disparities among ethnic minorities. *Psychological Services, 11*, 357–368. https://doi.org/10.1037/a0038122

Holman, E. A., & Silver, R. C. (2011). Health status and health care utilization following collective trauma: A 3-year national study of the 9/11 terrorist attacks in the United States. *Social Science and Medicine, 73*, 483–490. https://doi.org/10.1016/j.socscimed.2011.06.018

Hook, J. N., Davis, D. E., Owen, J., Worthington, E. L., & Utsey, S. O. (2016). Cultural humility: Measuring openness to culturally diverse clients. *Journal of Counseling Psychology, 60*, 353–366. https://doi.org/10.1037/a0032595

Human Rights Campaign. (2018, November 13). *New FBI statistics show increase in reported hate crimes.* Retrieved from https://www.hrc.org/blog/new-fbi-statistics-show-alarming-increase-in-number-of-reported-hate-crimes

John, A., Glendenning, A. C., Marchant, A., Montgomery, P., Stewart, A., Wood, S., . . . Hawton, K. (2018). Self-harm, suicidal behaviours, and cyberbullying in children and young people: Systematic review. *Journal of Medical Internet Research, 20*(4), e129. https://doi.org/10.2196/jmir.9044

Jordan, J. V. (2018). *Relational–cultural therapy* (2nd ed.). Washington, DC: American Psychological Association.

Krogstad, J. M., & Gonzalez-Barrera, A. (2019, May 17). *Key facts about U.S. immigration policies and proposed changes.* Retrieved from https://www.pewresearch.org/fact-tank/2019/05/17/key-facts-about-u-s-immigration-policies-and-proposed-changes/

LaJoie, A. S., Sprang, G., & McKinney, W. P. (2010). Long-term effects of Hurricane Katrina on the psychological well-being of evacuees. *Disasters, 34*, 1031–1044. https://doi.org/10.1111/j.1467-7717.2010.01181.x

McCormick, A., Scheyd, K., & Terrazas, S. (2018). Trauma-informed care and LGBTQ youth: Considerations for advancing practice with youth with trauma experiences. *Families in Society, 99*(2), 160–169.

McIntosh, P. (1989, July/August). White privilege: Unpacking the invisible knapsack. *Peace and Freedom Magazine*, 10–12.

McIntosh, P. (1992). White privilege and male privilege: A personal account of coming to see correspondences through work in women's studies. In M. L. Andersen & P. H. Collins (Eds.), *Race, class, and gender: An anthology* (pp. 70–81). Belmont, CA: Wadsworth.

Me Too. (n.d.). *About.* Retrieved from https://metoomvmt.org/about/

Mintz, S., & McNeil, S. (2018). Two accounts of the Trail of Tears: Wahnenauhi and Private John G. Burnett. *Digital History.* Retrieved from http://www.digitalhistory.uh.edu/disp_textbook.cfm?smtID=3&psid=1147

Mohatt, N. V., Thompson, A. B., Thai, N. D., & Tebes, J. K. (2014). Historical trauma as public narrative: A conceptual review of how history impacts present-day health. *Social Science Medicine, 106*, 128–136. https://doi.org/10.1016/j.socscimed.2014.01.043

Morning Consult. (2017). *National tracking poll #170916* [Data file and code book]. Retrieved from https://morningconsult.com/wp-content/uploads/2017/10/170916_crosstabs_pr_v1_KD.pdf

Nader, K., Dubrow, N., & Stamm, B. H. (2013). *Honoring differences: Cultural issues in the treatment of trauma and loss.* Abingdon, England: Routledge.

National Association for the Advancement of Colored People. (n.d.). *History of lynchings.* Retrieved from https://www.naacp.org/history-of-lynchings/

National Congress of American Indians. (2015). *Tribal Nations and the United States: An introduction.* Retrieved from http://www.ncai.org/resources/ncai_publications/tribal-nations-and-the-united-states-an-introduction

Neimeyer, R., Klass, D., & Dennis, M. R. (2014). Toward a social constructionist account of grief: Loss and the narration of meaning. *Death Studies, 38,* 485–498. https://doi.org/10.1080/07481187.2014.913454

Ojebode, A. (2017). Alan Kurdî, deaths in the desert and failed migrants' processing of dystopic images on social media. *Crossings: Journal of Migration and Culture, 8*(2), 115–130.

Onwuachi-Willig, A. (2016). The trauma of the routine: Lessons on cultural trauma from the Emmett Till verdict. *Sociological Theory, 34,* 335–357. https://doi.org/10.1177/0735275116679864

Ratts, M. J., & Greenleaf, A. T. (2018). Multicultural and social justice counseling competencies: A leadership framework for professional school counselors. *Professional School Counseling, 21*(1b), 1–9. https://doi.org/10.1177/2156759X18773582

Schweiger, G. (2016). The duty to bring children living in conflict zones to a safe haven. *Journal of Global Ethics, 12,* 380–397. https://doi.org/10.1080/17449626.2016.1247744

Siegel, D. J. (2012). *The developing mind: How relationships and the brain interact to shape who we are* (2nd ed.). New York, NY: Guilford Press.

Singh, A. A., & Gonzalez, M. (2014). ACA counseling brief: LGBTQQ-affirmative counseling. *American Counseling Association Practice Briefs.* Retrieved from https://isucounselingresources2017.weebly.com/uploads/1/1/3/4/11344496/aca_practice_brief_lgbtqq_coun.pdf

Snell, J., Rosenwald, R., & Robey, A. (1964). The wifebeater's wife: A study of family interaction. *Archives of General Psychiatry, 11,* 107–112. https://doi.org/10.1001/archpsyc.1964.01720260001001

Substance Abuse and Mental Health Services Administration. (2014a). *A Treatment Improvement Protocol: Improving cultural competence: TIP 59* (HHS Publication No. [SMA] 14-4849). Retrieved from https://store.samhsa.gov/system/files/sma14-4849.pdf

Substance Abuse and Mental Health Services Administration. (2014b). *Trauma-informed care in behavioral health services. Treatment Improvement Protocol (TIP) Series 57* (HHS Publication No. [SMA] 13-4801). Retrieved from https://www.integration.samhsa.gov/clinical-practice/SAMSA_TIP_Trauma.pdf

Sue, D. W. (2010). *Microaggressions and marginality: Manifestation, dynamics, and impact.* Hoboken, NJ: Wiley.

U.N. Educational Scientific and Cultural Organization. (2001, November). *Universal declaration on cultural diversity.* Retrieved from http://www.unesco.org/new/fileadmin/MULTIMEDIA/HQ/CLT/pdf/5_Cultural_Diversity_EN.pdf

U.N. Office on Drugs and Crime. (2018). *Global study on smuggling of migrants 2018.* Retrieved from https://www.unodc.org/documents/data-and-analysis/glosom/GLOSOM_2018_web_small.pdf

U.N. Refugee Agency. (2018). *Climate change and disaster displacement.* Retrieved from https://www.unhcr.org/en-us/climate-change-and-disasters.html

Union of Concerned Scientists. (n.d.). *Global warming impacts.* Retrieved from https://www.ucsusa.org/our-work/global-warming/science-and-impacts/global-warming-impacts

U.S. Department of Health and Human Services, Office of Minority Health. (2010a). *Cultural competency curriculum for disaster preparedness and crisis response.* Retrieved from https://cccdpcr.thinkculturalhealth.hhs.gov/default.asp

U.S. Department of Health and Human Services, Office of Minority Health. (2010b). *National Standards for Culturally and Linguistically Appropriate Services in Health and Health Care: Enhancement initiative environmental scan.* Washington, DC: Author.

U.S. Holocaust Memorial Museum. (n.d.). *Introduction to the Holocaust.* Retrieved from https://www.ushmm.org/learn/introduction-to-the-holocaust

U.S. House of Representatives Select Bipartisan Committee to Investigate the Preparation for Response to Hurricane Katrina. (2006). *A failure of initiative: Final report of the Select Bipartisan Committee to Investigate the Preparation for and Response to Hurricane Katrina* (U.S. Congress House Report 109-377). Retrieved from https://www.govinfo.gov/content/pkg/CRPT-109hrpt377/pdf/CRPT-109hrpt377.pdf

van der Kolk, B. (2014). *The body keeps the score: Brain, mind, and body in the healing of trauma.* New York, NY: Viking.

Waters, A., & Asbill, L. (2013, August). Reflections on cultural humility. *CYF News.* Retrieved from http://www.apa.org/pi/families/resources/newsletter/2013/08/cultural-humility.aspx

Yehuda, R., & Lehrner, A. (2018). Intergenerational transmission of trauma effects: Putative role of epigenetic mechanisms. *World Psychiatry, 17,* 243–257. https://doi.org/10.1002/wps.20568

Multiple-Choice Questions

1. Which best describes a "relational image?"
   a. A person's inner picture of what to expect from others and life formed from earlier, important relationships
   b. An image that a mother tells her daughter about
   c. A theory used in cognitive behavioral therapy
   d. A technique used in behavioral therapy

2. Counselors who hold a traditional mind-set about culture may
   a. Make degrading jokes.
   b. Create toxicity in professional settings.
   c. All be from a certain location.
   d. Both a and b

3. According to the authors, controlling images are similar to
   a. Biases.
   b. Stereotypes.
   c. Abuse.
   d. None of the above

4. Power dynamics, from a relational viewpoint, are an important tenet of crisis and trauma.
   a. False
   b. True
   c. True when the crisis and/or trauma involves a child
   d. False when the crisis and/or trauma involves a female

5. Birrell and Freyd (2006) posited that _____ groups in society tend to experience oppression and social exclusion.
   a. Diverse
   b. Marginalized
   c. American
   d. Large

6. The authors feel _____ is important for helping a client develop short- and long-term goals during and following crises or traumas.
   a. The counselor theory used
   b. An understanding of community
   c. An inpatient setting
   d. All of the above

7. According to the ecological-social model, what is associated with the interpersonal factors?
   a. Historical timeframes
   b. History of trauma
   c. Societal norms
   d. Period of time

8. According to the ecological-social model, what feature influences all areas of the model?
   a. Cultural influences
   b. Individual factors
   c. Work factors
   d. None of the above

9. Collective trauma refers to
   a. Traumas experienced by society at large.
   b. Traumas experienced by a collective group of any size.
   c. Traumas experienced by marginalized groups only.
   d. Traumas that occurred in the past.

10. What term is related to how people respond with ambiguity and believe in absolutes?
    a. Uncertainty-avoidance
    b. Avoidant
    c. Unsure avoidant
    d. Power-distance

11. Which two divisions of the American Counseling Association were developed with competencies for counselors working with diverse and marginalized groups?
    a. Association for Humanistic Counseling and the Association for Multicultural Counseling and Development
    b. Association for Multicultural Counseling and Development and Counselors for Social Justice
    c. Association for Creativity in Counseling and the Association for Assessment and Research in Counseling
    d. None of the above

12. According to this chapter, what is a step counselors can use toward being culturally effective?
    a. Studying every type of culture
    b. Studying abroad
    c. Collaborate with community leaders about your thoughts
    d. Check in with community leaders about legal aspects

13. What does Sue (2010) consider to be a *microassault*?
    a. Physical abuse
    b. Yelling at someone
    c. Intentional denigrating acts
    d. Nonintentional denigrating acts

14. J. Alexander et al. (2004) posited that cultural trauma
    a. Is not a real issue in today's society.
    b. Leaves a lasting impression on group consciousness.
    c. Is not relevant to collective cultures.
    d. Only exists in the past.

15. Which collective traumatic experience involved a hashtag to spread awareness for sexual assault?
    a. Me Too movement
    b. Me Also movement
    c. Pulse nightclub
    d. 9/11

Essay Questions

1. The authors explore the concepts of power and privilege. What types of power or privilege are you aware of in your life? What are the different ways in which you have used your power in a negative manner? How about ways in which you have used your power to create changes in society and foster social change? If so, how?

2. *Microinvalidations* can occur when counselors dismiss or minimize an experience of their clients. This behavior can be particularly upsetting to a client who has experienced trauma. How do you connect with your client authentically, and how do you notice those times in which you engage in microinvalidations?

3. Think and reflect on your life. Have you ever experienced some sort of event, regardless of whether it was traumatic, that affected your entire community? What happened to the community during this time? How did the community grow closer or more distant after the event?

4. This chapter explores the ecological-social model. Create an ecological-social model that represents your life. What did you notice about your model?

5. The chapter explores the case of the Martinez family and asks some questions about how a counselor may conceptualize the counseling process. How else do you envision working with the family using information provided in the chapter about cultural factors and social influences?

CHAPTER 4

Neurobiological, Psychological, and Relational Effects of Crisis and Trauma

Deborah Bergmann, Thelma Duffey, Shane Haberstroh, Mark Jones, Vincent Schroder, and J. Claire Gregory

Neurological studies indicate that the brain is an adaptive system of extraordinary plasticity. When coping with a real or perceived existential threat, the brain triggers a series of physiological reactions and behaviors primed for coping and psychological survival. However, this same protective neurological system often profoundly stymies vitality and may make life for a trauma survivor almost intolerable—that is to say, the neurology of trauma is both adaptive and maladaptive. Understanding this dual character of trauma can help normalize the experiences following a trauma and guide healing from a position of concrete hope. The brain can, in fact, shift from functioning in a state of trauma to functioning flexibly and joyfully. This shift occurs through the steady work of strengthening the neural pathways that have been understimulated in trauma and attenuating those that have been overstimulated. To understand what this work looks like in practice, we begin by putting the neurobiological description of trauma into the context of a broader understanding of brain development and functioning. This understanding is situated within relational neuroscience (Banks, 2016), a relatively new field of emerging research on the inextricable link between the relational environment and the brain.

Relational Neuroscience

Basis in Relational-Cultural Theory (RCT)

The pioneering work of psychiatrist Jean Baker Miller and colleagues at Wellesley College in the 1970s moved away from a self-sufficient, individualized model of personal development toward a relational one, in which authentic and mutually empathic connection with others was understood to be at the core of well-being. At that time, professional and popular psychological theory emphasized relational boundaries and independence as indicators of maturity and functionality. Miller and her colleagues' own clinical work suggested that the women they were seeing suffered not from a failure to mature into individuated selves but from a lack of supportive relationships. Frequently, these women had histories of relational deprivation or abuse beginning early in life. Being raised in undernurturing environments resulted in what Miller called *negative relational images,* in which they saw themselves as relationally deficient. The consequences of feeling relationally deficient lead to chronic disconnection or isolation from self and others. Jean Baker Miller, Judith Jordan, Irene Stiver, and Janet Surrey concluded that healthy human connection was both the means and the end of mental health. Their model, RCT, was a prescient voice that paved the way for the current relational understanding of the human brain.

Because relational neuroscience did not yet exist, and relational experience was not a subject of study in psychological research at the time, Miller and her colleagues stood not on scientific empirical ground but on the strength of their clinical experience and their theoretical work. As the neuroscience of human relationships emerged as an active field of study, it has become clear that understanding human beings as intrinsically relational is empirically defensible and prompts many interesting avenues of inquiry. Neuroscientific research on human relationality currently goes by many names—social neuroscience, interpersonal neurobiology, and relational neuroscience, to name a few. In this chapter, we refer to relational neuroscience, the term used by RCT psychiatrist and researcher Amy Banks in her work.

The Relational Brain

Psychiatrist Daniel J. Siegel (2015) called the mind an emergent property of the body and relationships. In this model, mental life emerges from the flow of energy between the embodied mind (brain) and its experiential environment, including, most importantly, relationships. The relationship between infant and mother has long been of interest in understanding the way that an individual moves from the relatively undifferentiated sensory experiences of the newborn to the variegated experience of the toddler.

Early empirical studies of caretaker-child relationships were done within attachment theory, beginning with John Bowlby and Mary Ainsworth in the 1950s and 1960s, supporting the importance of certain relationships for healthy psychosocial development. More recent developments bring new understanding that the brain is *essentially* relational. Children need a secure base for their brains to successfully run their own programming for such critical functions as memory and emotional regulation. Their developing brains directly adapt to the brain of the caretaker, mirroring its neural pathways and using the more mature brain as scaffolding for its own emerging structure.

Allan N. Schore (2012) identified brain regions and processes in a mother's right hemisphere that begin to affect the fetus brain in the third trimester. Reciprocal right hemispheric connections between caregivers and children create powerful bonds during early years of life. At no other time in the human life span is there this quantity of brain growth. Infants cry out to loved ones, and their reactions settle infants into physical satiation and emotional comfort or, conversely, bring more anxiety. Infants' formative relationships either downregulate or upregulate their growing nervous system. A downregulated baby, for example, may be unfocused and emotionally adrift. Caretakers and family members through their behaviors, speech, and play can help their child come online and experience life in connection.

Social Synapses

The relational environment of the developing mind is, therefore, contiguous with the developing mind itself. This structuring relationship between minds has been called the *social synapse* by psychologist Louis Cozolino (2014), who noted that our interpersonal verbal and nonverbal communication can be understood as operating as part of the same network as their own neurons, albeit at a different structural level. A smile or greeting on our part, Cozolino indicated, travels across the social synapse, is received as sensory information, and is converted to an electrochemical signal in the recipient's brain. The electrical signal in the recipient's brain will often initiate a downstream motor response, which will, in turn, travel back across the social synapse to stimulate a response in our own brain. Just as the neurons within a single brain form overlapping and interrelated webs of excitatory and inhibitory stimulation to create something greater than the sum of its parts, so do we as individual brains form an emergent social system through our networks of communication.

Mirror Neurons

Mirror neurons were accidentally discovered in the mid-1990s when a group of researchers noticed that the same neuron activated when a monkey ate a peanut was also activated when the monkey watched a researcher eat a peanut (Gallese, Fadiga, Fogassi, & Rizzolatti, 1996; Siegel, 2015). Since their initial discovery in nonhuman primates, the presence of mirror neurons in the human brain has been confirmed through single-neuron studies (Mukamel, Ekstrom, Kaplan, Iacoboni, & Fried, 2010). Mirror neurons effectively allow an observer to experience the intentional action of another individual, or to "feel" another person's brain through a kind of internal simulation. It has even been suggested that this automatic and pervasive simulation is what allows people to understand intentional behavior and to predict what someone will do next (Blakeslee, 2006). Mirror neuron properties have been found in the anterior cingulate and in the anterior insula of the ventrolateral region (Siegel, 2015). Notably, *interoception,* or the perception of our own internal visceral states, is also mediated by the insula. Siegel (2015) suggested that the same neural circuits may be implicated in other-awareness, such as self-awareness, supporting the idea that even people's perception of their own bodily experience is profoundly linked with their social experience. Mirror neurons are active from birth—newborns have been shown to stick out their tongues at adults doing the same—and are implicated in many functions, including language development, emotional regulation, autobiographical memory, and empathic attunement. This early, profound, and widespread mimicry seems to be integral to the development of mind, suggesting that, just as Jean Baker Miller and her colleagues claimed, relationality is identity.

Like much research in brain science, there is an ongoing need for further study into mirror neurons (Bekkali et al., 2019). In a meta-analysis, Bekkali et al. (2019) found that many studies included a small sample size and provided various definitions for mirror neuron actions; they also noted a lack of consistent methods for data collection. Mirror neurons may play varied roles than what was once believed to be true (Bekkali et al., 2019). As with any exciting discovery, we aim to increase literature and knowledge and remember that the intricate workings of the brain are immeasurably complex. See Sidebar 4.1 for more information on mirror neurons.

Neurological Effects of Trauma

PTSD is marked by the presence of symptoms that fall into three categories: re-experiencing, avoidance, and hyperarousal. The neurobiological mechanisms underlying each of these symptom categories are interconnected with each other and with other bodily systems. After an overview of some of these mechanisms, we will consider how these mechanisms can be understood in the context of relational neuroscience.

Amygdala

The amygdala, located roughly behind the eyes in the temporal lobes, is at the center of the body's stress response. The most highly studied function of the amygdala is in fear conditioning, but the amygdala is important in positive learning as well. In general, increased activation of the amygdala during learning leads to better retention of the learned response or information. The amygdala receives sensory information from the various sensory systems and processes it as either threatening or nonthreatening. In a fear response, a sufficiently threatening set of sensory inputs to the amygdala leads to several downstream stress responses (hypothalamic-pituitary-adrenal [HPA] axis, startle response, and activation of the sympathetic nervous system [SNS]) through projections to the hypothalamus and reticularis pontis (Banks, 2006). The amygdala has been found to be more reactive in people with posttraumatic stress disorder (PTSD) than in control participants, and amygdala responsivity is directly related to PTSD symptom severity (McLaughlin et al., 2014; Shin, Rauch, & Pitman, 2006).

Medial Prefrontal Cortex

Various studies have implicated the importance of the medial prefrontal cortex in development of PTSD (McLaughlin et al., 2014; Shin et al., 2006). Morphometric MRI studies have shown reduced frontal cortex volumes among PTSD participants (Cohen, Perel, De Bellis, Friedman, & Putnam, 2002; Meng et al., 2014). Neurochemical studies of N-acetyl aspartate/creatinine ratios point to reduced neuronal integrity in the prefrontal cortex of maltreated children and adolescents with PTSD (De Bellis & Zisk, 2014). Similarly, functional neuroimaging studies show reduced prefrontal cortex activation during presentation of negative emo-

Sidebar 4.1 • Mirror Neurons

Mirror neurons activate in the presence of others. Researchers are currently exploring mirror neurons more in depth. What might "mirror neurons" explain? How do mirror neurons and concepts such as neuroception and interoception frame the social-neurobiological and relational aspects of trauma and recovery?

tional stimuli or performance of learning and memory tasks under conditions of emotional interference (Bremner et al., 2004; Lanius et al., 2003; Shin et al., 2006).

Because the medial prefrontal cortex is involved in regulating amygdala's response through inhibitory inputs, these findings on compromised medial prefrontal cortex functioning, along with amygdala hyperreactivity in PTSD, suggest a functional relationship between these two areas in PTSD. However, two functional MRI studies on regional cerebral blood flow (rCBF) changes in the medial prefrontal cortex and amygdala in participants with PTSD produced opposite results. In one study, reduced rCBF changes in the medial prefrontal cortex correlated with increased rCBF changes in the amygdala (Shin et al., 2005), whereas in the other study, there was a direct relationship between rCBF changes in both brain regions (Shin et al., 2006). Both correlations were statistically significant. The study showing a reciprocal relationship between the two regions' activation looked at participants with chronic PTSD (Shin et al., 2005), and the study showing a direct relationship looked at participants with acute PTSD (Shin et al., 2006). A need exists for increased understanding of the way the amygdala and medial prefrontal cortex interact across the time course of PTSD.

HPA Axis

The HPA axis is a neuroendocrinological pathway that plays an important role in the fight-flight-freeze response. When threatening sensory stimuli relayed to the amygdala by one or more sensory systems reach a certain threshold, the amygdala starts a coordinated stress response through several projections, including the HPA axis. This pathway begins with amygdala-stimulated release of corticotropin-releasing factor (CRF) from the paraventricular nucleus (PVN) of the hypothalamus. This reaction stimulates the release of adrenocorticotropin hormone (ACTH) from the anterior pituitary, in turn stimulating the release of glucocorticoids, including cortisol, from the adrenal glands.

The binding of cortisol to receptors initiates cellular signal cascades, leading to wide-ranging systemic effects on glucose metabolism, cardiovascular function, inflammation, arousal, learning, and memory (Stephens & Wand, 2012). As cortisol levels mount, increased cortisol concentration in the system exerts a negative feedback effect on the hypothalamus to downregulate the stress response by reducing CRF release. In the absence of ongoing stimulation of the PVN by the amygdala (usually because of the cessation of incoming threatening sensory information), the HPA axis stress response ends.

Because of its prominent role in the physiology of stress reactions, cortisol was long assumed to be elevated in people suffering from PTSD. However, studies show a correlation between *lower* cortisol levels in the wake of a traumatic event and the development of PTSD (Bremner, Vermetten, & Kelley, 2007; Yehuda, Teicher, Trestman, Levengood, & Siever, 1996). This finding supports the hypothesis that the dysregulation of the negative feedback phase of the stress response may be an important determinative factor in PTSD.

Autonomic Nervous System (ANS)

The ANS is activated in a stress response and may lead to fight, flight, or freeze behaviors, depending on the interaction between the sympathetic and parasympathetic components of the ANS. The effects of activation of the SNS on target organs include pupil dilation, bronchodilation, increased heart rate, blood vessel dilation in skeletal muscle, and constriction in the gastrointestinal tract, among others.

Studies have shown that people suffering from PTSD have baseline autonomic hyperarousal when compared with control participants (Cohen et al., 2002). The role of the SNS in this baseline and stress-induced hyperarousal among participants with PTSD has been confirmed by numerous studies measuring heart rate, systolic blood pressure, and diastolic blood pressure (Zoladz & Diamond, 2016). The parasympathetic nervous system (PNS) may also play a significant role, with decreased PNS tone contributing to hyperarousal and ineffective arousal regulation (van der Kolk, 2014). Hyperarousal, therefore, is not simply a matter of reacting more intensely to a threat but also of a decreased ability to come down from that intense reaction. The PNS, however, enervates organs supporting functions carried out in nonstressful situations, such as the digestive and genitourinary systems.

The *smart vagus* is a term coined by Stephen Porges as part of his polyvagal theory, and it was adopted by Amy Banks (2016) in her writing on relational neuroscience. It refers to the myelinated ventral vagus nerve arising from the 10th cranial nerve that is related to, but distinct from, the SNS and PNS. The vagus nerve communicates with the SNS and PNS to inhibit their activity during times of safety and connection. When the smart vagus is activated, the facial muscles and the muscles that control the tympanic membrane relax as part of the body's move toward social engagement (Siegel, 2015). Porges (2014) discussed this process as *neuroception,* describing how, at autonomic levels, people read cues from their social surroundings. Mirror neurons alert people to danger and safety through their perceptions of others' body language and subtle expressions. Depending on these nuanced contextual cues, the ANS will respond accordingly.

Hippocampus

The hippocampus, located between the temporal lobes and limbic system, functions in memory consolidation, spatial contextualization, and learning. This structure assists with memory formation, and traumatic stress directly affects this area, leading to difficulties with memory encoding and recall (Bremner, 2006). Many neuroimaging studies have confirmed reduced hippocampal volume in research participants with PTSD compared with control participants (Bremner, 2006; Kasai et al., 2008; Levy-Gigi, Szabó, Kelemen, & Kéri, 2013), but the functional role of reduced hippocampal volume needs further study. In a recent study, Banks (2016) found that the degree of reduced hippocampal volume among participants with PTSD best predicted their performance on a generalization learning task; those with the most reduced hippocampal volume were most likely to overgeneralize negative context in the learning exercise. If we assume that reduced hippocampal volume correlates with reduced functioning, it helps to explain the neural mechanism that causes some trauma survivors to have difficulty distinguishing between relationally safe and unsafe environments, often leading to a series of unsupportive or abusive relationships (Banks, 2016).

Despite evidence for reduced hippocampal volume among people suffering from PTSD, there are no studies that discriminate between reduced hippocampal volume as an effect of trauma and as a risk factor for trauma. Whether trauma affects the hippocampus or reduced hippocampal volume predisposes a person to trauma is, therefore, an open question. The importance of the hippocampus in mediating the lived experience of PTSD, however, is clear. Understanding how impaired hippocampal function could be implicated in generalization of negative context and intrusive memories does not require that researchers know the direction of correlation.

Ventrolateral Periaqueductal Gray

Schore (2012) demonstrated that a subtype of PTSD involving less fight-flight activation and more dissociative, blunting, and submissive responses corresponded with a brain region called the ventrolateral periaqueductal gray. This region corresponds with the freezing that may happen when someone is under distress. As a normal process, this freezing helps conserve energy, avoid predators, and reduce blood volume to exposed extremities. For clients experiencing dissociation, right hemispheric connections in session help a person move from detachment to increased zest and creativity (Jordan, 2017). Conversations that bring people back to the here and now in safety create emotional healing, which, as Schore and Sieff (2015) wrote

> is not achieved by making the unconscious conscious: rather it depends on restructuring the emotional brain itself through building new neural networks. Achieving this requires relationally based, emotionally focused psychotherapy with an empathic therapist who is an active participant in the process. Healing occurs primarily through the nonverbal, right brain, implicit connection between a therapist and a patient. (p. 111)

Relational Effects of Trauma

The effects of trauma on the brain, as we have seen, are numerous. The way these effects come together in the experience of each trauma survivor varies. The "amygdala hijack" that can lead to heightened anger, impulsivity, and fear may work in concert with a diminished ability to discern between safe and unsafe situations. Traumatic memories may be fragmented and emerge as flashbacks, setting the fight-flight-freeze response into action. Emotional disconnection and dissociative experiences can leave a trauma survivor with an unreliable sense of self and anxiety about their social interactions. Compromised memory and attentional focus can interfere with a person's ability to participate fully in a social moment, and the need to avoid situations that may trigger reexperiencing of trauma can also constrict a person's social world.

Neurology of Compassion and Connection

The prefrontal cortex, responsible for emotional regulation, remains neuroplastic across the life span (Siegel, 2015). This concept presumes that what may go wrong during early brain development is not doomed to remain so. Early experiences are tremendously important, but they are not set in stone. An abusive or even just mis-attuned caretaker can create insecurity, confusion, and an unreliable sense of self in the child. A discrete traumatic experience at any age can lead to similar experiences of lost meaning and impaired functioning, particularly in cases of interpersonal and intentional trauma. Thankfully, the therapeutic experience of a well-attuned counselor and a move toward relational health through growth-fostering relationships can restore much of what is lost in trauma (Banks, 2016). See Sidebar 4.2 for more information on the effects of childhood trauma.

We know that the therapeutic relationship is the most determinative factor in the success of therapy (Norcross & Wampold, 2011); how exactly that relationship serves as a substratum or locus for neurological change remains an open question.

Allan N. Schore emphasized the importance of affective enactments in the process of therapy—whereby emotional transactions between client and counselor create the opportunity for both parties to grow and integrate a greater level of self-awareness. This awareness is not psychoeducational or metacognitive—it is deeply emotional. Schore (2009) described these enactments as occurring "at the edges of the regulatory boundaries of both high and low arousal in the intersubjective fields" (p. 138). In other words, when the here and now of a therapy session with an attuned counselor is uncomfortable, something is happening and, depending on how that is handled in the relationship between client and counselor, this discomfort can be part of a therapeutic rewiring. Schore noted that using interpretation in such a situation can be damaging, because it represents a turn away from the affective moment and toward a distancing intellectualization.

A person's conscious experience of emotion is just the tip of the iceberg when it comes to the unconscious processing generating those emotions and their attendant behavioral responses (LeDoux, 1998). Enactments in therapy—which may take many forms, such as an argument, withdrawal into silence, or bursting into tears, for example (Mucci, 2013)—involve the affective brain in ways both conscious and unconscious. Schore (2012) considered the rewiring that occurs in effective enactments to be a reorganization of orbitofrontal-amygdala connectivity, which is implicated in the neurobiological changes of traumatic experience. Before this kind of work can be done, however, safety and presence have to be established. Banks (2016) noted that the work of psychoeducation, distress tolerance, and reconnection to self precede traditional trauma work in relational therapy for trauma.

Factors, Approaches, and Interventions That Foster Healing and Resiliency

Amy Banks (2016) outlined ways in which the neurobiological effects of traumatic experience can affect the working relationship between client and counselor. Banks noted that, in working with trauma survivors, we can expect challengingly abrupt relational movements from intimate connection to isolating disconnection. This behavior is often attributable to the trauma survivor's diminished ability to discern between safe and unsafe relational moments as well as the hyperarousal of the trauma survivor's fear-conditioning systems. It is the work of the well-attuned relational counselor to hold the relationship in times of disconnection, honoring the client's need to disconnect and recognizing that this disconnection is, in some sense, both adaptive and preserving of the therapeutic relationship in the long term. Integrating Banks's insights on relational therapy for trauma with the emerging body of research and theory on relationality and the brain, we attempt a relational neurobiological understanding of how the therapeutic relationship mediates the recovery process for survivors of trauma.

Relational Empowerment and Attunement

Nonverbal communication is deeply seated in the brain. Infants receive and send messages nonverbally long before they acquire speech, and in the evolutionary history of the human species, gestural communication precedes spoken language (Burgoon, Guerrero, & Floyd, 2016). Studies show that when a spoken message is incongruent with its nonverbal accompaniment, people tend to believe the unspoken semantic content over the spoken (Burgoon et al., 2016). Generally, nonverbal communication is referred to as "right brain," but both hemispheres can be involved in nonverbal communication processing.

Nonverbal communication is well established as an important factor in therapy. Eye contact, body position, silence, voice tone, facial expressions and gestures, physical distance, and touching have been identified as the seven forms of nonverbal communication (Gladstein, 1974). The way that these come together in the embodied and fluid expression between counselor and client is difficult to analyze. Daniel J. Siegel (2015) spoke of "contingent collaborative communication that involves sensitivity to signals, reflection on the importance of mental states, and the nonverbal attunement of states of mind" (p. 114). This combination of verbal and nonverbal attunement is what is at play in growth-fostering relationships and mutual empathy (Jordan, 2017).

From a neurobiological perspective, attunement helps the trauma counselor to feel the brain of the client in a way that allows the counselor to proceed while preserving the client's safety and deepening trust. Siegel described a sense of distance and boredom with clients who are detached from their own emotional experience (Wylie & Turner, n.d.). Although not unique to trauma survivors, disconnection from emotion is one adaptive element of traumatic coping that allows the individual dealing with PTSD to function in the face of overwhelming stress.

Trauma and the Body

The intrusive memories, dissociative experiences, avoidant behaviors, and baseline stress of the trauma survivor are in themselves disturbing experiences. Bessel A. van der Kolk (2006) has described the trauma survivor as having subjectively "lost their way in the world," and the work of healing from trauma involves a return to self, world, and relationship. Because this return to intimacy with self and other can be so intimidating to the trauma survivor who is on guard against her own experience, structured practices of attending to her bodily state and to stimuli not associated with trauma can be a gentle place to start. Mindfulness meditation and yoga guide the trauma survivor toward being present in the here and now and achieving a greater degree of self-awareness. Reconnecting with bodily experience and exercising nonjudgmental recognition of her bodily state and stream of consciousness, the trauma survivor has a path toward reorientation, or finding her way in the world she inhabits today and reconnecting with others in growth-fostering relationships.

Although verbal processing of traumatic experience is a necessary part of healing and posttraumatic growth for some trauma survivors, others may have a more somatic path to feeling well again, and reconnecting to self through finding physical integration may represent full recovery. In either case, a sensitivity to the unique experience of each client and a well-attuned relational approach allow the wisdom inherent in trauma to come full circle. See Sidebar 4.3 for more information on disassociation.

Case Examples and Applications for Hope and Healing

Case Example One

Neurobiology provides a rich frame for counseling. Chelsea came to my (Vinny's) counseling practice expressing feeling afraid at work after a recent breakup with her partner. Chelsea was a mechanical engineering graduate student, putting herself through school. With her workload and studies bearing down on her, Chelsea recently broke it off with her abusive partner, Bob. However, they still worked at the same restaurant together, and she dreaded seeing Bob at work. Given her demanding school schedule, Chelsea could not afford to job hunt for the next few months, and she felt trapped by these circumstances. She would feel gut punched when he walked in the room, and she would feel like she was out of her body, floating numbly through the workday, seemingly on autopilot. Given her many strengths, exceptionally bright mind, and persevering grit, these feelings felt uncontrollable and really bothered her.

As we formed our relationship, we explored Chelsea's current struggles and other salient moments from her life and identified how past experiences were similarly laden with anxiety. Chelsea revealed stories about her father's explosive temper and her mother's emotional invisibility because of her drinking. Chelsea's present-day turmoil was superimposed over her early life wounding. Her family dysfunction, abuse, and neglect—etched into her ANS—forged a baseline arousal level. Her dysregulated ANS seemed prone to locking in and defending against perceived immediate threats.

In our discussions about how past traumas imprint on the nervous system, I shared a metaphor of tree rings. Metaphor and imagery emerge from the right hemisphere and speak to the affective substrate of left hemisphere. Chelsea and I talked about how the cross-section of rings in a tree document past storms, wounds, and the growth that occurred despite these inflictions. We also explored how tree rings can shape future growth. Discussing neuroplasticity, we discussed

Sidebar 4.3 • Disassociation

Some counselors wonder why a person disconnects from their body after a trauma or when remembering a traumatic event. This reaction is natural and safe for someone who has experienced a trauma. The mind disconnects from the body as a protective measure. For this reason, it is important not to push a client too quickly into being emotionally connected to their trauma stories until they are ready; otherwise, clients may experience distress and greater disassociation. What can counselors do to create a safe space to explore traumatic events?

how supportive relationships, as well as new experiences and activities, that retrain the ANS can lessen the depth of historical grooves.

Chelsea's distressing stalemate reflects the "freeze" process. Another phase in threat detection, "fold/faint" has the power to drop respiration, heart rate, and blood pressure and cause fainting. Some animals use it to play dead. This process is believed to be modulated by a combination of the PNS and other components of the dorsal vagus. Chelsea expressed relief as we discussed the power of faint/fold as an autonomic response rather than personal weakness or flaw. I shared with her that mild levels of dissociation are more common than most realize and can contribute to inaction and to people foregoing counseling for years despite intense suffering.

Clients who come to counseling "know" by way of their left hemisphere that they are bodily safe. The inner safety they seek is nuanced and complex and involves true connection. Through a right hemispheric–based empathic connection, counselors can cultivate mutual empathy. This capacity may seem like intuition, but there is much more at work and in play, including curiosity, imagination, risk taking, and creativity. In counseling, Chelsea began to feel free to zig zag and to go off script; however, as is common, she felt worse before she felt better because she was freer to fully experience her past pain. She brought in photos, made drawings, and worked through challenging feelings and memories. She walked me through what it was like to be her as a child, a teenager, and fluidly in the present in the chair facing me. Counseling for her became a place to confront tremendous pain at her own speed and to develop freer, playful capacities.

Case Example Two

"Alex" was 7 years old when he first came to my (Mark's) office for treatment of developmental trauma, a syndrome proposed by Bessel A. van der Kolk (2005). We used neurofeedback, a biofeedback method that trains brain waves using classical and operant conditioning. Treatment involved an approach developed by Sebern Fisher (2014) as well as protocols based on a quantitative assessment of the electroencephalogram, three-dimensional localization of brain wave activity, and normative database values for feedback.

Initial Assessment

The initial clinical assessment included history and symptomatology, reports from various agencies, adoptive parents' reports and symptom scale, and clinician impressions. Alex's parents have given written consent for nonidentifying aspects of the treatment process to be published for the sake of research. On the basis of Alex's adoptive parents' report, a recent psychological evaluation, and state Child Protective Services caseworker reports, we ascertained the following about Alex's history. Born to a mother addicted to heroin and pain medication and diagnosed with multiple *Diagnostic and Statistical Manual of Mental Disorders* (5th ed.; *DSM-5*; American Psychiatric Association, 2013) conditions and to a biological father with a criminal history of theft, assault on a family member, and trespassing, Alex had profoundly turbulent early years. Alex was exposed to alcohol, heroin, cocaine, nicotine, and possibly other substances prenatally.

Alex's paternal grandmother assumed responsibility for his care as an infant, but records indicated that he was often neglected and left alone for long periods of time without supervision or nutrition. Alex experienced periods of malnutrition and was found digging through the garbage for food—eating playdough on one occasion. His home environment included the sale and use of drugs, and his grandmother reportedly forced him to perform sexual acts with men for money on numerous occasions. Alex was exposed to violence and murder as well as repeated beatings. When Alex's younger sister was born addicted to drugs, Child Protective Services removed the children from the home. Alex was 4 years old at the time they were placed in foster care.

Alex was sexually abused at his first foster home by an older boy, beaten by his foster parents with a belt, locked in a closet, and deprived of food. There is no record of his experience in a second foster home. He and his younger sister were adopted by his current parents when he was 5 years old. After adoption, Alex was diagnosed with autism spectrum disorder, but after several months of counseling with a child sexual abuse specialist, his diagnoses were changed to PTSD, attention-deficit/hyperactivity disorder (ADHD), obsessive-compulsive disorder, and anxiety disorder. At that time, his symptoms included night terrors, flashbacks, dissociation, and panic attacks. In addition to individual therapy, Alex received family therapy and psychiatric treatment with psychotropic medications. Both adoptive parents were present in our interview and subsequent sessions and were invested in providing him and his sister with love and concern as well as a stable and nurturing home environment.

On the basis of parent report (via verbal report and symptom checklist) and clinical appraisal, Alex's key symptoms—in order of severity on a 7-point Likert scale—were fearfulness, anxiety, obsessive thoughts, not feeling calm or relaxed, being hyper-focused, expressing negative thoughts, inconsistent energy levels, and poor concentration. Because of his parents' concern for his academic progress, treatment initially targeted Alex's ADHD symptoms.

Alex's harsh early years left an imprint on his brain physiology. The electroencephalogram reflected overall slowing, indicative of cognitive functioning problems that would include symptoms of ADHD. Slowing was predominant in the right hemisphere, the anterior cingulate, and right parietal-temporal junction. There were indications of right limbic overarousal. Taken together, these findings are consistent with brain scan research on chronic PTSD.

Neurofeedback Plan

Treatment protocols initially focused on decreasing the cortical slowing and decreasing fast wave activity to improve attention and reduce anxiety. At Session 23, a temporal lobe placement was added to improve emotional regulation. At Session 37, a placement targeting the right prefrontal cortex was included to further address emotional regulation and to reduce the fear response. Beginning at Session 42, a follow-up electroencephalogram was performed to assess PTSD markers in preparation for the final five sessions using a 19-channel, three-dimensional, normative database-driven neurofeedback approach, known as low-resolution brain electromagnetic tomography (LORETA Z-score). This approach was used to target overarousal of the right limbic area to reduce fear and improve emotional regulation.

Progress

By Session 10, Alex was sleeping better and seemed calmer during the day. At Session 15, he had improved handwriting and focus when studying. At Session

29, symptoms were improving overall, but Alex continued to experience episodes of dissociation. After Session 38, he showed improvement in all eight symptoms initially prioritized on the checklist.

After one session of right prefrontal training, Alex had an abreaction of a traumatic memory, and his sensitivity to odors was heightened. After subsequent sessions, he was calmer. After the first session of LORETA Z-score training, Alex began sleeping more at night and taking daytime naps. After the fourth LORETA Z-score session, he took a 4-hour nap when he returned home. The average symptom checklist severity score completed at the beginning of treatment (average = 5.6/7), midtreatment (average = 3.9/7), conclusion of treatment (average = 2.3/7), and 1-year follow-up (average = 1.5/7) showed continual reduction in symptoms.

Two months after the conclusion of Alex's neurofeedback treatment, his parents sent a video of him unreservedly scaling a 30-foot climbing wall at a local children's museum and letting himself fall back to earth using his harness and support cord. This behavior is in stark contrast to the fearful child that Alex was at the beginning of neurofeedback treatment.

Connections and Disconnections in Neurofeedback

Alex entered my (Mark's) waiting room for the initial assessment with his adoptive family, appearing to be truly uncomfortable in his own skin as well as with his surroundings. As I emerged from my office to greet him, he glanced tentatively at me with fearful eyes but managed a polite greeting. That began a journey he and I would embark on together—a sojourn that deeply enriched both our lives.

If we were to use traditional psychodynamic terms, I would say that I unreservedly acknowledged my "countertransference" with Alex. As I have learned from deeply traumatized clients, such transference reactions on the part of the counselor are more the norm, if not a necessary part of the therapeutic environment. Borrowing from an RCT lens, I embraced my work with Alex truly appreciative of his courage to attend neurofeedback counseling with me and immensely hopeful that my genuine care and desire to help would be well received. Recognizing the context of Alex's history, and the historical abuse at the hands of men and women alike, I hoped to be a male figure he could one day trust—a person invested in building a trustworthy connection.

In reflecting on my work with Alex, I can best describe my sentiments at our first meeting, and throughout our work, as those of deep respect. To work with a person who has undergone such profound traumatic experiences as a young child and to know he is taking such risks by coming to our sessions created a dynamic in our therapeutic relationship I to this day cherish. Obviously, as the person with training, I provided the technical treatment. However, on a much more personal level, Alex became my teacher on matters of the human condition. He is an old soul.

I truly believe it was my level of respect for Alex and the connection we forged that helped create a relationship in which we could build trust. One of the ways I conveyed this stance was by consistently addressing him as "Mr. Alexander" with a smile and conversing with him about the rationale of therapy as well as maintaining an air of playfulness. At a spiritual level, our time together felt like holy ground.

At the beginning of treatment, Alex was wary of the office environment and the neurofeedback wires. His tendency to perseverate was apparent, as he would anxiously fixate on a word or concept, such as when he read about snakes in his geography lesson. The treatment situation only provided additional sources of anxiety. Dialog with Alex or his parents had to be done carefully, recognizing that some aspect of his diagnoses or treatment would become the focus of his perseveration. For example, in responding to his questions about the nature of neurofeedback, and why he was being brought to treatment, I would frame my responses positively ("to make your brain better" or "so that you will be happier"). Engaging Alex in the process of hooking up the sensors, checking connection measures, and picking the feedback (such as which game or cartoon) helped him to be less preoccupied about neurofeedback.

Alex could be articulate in his questions about the therapeutic process and about me. Initially, he presented with anxiety in the sessions, constantly querying me about how he was doing and what was normal. As treatment continued, our discussions were more about life.

There were setbacks. As Alex became confident enough to travel to visit his adopted relatives, two men got into an ugly argument over seat assignments across the aisle on the airplane. A visit to a local park was interrupted when the family's window was smashed by a group from the neighborhood. St. Patrick's Day pinching by other children at a restaurant play area triggered Alex into a panic attack with psychogenic seizures, resulting in a trip to the emergency department and extensive testing. In Alex's world, it felt untenable to me to reassure him that this was not the nature of life. It was the nature of his life. Following one of these crises, I wrote to his mother expressing my concern. When she shared it with him, he replied, "I don't think I have every mattered to anyone."

Toward the end of the treatment regimen, I gave Alex a can of black-eyed peas—an impromptu notion that arose out of our playful discussions about food. He reciprocated with a can of pork and beans. In this action, Alex demonstrated an ability to form positive connections.

During our time together, there were times when, seemingly out of the blue, Alex would comment on some horrific experience in his earlier childhood. Digging through the trash to feed his baby sister. Seeing the body of a neighbor who'd been shot. Being burned by a cigarette. Admittedly, I was taken aback by these statements and struggled with how to respond. I let him see my sadness. Later, I would learn that doing so reflected the RCT concept of mutual empathy. We talked about these experiences with the parent who was in the room, and they would reassure him. Ultimately, I redirected us back to the neurofeedback with a realization that these are the wounds we are treating. These were the most challenging experiences for me. These were the times I especially wanted him to feel my care.

Alex has continued individual counseling with a gentle male colleague of mine, trained in child and adolescent psychiatric settings and well versed in trauma treatment, including eye movement desensitization and reprocessing. I still see him occasionally in the office complex. He'll call out my name and give me a hug.

Future Directions and Emerging Research

What began as the insistence of Jean Baker Miller and her colleagues on the relevance of relationships to mental health has become a field of research and practice (Banks, 2016). Relational neuroscience deepens the way we understand trauma and, most importantly, broadens the tools we have to support individuals who have survived traumatic experiences. Allan N. Schore (2014) declared the totality of these emerging lines of research and clinical work to be a "paradigm shift." Here, we wish to draw special attention to two frontiers in the research opened by the relational turn in trauma theory and therapy: neurofeedback and somatic approaches. Both seek to intervene on traumatic dysregulation at the level of biological sequelae and, thus, provide novel avenues for working within and beyond traumatic experience.

Neurofeedback is emerging as a powerful mental health tool found effective in trauma therapy. By translating real-time electroencephalography measurements of brain activity into a visual image that the client can manipulate through self-regulation of brain function, neurofeedback gives clients a way to gauge their own efforts and learn how to regulate brain processes. For some, this method may be the safest and most effective way into healing. Somatic approaches, although they have a long clinical history, have emerged more recently in the empirical literature. The mind-body connection is now undeniable, and the use of practices such as trauma-sensitive yoga to build mind-body awareness can give individuals who feel constricted by their brain's adaptation to past traumas a way back to greater neural integration and flexibility.

In addition to the neurological and somatic frontiers, a relational perspective on trauma can also shed light on the ways in which many other approaches effect change. Research on the relational neuroscientific bases of creativity in counseling, for example, can help us better understand and support the widespread use of interventions that activate collaborative creativity as a healing practice for trauma survivors. We advocate for continued research into the science and clinical practice of these and other emergent approaches from a commitment to relationship as the heart of well-being.

References

American Psychiatric Association. (2013). *Diagnostic and statistical manual of mental disorders* (5th ed.). Arlington, VA: Author.

Banks, A. (2006). Relational therapy for trauma. *Journal of Trauma Practice, 5*(1), 25–47. https://doi.org/10.1300/J189v05n01_03

Banks, A. (2016). *Wired to connect: The surprising link between brain science and strong, healthy relationships.* New York, NY: Penguin.

Bekkali, S., Youssef, G. J., Donaldson, P. H., Albein-Urios, N., Hyde, C., & Enitcott, P. G. (2019, March 20). *Is the putative mirror neuron system associated with empathy? A systematic review and meta-analysis.* Manuscript submitted for publication. https://doi.org/10.31234/osf.io/6bu4p

Blakeslee, S. (2006, January 10). Cells that read minds. *The New York Times.* Retrieved from https://www.nytimes.com/2006/01/10/science/cells-that-read-minds.html

Bremner, J. D. (2006). Traumatic stress: Effects on the brain. *Dialogues in Clinical Neuroscience, 8,* 445–461.

Bremner, J. D., Vermetten, E., & Kelley, M. E. (2007). Cortisol, dehydroepiandrosterone, and estradiol measured over 24 hours in women with childhood sexual abuse-related posttraumatic stress disorder. *The Journal of Nervous and Mental Disease, 195,* 919–927. https://doi.org/10.1097/NMD.0b013e3181594ca0

Bremner, J. D., Vermetten, E., Vythilingam, M., Afzal, N., Schmahl, C., Elzinga, B., & Charney, D. S. (2004). Neural correlates of the classic color and emotional Stroop in women with abuse-related posttraumatic stress disorder. *Biological Psychiatry, 55*, 612–620. https://doi.org/10.1016/j.biopsych.2003.10.001

Burgoon, J. K., Guerrero, L. K., & Floyd, K. (2016). *Nonverbal communication.* New York, NY: Routledge.

Cohen, J. A., Perel, J. M., De Bellis, M. D., Friedman, M. J., & Putnam, F. W. (2002). Treating traumatized children: Clinical implications of the psychobiology of posttraumatic stress disorder. *Trauma, Violence, and Abuse, 3*(2), 91–108. https://doi.org/10.1177/15248380020032001

Cozolino, L. (2014). *The neuroscience of human relationships: Attachment and the developing social brain* (Norton Series on Interpersonal Neurobiology). New York, NY: Norton.

De Bellis, M. D., & Zisk, A. (2014). The biological effects of childhood trauma. *Child and Adolescent Psychiatric Clinics of North America, 23*(2), 185–222. https://doi.org/10.1016/j.chc.2014.01.002

Fisher, S. (2014). In consultation. *Psychotherapy Networker, 38*(3). Retrieved from https://www.questia.com/magazine/1P3-3312415521/in-consultation

Gallese, V., Fadiga, L., Fogassi, L., & Rizzolatti, G. (1996). Action recognition in the premotor cortex. *Brain, 119*, 593–609. https://doi.org/10.1093/brain/119.2.593

Gladstein, G. A. (1974). Nonverbal communication and counseling/psychotherapy: A review. *The Counseling Psychologist, 4*(3), 34–57. https://doi.org/10.1177/001100007400400307

Jordan, J. (2017). Relational-cultural theory: The power of connection to transform our lives. *Journal of Humanistic Counseling, 56*, 228–243. https://doi.org/10.1002/johc.12055

Kasai, K., Yamasue, H., Gilbertson, M. W., Shenton, M. E., Rauch, S. L., & Pitman, R. K. (2008). Evidence for acquired pregenual anterior cingulate gray matter loss from a twin study of combat-related posttraumatic stress disorder. *Biological Psychiatry, 63*, 550–556. https://doi.org/10.1016/j.biopsych.2007.06.022

Lanius, R. A., Williamson, P. C., Hopper, J., Densmore, M., Boksman, K., Gupta, M. A., . . . Menon, R. S. (2003). Recall of emotional states in posttraumatic stress disorder: An fMRI investigation. *Biological Psychiatry, 53*, 204–210. https://doi.org/10.1016/S0006-3223(02)01466-X

LeDoux, J. (1998). *The emotional brain: The mysterious underpinnings of emotional life.* New York, NY: Simon & Schuster.

Levy-Gigi, E., Szabó, C., Kelemen, O., & Kéri, S. (2013). Association among clinical response, hippocampal volume, and FKBP5 gene expression in individuals with posttraumatic stress disorder receiving cognitive behavioral therapy. *Biological Psychiatry, 74*, 793–800. https://doi.org/10.1016/j.biopsych.2013.05.017

McLaughlin, K., Busso, D., Duys, A., Green, J., Alves, S., Way, M., & Sheridan, M. (2014). Amygdala response to negative stimuli predicts PTSD symptom onset following a terrorist attack. *Depression and Anxiety, 31*, 834–842. https://doi.org/10.1002/da.22284

Meng, Y., Qiu, C., Zhu, H., Lama, S., Lui, S., Gong, Q., & Zhang, W. (2014). Anatomical deficits in adult posttraumatic stress disorder: A meta-analysis of voxel-based morphometry studies. *Behavioural Brain Research, 270*, 307–315. https://doi.org/10.1016/j.bbr.2014.05.021

Mucci, C. (2013). *Beyond individual and collective trauma: Intergenerational transmission, psychoanalytic treatment, and the dynamics of forgiveness.* New York, NY: Karnac Books.

Mukamel, R., Ekstrom, A. D., Kaplan, J., Iacoboni, M., & Fried, I. (2010). Single neuron responses in humans during execution and observation of actions. *Current Biology, 20,* 750–756. https://doi.org/10.1016/j.cub.2010.02.045

Norcross, J. C., & Wampold, B. E. (2011). Evidence-based therapy relationships: Research conclusions and clinical practices. *Psychotherapy, 48,* 98–102. https://doi.org/10.1037/a0022161

Porges, S. (2014). The polyvagal theory: Demystifying the link between social behavior and health. *Applied Psychophysiology and Biofeedback, 39*(2), 141.

Schore, A. N. (2009). Right-brain affect regulation: An essential mechanism of development, trauma, dissociation, and psychotherapy. In D. Fosha, D. J. Siegel, & M. F. Solomon (Eds.), *The healing power of emotion: Affective neuroscience, development and clinical practice* (pp. 112–144). New York, NY: Norton.

Schore, A. N. (2012). *The science of the art of psychotherapy* (Norton Series on Interpersonal Neurobiology). New York, NY: Norton.

Schore, A. N. (2014). The right brain is dominant in psychotherapy. *Psychotherapy, 51,* 388–397.

Schore, A. N., & Sieff, D. F. (2015). On the same wavelength: How our emotional brain is shaped by human relationships. In D. F. Sieff (Ed.), *Understanding and healing emotional trauma: Conversations with pioneering clinicians and researchers* (p. 111–136). East Sussex, London: Routledge.

Shin, L. M., Rauch, S. L., & Pitman, R. K. (2006). Amygdala, medial prefrontal cortex, and hippocampal function in PTSD. *Annals of the New York Academy of Sciences, 1071,* 67–79. https://doi.org/10.1196/annals.1364.007

Shin, L. M., Wright, C. I., Cannistraro, P. A., Wedig, M. M., McMullin, K., Martis, B., . . . Krangel, T. S. (2005). A functional magnetic resonance imaging study of amygdala and medial prefrontal cortex responses to overtly presented fearful faces in posttraumatic stress disorder. *Archives of General Psychiatry, 62,* 273–281. https://doi.org/10.1001/archpsyc.62.3.273

Siegel, D. J. (2015). *The developing mind: How relationships and the brain interact to shape who we are.* New York, NY: Guilford Press.

Stephens, M. A. C., & Wand, G. (2012). Stress and the HPA axis: Role of glucocorticoids in alcohol dependence. *Alcohol Research: Current Reviews, 34,* 468–483.

van der Kolk, B. A. (2005). Developmental trauma disorder: Towards a rational diagnosis for children with complex trauma histories. *Psychiatric Annals, 35,* 401–408.

van der Kolk, B. A. (2006). Clinical implications of neuroscience research in PTSD. *Annals of the New York Academy of Sciences, 1071,* 277–293. https://doi.org/10.1196/annals.1364.022

van der Kolk, B. A. (2014). *The body keeps the score: Brain, mind, and body in the healing of trauma.* New York, NY: Viking.

Wylie, M. S., & Turner, L. (n.d.). *Adult attachment disorder: 3 detours to the right hemisphere.* Retrieved from https://www.psychotherapynetworker.org/blog/details/18/adult-attachment-disorder-3-detours-to-the-right-hemisphere

Yehuda, R., Teicher, M. H., Trestman, R. L., Levengood, R. A., & Siever, L. J. (1996). Cortisol regulation in posttraumatic stress disorder and major depression: A chronobiological analysis. *Biological Psychiatry, 40,* 79–88. https://doi.org/10.1016/0006-3223(95)00451-3

Zoladz, P. R., & Diamond, D. (2016). Psychosocial predator stress model of PTSD based on clinically relevant risk factors for trauma-induced psychopathology. In J. D. Bremner (Ed.), *Posttraumatic stress disorder: From neurobiology to treatment* (pp. 125–144). Hoboken, NJ: Wiley. https://doi.org/10.1002/9781118356142.ch6

Multiple-Choice Questions

1. According to the author, trauma is both adaptive and
   a. Harmful.
   b. Maladaptive.
   c. Reactive.
   d. All of the above

2. Relational neuroscience is also known as social neuroscience.
   a. False
   b. True, until a few years ago
   c. True
   d. False, because these concepts are very different

3. What theory talks about caretaker-child relationships?
   a. CBT
   b. Gestalt
   c. Attachment theory
   d. None of the above

4. What type of neuron was accidently discovered?
   a. Mirror neuron
   b. Twin neuron
   c. Single neuron
   d. Excitatory neuron

5. Siegel (2015) posited that our view of our own physical experience is profoundly connected to our social experience.
   a. True
   b. False
   c. True, for only children
   d. True, for only adults

6. Polyvagal theory highlights the role of
   a. Adrenaline secretion as a response to an inner memory.
   b. The role of the vagus nerve in disassociation.
   c. How the nervous system responds to social cues, especially facial expressions.
   d. None of the above

7. The most highly studied function of the amygdala is in the
   a. Trust conditioning.
   b. Fear conditioning.
   c. Response conditioning.
   d. Ego conditioning.

8. When the brain senses fear, which happens first?
   a. Release of adrenocorticotropin hormone (ACTH)
   b. Release of endorphins
   c. Release of GABA
   d. Release of corticotropin-releasing factor (CRF)

9. Which is part of the sympathetic nervous system (SNS)?
   a. Increased heart rate
   b. Digestive system
   c. Genitourinary systems
   d. None of the above

10. The "smart vagus" is a term created by
    a. Amy Banks.
    b. Stephen Porges.
    c. Judith Jordan.
    d. Jean Baker Miller.

11. What is important in mediating the lived experience of PTSD?
    a. The amygdala
    b. The heart
    c. The hippocampus
    d. The stomach

12. Siegel (2015) believed that if trauma happens during early brain development,
    a. Social bonds will always be hard to manage.
    b. The brain can still heal.
    c. The brain is stuck at a certain age.
    d. None of the above

13. Affective enactments in counseling mirror which RCT principle
    a. Strategies of disconnection.
    b. Mutual empathy.
    c. Perspective valuation.
    d. Cognitive restructuring.

14. Which is a component of trauma-informed care?
    a. Exposure
    b. Self-control
    c. Emphasis on safety
    d. Behavioral therapy

15. Neurofeedback may be an effective treatment for trauma symptoms.
    a. False
    b. True
    c. False, because neurofeedback can only be used with ADHD symptoms
    d. True, if the trauma symptoms are not too severe

Essay Questions

1. You have probably learned about trauma theories and how trauma affects the brain during your master's degree or trainings. However, have you ever considered the relational impact that trauma can have on a person's brain? Trauma does not simply affect the brain and how clients relate to their counselor but also how clients relate to their physical self. Is this surprising to you? Have you worked with clients who feel disconnected from their bodies?

2. Learning about the neurobiological effects of trauma can feel daunting. After all, we are counselors and not neuroscientists. However, we are in a unique position to help our clients understand more about their brain and the effects of trauma. Do you talk with your clients about the neurobiological effects of trauma, and if so, how do you do this?

3. Research and scientists used to believe that the brain could not change or create new neuron connections later in life. We now know this is incorrect, and our brains have neuroplasticity. This finding can instill hope for clients with past trauma, addictions, or other issues that may have negatively affected their brain. How do you use this information to instill hope for your clients?

4. According to the chapter, nonverbal behavior is more believable than verbal communication. How do you validate your client and support your client in nonverbal ways? How do you use nonverbal behavior with your friends or family to communicate caring?

5. Trauma research is increasing, and we have a better understanding of trauma every day. PTSD was first added in the *DSM-III* and became its own diagnosis in the *DSM-5*. What would you predict the next step for PTSD knowledge to be?

CHAPTER 5

Fundamental Theories and Skills
for Crisis Counseling

Shane Haberstroh

On a beautiful south Texas morning, I walked into our university community counseling clinic. I learned of a woman who was on the verge of killing herself, and my morning swiftly shifted into listening to Marcelle share her suicidal thoughts, plans, hesitations, and history of abuse and neglect. The conversation was fluid and did not follow the linear flow of suicide screening instruments. My most pressing concern was to stay connected. I feared she could hang up at any moment. To be honest, I feared I might make a misstep in the conversation—not really hear the nuances and pain in her story, but I kept listening with all the compassion I had. Being heard and cared for sparked a hazy possibility of hope, and she expressed a faint modicum of relief. I interspersed suicidal screening questions, affirmed her courage to make the call, explored her reasons for living, ascertained any protective factors, and quickly scribbled instructions for the staff to connect with the mobile crisis team. After we rallied our resources, we planned for our next steps. The mobile crisis team connected with Marcelle and provided stabilization services, and she followed up with individual counseling.

Moments of crisis call on our presence and genuine care for a person who is suffering as well as knowing about what to ask and what steps to take. Crisis situations feel tumultuous, and many are sudden and extreme events in someone's life. However, not all crisis situations involve the potential for violence. Many life crises are sublime in their misery and exact tolls that weave through the threads of life. Our hope is to provide you with conceptual frameworks and some practices to help guide you during these critical moments.

The Nature of Crises

A crisis is a shock to internal and external systems. These events can take many shapes, with many factors determining their personal and social impact. James and Gilliland (2017) defined a *crisis* as a "perception or experiencing of an event or situation as an intolerable difficulty that exceeds the person's current resources and coping mechanisms" (p. 26). Events that can create crisis reactions range in intensity and scope. According to the Substance Abuse and Mental Health Services Administration (SAMHSA, 2014b), crises and traumatic events can be natural disasters such as hurricanes, earthquakes, or fires. Human-driven catastrophes include examples such as accidental gun shootings, oil spills, building collapses, and train derailments. These events represent accidents and unintentional structural failures. However, people can inflict considerable suffering on each other. Terrorism, sexual assault, abuse, genocide, robberies, and school violence are exemplars of intentional acts committed to hurt others. Other transitional and situational life crises and losses can also bring a person to the brink of despair.

Perception, Proximity, and Intentionality

How a person and a counselor both perceive a crisis or traumatic event plays an important role in how people respond. Certainly, many of the events listed in the previous section represent world-shattering experiences. Imagine working as a disaster mental health worker with the American Red Cross, and you are standing next to a father surveying the ruins of his smoldering house. Family memories reduced to charred picture frames, melted toys, and heaps of rubble. The events of that night seared in memories and guilt because he could not get to his daughter's room fast enough. A couple of glasses of wine might have slowed his reaction time. His healing, like his daughter's burns, will be long and punctuated by points of agony, moments of hope, and maybe—in the future—days without pain. Over time, this father and daughter will adjust, fight, feel despair, hope, and try to make some sense of their tragedy. The next day, you work with a college student recently dumped by his boyfriend, and you struggle to access the same compassion you had yesterday. You think to yourself, "At least you didn't lose everything in a fire and have to listen to the agony of your 6-year-old daughter in the burn ward. You'll get over this." This kind of thinking is a mistake. For your client, this is a true crisis and a potentially dangerous one as well. In examining the factors leading to death by suicide, the Centers for Disease Control and Prevention (CDC, 2018) found that relationship problems were a predictive factor for 42% of people who committed suicide. In this instance, the perception of the breakup and resulting heartbreak can bring about feelings of hopelessness. Unfortunately, outsiders can unintentionally minimize the true pain people feel.

Proximity also plays an important role in how people respond to perilous situations (Pfeifer & Haeffel, 2014). Proximity can be seen as both physical and relational. For example, children experienced higher rates of posttraumatic stress disorder (PTSD) when they were physically close to a disastrous event on school campuses (Brock et al., 2016). Relational proximity can be understood when someone with whom we are close suffers a tragedy. Imagine the despair, pain, and profound sadness that parents feel when their learn that their child has been hurt thousands of miles away. Distance may increase their sense of anguish. Interestingly, social support may be a powerful factor in mediating the brunt of loss. Pfeifer and Haeffel (2014) found that students who learned of a classmate's death felt more distress when they lived farther away, even when the relationship was less close than those proximal to the tragedy.

Crises and Emergencies

It is important to differentiate between a crisis and an emergency (James & Gilliland, 2017). Depending on the circumstances, a crisis can surely be an emergency situation. An emergency requires that we act quickly and a life is on the line. An example of how these terms differentiate in practice drove several items on the development of the Columbia Suicide Severity Rating Scale (Posner et al., 2011). In many instances, people who engaged in self-injurious behaviors without intent to commit suicide were treated as active suicide risks. They engaged in self-harm to express relief due to internal pain (Haberstroh & Moyer, 2012; Posner et al., 2011), but many did not express suicidal intent. Not all crises are emergencies, and distress can be mitigated through expressing care, connecting people with resources, and developing plans that increase coping and linkages to community supports (James & Gilliland, 2017).

There are many times when a crisis event is an emergency situation. These events include suicidal ideation with a plan and means; active abuse of children, older adults, or those with disabilities; homicidal ideations and plans; medical emergencies; destabilizing psychiatric conditions; alcohol, opiate, and benzodiazepine withdrawals; drug overdoses; and active disaster situations. These kinds of situations require involving medical and law enforcement personnel and potentially arranging involuntary placements.

A Life in Crisis and Crises of Everyday Living

Life crises range from expected transitions to unexpected and traumatic life-changing events. According to G. A. Miller (2012), *situational crises* are episodes that take people by surprise and tax their resources. *Developmental crises* include life events and common struggles that people endure. For example, some people may be surprised at their bittersweet feelings of joy, nostalgia, and sadness as they send their children off to college, retire, or make major life decisions. Others may endure many crisis moments when parenting children with special needs, helping a friend who suffers from addiction, or coming to terms with their own failing health. Likewise, people may seek counseling after the death of a loved one, loss of an important relationship, loss of a job, or an academic failure. Moments of crisis flare from these simmering stresses, and situational crises can strike at any time, complicating matters. In Chapter 9, we explore the varying situational, maturational, and identity crises that people endure.

The Relational Foundations for Crisis Counseling

Depending on the type of crises, and the reactions to these events by your clients, you will vary in your approach and style. Regardless of your first steps, the counseling relationship in crisis work begins at the first contact with you and a person in distress. A person's resilience grows from the act of reaching out for help

(Jordan, 2017). Our relational reciprocity (van der Kolk, 2014) in those key moments set the foundation for effective helping. Some crisis intervention models list risk assessment as the first task and rapport building secondary. We contend that your first contact and risk assessment methods are relationally bound. As someone hangs onto the fraying threads of their life, connection through compassion during these critical junctures can be a source of strength. Given the circumstances, crisis counselors may need to engage in life-saving measures. Depending on your client's physical and mental states, you may need to take an active and instructive role in referring clients to services and engaging with mental health facilities, law enforcement professionals, and medical personnel.

Overview of Crisis Intervention Theories and Models

Several models define the nature of crises and provide counselors with a roadmap to provide interventions. Like most theories, many of these approaches emphasize certain dimensions of the human experience, and the original theories were developed decades ago. As crisis counseling evolved into a specialty practice, new models offered stepwise approaches, whereas others provided important tasks for you to cover in session. Progressive approaches to crisis intervention integrate elements from traditional models and add environmental, social, contextual, and developmental factors. Finally, grief models may help articulate the processes of chronic life stresses. These models make sense when people seem to barely tread the waters of their lives. James and Gilliland (2017) described several foundational crisis intervention theories. These approaches range from considering a crisis as an internal deficiency in coping and cognition to recognizing the crux of crises lying within systems and social interactions. Integrated models allow you flexibility to conceptualize the complex and nuanced factors in a crisis situation while offering structured guidelines to follow in chaotic times.

Internally Focused Cognitive and Coping Models

Early theories of crisis counseling illustrated crisis responses as dysregulation or dysfunction within the coping or belief systems of an individual. The *cognitive model,* based in cognitive-behavioral therapy, focuses on how people develop and sustain irrational beliefs that serve as perceptual filters during times of crisis (James & Gilliland, 2017). These beliefs may serve as wellsprings of cognitive dysfunction that can exacerbate stressful times. Basically, negative thinking spirals can lead people away from constructive problem solving and objective perspective taking before, during, and after a destabilizing event. For example, clients who suffer through a heart-wrenching divorce may share they will never find another gratifying relationship. A cognitive-focused counselor would focus in on the potential distortions in this thinking.

Many cognitive therapies for trauma work include discussion of the interrelationships and evaluation of thoughts, feelings, and emotions (James & Gilliland, 2017). From this perspective, the counselor may ask probing questions to help people articulate alternative perspectives. For example, a counselor could reflect that these statements seem like a worst case scenario. To expand their client's cognitive perspective, a counselor might inquire about what the best case outcome might be and what the most probable outcome might look like (Jaycox, Langley, & Hoover, 2018). This might not be the best approach for someone in an immediate life-threating emergency. However, this work may help interrupt destructive cognitive schemas in longer term work with clients and is a mainstay of cognitive therapies for PTSD.

Likewise, the *equilibrium* approach first described by Caplan (1961) contends that before a crisis, a person maintains a repertoire of coping responses that become challenged during vexing times. As a result, people enter a state of disequilibrium, and the tensions they feel overpower their natural capacities to cope. As internal pressures build, people may sink into depression and eventually suffer a mental breakdown. The goal is to help restore people to their previous homeostatic functioning though problem solving and developing new coping strategies.

One of the predisposing factors for developing PTSD is a sense of helplessness and inescapability from a threatening situation (van der Kolk, 2014). Exploring resources, support systems, and potential power to make changes, no matter how small, can remind people of their control. After people have a sense of control and direction, they experience *psychological mobility*, which allows them to make decisions and work toward solutions. Much literature and professional guidance materials support the equilibrium model with people experiencing acute distress, because this approach seeks to remedy immediate concerns and restore a person's functional capacity (James & Gilliland, 2017).

Biopsychosocial and Psychosocial Transition Models

The biopsychosocial approach highlights interactions among personal, genetic, and demographic factors with psychological and social influences (SAMHSA, 2014b). These interactions are recursive, and each of these domains influences the other domains. The CDC (2019) used this model to frame their violence-prevention programs. Although crisis and disasters can strike anyone, causing disequilibrium and taxing resources (James & Gilliland, 2017), certain demographic and genetic factors may be important to explore. At the genetic level, studies of heritable predisposition find that many addictive and mental health disorders share genetic backgrounds (National Institute on Drug Abuse [NIDA], 2018). Clearly, addiction and co-occurring disorders can lead to physiological, mental, and social crises (NIDA, 2018). The severity of a co-occurring disorder also predicts how well someone can cope in the face of a crisis or traumatic event (SAMHSA, 2014b). Moreover, age, biological sex, and gender are demographic important factors under study. For example, men face greater odds of experiencing traumatic stressful events related to violence and crime victimization, whereas women experience physical and sexual assault more frequently and are twice as likely to develop PTSD (SAMHSA, 2014b). As we discussed in Chapter 2, sexual minority individuals face increased harassment, hate crimes, and sexual assaults. Keep in mind that people's identity occurs within the context of social and cultural systems that can either hinder or support recovery.

Age plays a factor in how a crisis or traumatic event interacts with developmental and situational variables. For example, traumas experienced at younger ages can affect development, connection, relational images, and beliefs about trust and safety (SAMHSA, 2014b). Crises that occur during midlife can burden people as they navigate multiple adult roles and care for others while under the strain of unexpected predicaments. Finally, as people age, they may not recover as quickly from physical injuries, or they could lose access to medications and medical care during a disaster and face increased traumas from medical practices (van der Kolk, 2014).

Systemic and Ecological Approaches

As we discussed in Chapter 3, social and cultural forces play a significant role in the conceptualization of a crisis and factors that can impede or worsen a crisis situation. Systemic and ecological approaches explore the dynamics, roles, and normative functions within small systems and larger organizations and communities. Systems theory (MacKay, 2012) can help us understand the interactional patterns, normative emotional expressions, role adherence, and boundaries within a group, community, or family system. Of note, Jordan (2017) conceptualized boundaries as points of contact and energy rather than walls of separation. Equally important is the concept of homeostasis, which posits that people in systems will gravitate toward familiar ways of acting and responding to each other, even when these styles appear harmful and counterproductive to an outside observer. Moreover, as a destabilizing event shatters familiar interactional and behavioral patterns, a crisis can serve as a touchpoint for a group, community, or family to evaluate how ways of coping and supporting one another can change. For example, Tyler found his daughter unresponsive after she overdosed. While waiting in the emergency room, Tyler plays back all the times he ignored his daughter and became lost in work stress and personal ambition. He finally sees his neglect and emotional abandonment. He vows to change. See Sidebar 5.1 for more information on navigating crises.

SAMHSA Core Elements for Responding to Mental Health Crises

The millions of people living with mental health issues and co-occurring substance use problems face social and intrapersonal challenges that place them at high risk for experiencing multiple crises (SAMHSA, 2009). Many people suffering from mental health and behavioral problems experienced high levels of childhood trauma, increased homelessness, poor health, and high levels of criminal justice involvement (SAMHSA, 2009). To provide guiding principles for practitioners working with individuals with these traumatic history and complex needs, SAMHSA published guidelines outlining core elements for responding to mental health crises.

Sidebar 5.1 • Navigating Crises

According to the biopsychosocial and psychosocial models, many factors can contribute to how a person experiences a crisis. The ecological-social model is another model that explores how areas of a person's life influence all other areas. With all these varying factors, it can be challenging to help others productively navigate crises. This challenge is one reason a relational lens may be helpful. A relational approach may help a counselor better understand their client's overall life context.

These guidelines advocate for systems and counselors to (a) avoid harm, (b) use person-centered approaches, (c) share responsibility, (d) address trauma, (e) establish safety, (f) view people holistically, (g) see people as credible, and (h) activate natural recovery supports and resources. To achieve these principles in action, programs and staff provide timely and least restrictive services. Instead of immediately restraining someone, SAMHSA recommends watchful waiting to see whether a person in crisis can deescalate without the use of physical restraints. Other elements of effective programs involve ready peer support and quality time with qualified counselors who focus on strength-based approaches—counselors who seek to understand the context of a client's life when making treatment recommendations. This means identifying and remedying service gaps, psychosocial needs, and environmental situations that precipitate mental health crisis. When counselors respect a person's life context and trust them as credible, they can begin to plan comprehensive and culturally appropriate treatment interventions to reduce the issues and circumstances that lead to repeated hospitalizations or mental health crises.

Grief Models and Processes

A crisis or trauma represents loss in many ways. People can lose their sense of control, familiar routines, homes, jobs, loved ones, and physical capabilities. Counselors can understand how people navigate myriad losses by conceptualizing clients' situations integrating the various models of grieving and crisis intervention. *Ambiguous losses* (Bloom & Farragher, 2010) have no definite answer, often persist without a clear end, and weave themselves into the daily lives of those who experience them. For example, an older adolescent who suffers from addiction might disappear for lengthy periods, leaving his parents to live with the ambiguity surrounding his safety and health. The parents also live with the loss of their initial dreams for their family (Duffey, 2007). Although this example speaks to ambiguous loss, the parents also may experience disenfranchisement because of the stigma surrounding addiction, judgment of their parenting skills, and the addictive behaviors of their son in their community. Each night he goes missing and every phone call from the police become moments of crisis that boil from the toxic stresses and losses this family endures.

Disenfranchised losses (Bloom & Farragher, 2010; Duffey, 2007) and grief arise when people cope with losses that are not socially sanctioned and bear the weight of stigma. Feelings of shame, humiliation, and exclusion isolate individuals and groups from meaningful contact with others. It is during these times that counselors can reach out to, advocate for, and connect with their clients. Much of a counselor's work focuses on being with people as they adjust to challenging situations and find meaning in an often confusing and complex world. Although many losses and crises do not reach the diagnostic thresholds for acute stress disorder or PTSD, they may be considered traumatic events according to SAMHSA (2014a) because they can create intense feelings and stress as a result of the harm perceived. With authenticity, counselors can honor the real losses and pain that people feel after they may have suffered from countless empathic failures from others (Neimeyer, Klass, & Dennis, 2014).

Early Models Explaining the Grief and Loss Process
Early models of the human grief process focused on severing the intrapsychic re-

lationships with those who died (Freud, 1917; Lindemann, 1944). The goal for successfully navigating grief focused on eliminating connections by sharing every memory of the person lost. After these memories are purged from the intrapsychic tension, a person can then establish new relationships (Freud, 1917). This notion was reiterated by Lindemann (1944), who similarly focused on the process of letting go of the past and creating new relationships in the present. However, Lindemann's work gave voice to postcrisis and grief experiences as natural and nonpathological processes. Given the popular assumptions of gaining closure, letting go, and moving on, these models influence collective thoughts about crises, grief, and loss and may create unrealistic expectations for people.

As the helping professions evolved, Kübler-Ross (1969) conceptualized the grief process as an experience for the *terminally ill* who traversed different stages of denial, anger and rage, bargaining, sadness, and eventually acceptance. Although this model was not intended to chart the course of the grieved, this approach was subsumed into the zeitgeist of counseling to provide a roadmap for grief. Likewise, Worden (2009) theorized that grief work included a series of tasks to complete that included feeling the emotions, adjusting to a new life, and investing energy into new relationships. These linear and task-based processes still frame approaches used to conceptualize grief. Although these models help people name feelings and experiences, they may also provide messages that a person may not be doing their "grief work" right. People may feel that they should be more accepting of the loss years later, or a community may promote messages that people do not need to talk anymore about their trauma. People should move on and rebuild. In contrast, contemporary models of grief work explore the dynamic and personal factors involved with the range of feelings, thoughts, and approach to living in a new and unfamiliar world. Stage-based models, although convenient and understandable, do not pan out when researchers follow the processes of bereaved individuals (Bonanno, 2009).

The Dual Process Model

As the research and theoretical base for grief work expanded, new models focused on the complexities of adjusting to loss and living in a new reality while finding ways to make meaning of loss. Current research shows that when people endure a loss, there is pain that does not exist on a predetermined timeline (Bonanno, 2009). Current literature on grief dispels the myth of closure (Bonanno, 2009) and recognizes that grief involves maintaining connection to memories, lost hopes, and accounts for many of these dynamics from a personal process model. The dual process model (Stroebe & Schut, 2008) explores how people move between their new life (restoration) and living with their experience of loss. In this model, individuals vacillate between the cognitive and emotional aspects of their grief while forging new relationships and life patterns. Although the pain never leaves entirely, it may ebb and flow throughout a person's life as they move into new situations, relationships, and understanding. See Sidebar 5.2 for more information on grief.

Meaning Making

Neimeyer et al. (2014) promoted a constructivist theory focused on creating meaning from loss by engaging in validation, honest storytelling, exploring metaphors, creativity, and eclecticism. Neimeyer et al. posited that counselors may find this approach especially useful for people haunted by protracted grief. In this process,

Sidebar 5.2 • Grief

Grief models previously viewed grief as a linear process in which people work their way through stages of different emotions. However, we now know that grief is much more complex. The pain of loss may not completely leave a person; rather, the loss shapes their new life, new life patterns, and thoughts about others. We can support others through their experience of grief by connecting with them and honoring the memories of their loved ones.

the counselor listens to a client retell their story in an empathic and safe space. Given the many ways that a person's experiences may be invalidated by others, it is especially important that clients see that their story is heard, received, and validated. As the narrative unfolds, counselors listen for themes and metaphors, and explore the stories of coping and meaning making. Counselors then help people evaluate the strategies they use to make sense of their loss. From a relational-cultural theory perspective, these conversations can illuminate a person's historical and current relational strategies of survival and connection while co-creating narratives of resilience (Jordan, 2017). As counselors work with people experiencing acute and chronic crises, they can integrate elements of crisis intervention, grief counseling, and trauma work into their conceptualization of their clients' situations as they work in longer term settings. Approaches for working with grieving people do remind us of important skills when listening to others in the midst of crushing loss. The act of *companioning with* (Wolfelt, 2014) speaks to your presence during tumultuous events, when the immediate need for compassionate company supersedes platitudes and action planning.

Crisis Counseling Skills and Approaches

Theories and models define the nature of crises, provide a rationale for interventions, and give words to client's experiences. However, in the midst of a suicidal call, community shooting, natural disaster, or the aftermath of abuse, what do we do? These are not times to pontificate or be paralyzed by confusion or uncertainty. Procedural clarity, compassionate responsiveness, and triage acuity can serve you and your clients in the midst or aftermath of chaotic and traumatic incidents. The first step in crisis response is preparing your tool kit and identifying available resources before a catastrophe strikes or between crisis events. The work does not stop after a situation is resolved, and each crisis will involve a complex mix of many variables.

Preparation

The PREPaRE model of crisis prevention and intervention in schools (Brock et al., 2016) outlines the many needed aspects of a comprehensive crisis plan for school systems. From this model, we learn that crisis preparation includes developing and training response teams, crafting policies, outlining chain of command activities, creating annexes, training staff and students in procedures, and establishing communication protocols. Likewise, one of the major activities of the American Red Cross is to help people and communities prepare for disasters and emergencies. For example, given that home and apartment fires represent the most frequent emergencies (Federal Emergency Management Agency, n.d.), the Red Cross provides free smoke detector installations as a prevention activity. Enacting simple and strategic resources before a crisis hits can provide you the structure and materials you may need in responding to crisis or emergency situations. James and Gilliland (2017) have named this practice *predispositioning.* In your practice, consider the following preparation steps:

1. Review and gain clarity on the policies at your agency or institution related to (a) threat assessments; (b) suicide screenings; (c) evacuation plans; (d) abuse of children, older adults, or those with disabilities; (e) domestic violence screenings; and (f) verbal or physical de-escalation procedures. If you work in a private practice, these may be helpful topics to explore, especially with colleagues in a group setting.
2. Create your office space so that you have a means to escape a potentially violent situation. Create code words to notify staff for situations in which you may feel threatened. For example, when I worked in a hospital and Dr. Strongarm was paged, the staff knew someone was in danger.
3. Develop resource materials that include suicide and violence screening instruments, safety plans, and a list of verified resources you can use in the office or the field. I provide a few national examples of free resources to help build your resource kit:
   a. The Columbia Suicide Screening Severity Rating Scale includes many versions of screeners for use across multiple settings as well as a full-length suicide assessment tool. You can access these free materials and online training at http://cssrs.columbia.edu/. Other evidence-based suicide screening materials, such as the Patient Health Questionnaire–9 and SAFE-T, can be found at https://www.integration.samhsa.gov/clinical-practice/suicide-prevention-update.
   b. The Suicide Prevention Resource Center includes a free safety planning instrument at http://www.sprc.org/resources-programs/patient-safety-plan-template.
   c. SAMHSA (2019) offers mental health and substance abuse treatment locators at https://findtreatment.samhsa.gov/.
4. Develop plans for your self-care and strategies to mitigate compassion fatigue. The Professional Quality of Life Scale (SAMHSA, 2014b) is a free tool to assess your level of burnout and secondary trauma. Find supportive colleagues to share about your work stress without diverging into complaining and gossip. Proactive self-care and wellness help counselors maintain a calm presence and perspective during crises.

With preparation, you will be equipped with some basic tools to help you make decisions about the severity of a crisis and have resources handy to make referrals as needed.

Task- and Step-Based Approaches to Crisis Intervention

James and Gilliland (2017), Roberts and Ottens (2005), and Jackson-Cherry and Erford (2018) developed step- and task-based approaches to working with people in crisis. James and Gilliland cautioned that because of the chaotic nature of crises, following a linear protocol may not be the best approach. Instead, you may weave throughout each of these tasks as the situation demands. Each of these task approaches contains elements of (a) relationship building; (b) assessing a person's status and potential threats; (c) providing psychological, social, informational, and physical supports; (d) exploring alternatives; (e) developing an action plan and obtaining commitment; and (f) providing follow-up resources and contacts. Table 5.1 provides a synthesis of the models according to these domains. In the following section, we outline important tasks for the crisis work to focus on when providing responsive services.

Table 5.1 • Comparison and Synthesis of Crisis Approach Models

Author, Task Model, and Steps or Tasks	Approach					
	1	2	3	4	5	6
Roberts and Ottens's (2005) Seven-Step Model						
Step 1: Plan and Conduct a Thorough Biopsychosocial and Lethality/Imminent Danger Assessment		✔				
Step 2: Make Psychological Contact and Rapidly Establish the Collaborative Relationship	✔					
Step 3: Identify the Major Problems, Including Crisis Precipitants		✔				
Step 4: Encourage an Exploration of Feelings and Emotions			✔			
Step 5: Generate and Explore Alternatives and New Coping Strategies				✔		
Step 6: Restore Cognitive Functioning Through Implementation of an Action Plan					✔	
Step 7: Plan Follow-Up and Booster Sessions						✔
James and Gilliland's (2017) Seven Task Model						
Task 1: Predispositioning and Engaging	✔					
• Initiating Contact						
• Establishing Psychological Connection						
• Clarifying Intentions						
Task 2: Problem Exploration		✔				
• Defining the Crisis						
Task 3: Providing Support			✔			
• Psychological						
• Logistical						
• Informational						
Task 4: Examining Alternatives				✔		
Task 5: Planning in Order to Reestablish Control					✔	
• Psychoeducation						
Task 6: Obtaining Commitment					✔	
Default Task: Safety		✔				
Jackson-Cherry and Erford's (2018) Assessment Tasks						
Task 1: Address Safety, Stabilization, and Risk		✔				
Task 2: Follow a Holistic Bio-Psycho-Social-Spiritual Approach		✔				
Task 3: Clarify the Problem(s)		✔				
Task 4: Explore Coping Skills, Resources, and Supports			✔			
Jackson-Cherry and Erford's (2018) Intervention Tasks						
Task 1: Normalize and Educate			✔			
Task 2: Explore Options				✔		
Task 3: Develop a Plan and Obtain a Commitment					✔	
Task 4: Prepare Documentation, Follow Up, and Provide Referrals						✔

Note. Approaches: 1 = relationship building; 2 = assessment of status and risk assessment; 3 = provide psychological, social, informational, and physical support; 4 = explore alternatives; 5 = develop an action plan and obtaining commitment; 6 = provide follow-up resources and contacts.

Relationship Building and Engagement

Roberts and Ottens's (2005) seven-step model and James and Gilliland's (2017) task approach specifically address the role and activities focused on engaging clients and relationship building. Roberts and Ottens emphasized quickly establishing rapport and connection with clients in crisis. James and Gilliland explored these initial conversations in some more detail and proposed that the directivity of the crisis intervention session is guided by the client's mobility. If a client is *immobile* (e.g., in a profound state of panic, disassociation, rage, actively suicidal or violent, under the influence of substances), then the counselor becomes more directive and concrete in communication style and recommendations (James & Gilliland, 2017). For clients who are able to engage and partner somewhat in the process (*partially mobile*), then the relationship becomes more collaborative, and the crisis counselor serves in a consultant role. For those clients who demonstrate *mobility,* counselors use broad open-ended questions and more complex reflections of meaning and feeling that engage a client's repertoire of problem-solving skills, self-reflection, and personal awareness as resources to address their current stresses (James & Gilliland, 2017).

Triage and Assessment

If you have ever been to an emergency room for a sickness, you hopefully met with a nurse first who asked a series of questions. Depending on your answers, you either sat miserably in the waiting room for hours or they quickly rushed you in for an evaluation. Triage in crisis situations works the same way. Roberts (2002) defined *triage* as

> The immediate decision-making process in which the mental health worker determines lethality and referral to one of the following alternatives: (a) emergency inpatient hospitalization, (b) outpatient treatment facility or private therapist, (c) support group or social service agency, or (d) no referral needed. (p. 5)

In crisis assessment situations, lethality screening occurs soon in the initial dialogue. James and Gilliland (2013) included assessing safety as a default task that occurs thought the entire encounter with a person in distress. Other models place risk assessment as a core task to complete when defining the crisis, conducting a biopsychosocial assessment, and examining the scope of the crisis event. The Triage Assessment Form (Myer, Williams, Ottens, & Schmidt, 1992) and the Individual/Family Crisis Counseling Services Encounter Log (SAMHSA, n.d.) provide structure to determine the affective cognitive, behavioral, and physical reactions to a crisis to help you ascertain the severity of a person's reaction and referral for ongoing services. The main focus of a crisis screening and assessment is to determine lethality risks and to attend to the crisis situation by exploring the immediate precipitants of the crisis, the scope and impact of the event, a person's reactions to the event, and any natural supports or resources available.

Providing Supportive Interventions

Although crisis counseling is not brief therapy (James & Gilliland, 2017), several supportive time-limited interventions can be helpful. Active listening, normalizing, brief psychoeducation, relevant information resources, and connecting people to resources are all interventions we can provide in person, over the phone, and online in a time-limited manner. Roberts (2005) recommended exploring thoughts and feelings through posing open-ended questions and offering reflections to help clients clarify their perspectives and feel heard. Psychoeducation is a valuable tool that can help people gain important content and provide some normalizing information that can help reduce shame and self-blame in many situations. Psychoeducational activities also center on educating clients about relevant resources and other sources of support in their community and within larger systems of care.

Action Planning and Commitment

For clients who are immobile or incapacitated, action planning and commitment activities may be involuntary processes. At other times, the action planning stage represents the next phase for trying out different behaviors, exploring programs, and concretizing these plans in writing if possible. Many safety plans include detailed informational sections including contact phone numbers, places to seek refuge, and lists of people who can provide support. However, these are useless if clients have not committed to follow through.

Motivational interviewing is a counseling approach that focuses on how and why people change. One of the main goals of motivational interviewing is to elicit client change talk. The acronym DARNCAT (i.e., desire, ability, reasons, need, commitment, activation, and taking steps) can help you identify change talk (W. R. Miller & Rollnick, 2013). For example, Tyler's daughter says, "Yeah, I think I need treatment, but I've got too much going on right now." Rather than arguing, explore her need statement. Your goal in helping people change is to elicit and expand on their change talk through active listening and a collaborative relational style. Finally, an important aspect of planning is not to overpromise services (e.g., PREPaRE, American Red Cross). Only promise activities you can reasonably accomplish, and then follow up with your client as soon as possible. For example, when working at the shelter after Hurricane Katrina, many people asked us about their pets. Rather than saying we will find them, we set a time to meet up later, after we explored how pets were being housed and cared for. See Sidebar 5.3 for more information on motivational interviewing.

Follow-Up

Finally, in many situations, establishing quick follow-up to address immediate concerns helps resolve some issues. Follow-up in crisis settings is unlike other mental health and counseling processes. Usually follow-up occurs within hours or, at most, days (James & Gilliland, 2017). For example, after referring clients to emergency placement, you may ask clients to put your name on their contact list and to also sign a consent to release information. You can then follow up, touch base when appropriate, and maintain a connection with them while they are in inpatient care. See Figure 5.1 for more information.

Sidebar 5.3 • Motivational Interviewing (MI)

The centrality of MI is helping people to explore their motivation and, in a collaborative manner, to help them change toward their goals. When using MI, it is important to remember not to argue with a client or forcefully point out a cognitive discrepancy. Instead, the counselor can guide the client to change by eliciting change talk and supporting clients as they navigate their values. How do you perceive MI working with clients?

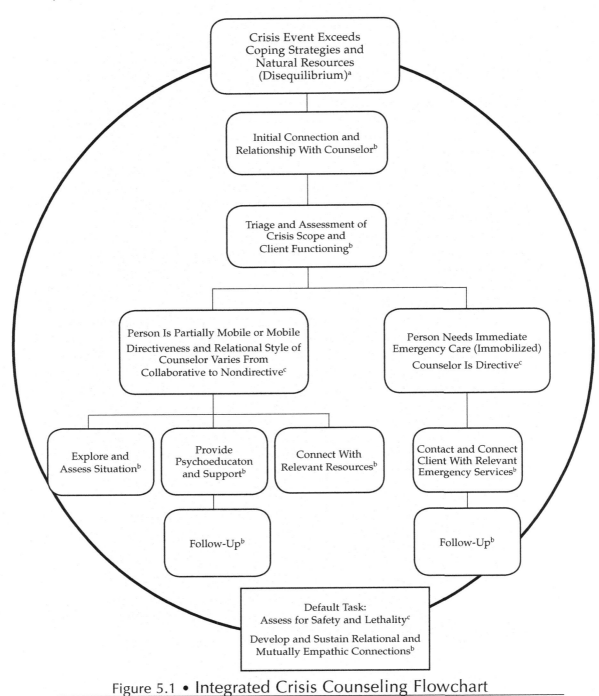

Figure 5.1 • Integrated Crisis Counseling Flowchart

[a]Source models are: Caplan (1961) and James and Gilliland (2017). [b]Source models are: Jackson-Cherry and Erford (2018), James and Gilliland (2017), and Roberts and Ottens (2005). [c]Source model is: James and Gilliland (2017).

Introduction to Disaster Counseling

Disasters can strike suddenly and grow into calamities that create mass havoc, confusion, and loss. Often profoundly destructive, disasters shatter social systems and can overwhelm people with trauma and loss. SAMHSA (2019) has defined many natural catastrophes and mass shootings as different types of disasters. These events are horrific and often garner social media and news attention, evoking national attention to the misery of those suffering on the ground. To respond to these events, the American Red Cross uses thousands of volunteers to provide basic needs as well as medical and mental health services (American Red Cross, n.d.). For licensed counselors and certified school counselors, the American Red Cross provides disaster mental health training to prepare the counseling workforce to deploy across the nation. In Chapter 11, we explore the many facets of community disasters and recovery processes. If you feel the call to serve as a disaster mental health worker, you can find more information at https://www.redcross.org/volunteer/volunteer-opportunities/disaster-health-mental-health-volunteer.html. In the meantime, the National Child Traumatic Stress Network offers free online training focused on psychological first aid (PFA).

PFA

The National Child Traumatic Stress Network and the National Center for PTSD developed PFA as an approach to help disaster and terrorism survivors in the immediate aftermath of exposure (Ruzek et al., 2007). Counselors practicing the core elements of PFA actively engage with people by request or by observing those who may be distressed. PFA counselors provide physical and psychological comfort and safety while working to stabilize those who may be emotionally distressed. Helpers then gather pertinent information to determine pressing needs and offer practical assistance to meet those needs. During the process of information gathering, counselors establish connections with support systems and community programs. Helpers provide relevant information and psychoeducation about stress and coping strategies and seek to link clients to collaborative services to address current and future needs. As you can see, PFA reflects many of the processes outlined in traditional crisis intervention approaches and harnesses your compassion, access to helpful resources, counseling skills, and advocacy to help people through moments of terror and despair.

Critical Incident Stress Debriefing (CISD) and Critical Incident Stress Management

For many years, the standard of practice was to enroll people into semi-mandatory group debriefing sessions after a traumatic event (Paterson, Whittle, & Kemp, 2015). This intervention was predicated on the idea that first responders, victims, and others affected by a trauma should receive immediate debriefing services. In 2010, the American Red Cross conducted a review of the available evidence and did not recommend CISD as an approach to use with traumatized people. More recent research (Paterson et al., 2015) found that police officers who attended these sessions fared worse than those who did not. When services are mandatory and people are faced with additional details of horrific events, they may develop secondary traumatization. Furthermore, when mandated to attend sessions, people lose a sense of agency and control over their natural recovery processes. Most people do not develop PTSD after a traumatic event (U.S. Department of Veterans Affairs, 2019). Therefore, approaches such as PFA serve as a current best practice, because we offer compassionate listening, provide connection with resources, and respect the choices of people to engage or not.

Case Example and Applications for Hope and Healing

Nate, a survivor of a mass shooting incident, called the phone crisis line after telling himself he was going crazy because of his reactions and seemingly fragile state of being after the shooting. He shared, "I don't know, I don't know what's *wrong* with me. I'm educated, professional, and am good at managing my life. I put myself through college while working full time and raising a family. I'm just losing my mind, I just think I'm going crazy!" After exploring his situation further and listening to his life context, I reaffirmed his many strengths, perseverance, and clear ability to problem solve throughout his life. He was not in any danger to himself or others; he just wanted to stop feeling so afraid. His reactions were interfering with his productivity, and his workplace was seemingly unsympathetic. His friend who was with him at the time of the disaster was seemingly unfazed and did not understand his reactions. He felt ashamed and could not reach out to his friend any more about this situation.

Throughout our conversation, I appreciated the context of his life and shared some education about the neurobiological effects of trauma. Rather than being crazy, we discussed how his response was a natural expression of his fight-or-flight system, and when activated, it works much faster than rational thinking processes. We also explored local resources to help him with ongoing free counseling and legal assistance to help address his work situation. We left the conversation with him feeling more informed and ready to access local services. This encounter reminded me that helpful information can reframe frightening responses to stressful crisis situations.

Future Directions and Emerging Research

The Opioid Crisis

Driven by increased access to opiates such as fentanyl, which is 50 times more potent than morphine, opiate overdoses have reached epidemic proportions (NIDA, 2019). From overdoses of legally prescribed medication to deaths from illicit use, opiates take the lives of seasoned users and neophytes alike. Overdoses and death by overdose affect millions of people and bring medical and psychosocial crises, stress, and loss to loved ones and communities. Likewise, abrupt detoxification from opiates can lead to profound physical and psychological distress (NIDA, 2019). Addiction creates chaos within all realms of a person's life and is one of the major public health crises facing the world.

Bred in isolation, shame, manipulation, and trauma, addiction saps creative energy and creates physiological and psychological conditions that further drive people from healing resources. Coupled with the stigma and private shame surrounding addiction, people may not reach out until life has fallen apart or authorities intervene. Unfortunately, many mental health and medical systems are ill equipped to provide the level of care needed as the opioid epidemic blossoms. There are people and groups, however, that are making radical changes. For example, in Vancouver (British Columbia, Canada), supervised injection sites create a welcoming connection, safe practices, and caring relationships with staff as those addicted to substances are treated with dignity and respect.

Rising Suicide Rates and Nevada's Response

According to the CDC (2018), every state except Nevada reported increased suicide rates, and half of all suicides were not related to a known mental health condition. As a leading cause of death, suicide speaks to the utter isolation and pain that millions of people feel in the United States. The CDC calls for a national effort to intervene in the toll of suicide. Nevada saw a decrease in suicide rates, and the experience in that state can shed light on how we can provide help for those who need it desperately. In an interview about suicide prevention in Nevada (Bzdek, 2018), Misty Vaughan Allen, the Nevada state suicide prevention coordinator, emphasized the power of a collective and consistent approach to suicide prevention. Nevada requires all schools to provide suicide screening to all students, and the state connects many agencies and stakeholders in communal efforts to screen for suicide and to provide resources. These examples speak to how vision, creativity, and work to link people and systems of care can save lives.

References

American Red Cross. (n.d.). *Disaster training.* Retrieved from https://www.redcross.org/take-a-class/disaster-training

Bloom, S. L., & Farragher, B. (Eds.) (2010). Unresolved grief, reenactment, and decline. In *Destroying sanctuary: The crisis in human delivery systems* (pp. 327–355). New York, NY: Oxford University Press.

Bonanno, G. A. (2009). *The other side of sadness: What the new science of bereavement tells us about life after loss.* New York, NY: Basic Books.

Brock, S., Nickerson, A., Reeves, M., Conolly, C., Jimerson, S., Pesce, R., & Lazzaro, B. (2016). *School crisis prevention and intervention: The PREPaRE model* (2nd ed.). Bethesda, MD: National Association of School Psychologists.

Bzdek, V. (2018, December 1). Nevada's suicide rate is decreasing. What can Colorado learn from it? *The Gazette.* Retrieved from https://gazette.com/news/column-nevada-s-suicide-rate-is-decreasing-what-can-colorado/article_a9e7f404-f4e1-11e8-bb3f-8f2f6a0569d1.html

Caplan, G. (1961). *An approach to community mental health.* New York, NY: Grune & Stratton.

Centers for Disease Control and Prevention. (2018, June 7). *Suicide rates rising across the U.S.* [Press release]. Retrieved from https://www.cdc.gov/media/releases/2018/p0607-suicide-prevention.html

Centers for Disease Control and Prevention. (2019, January 16). *The public health approach to violence prevention.* Retrieved from https://www.cdc.gov/violenceprevention/pdf/PH_App_Violence-a.pdf

Duffey, T. (Ed.). (2007). *Creative interventions in grief and loss therapy: When the music stops, a dream dies.* New York, NY: Haworth Press.

Federal Emergency Management Agency. (n.d.). *U.S. fire statistics.* Retrieved from https://www.usfa.fema.gov/data/statistics/

Freud, S. (1917). Mourning and melancholia. In S. Freud (Ed.), *The standard edition of the complete psychological works of Sigmund Freud, Volume XIV (1914–1916): On the history of the psycho-analytic movement, papers on metapsychology and other works* (pp. 243–258). London, England: Hogarth Press.

Haberstroh, S., & Moyer, M. (2012). Exploring an online self-injury support group: Perspectives from group members. *The Journal for Specialists in Group Work, 37*, 113–132.

Jackson-Cherry, L. R., & Erford, B. T. (2018). *Crisis assessment, intervention, and prevention* (3rd ed.). London, England: Pearson.

James, R. K., & Gilliland, B. E. (2013). *Crisis intervention strategies* (7th ed.). Belmont, CA: Thomson Brooks/Cole.

James, R., & Gilliland, B. (2017). *Crisis intervention strategies* (8th ed.). Pacific Grove, CA: Thomson Brooks/Cole.

Jaycox, L. H., Langley, A. K., & Hoover, S. (2018). *Cognitive behavioral intervention for trauma in schools (CBITS)* (2nd ed.). Santa Monica, CA: RAND Corporation.

Jordan, J. (2017). Relational-cultural theory: The power of connection to transform our lives. *The Journal of Humanistic Counseling, 56*, 228–243. https://doi.org/10.1002/johc.12055

Kübler-Ross, E. (1969). *On death and dying*. New York, NY: Collier Books/Macmillan Publishing Company.

Lindemann, E. (1944). Symptomatology and management of acute grief. *American Journal of Psychiatry, 101*, 141–148.

MacKay, L. (2012). Trauma and Bowen family systems theory: Working with adults who were abused as children. *Australian and New Zealand Journal of Family Therapy, 33*, 232–241.

Miller, G. A. (2012). *Fundamentals of crisis counseling*. Hoboken, NJ: Wiley.

Miller, W. R., & Rollnick, S. (2013). *Motivational interviewing: Helping people change* (3rd ed.). New York, NY: Guilford Press.

Myer, R. A., Williams, R. C., Ottens, A. J., & Schmidt, A. E. (1992). Crisis assessment: A three dimensional model for triage. *Journal of Mental Health Counseling, 14*, 137–148.

National Institute on Drug Abuse. (2018, August). *Comorbidity: Substance use disorders and other mental illnesses*. Retrieved from https://www.drugabuse.gov/publications/drugfacts/comorbidity-substance-use-disorders-other-mental-illnesses

National Institute on Drug Abuse. (2019, January). *Opioid overdose crisis*. Retrieved from https://www.drugabuse.gov/drugs-abuse/opioids/opioid-overdose-crisis

Neimeyer, R., Klass, D., & Dennis, M. (2014). Toward a social constructionist account of grief: Loss and the narration of meaning. *Death Studies, 38*, 485–498.

Paterson, H. M., Whittle, K., & Kemp, R. I. (2015). Detrimental effects of post-incident debriefing on memory and psychological responses. *Journal of Police and Criminal Psychology, 30*, 27–37.

Pfeifer, B. J., & Haeffel, G. J. (2014). Proximity, relationship closeness, and cognitive vulnerability: Predicting enduring depressive reactions to a college campus tragedy. *Journal of Clinical Psychology, 70*, 1196–1210. https://doi.org/10.1002/jclp.22078

Posner, K., Brown, G. K., Stanley, B., Brent, D. A, Yershova, K. V., Oquendo, M. A., . . . Mann, J. J. (2011). The Columbia-Suicide Severity Rating Scale: Initial validity and internal consistency findings from three multisite studies with adolescents and adults. *The American Journal of Psychiatry, 168*, 1266–1277. https://doi.org/10.1176/appi.ajp.2011.10111704

Roberts, A. R. (2002). Assessment, crisis intervention, and trauma treatment: The integrative ACT intervention model. *Brief Treatment and Crisis Intervention, 2*(1), 1–21.

Roberts, A. (2005). *Crisis intervention handbook: Assessment, treatment, and research* (3rd ed.). New York, NY: Oxford University Press.

Roberts, A., & Ottens, A. (2005). The seven-stage crisis intervention model: A road map to goal attainment, problem solving, and crisis resolution. *Brief Treatment and Crisis Intervention, 5,* 329–339. https://doi.org/10.1093/brief-treatment/mhi030

Ruzek, J. I., Brymer, M. J., Jacobs, A. K., Layne, C. M., Vernberg, E. M., & Watson, P. J. (2007). Psychological first aid. *Journal of Mental Health Counseling, 29,* 17–49. https://doi.org/10.17744/mehc.29.1.5racqxjueafabgwp

Stroebe, M. S., & Schut, H. (2008). The dual process model of coping with bereavement: Overview and update. *Grief Matters: The Australian Journal of Grief and Bereavement, 11*(1), 4–10.

Substance Abuse and Mental Health Services Administration. (n.d.). *Individual/family crisis counseling services encounter log.* Retrieved from https://www.samhsa.gov/sites/default/files/dtac/ccptoolkit/individual-family-log-exp-09-30-2018.pdf

Substance Abuse and Mental Health Services Administration. (2009). *Practice guidelines: Core elements for responding to mental health crises* (HHS Publication No. SMA-09-4427). Retrieved from https://store.samhsa.gov/system/files/sma09-4427.pdf

Substance Abuse and Mental Health Services Administration. (2014a). *SAMHSA's concept of trauma and guidance for a trauma-informed approach* (HHS Publication No. SMA-14-4884). Rockville, MD: Author.

Substance Abuse and Mental Health Services Administration. (2014b). *Trauma-informed care in behavioral health services* (HHS Publication No. SMA-14-4816). Rockville, MD: Author.

Substance Abuse and Mental Health Services Administration. (2019, May 17). *Types of disasters.* Retrieved from https://www.samhsa.gov/find-help/disaster-distress-helpline/disaster-types

U.S. Department of Veteran's Affairs. (2019, October 17). *How common is PTSD among adults?* Retrieved from https://www.ptsd.va.gov/understand/common/common_adults.asp

van der Kolk, B. (2014). *The body keeps the score: Brain, mind, and body in the healing of trauma.* New York, NY: Viking.

Wolfelt, A. (2014). *Reframing PTSD as traumatic grief: How caregivers can companion traumatized grievers through catch-up mourning.* Fort Collins, CO: The Companion Press.

Worden, J. W. (2009). *Grief counseling and grief therapy* (4th ed.). New York, NY: Springer.

Multiple-Choice Questions

1. Crisis counseling is a set of techniques that counselors apply to people.
   a. True, there is a certain way to work with suicide
   b. True, the techniques have been applied since the 1930s
   c. False, counselors do not apply techniques *to* people
   d. False, there are two sets of techniques

2. Relationship problems can be a predictive factor for _____ of people who committed suicide.
   a. 42%
   b. 10%
   c. 75%
   d. 3%

3. Which of the following are emergency crisis situations?
   a. Suicidal ideation
   b. Alcohol withdrawal
   c. Active abuse to a child
   d. All of the above

4. According to the chapter, risk assessments and _____ should occur concurrently.
   a. Rapport building
   b. Mental health assessments
   c. Inpatient
   d. None of the above

5. The cognitive model for crisis response is based on
   a. Potential distortions in thinking.
   b. Cognitive-behavior therapy.
   c. Freud.
   d. Both a and b

6. The equilibrium approach to crisis was first described by Caplan in
   a. 2018.
   b. 1961.
   c. 2000.
   d. 1984.

7. Research shows the equilibrium approach to work well with which kind of distress?
   a. Extreme
   b. Severe
   c. Acute
   d. Moderate

8. Which violence prevention model does the Centers for Disease Control and Prevention use for their framework?
   a. Cognitive model
   b. Response model
   c. Violence prevention approach
   d. Biopsychosocial and psychosocial model

9. A few of the Substance Abuse and Mental Health Services Administration's (2009) guidelines for counselors working with mental health crises include
   a. Use a person-centered approach and establish safety.
   b. Use a person-centered approach and set strong boundaries.
   c. Help the client develop self-awareness.
   d. Both a and b

10. Disenfranchised losses develop when people cope with losses that include
    a. Extended family.
    b. Stigma.
    c. Pets.
    d. None of the above

11. The PREPaRE model of crisis _____ and _____ in schools includes training response teams and outlining a chain of command activities.
    a. Prevention, awareness
    b. Preparedness, intervention
    c. Prevention, intervention
    d. None of the above

12. Which is a good prevention step to include in a counseling office?
    a. Create office space so that you have a way to escape
    b. Review policies at your agency
    c. Wait for fire alarm batteries to expire
    d. Both a and b

13. For an immobile client, counselors become more directive and use clear communication.
    a. False, this will upset the client
    b. True, this helps stabilize the client
    c. False, the counselor becomes a consultant
    d. True, as long as the counselor only is directive for 2 minutes

14. What are some supportive interventions that can be provided over the phone?
    a. Normalizing
    b. Active listening
    c. Connecting people to resources
    d. All of the above

15. The American Red Cross does not recommend
    a. Critical incident stress debriefing (CISD).
    b. CCCD.
    c. Preparation for a natural disaster.
    d. Relocating.

Essay Questions

1. When working with your clients or talking with a friend about their crisis, have you ever minimized their situation? Have you ever minimized their situation maybe not externally but internally? If so, in what way?

2. If you were a counselor working with clients who experienced a crisis, which model or approach would you use? Why?

3. A person or client may be confused about his or her grief and how he or she cannot get past it. How could you creatively help clients explore their grief?

4. Self-care is important for every counselor. Creating a self-care plan is a great practice to prevent burnout. What does your self-care plan look like?

5. Think about the case example of Nate. Have you ever worked with a client who felt ashamed or embarrassed by an experience? How did you respond?

CHAPTER 6

Fundamental Theories and Skills for Trauma Counseling

Allison Marsh Pow and Hope Schuermann

A Relational Approach to Trauma Counseling

Although trauma counseling is markedly different from traditional counseling in many ways, the relationship remains central to effective treatment. Trauma lays open the most hurt and vulnerable parts of oneself. Thus, a counselor who is warm, empathic, caring, and genuine is all the more important. Tenets from person-centered theory (Rogers, 1957) and relational-cultural theory (Miller & Stiver, 1997) can be infused into trauma care to form a solid relational foundation, regardless of the technique or approach used. This connection can be seen in situations in which counselors use a nondirective play therapy approach with children.

In one of my (Hope's) cases, a 5-year-old client, who refused to disclose details of an abuse situation, spent her time in counseling building, painting, and then de-stroying versions of a cage for more than 6 weeks. During this time, I helped build the relationship and used tracking skills to let my client know she was present and cared for her. After 6 or 7 weeks, the cage theme disappeared, and her mom reported symptom relief at home as well. Positive therapeutic relationships change lives—and change is essential after trauma. Thus, all of the information presented in this chapter, and in this entire book, should be assimilated into practice knowing that the first thing the counselor must do is form a solid therapeutic relationship.

Empathy and Mutual Empathy

Early conceptualizations of empathy boil down to "walking a mile in another's shoes" (Rogers, 1957, p. 99). We know now that empathy is not quite that simple.

It can be challenging to imagine ourselves in any number of situations that we have not encountered in our personal lives; however, imagining ourselves going through a trauma may be even more difficult. The depth of feeling a person experiences when losing a loved one, suffering through an act of terror, or witnessing violence or other traumatizing events is complicated and hard to fathom for those who have not experienced similar losses. Even so, making the effort to understand the client's experiences through his or her lens of core beliefs, values, relationships, and life experiences and relaying to the client that you are there, serving as a witness to the heartache and recovery, will improve the client's overall chances of positive progress.

Relational-cultural theory, originally a feminist theory that has since been applied to multiple populations, posits that people develop through connection with each other, and it expands the conceptualization of empathy to one of mutual empathy (Duffey & Somody, 2011). Miller and Stiver (1997) suggested that empathy flowing in one direction—from counselor to client—is not sufficient for meaningful change; thus, mutual empathy, wherein clients know they have actually moved their counselor by sharing their experiences, allows the client to know their impact on others. Empathy is indispensable to a solid therapeutic relationship.

Introduction to Trauma Counseling

The term *trauma counseling* encompasses many topics, types of trauma, and techniques. It can be overwhelming for a new professional counselor or even a seasoned veteran to contemplate all of the ways in which trauma may present. Briere and Scott (2015) have made a strong case for conceptualizing trauma beyond the current definition in the *Diagnostic and Statistical Manual of Mental Disorders* (5th ed.; *DSM-5*; American Psychiatric Association [APA], 2013). This expanded definition includes the physical threat of harm or death to self or others from the *DSM-5* and adds that trauma may also include events "that are extremely upsetting, at least temporarily overwhelm[ing] the individual's internal resources, and produc[ing] lasting psychological symptoms" (Briere & Scott, 2015, p. 10). This definitional expansion is also a shift in focus, bringing the client's experience to the foreground as a criterion for identifying trauma. Expanding our working definition of what constitutes a traumatic event supports phenomenological assessment and encourages counselors to focus on the lived experience of the client.

Beyond traumatic reactions, traumas can also be typed by the person's relationship to the traumatic event, and, here too, an expanded understanding supports the relational counselor. In addition to primary trauma, we may see secondary trauma, vicarious trauma, and shared trauma. We begin with a brief overview of these types of trauma before discussing trauma reactions, including acute stress disorder (ASD), posttraumatic stress disorder (PTSD), and complex trauma.

Types of Trauma

Trauma can be categorized on the basis of a person's relationship to the traumatic event. *Primary trauma* refers to direct trauma exposure and applies to a person who experienced the trauma firsthand. *Secondary trauma* refers to indirect exposure through being a part of a trauma-affected community or group. Secondary trauma often affects people as if they were primary victims, and it may affect first responders, health care and mental health care professionals, neighborhoods, and communities (Arvay, 2001; Phelps, Lloyd, Greamer, & Forbes, 2009). When Newtown, Connecticut, suffered the terrible tragedy of an elementary school shooting in 2012, many in the town were traumatized even though they were not at the school during the shooting and did not have a direct link to a shooting victim. This type of trauma is categorized as secondary.

Vicarious trauma can occur in mental health professionals when beliefs and values begin to change as a result of working with trauma survivors, and it results from an empathic connection with clients (McCann & Pearlman, 1990). Mental health practitioners working solely with traumatized clients may be at a greater risk for vicarious trauma. Thus, they must be more vigilant for signs of shifting beliefs and emotions. Finally, *shared trauma* occurs when an entire group experiences the same trauma at the same time, as in the case of natural disasters or acts of terrorism (Bell & Robinson, 2013). Shared trauma can be particularly difficult for mental health professionals to navigate because they are often treating the trauma in others while dealing with its effects as a primary victim as well. Tosone collaborated with many of her social work students to explore this phenomenon following the September 11, 2001, terrorist attacks (Tosone et al., 2003), whereas Baum (2010) discussed shared trauma in the context of New Orleans, Louisiana, during Hurricane Katrina.

Traumatic Reactions

Individuals' traumatic reactions to events can vary widely. This variance may be due to internal and external resources, the extent of physical and psychological harm involved in the trauma, and experiencing multiple traumatic events. Thus, a similar event may bring one person to counseling, another into crisis, and another only a sleepless night of anxiety. Every person's trauma is as unique and individual as they are. Some of the most common trauma reactions seen by counselors manifest as ASD, PTSD, and complex trauma, although trauma may also present as depression, anxiety, substance abuse, and personality disorders. A brief overview of these trauma reactions is provided next.

ASD

ASD is diagnosed when symptoms begin between 3 days and 1 month following a trauma. Symptoms of ASD will often fall under the categories of intrusion, negative mood, dissociation, avoidance, and arousal. Events causing ASD may include, but are not limited to, personal assault or being witness to injury to others, war, car accidents, and natural disasters. People with ASD experience consistent symptoms for at least 3 days after the trauma and up to 1 month, and they often show signs of dissociation, depersonalization, and sleep disruption (APA, 2013).

PTSD

PTSD is a common diagnosis used in trauma reactions lasting beyond 1 month. Similar in symptomology to ASD, PTSD is unique in that the symptoms of intrusion, avoidance, and arousal persist while negative thoughts and beliefs form in relation to the trauma. These symptoms culminate in significant levels of distress that interfere with an individual's usual level of functioning. PTSD may be caused by the same events as ASD. Emotional states will vary in people suffering from PTSD. Some may exhibit fear, whereas others may appear angry or apathetic. Reexperiencing the trauma or traumatic events may occur through nightmares, flashbacks, rumination, and dissociative states. Additionally, a person suffering from PTSD will typically avoid triggers (i.e., stimuli associated with the traumatic event) either intentionally or unintentionally (APA, 2013). It is of note that different criteria are given for a diagnosis of PTSD in children younger than 6 years old. You can learn more about PTSD in the *DSM-5* (APA, 2013), and through the National Center for PTSD (https://www.ptsd.va.gov/), the National Institute of Mental Health (https://www.nimh.nih.gov/index.shtml), and numerous research articles and books.

Complex Trauma

Complex trauma reactions may occur when a person suffers multiple traumas over a period of time, culminating in severe symptomology not attributable to one traumatic incident alone (Briere & Spinazzola, 2005; Herman, 1992). Often, these multiple traumas began early in life and were interpersonal in nature, such as childhood abuse (Herman, 1992; van der Kolk, Roth, Pelcovitz, Sunday, & Spinazzola, 2005). Complex trauma may result in dissociation and somatic issues as well as difficulty identifying and using healthy boundaries. People who suffer from complex trauma may have difficulty with self-regulation or with building lasting, meaningful relationships. In addition, coping with complex trauma may overwhelm one's natural coping abilities, leading to coping through substance abuse, cutting, or engaging in high-risk sexual behaviors (Briere & Scott, 2015).

Theories and Skills for Trauma Counseling

Trauma cements the survivor in a space where time seems to stand still, and the horror of the traumatic event feels ever present and constantly looming. It is as if the sufferer's mind, emotions, and body get stuck in the moment of traumatization, unable to fully process something previously unprecedented in their life experience (van der Kolk, 2014). In a sense, the memory is frozen in time by neurological mechanisms tied to the person's most primitive stress response system (Levine, 1997). The long-term effects of these mechanisms can backfire, leading to dysregulation of the autonomic nervous system and an impaired ability to contextualize old and new experiences (Levine, 1997; van der Kolk, 2014). Thus, people's ability to process traumatic experiences is essential to healing.

We must be able to integrate these experiences into our existing schemas or to create new schemas to accommodate them, allowing our worldviews to shift under the weight of their significance (Triplett, Tedeschi, Cann, Calhoun, & Reeve, 2012). It is this shift that allows for deep healing and growth. Just as the impact of a traumatic event fractures multiple dimensions of a survivor's life experience (i.e., cognitive, affective, behavioral, and relational), the processing of that event must occur on multiple levels as well. The theories we use to understand trauma and how it affects the ways in which we think, behave, feel, and interact are each based on a different view of how processing occurs. Next, we explore some of the most common theories of trauma and its etiology as well as the core elements and skills of each. See Sidebar 6.1 for more information on trauma responses.

Sidebar 6.1 • Trauma Responses

Clients may sometimes feel shame or embarrassment about their natural autonomic responses to trauma. Traumatic memories can produce crying, shaking, dissociating, trouble sleeping, and many other physiological effects. Counselors can educate their clients about trauma's effect on the body. No reaction is right or wrong. Everyone experiences and manifests trauma differently.

Assessing Trauma

Assessing the etiology and implications of trauma is a complex task that takes place over time as, together with the trauma survivor, we explore new levels of impact and the meaning that these changes hold in his or her life. The first phase of assessment usually occurs when we meet our clients. Typically, a full biopsychosocial assessment is indicated at intake. However, there are a few aspects of this assessment to which we may want to pay particular attention when working with trauma survivors.

In my work, I (Allison), typically begin with a brief exploration of five key areas of the client's life and current functioning: (a) most immediate presenting concerns, (b) current functioning (including mental status and immediate medical needs), (c) risk assessment (i.e., presence of suicidal or homicidal ideation, acute substance use, and other types of psychological impairment that may leave the client at imminent risk), (d) current social support, and (e) past and current coping skills. These areas of emphasis are based in crisis intervention models that conceptualize crisis as a balance between a client's perceived level of distress and the coping resources available to help them process their distress (Greenstone & Leviton, 2011). Counselors must closely monitor clients' potential for crisis and risk at every stage of treatment, and continual assessment in these key areas will help them detect early signs of crisis and protect against further emotional damage.

Additionally, several standardized assessment tools may come in handy in the pursuit of a holistic understanding of the way trauma has affected your client's life, outlook, and coping resources. The U.S. Department of Veterans Affairs (https://www.ptsd.va.gov) offers a thorough list of available standardized assessments for trauma and trauma-related symptoms that can be accessed at https://www.ptsd.va.gov/professional/assessment/screens/index.asp. The Adverse Childhood Experiences questionnaire, which is based on the largest longitudinal study of child trauma and its impact on adult health and well-being, can help you and your client explore early life experiences that may be contributing to current difficulties (Centers for Disease Control and Prevention, 2019).

In addition, the Posttraumatic Growth Inventory can help you assess trauma-related growth and wellness and mark strength-based therapeutic gains (Tedeschi & Calhoun, 1996). Assessments of coping style, such as the COPE Inventory (Carver, Scheier, & Weintraub, 1989) and the Coping Responses Inventory (Moos, 1993), can also offer a broader understanding of how clients tend to cope with life challenges and where you could work to help them develop more diverse and adaptive coping skills.

Cognitive Processing Therapy (CPT)

Many of the most popular evidence-based approaches to treating trauma stem from a foundational belief that trauma anchors the brain in the cognitive and emotional context of the traumatic event. Thus, when triggered, the survivor travels mentally back to the time and place when the trauma occurred and acts within the context of assumptions, beliefs, and perceptions that were encoded at that time (Briere & Scott, 2015). To free themselves from this state, trauma survivors must work to reframe and restructure old fear-laden beliefs into new, more adaptive beliefs and perceptions that are grounded in the reality of the present moment (Briere & Scott, 2015). In this way, the related emotions are also targeted so as to detach them from the state-based, fear-driven context of the trauma itself. Known as the information processing theory of trauma (Foa, Steketee, & Olasov-Rothbaum, 1989), this approach frames most cognitive-behavioral trauma interventions.

CPT is a cognitive-behavioral approach designed to aid trauma survivors in processing traumatic material by "unsticking" state-based thoughts, behaviors, and feelings (Resick & Schnicke, 1992). The counselor facilitates a structured 12-week protocol with four main goals in mind: (a) psychoeducation about the information processing model of trauma, (b) increasing awareness of thoughts and feelings and their connection with each other and with the traumatic event, (c) training in specific skills to help clients challenge distorted thoughts and beliefs and to cope more effectively with the reality of the trauma, and (d) understanding subsequent changes in beliefs and worldview (Resick & Schnicke, 1992). Each strategy is geared toward helping the client identify "stuck points," or areas of incomplete processing, and to work through those blocks effectively (Resick & Schnicke, 1992).

Originally developed for use with survivors of sexual assault (Resick & Schnicke, 1992), CPT is commonly used today in work with military personnel (for more information, see https://www.ptsd.va.gov) as well as with survivors of a variety of traumatic experiences. A strong evidence base supports its effectiveness. Resick and Schnicke (1992) reported clinically and statistically significant changes in PTSD and depression symptoms among their original sample of sexual trauma survivors when compared with a waitlist control group. In a meta-analysis of 11 more recent quantitative studies, Lenz, Bruijn, Serman, and Bailey (2014) found that, when compared with waitlist and alternative treatment groups (i.e., other cognitive and exposure therapies and supportive nondirective approaches), clients receiving CPT showed greater decreases in severity of PTSD symptoms as well as related symptoms of depression.

Two core skill sets compose the basis of the CPT approach: (a) cognitive processing and (b) exposure to traumatic material through reflection and writing (Resick, Nishith, Weaver, Astin, & Feuer, 2002). Cognitive processing strategies help the client examine and deconstruct dysfunctional beliefs that are grounded in the fear state of trauma and to rebuild those beliefs into more balanced and realistic ideas about the self and the traumatic event (Resick et al., 2002). This process may be done through Socratic questioning, daily worksheets, homework assignments, and evaluation of self-statements (Resick et al., 2002). For example, in working with a sexual assault survivor, I (Allison) identified her dysfunctional belief, "I am unlovable." By gently and supportively asking her to evaluate the evidence for this belief, she was able to see that it was tied to the experience of the rape and was not actually a global truth. She then worked to replace that belief with a new, more self-sustaining and realistic belief—"I am worthy of love, and my perpetrator violated my safety."

As we worked through this and similar trauma-based beliefs, we began to slowly expose her to material related to the trauma that she previously avoided. Briere and Scott (2015) suggested that this step can be done through telling the trauma narrative—describing details of the traumatic events aloud—or by writing or journaling about elements of the experience. Creative approaches such as art therapy and sand tray therapy can also be used. Telling the trauma story or narrative is a common intervention among many treatment modalities, and it seems to be central to successful cognitive and emotional processing. Counselors new to trauma treatment, however, should use caution. Clients should be invited and never pressured to tell their trauma story, and they should only be asked to do so in a supportive environment with adequate coping mechanisms to support self-regulation and emotional safety.

Exposure Therapy

Along with intrusion and hyperarousal, avoidance is one of the hallmarks of a traumatic response (van der Kolk, 1987). It is a self-protective mechanism designed to cushion the impact of intense emotional and physical threat and, in the short term, can help people safely escape a threat without being distracted by overwhelming thoughts and feelings. However, sustained avoidance over time can block trauma survivors from one of their most important tasks—processing the thoughts and feelings that they so deeply fear. Triplett et al. (2012) suggested that healing and growth following a traumatic experience necessitate active processing, or *deliberate rumination.* As opposed to *intrusive rumination,* which happens beyond the survivor's will and can leave them inundated with vivid memories of the traumatic event, deliberate rumination requires slow, progressive exposure to those memories in a controlled and intentional way (Triplett et al., 2012). Thus, exposure therapy involves a highly structured and deliberate process of exposing survivors to the details of their traumatic experience in a physically safe and emotionally therapeutic environment so as to disassociate the fear response from otherwise nonthreatening stimuli.

There are several approaches to exposure therapy—all with the ultimate goal of unpairing a conditioned fear response from stimuli associated with the trauma. Prolonged exposure (PE) therapy is a structured exposure approach in which a trauma survivor uses in vivo and imaginal exposure to approach previously feared people, places, thoughts, memories, and other associations related to the traumatic experience (Foa & Rothbaum, 1998). Over the course of 8–15 sessions, the counselor pairs these exposure techniques with deep breathing exercises that assist the client in self-regulatory coping as trauma triggers are systematically activated and ultimately extinguished (McLean & Foa, 2011). Researchers have demonstrated PE's effectiveness in diminishing symptoms of PTSD and depression (Foa et al., 1999; Foa, Rothbaum, Riggs, & Murdock, 1991), and it has yielded similar treatment outcomes to CPT (Resick et al., 2002). Some researchers, however, have also noted the potential for PE to exacerbate PTSD symptoms in the short term, especially if not implemented correctly or with adequate coping support

(Foa, Zoellner, Feeny, Hembree, & Alvarez-Conrad, 2002; McLean & Foa, 2011). In a study of 76 women with chronic PTSD, Foa et al. (2002) reported that a minority of participants experienced exacerbated trauma symptoms but that those who reported symptom exacerbation still benefited from treatment. See Sidebar 6.2 for more information on PE.

Systematic desensitization offers one alternative to PE (Wolpe, 1958). In this approach, the counselor exposes the client to trauma-related stimuli, first inviting them to recall experiences that are not overwhelming but are moderately distressing, and then to build, over time, to more and more distressing associations after the client has seen success at lower levels of intensity (Briere & Scott, 2015). This approach promotes briefer periods of exposure and keeps close pace with the individual needs of the trauma survivor (Briere & Scott, 2015).

Trauma-Focused Cognitive-Behavioral Therapy (TF-CBT)

Cohen, Mannarino, and Deblinger (2006) developed TF-CBT as an adaptation of the popular cognitive-behavioral counseling approaches, tailored specifically to treat trauma in children, adolescents, and their families. The approach is time limited and emphasizes a set of central skills designed to build a child's coping strengths, and it facilitates the cognitive and behavioral processing of the traumatic experience with an emphasis on family involvement (Cohen et al., 2006). TF-CBT incorporates elements of cognitive processing as well as exposure therapy, introduced in a developmentally attuned way that helps to ensure that the trauma survivor has adequate coping mechanisms in place to support them through the exploration and processing of traumatic material.

Key components of the TF-CBT approach are outlined in the acronym PRACTICE (Cohen et al., 2006). These components include (a) psychoeducation and parenting strategies, (b) relaxation strategies, (c) affective expression and regulation, (d) cognitive coping strategies, (e) trauma narrative and processing, (f) in vivo exposure, (g) conjoint parent-child sessions, and (h) enhancing personal safety and future growth. Thus, the counselor walks the trauma survivor and their family safely into and through the trauma narrative while training specific skills in relaxation, emotion regulation, cognitive coping, and behavioral exposure, with an ultimate goal of empowering and facilitating growth through agency over present-oriented life experiences.

According to the National Child Traumatic Stress Network (2012), TF-CBT has the strongest research evidence of any treatment model for traumatized children on the basis of numerous randomized controlled trials and replication studies (e.g., Cohen, Deblinger, Mannarino, & Steer, 2004; Cohen & Mannarino, 1996; Cohen,

Sidebar 6.2 • Prolonged Exposure

Prolonged exposure can be a powerfully healing method for helping clients work through trauma. However, the text also states that counselors respect their client's space when they process trauma and not force exposure. There are other creative ways to help clients slowly heal from trauma. For example, sharing music, poetry, and art are other ways for clients to tell their stories.

Mannarino, & Iyengar, 2011). Although it is intended specifically for children and youth, researchers support its use up to age 21, and it has been modified for use in military settings (National Child Traumatic Stress Network, 2012). Some training and supervision is required and can be initiated through the TF-CBT training website at https://tfcbt2.musc.edu/.

Eye Movement Desensitization and Reprocessing (EMDR)

When you are stressed and trying to process major life decisions or unexpected events, do you ever find that it helps to take a walk? Psychologist Francine Shapiro had a similar experience that ultimately led to the creation of one of the most popular evidence-based approaches to trauma treatment (Shapiro, 2018). EMDR emerged from Shapiro's discovery that her own emotional distress seemed to lessen as she moved her eyes back and forth spontaneously during a walk (Lipke, 2012). In 1989, Shapiro published the results of her first study on the procedure, reporting a reduction in the intensity of traumatic memories among a group of 22 trauma survivors after only one session of EMDR. She reported that the results were maintained at a 3-month follow-up and led to behavioral changes that alleviated many of the participants' primary symptoms (Shapiro, 1989).

This groundbreaking work led to the formalization of Shapiro's EMDR protocol, which was later endorsed by behaviorist Joseph Wolpe and others who observed accelerated results when the protocol was used with their own clients (Lipke, 2012). The systematic eye movements that Shapiro discovered on her walk drive the effectiveness of the treatment. These eye movements and other forms of *bilateral stimulation*—repeated sensory stimulation that alternates between the left and right sides of the brain and body—seem to catalyze cognitive and emotional processing and aid in resetting physiological and neurological rhythms that are disrupted by trauma (Lipke, 2012; Shapiro, 2018). Thus, bilateral stimulation can help desensitize the trauma survivor to fear-laden traumatic associations while expediting reprocessing of the memory.

Shapiro (2018) distinguished between the technique of EMDR and the treatment protocol. In the basic technique, the counselor asks the client to bring a painful image or memory to mind, to connect that memory with related thoughts or beliefs as well as emotions and physical sensations (similar to cognitive-behavioral approaches), and then to hold that awareness as the counselor prompts bilateral stimulation through successive eye movements (Lipke, 2012; Shapiro, 2018). Typically, the counselor does this technique by holding their hand in the client's line of sight and moving it left to right across the full range of vision, about a foot and a half in front of the client's face, for about 25 repetitions (Lipke, 2012). Other variations include bilateral auditory or tactile stimulation, such as moving a sound from one side of the client's body to another or using hand-held buzzers that alternate stimulation (Lipke, 2012). After each episode of eye movement or bilateral stimulation, the counselor invites the client to breathe and to notice what emerges next.

Many clients favor this approach because they are not required to talk openly about their recollections of the traumatic event—a point of divergence from other trauma treatment models (Lipke, 2012). Instead, they can simply call the memory to mind while much of the processing is done internally. Counselors practice this technique within the larger protocol of EMDR, which includes eight phases: (a) history and treatment planning, (b) preparation (training in relaxation and other self-regulatory coping skills), (c) assessment, (d) desensitization, (e) installation of positive beliefs, (f) body scan, (g) closure, and (h) reevaluation (http://www.emdria.org). If you are interested in practicing EMDR, you will need to get formal training and supervision. You can learn more through the EMDR International Association (http://www.emdria.org), which certifies counselors in EMDR, and through Dr. Shapiro's EMDR Institute (http://www.emdr.com).

Medication Intervention

Researchers have identified medications that may help mitigate dysregulation of the autonomic nervous system, a central mechanism of the trauma response. These medications act on the hypothalamic-pituitary-adrenal axis and the sympathetic nervous system to ameliorate some of the adverse effects of sympathetic hyperactivation and trauma-related hormone release (Briere & Scott, 2015). They are most effectively used as an adjunctive treatment, along with evidence-based psychotherapeutic approaches such as the ones outlined in this chapter. For some trauma survivors, the physiological and psychological impact of trauma becomes so severe that it can inhibit cognitive, behavioral, and affective processing. Medications may go a long way in the short term to relieve the intensity of this impact and to enable and empower clients to engage more actively in counseling. Typically, the first line of defense is psychopharmacological intervention, in which selective serotonin reuptake inhibitors and other antidepressants address underlying symptoms of depression that can interfere with progress in trauma treatment (Conrad & Pejic, 2012). Other medications such as morphine, hydrocortisone, betablockers, and benzodiazepines may help lower acute anxiety and sympathetic nervous system activation (Conrad & Pejic, 2012).

Although some medications have proven useful in addressing acute symptoms of PTSD, strong evidence suggests that psychopharmacological intervention alone is not sufficient for healing from trauma and, when compared with psychotherapeutic interventions, may be less effective overall (Cahill, Rothbaum, Resick, & Follette, 2009; Friedman, Davidson, & Stein, 2009). Briere and Scott (2015) have cautioned counselors about the risks associated with medication use, including compliance, sedation, sleep disturbance, impairment in memory processing, and risk of medication abuse. Some of these effects may exacerbate existing trauma symptoms or present obstacles to successful treatment. Counselors should work closely with prescribing psychiatrists to ensure that any psychopharmacological interventions are appropriate for their individual clients and are closely monitored in the context of supportive trauma counseling.

Group Interventions

We know that trauma disrupts important functions and rhythms within the body's autonomic nervous system (van der Kolk, 2014). This part of the central nervous system is responsible for signaling the body to be calm and rest when things are safe and to fight, flee, or freeze under threat of imminent harm. However, one branch of the autonomic nervous system—the parasympathetic branch—also plays an important role in allowing people to socialize, build relationships, and to turn to others as sources of comfort and support when things get stressful (Porges,

2011; van der Kolk, 2014). In his polyvagal theory of trauma, Stephen W. Porges (2011) suggested that socializing and interpersonal connection may be central to the healing process following trauma because they help to bring back "online" parts of the parasympathetic nervous system that let people know when they are safe and no longer in danger. Thus, interpersonal connection may be vital to processing and healing on even the deepest physiological levels.

Group approaches to trauma treatment became popular following the Vietnam War (Foy et al., 2000) and remain common as an adjunctive approach to trauma treatment today. When incorporated into an individualized treatment plan, treatment and support groups can help trauma survivors practice and strengthen skills in empathy, emotion regulation, and interpersonal attunement that help to normalize the often isolating experience of trauma; these approaches also re-regulate important functions of the parasympathetic nervous system essential to posttraumatic growth. The most common treatment groups adopt a cognitive-behavioral approach, translating elements of CPT and PE into the group modality (Sloan & Beck, 2016). Many counselors also use groups to address comorbid concerns such as depression, anxiety, and substance use.

Common approaches include psychoeducation and interpersonal therapy groups as well as Seeking Safety groups for survivors who struggle with substance abuse (Sloan & Beck, 2016). Dialectical behavior therapy, which includes both individual and group components, also has been widely used to build self- and co-regulatory coping skills among survivors of complex trauma (Linehan, 1993). There is limited evidence to support the relative efficacy of group trauma treatment compared with other forms of individual therapy, in part because of a lack of randomized clinical trials (Sloan & Beck, 2016). Theoretically, however, the group modality may offer a unique therapeutic experience that targets key areas of traumatic impact not inherent to individual counseling.

Family Interventions

Bowlby's (1958) attachment theory reminds us that our earliest relationships with caregivers dramatically influence the ways in which we, as individuals, learn to cope with unexpected and threatening situations throughout life. Many trauma researchers have turned to Bowlby's work as a way of explaining why close family relationships and attachment patterns are so important to consider in treating trauma (e.g., Gore-Felton et al., 2013; O'Connor & Elklit, 2008). It is through these relationships that we learn how to seek comfort and safety in times of turmoil and we come to see ourselves and others as either reliable and trustworthy sources of support or—in the case of abuse, neglect, or other traumatic experiences within the home environment—as unreliable and untrustworthy in meeting these needs (Bartholomew & Horowitz, 1991).

Several treatment approaches have been designed to incorporate the trauma survivor's family members and collaterals and to address the systemic needs of families affected by trauma. TF-CBT, mentioned previously, is one popular approach that is especially relevant for work with children and teens. Other psychoeducational and cognitive-behavioral models have proven useful with couples and families, including the partners and families of returning service members (Monson, Fredman, & Adair, 2008). Figley's (1998) systemic family therapy model helps families affected by trauma to develop new means of coping while empowering family members to confront and actively process through the obstacles created by trauma in their lives and relationships. Susan M. Johnson (2002), creator of emotionally focused therapy for couples, also offers an attachment-based treatment model to help trauma survivors and their partners reprocess the attachment-related emotional responses that are often amplified during and after a trauma.

Brief Therapies

Treating trauma is a long-term commitment for client and counselor alike. Brief interventions in the context of trauma work generally target the acute crises that commonly arise throughout this process. In the immediate aftermath of a traumatic event, psychological first aid (PFA) provides concrete guidelines for counselors that will help to stop clients' emotional bleeding and promote adaptive coping—that is, empower clients to take control back in an otherwise chaotic and uncontrollable situation (National Child Traumatic Stress Network & National Center for PTSD, 2006). The eight core actions of PFA are (a) contact and engagement, (b) safety and comfort, (c) stabilization, (d) information gathering, (e) practical assistance, (f) connection with social supports, (g) information on coping strategies, and (h) linkage with collaborate services.

Stabilization skills, in particular, can assist counselors when their clients become activated or are in the midst of an acute panic attack or flashback. These skills may include breathing techniques as well as mindfulness strategies, such as visual relaxation, body awareness practices, and simple questions, that help ground a trauma survivor in the here and now, reminding them that they are safe in the current moment (National Child Traumatic Stress Network & National Center for PTSD, 2006). It is important for counselors working with trauma survivors to familiarize themselves with at least one good crisis intervention model. This knowledge will help in those moments of unexpected client crisis when it is vital for the counselor to manage their own stress reactions effectively so that they may accurately assess client needs and make informed decisions regarding immediate treatment and intervention. I like Greenstone and Leviton's (2011) model because it is clear, concrete, and easy to remember. For further reading on crisis intervention skills and strategies as well as PFA, see Greenstone and Leviton's book, *Elements of Crisis Intervention*, as well as the *PFA Field Operations Guide* (National Child Traumatic Stress Network & National Center for PTSD, 2006).

Contraindications

Trauma's inherent complexity necessitates a careful hand and cautious implementation of strategies that have the potential to exacerbate symptoms if used incorrectly. If exposed to traumatic triggers too soon or without adequate coping and support, survivors may feel unsafe or overly activated and ultimately disengage from treatment. In this section, we discuss contraindications in trauma treatment—that is, approaches and interventions that are not recommended or should be used with extreme caution because of their potential for harm.

Following major disasters and other large-scale traumas, helping professionals may use critical incident stress debriefing (CISD), a structured protocol designed to provide coping support and the opportunity for small-group debriefing for responders and personnel (Briere & Scott, 2015; Mitchell, 1983). CISD is specifically intended for use with disaster responders and trauma relief personnel, and it has been used successfully with rescuers, first responders, and members of law enforcement following large-scale traumatic events such as the September 11, 2001, terrorist attacks and Hurricane Katrina (Briere & Scott, 2015). The protocol invites participants to recall and share details of their experiences during trauma response with the goal of normalizing and facilitating cognitive appraisal and emotional processing (Briere & Scott, 2015).

It has been criticized, however, for its potential to retraumatize participants through exposure to others' traumatic material too soon after an event and for its frequent misuse with primary trauma survivors (Briere & Scott, 2015). CISD is not appropriate for use with individual clients, primary survivors (i.e., those who are not exposed in a professional capacity), or by counselors who are not properly trained in the modality. CISD should never be mandatory, even for response personnel, because this requirement violates an individual's right to personal agency—a core need for successful trauma processing. Finally, CISD is a structured prevention program and is not intended as a psychotherapeutic approach (Briere & Scott, 2015).

Similarly, counselors should use exposure therapies with caution because of the potential for these approaches to retraumatize survivors through excessive exposure too soon or without adequate support. If used correctly, exposure therapies, such as PE and systematic desensitization, can be highly effective and are among the strongest evidence-based approaches to trauma treatment. However, in the hands of a counselor who is new to trauma intervention or to these treatment protocols, they can lead to lasting negative effects that may harm clients and deter them from further treatment. If you plan to use exposure techniques in your practice, we advise that you seek additional training in these techniques and their appropriate use; you should also seek supervision from a trauma specialist who is well versed in these approaches.

Counselor Self-Care

Self-care is a foundational part of serving as a mental health professional. When working with survivors of trauma, self-care is paramount. As discussed in earlier sections, counselors working with trauma are at greater risk of secondary and vicarious trauma. We may begin seeing symptoms similar to our clients', and our values and beliefs may begin to shift as a result of exposure to trauma narratives. One of the challenges I (Hope) witnessed while working at a child advocacy center was the revolving door of professionals. Listening to children detail the abuse they have suffered day in and day out can be an exhausting job, and, if left unaddressed, this exhaustion can lead to disillusionment and resentment. I found that only through self-care strategies was I able to maintain my passion and continue serving children in need. Self-care is the balm that prevents and treats trauma symptoms, burnout, and compassion fatigue in counselors.

Self-care can cover many different activities, as long as it meets the needs of the individual person by allowing them to feel renewed and refreshed. During my time at the child advocacy center, I used supervision sessions for self-care but also made sure to take my dogs for walks and read lighthearted fiction books. Many people seek self-care through exercising, massages, or reality television. Although reinforced in graduate programs, once in practice, fully licensed and unsupervised counselors may forget the importance of self-care. Making a plan, setting boundaries around personal time, and remembering to put yourself first at times will assist in maintaining self-care. We cannot give to others when we are empty; thus, it is of utmost importance to find a way to "fill up your own cup."

Factors, Approaches, and Interventions That Foster Healing

A strong therapeutic relationship when counseling trauma victims should serve as the foundation for trauma treatment. Counselors then weave theory and skills intentionally into sessions to promote growth and healing. Beyond the relationship, individual factors within the client's life can assist in promoting healing, whereas specific approaches and interventions from the counselor's expertise may contribute to greater success in treatment.

Individual Factors

Safety and social support are key individual factors in promoting healing in trauma survivors. Physical and emotional safety are paramount in trauma treatment. Clients who remain in violent relationships, continue to live in unsafe conditions, or cannot feel emotionally safe face serious roadblocks to recovery. Although emotional safety can be built in session, physical safety can only be discussed in counseling in terms of resources, options, and safety planning because the client may choose to return to an unsafe home. Although taking actions to promote their own safety may seem scary, stressful, or retraumatizing, clients face a difficult journey to healing when they remain in physical danger. Biologically, the body cannot move forward to process trauma while it is still in a hyperalert state. Thus, expressing the need and importance for clients to remove themselves from unsafe situations cannot be overstated.

Posttraumatic social support is one of the most important factors in promoting healing (Ozer, Best, Lipsey, & Weiss, 2008). Counselors can assess for existing social support in the intake session and continue to reinforce the importance of social support throughout treatment. If direct family support is not available, clients can seek social support through friendships, religious affiliations, volunteer opportunities, or group counseling, to name a few. Counselors can promote use of social support through regular check-ins with the client, referrals, and homework assignments.

Approaches and Interventions

Several empirically based treatments were discussed earlier in the chapter. However, several overarching approaches may assist in the healing process. Trauma treatment, like counseling in general, is not one size fits all. Thus, as ethical and invested mental health professionals, we must have an arsenal of tools at our side to assist our clients. Some broader approaches specific to trauma treatment, including emotion regulation, mindfulness, creativity, and brain-based interventions, can help counselors supplement their trauma toolbox.

Emotion Regulation

Emotion regulation has strong empirical support in addressing many symptoms of trauma (e.g., Lilly & Lim, 2013). Emotion regulation in trauma treatment encompasses an awareness of, and intentional reaction to, emotions that stem from the traumatic event. Counselors can teach clients about identifying emotions, triggers, or stimuli that may cause an emotional reaction, current actions when feeling a particular emotion, and desired actions when experiencing the emotion. Treatment can address these topics to create a change in thoughts and behaviors around an emotion associated with the trauma. Emotion regulation is a foundational step in treating trauma because it allows the client to feel some control over his or her previously uncontrollable reactions; and in doing so, it sets a safe stage in which trauma can be further processed.

Mindfulness

The practice of mindfulness encompasses bringing awareness to and observing a phenomenon without judgment in the present moment (Baer, 2003). Mindfulness can be helpful in establishing emotion regulation, grounding a client when triggered, and creating healthy coping skills. Many techniques make up a mindfulness approach, including meditation (e.g., Zen, transcendental, loving-kindness), deep breathing, nonjudgmental awareness, yoga, and developing compassion for self and others. Although mindfulness can be used in conjunction with other treatment modalities, mental health professionals may also find it helpful to use a mindfulness-based treatment protocol such as acceptance and commitment therapy or mindfulness-based stress reduction (Kabat-Zinn, 2003). See Sidebar 6.3 for information on loving-kindness meditation.

Creativity

Creativity helps counselors to think "outside of the box" with clients. Creative interventions are particularly helpful in trauma treatment when clients may struggle to verbally express the depth of emotion they are experiencing (Gladding, 2008). Creative methods include, but are not limited to, art, music, play activities, bibliotherapy, and using a sand tray. The use of a sand tray may be particularly appropriate as a creative intervention because the client can tell the story of their trauma through real or metaphorical scenes in the sand. A sand tray also offers the client an opportunity to create a past, present, and future description of him- or herself in relation to the traumatic event. Creative approaches can be used to complement and enhance other theoretical approaches and may assist in helping a "stuck" client move forward (Duffey, Haberstroh, & Trepal, 2016).

One of my (Hope's) favorite examples of using creativity to assist a client in moving forward took place within a family system. I was working with two

Sidebar 6.3 • Loving-Kindness Meditation

Throughout this book, the importance of counselor self-care is emphasized. The loving-kindness meditation is a guided meditation used by counselors to practice self-care. Is this something you would consider using? What might be the benefits?

children—a male, age 11, and a female, age 8—and their mother. They came in because of suspected abuse by the children's father, and the entire family was consumed with sadness, guilt, and responsibility. Over time, I knew that a traditional approach was not as effective because the family could not see past the trauma and personal blame to recapture the strengths that held them together.

Using a framework of TF-CBT and narrative therapy, I began a project with the family in which they created a storybook—complete with illustrations—about their trauma. I instructed them, however, that they were each a hero in the story and, thus, must reframe the story to show themselves in that light. As a whole, the family rewrote their trauma narrative and formed new ideas about themselves through telling the trauma narrative and reframing the experience. Each person took great pride in the story and the illustrations. This project fostered the momentum the family needed to heal and grow. For our termination session, I presented them with their story, spiral bound, as a reminder to always see the strengths in each other.

Brain-Based Approaches

Recent advances in brain science have opened doors to new and exciting interventions in trauma therapy. Neurofeedback, an advanced intervention that uses brain waves during counseling, is empirically supported for treating anxiety, depression, attention-deficit/hyperactivity disorder, and trauma (Marzbani, Marateb, & Mansourian, 2016). Neurofeedback works through operant conditioning to teach clients self-regulation. In addition, a technique known as brainspotting uses the principles of EMDR to activate traumatic memories through specific eye positions (i.e., brainspots). Although less researched, brain spotting does have strong anecdotal support for trauma treatment. For more information on brainspotting, visit https://brainspotting.pro.

Case Example and Applications for Hope and Healing

Ana is a 20-year-old female college student who identifies as Mexican American. She has come to counseling at her family's urging because of their concerns about her behavior following a recent traumatic event. About 6 months ago, Ana discovered her roommate dead in their shared apartment. Her roommate died by suicide after overdosing on medication. Since this incident, Ana reports elevated anxiety, fear of being alone, frequent worry—especially about the whereabouts and safety of her friends and family—and weekly recurring nightmares. Her family describes her as a "jittery," "anxious," and "always in her own head." Today, Ana is recounting a panic attack that occurred just hours ago. She states that she had plans to meet a friend after class, but when she got to her friend's apartment, there was no answer. Ana knocked on the door for 15 minutes and called her friend at least 10 times. She states that, at that point, she started to feel like she could not breathe. Her chest tightened, and she feared she was having a heart attack. The panic was relieved when her friend finally came to the door, stating that she had accidentally fallen asleep. This occasion is the first time Ana has experienced a panic attack.

In working with Ana, we have chosen TF-CBT as the primary treatment approach because of its strong evidence base, structure, and ability to address cognitive, behavioral, and affective processing needs. TF-CBT is appropriate for her age, and we like the fact that it emphasizes family involvement. Ana is close to her family and friends, and we can begin by maximizing the effectiveness of social supports and the co-regulatory coping skills on which Ana already relies in times of distress. This is Ana's fourth counseling session. During the first and second sessions, we worked on psychoeducation around what trauma is and how the experience of finding her roommate following her suicide has affected Ana's functioning on cognitive, behavioral, affective, physiological, and social dimensions. We have also been in touch with her parents and sister who live about an hour away, and, together with Ana, we have talked to them about the plan for Ana's counseling and about how they might be involved. Ana would like them to come periodically to join her for sessions so that they can learn more about what she is experiencing and how best to support her. During the last session, we integrated a mindfulness approach to foster healing.

First, we worked on teaching Ana some simple breathing techniques for relaxation to help her regulate her autonomic nervous system when she is activated (e.g., Healthwise, 2018). We also practiced a new mindfulness strategy—mindful awareness of the five senses—designed to help Ana relax her mind and body when she feels anxious. Mindfulness techniques will be interwoven with the TF-CBT approach throughout her treatment. Today, Ana shares that she did not think to try these strategies until after her panic had escalated this morning, but we practice them again in session today, which helps her to self-regulate as she recounts this morning's events. In terms of the PRACTICE model (Cohen et al., 2006), we have now addressed Steps 1 and 2, psychoeducation and relaxation. We will continue to revisit these as we progress through counseling.

Given Ana's recent panic attack, our focus today and for the next couple of sessions will be on establishing Ana's sense of "safe space" and continuing to build and practice her self-regulatory coping strategies to give her tools and a sense of agency over her physiological response to trauma triggers. Next, we will move to affective expression and regulation and help Ana identify the emotions she is experiencing when she is both activated and calm. She will learn emotion regulation and cognitive coping strategies to show her how her thoughts and feelings are connected and how she can manage them effectively and intentionally. Ultimately, we will move into helping Ana tell her trauma story—perhaps through a creative technique such as sand tray use (Blankenship, 2017) or musical chronology (Duffey, 2005; Duffey, Lumadue, & Woods, 2001)—as we begin to reintroduce trauma-related associations in a new and safer context. Throughout, she will practice her new skills in self-regulatory coping and will work together with her family to reestablish a sense of security in her world.

Future Directions and Emerging Research

From traditional cognitive-behavioral approaches to the newer brain-based techniques, a recent shift in how we understand and treat trauma marks a new wave of treatment approaches that integrate cutting-edge neurophysiological research with time-tested strategies known to promote cognitive, behavioral, and affective processing. Thus, the study of trauma and its treatment grows richer through a deeper understanding of the brain-body connection and its role in traumatic response. Researchers—including Bessel A. van der Kolk (2014), Peter A. Levine (2008), and Stephen W. Porges (2011)—are paving the way for these new intersections through innovative theories of trauma that tie its lasting effects to dysregulation of the human body's primitive stress response system. Somatic experiencing (Levine, 2008) and the polyvagal theory (Porges, 2011) are gaining traction among trauma-focused practitioners, and van der Kolk's advocacy for mind-body interventions can be at least partially credited with the growing popularity of yoga and mindfulness in trauma work.

Additionally, more trauma counselors are using creative approaches with their clients. Techniques borrowed from art and music therapy, as well as bibliotherapy and cinema therapy, are giving survivors new languages through which to tell their stories. From a neurological perspective, it makes sense that many trauma survivors have trouble finding words to communicate their experiences because the brain's prefrontal cortex (responsible for problem solving, decision making, and contextualizing experiences) and hippocampus (responsible for memory storage) are heavily affected by traumatic response (van der Kolk, 2014). Creative interventions and play therapy techniques are particularly well suited to work with trauma survivors. Specifically, we have found sand tray, musical chronology, and creative approaches to narrative counseling (e.g., asking the client to create a photo collage or short flip book about their story) to be particularly powerful.

Finally, researchers are paying increasing attention to the construct of posttraumatic growth, or the belief that trauma can promote growth through positive psychological change (Tedeschi & Calhoun, 1996). This method may seem counterintuitive to many deficiency-based models of trauma that focus on symptom identification and alleviation. However, researchers are discovering that, when processed successfully in a safe and supportive environment, the traumatic experience can actually lead to improvements in life satisfaction and well-being. This area of study is ripe for counselors and counselor researchers because it aligns so nicely with the wellness- and strength-based philosophy on which the field was founded. To quote Ernest Hemingway (1929), "The world breaks everyone and afterward many are strong in the broken places" (p. 267).

References

American Psychiatric Association. (2013). *Diagnostic and statistical manual of mental disorders* (5th ed.). Arlington, VA: Author.

Arvay, M. J. (2001). Secondary traumatic stress among trauma counsellors: What does the research say? *International Journal for the Advancement of Counselling, 23,* 283–293.

Baer, R. A. (2003). Mindfulness training as a clinical intervention: A conceptual and empirical review. *Clinical Psychology: Science and Practice, 10,* 125–143. https://doi.org/10.1093/clipsy.bpg015

Bartholomew, K., & Horowitz, L. M. (1991). Attachment styles among young adults: A test of a four-category model. *Journal of Personality and Social Psychology, 61,* 226–244. https://doi.org/10.1037/0022-3514.61.2.226

Baum, N. (2010). Shared traumatic reality in communal disasters: Toward a conceptualization. *Psychotherapy: Theory, Research, Practice, Training, 47,* 249–259. https://doi.org/10.1037/a0019784

Bell, C. H., & Robinson, E. H. (2013). Shared trauma in counseling: Information and implications for counselors. *Journal of Mental Health Counseling, 35,* 310–323. https://doi.org/10.17744/mehc.35.4.7v33258020948502

Blankenship, D. (2017). Five efficacious treatments for posttraumatic stress disorder: An empirical review. *Journal of Mental Health Counseling, 39,* 275–288. https://doi.org/10.17744/mehc.39.4.01

Bowlby, J. (1958). The nature of the child's tie to his mother. *International Journal of Psycho-Analysis, 39,* 350–373. https://doi.org/10.4324/9780429478931-15

Briere, J. N., & Scott, C. (Eds.). (2015). *Principles of trauma therapy: A guide to symptoms, evaluation, and treatment* (2nd ed.). Thousand Oaks, CA: Sage.

Briere, J., & Spinazzola, J. (2005). Phenomenology and psychological assessment of complex posttraumatic states. *Journal of Traumatic Stress, 18,* 401–412. https://doi.org/10.1002/jts.20048

Cahill, S. P., Rothbaum, B. O., Resick, P. A., & Follette, V. M. (2009). Cognitive behavioral therapy for adults. In E. B. Foa, T. M. Keane, M. J. Friedman, & J. A. Cohen (Eds.), *Effective treatments for PTSD: Practice guidelines from the International Society for Traumatic Stress Studies* (pp. 139–222). New York, NY: Guilford Press.

Carver, C. S., Scheier, M. F., & Weintraub, J. K. (1989). Assessing coping strategies: A theoretically based approach. *Journal of Personality and Social Psychology, 56,* 267–283. https://doi.org/10.1037/0022-3514.56.2.267

Centers for Disease Control and Prevention. (2019, April 2). *Adverse childhood experiences (ACEs).* Retrieved from https://www.cdc.gov/violenceprevention/acestudy/index.html

Cohen, J. A., Deblinger, E., Mannarino, A. P., & Steer, R. (2004). A multisite, randomized controlled trial for children with sexual abuse-related PTSD symptoms. *Journal of the American Academy of Child and Adolescent Psychiatry, 43,* 393–402. https://doi.org/10.1097/00004583-200404000-00005

Cohen, J. A., & Mannarino, A. P. (1996). A treatment outcome study for sexually abused preschool children: Initial findings. *Journal of the American Academy of Child and Adolescent Psychiatry, 35*(4), 42–50. https://doi.org/10.1097/00004583-199601000-00011

Cohen, J. A., Mannarino, A. P., & Deblinger, E. (2006). *Treating trauma and traumatic grief in children and adolescents* (2nd ed.). New York, NY: Guilford Press.

Cohen, J. A., Mannarino, A. P., & Iyengar, S. (2011). Community treatment of posttraumatic stress disorder for children exposed to intimate partner violence: A randomized controlled trial. *Archives of Pediatrics and Adolescent Medicine, 165,* 16–21. https://doi.org/10.1001/archpediatrics.2010.247

Conrad, E. J., & Pejic, N. G. (2012). Psychopharmacology, psychiatry, and trauma. In C. R. Figley (Ed.), *Encyclopedia of trauma: An interdisciplinary guide* (pp. 502–504). Thousand Oaks, CA: Sage. https://doi.org/10.4135/9781452218595.n168

Duffey, T. (2005). A musical chronology and the emerging life song. *Journal of Creativity in Mental Health, 1*(1), 140–147. https://doi.org/10.1300/J456v01n01_09

Duffey, T., Haberstroh, S., & Trepal, H. (2016). Creative approaches in counseling and psychotherapy. In D. Capuzzi & M. D. Stauffer (Eds.), *Counseling and psychotherapy: Theories and interventions* (pp. 445–468). Alexandria, VA: American Counseling Association.

Duffey, T., Lumadue, C., & Woods, S. (2001). A musical chronology and the emerging life song. *The Family Journal, 9,* 398–406. https://doi.org/10.1177/1066480701094007

Duffey, T., & Somody, C. (2011). The role of relational-cultural theory in mental health counseling. *Journal of Creativity in Mental Health, 3,* 223–242. https://doi.org/10.17744/mehc.33.3.c10410226u275647

Figley, C. R. (1998). A five-phase treatment of PTSD in families. *Journal of Traumatic Stress, 1,* 127–141. https://doi.org/10.1007/bf00974909

Foa, E. B., Dancu, C. V., Hembree, E. A., Jaycox, L. H., Meadows, E. A., & Street, G. P. (1999). A comparison of exposure therapy, stress inoculation training, and their combination for reducing posttraumatic stress disorder in female assault victims. *Journal of Consulting and Clinical Psychology, 67,* 194–200. https://doi.org/10.1037/0022-006x.67.2.194

Foa, E. B., & Rothbaum, B. O. (1998). *Treating the trauma of rape: Cognitive-behavioral therapy for PTSD.* New York, NY: Guilford Press.

Foa, E. B., Rothbaum, B. O., Riggs, D., & Murdock, T. (1991). Treatment of posttraumatic stress disorder in rape victims: A comparison between cognitive-behavioral procedures and counseling. *Journal of Consulting and Clinical Psychology, 59,* 715–723. https://doi.org/10.1037/0022-006x.59.5.715

Foa, E. B., Steketee, G., & Olasov-Rothbaum, B. (1989). Behavioral/cognitive conceptualizations of post-traumatic stress disorder. *Behavior Therapy, 20,* 155–176. https://doi.org/10.1016/S0005-7894(89)80067-X

Foa, E. B., Zoellner, L. A., Feeny, N. C., Hembree, E. A., & Alvarez-Conrad, J. (2002). Does imaginal exposure exacerbate PTSD symptoms? *Journal of Consulting and Clinical Psychology, 70,* 1022–1028. https://doi.org/10.1037/0022-006x.70.4.1022

Foy, D. W., Glynn, S. M., Schnurr, P. P., Jankowski, M. K., Wattenberg, M. S., Weiss, D. S., . . . Gusman, F. D. (2000). Group therapy. In E. Foa, T. Keane, & M. Friedman (Eds.), *Effective treatments for PTSD: Practice guidelines from the International Society for Traumatic Stress Studies* (pp. 155–175). New York, NY: Guilford Press.

Friedman, M. J., Davidson, J. R. T., & Stein, D. J. (2009). Psychopharmacotherapy for adults. In E. B. Foa, T. M. Keane, M. J. Friedman, & J. A. Cohen (Eds.), *Effective treatments for PTSD: Practice guidelines from the International Society for Traumatic Stress Studies* (pp. 139–222). New York, NY: Guilford Press.

Gladding, S. T. (2008). The impact of creativity in counseling. *Journal of Creativity in Mental Health, 3,* 97–104. https://doi.org/10.1080/15401380802226679

Gore-Felton, C., Ginzburg, K., Chartier, M., Gardner, W., Agnew-Blais, J., McGarvey, E., . . . Koopman, C. (2013). Attachment style and coping in relation to posttraumatic stress disorder symptoms among adults living with HIV/AIDS. *Journal of Behavioral Medicine, 36,* 51–60. https://doi.org/10.1007/s10865-012-9400-x

Greenstone, J. L., & Leviton, S. C. (2011). *Elements of crisis intervention: Crises and how to respond to them.* Belmont, CA: Brooks-Cole.

Healthwise. (2018, June 28). *Stress management: Breathing exercises for relaxation.* Retrieved from https://www.uofmhealth.org/health-library/uz2255

Hemingway, E. (1929). *A farewell to arms.* New York, NY: Scribner.

Herman, J. L. (1992). *Trauma and recovery: The aftermath of violence—From domestic abuse to political terror.* New York, NY: Basic Books.

Johnson, S. M. (2002). *Emotionally focused couple therapy with trauma survivors: Strengthening attachment bonds.* New York, NY: Guilford Press.

Kabat-Zinn, J. (2003). Mindfulness-based interventions in context: Past, present, and future. *Clinical Psychology: Science and Practice, 10,* 144–156. https://doi.org/10.1093/clipsy.bpg016

Lenz, S., Bruijn, B., Serman, N. S., & Bailey, L. (2014). Effectiveness of cognitive processing therapy for treating posttraumatic stress disorder. *Journal of Mental Health Counseling, 36,* 460–376. https://doi.org/10.17744/mehc.36.4.1360805271967kvq

Levine, P. A. (1997). *Waking the tiger—Healing trauma.* Berkeley, CA: North Atlantic Books.

Levine, P. A. (2008). *Healing trauma: A pioneering program for restoring the wisdom of your body.* Boulder, CO: Sounds True.

Lilly, M. M., & Lim, B. H. (2013). Shared pathogeneses of posttrauma pathologies: Attachment, emotion regulation, and cognitions. *Journal of Clinical Psychology, 69,* 737–748. https://doi.org/10.1002/jclp.21934

Linehan, M. M. (1993). *Skill training manual for borderline personality disorder.* New York, NY: Guilford Press.

Lipke, H. (2012). Eye movement desensitization and reprocessing: Theory and research. In C. R. Figley (Ed.), *Encyclopedia of trauma: An interdisciplinary guide* (pp. 249–253). Thousand Oaks, CA: Sage. https://doi.org/10.4135/9781452218595.n86

Marzbani, H., Marateb, H. R., & Mansourian, M. (2016). Neurofeedback: A comprehensive review on system design, methodology and clinical applications. *Basic and Clinical Neuroscience, 7,* 143–158. https://doi.org/10.15412/J.BCN.03070208

McCann, I. L., & Pearlman, L. A. (1990). Vicarious traumatization: A framework for understanding the psychological effects of working with victims. *Journal of Traumatic Stress, 3,* 131–149. https://doi.org/10.1007/bf00975140

McLean, C. P., & Foa, E. B. (2011). Prolonged exposure therapy for post-traumatic stress disorder: A review of evidence and dissemination. *Expert Review of Neurotherapeutics, 11,* 1151–1163. https://doi.org/10.1586/ern.11.94

Miller, J. B., & Stiver, I. (1997). *The healing connection.* Boston, MA: Beacon.

Mitchell, J. T. (1983). When disaster strikes: The critical incident stress debriefing process. *Journal of Emergency Medical Services, 8*(1), 36–39.

Monson, C., Fredman, S. J., & Adair, K. C. (2008). Cognitive-behavioral conjoint therapy for posttraumatic stress disorder: Application to Operation Enduring and Iraqi Freedom veterans. *Journal of Clinical Psychology, 64,* 958–971. https://doi.org/10.1002/jclp.20511

Moos, R. H. (1993). *Coping responses inventory.* Odessa, FL: Psychological Assessment Resources.

National Child Traumatic Stress Network. (2012). *Trauma-focused cognitive behavioral therapy.* Retrieved from https://www.nctsn.org/interventions/trauma-focused-cognitive-behavioral-therapy

National Child Traumatic Stress Network & National Center for PTSD. (2006). *Psychological first aid (PFA) field operations guide* (2nd ed.). Retrieved from https://www.nctsn.org/resources/psychological-first-aid-pfa-field-operations-guide-2nd-edition

O'Connor, M., & Elklit, A. (2008). Attachment styles, traumatic events, and PTSD: A cross-sectional investigation of adult attachment and trauma. *Attachment and Human Development, 10,* 59–71. https://doi.org/10.1080/14616730701868597

Ozer, E. J., Best, S. R., Lipsey, T. L., & Weiss, D. S. (2008). Predictors of posttraumatic stress disorder and symptoms in adults: A meta-analysis. *Psychological Trauma: Theory, Research, Practice, and Policy, 1,* 3–36. https://doi.org/10.1037/1942-9681.S.1.3

Phelps, A., Lloyd, D., Greamer, M., & Forbes, D. (2009). Caring for carers in the aftermath of trauma. *Journal of Aggression, Maltreatment and Trauma, 18,* 313–330. https://doi.org/10.1080/10926770902835899

Porges, S. W. (2011). *The polyvagal theory: Neurophysiological foundations of emotions, attachment, communication, and self-regulation.* New York, NY: Norton.

Resick, P. A., Nishith, P., Weaver, T. L., Astin, M. C., & Feuer, C. A. (2002). A comparison of cognitive-processing therapy with prolonged exposure and a waiting condition for the treatment of chronic posttraumatic stress disorder in female rape victims. *Journal of Consulting and Clinical Psychology, 70,* 867–879. https://doi.org/10.1037/0022-006x.70.4.867

Resick, P. A., & Schnicke, M. K. (1992). Cognitive processing therapy for sexual assault victims. *Journal of Consulting and Clinical Psychology, 60,* 748–756. https://doi.org/10.1037/0022-006x.60.5.748

Rogers, C. R. (1957). The necessary and sufficient conditions of therapeutic personality change. *Journal of Consulting Psychology, 21,* 95–103. https://doi.org/10.1037/h0045357

Shapiro, F. (1989). Efficacy of eye movement desensitization procedure in the treatment of traumatic memories. *Journal of Traumatic Stress, 2,* 199–223. https://doi.org/10.1002/jts.2490020207

Shapiro, F. (2018). *Eye movement desensitization and reprocessing (EMDR) therapy: Basic principles, protocols, and procedures* (3rd ed.). New York, NY: Guilford Press.

Sloan, D. M., & Beck, J. G. (2016). Group treatment for PTSD. *PTSD Research Quarterly, 27*(2), 1–9. Retrieved from https://www.ptsd.va.gov/publications/rq_docs/V27N2.pdf

Tedeschi, R. G., & Calhoun, L. G. (1996). The Posttraumatic Growth Inventory: Measuring the positive legacy of trauma. *Journal of Traumatic Stress, 9,* 455–471. https://doi.org/10.1007/bf02103658

Tosone, G., Bialkin, L., Gampbell, M., Gharters, M., Gieri, K., Gross, S., & Stefan, A. (2003). Shared trauma: Group reflections on the September 11th disaster. *Psychoanalytic Social Work, 10,* 57–77. https://doi.org/10.1300/j032v10n01_08

Triplett, K. N., Tedeschi, R. G., Cann, A., Calhoun, L. G., & Reeve, C. L. (2012). Posttraumatic growth, meaning in life, and life satisfaction in response to trauma. *Psychological Trauma: Theory, Research, Practice, and Policy, 4,* 400–410. https://doi.org/10.1037/a0024204

van der Kolk, B. A. (1987). *Psychological trauma.* Washington, DC: American Psychiatric Press.

van der Kolk, B. A. (2014). *The body keeps the score: Brain, mind, and body in the healing of trauma.* New York, NY: Viking.

van der Kolk, B. A., Roth, S., Pelcovitz, D., Sunday, S., & Spinazzola, F. (2005). Disorders of extreme stress: The empirical foundation of a complex adaptation to trauma. *Journal of Traumatic Stress, 18,* 389–399. https://doi.org/10.1002/jts.20047

Wolpe, J. (1958). *Psychotherapy by reciprocal inhibition.* Stanford, CA: Stanford University Press.

Multiple-Choice Questions

1. The *DSM-5* added which concept to the definition of trauma?
   a. Trauma is only related to multiple events.
   b. Trauma may include an extremely upsetting event that leads to lasting psychological symptoms.
   c. Trauma may include an extremely upsetting event that has no effect on the brain.
   d. None of the above

2. Categories of trauma include
   a. Secondary trauma.
   b. Primary trauma.
   c. Vicarious trauma.
   d. All of the above

3. A symptom of acute stress disorder is
   a. Avoidance.
   b. Happiness.
   c. Tremors.
   d. Psychosis.

4. Complex trauma may affect a person's ability to
   a. Self-regulate.
   b. Walk.
   c. Contribute to society.
   d. Receive medical treatment.

5. Trauma may feel like a person's mind, emotions, and _____ are stuck in the moment when the trauma happened (van der Kolk, 2014).
   a. Thoughts
   b. Body
   c. Senses
   d. None of the above

6. Which is not a step of the authors' initial assessment?
   a. Immediate presenting concerns
   b. Mental status examination
   c. Risk assessment
   d. Current social support

7. The _____ can help a counselor identify trauma-related growth and wellness gains.
   a. *DSM-5*
   b. Columbia Assessment
   c. Posttraumatic Growth Inventory
   d. AUDIT

8. Which theory helps clients struggling with trauma to "unstick" their state-based thoughts?
   a. Cognitive-behavior therapy (CBT)
   b. Psychoanalysis
   c. Gestalt
   d. Cognitive processing therapy (CPT)

9. What is a theory that uses imaginal exposure for clients to process through memories associated with trauma or PTSD?
   a. Prolonged exposure (PE)
   b. Imagine therapy
   c. REBT
   d. Mindfulness

10. Eye movement desensitization and reprocessing (EMDR) highly relies on which technique for treating trauma?
    a. Telling trauma stories quickly
    b. Bilateral stimulation
    c. Only talk therapy
    d. None of the above

11. A curriculum used for treating trauma and substance abuse is
    a. Anger management.
    b. Safety after trauma.
    c. Seeking Safety.
    d. The SUD/Trauma Book.

12. In the aftermath of a traumatic event, stabilization skills may be used, and these can include
    a. Breathing techniques.
    b. Body awareness practices.
    c. Mindfulness skills.
    d. All of the above

13. When a client is exposed to trauma triggers too soon in counseling, they may
    a. Heal quicker.
    b. Feel unsafe and disengage from treatment.
    c. Appreciate the counselor's stern approach.
    d. None of the above

14. Mindfulness techniques may include
    a. Loving-kindness meditation.
    b. Acceptance and commitment therapy (ACT).
    c. Psychoanalysis.
    d. Both a and b

15. What may be a particularly appropriate creative approach for clients wanting to tell their trauma story using play?
    a. Sand tray therapy
    b. Bibliotherapy
    c. Walking meditation
    d. Neurofeedback

Essay Questions

1. Imagine you experienced an intense event that has been affecting you daily. What intervention would fit best with your personality and needs? Prolonged exposure? EMDR?

2. The chapter talks about individual and group techniques for working with trauma. Which modality would you favor if you were working through your own trauma? Why would that be?

3. If you were to seek training in a trauma theory (e.g., PE, CPT), which one would you choose? Why would you choose this one over others?

4. Trauma is systemic in that it can have a ripple effect throughout communities and extended family. Can you think of an experience that did not directly affect you but that left an imprint on your life?

5. Think about the case of Ana. What are your own ideas about how to best help Ana?

CHAPTER 7

Suicide Prevention and Intervention

Derrick A. Paladino

It was my first suicide call as a neophyte crisis phone volunteer. The caller's voice was aged and disheartened, revealing profound exhaustion. She brought me into a world that held loneliness, sadness, and shame. I began reflecting and attempting to build a relationship while anticipating that she was going to say "yes" to my question about her desire to die. And then she did. She spoke about hanging herself from the ceiling of her front porch. It would be nighttime, with her feet hanging heavily above the porch floorboards as her body swayed in the breeze. Eventually, people would find her on their evening walk or as they drove down the darkened street. Her vivid description of this desire was haunting and powerful, but more important, it was genuine. She had ruminated about this experience during a lifetime of distress. I sat on the phone, with my abilities feeling greener as every moment passed. I relied on my crisis center training, which taught me to create shared space with her to exist in the genuineness of the moment. I needed to see within her words and to understand her world if I was to make a connection. I needed to become someone familiar in her life.

Since that experience, I have worked with individuals living with suicidal ideation and behavior on the phone; sitting next to their hospital beds; in college residence halls; on a cot in an arena of evacuees after a natural disaster; at a field memorial after the Pulse tragedy in Orlando, Florida; in a traditional counseling room; and even at a table using a vase of flowers as privacy because every crisis counseling room was taken. These individuals' lethality ranged from nil to high. Some had no known means or methods to die, and others had the means to kill themselves in their hands. As I reflect on my time sharing space with these individuals, I recognize that building a strong relationship has always been my guiding principle. In every crisis intervention, I wanted my client to know that I saw and heard her so that, together, we could discover hope.

My wife, Amanda, who is an amazing writer (and an amazing person), told me that my experience reads as "flowery, and verbose . . . more like a suspense novel than a genuine tale of struggling to help those grappling with depression." And she is absolutely right, because that's exactly how that moment felt for me—being my first time. I was worried that my skills were lacking, an experience common for those new to this field (Douglas & Wachter Morris, 2015).

Unless you have specific training in suicide assessment and intervention, you are most likely going to have one class or one chapter of a textbook—if you are lucky—and that will not feel like enough when you are sitting across from your first client who is living with suicidal ideation. This chapter will be a primer for you, and my hope is that through this chapter you will increase your comfort with the topic of suicide and gain tools to pull from.

Understanding Those Living With Suicidal Thoughts and Behaviors

It is evident that those who engage in suicidal behavior are suffering emotionally, psychologically, or physically (Gramaglia et al., 2016). To understand the individual's unique pain, the counselor appreciates the client's perception with full empathy. Edwin S. Shneidman, the father of contemporary suicidology, believed that "the author of suicide is pain" (Shneidman, 1998, p. 246), and he introduced the idea of those engaging in suicidal behavior as experiencing *psychache*. Psychache is the aching psychological pain that can take over the mind (Shneidman, 1999). Shneidman (1999) suggested that suicidal behavior occurs when an individual deems their psychache to be intolerable and begins to see death as an active option to be rid of their pain. Indeed, those living with suicidal ideation are struggling to find connection and hope. Riethmayer (2004), in her discussion on trauma, stated:

> Trauma's initial impact brings four very powerful messages to a trauma survivor and the community. It tells the survivor that the world is no longer safe, kind, predictable, and trustworthy. Each of these has been taken away, or at the very least has been violated and/or damaged through the traumatic experience. (p. 219)

Individuals living with suicidal behavior experience a sense of the world as unsafe, unkind, unpredictable, and untrustworthy (National Suicide Prevention Lifeline, 2017a). In a suicide assessment and intervention, a counselor remembers that this perspective is likely how their client is experiencing the world, and the counselor should actively look for hope and stability as they move toward a treatment decision.

Myths

The word "suicide" feels heavy for many. This feeling may be due to the taboo nature of the act, personal and societal moral and philosophical views, or simply the fear of not knowing what to do after a client states, "I want to die." Society and culture have a large impact on the narrative of suicide. In addition, the act of suicide is so personal that those affected by it may create their own narrative about it (American Association of Suicidology [AAS], 2014). As a result, several myths abound (Moskos, Achilles, & Gray, 2004; World Health Organization [WHO], 2014). The WHO (2014) published six common myths in a report on suicide:

1. "Once someone is suicidal, he or she will always remain suicidal" (p. 69). According to the WHO report, this assumption is not the case: "Heightened suicide risk is often short-term and situation-specific" (p. 69). Although it is true that those with suicidal ideation may reexperience suicidal ideation, these thoughts need not be permanent, and individuals with previous ideations and attempts can continue their life without existing in this state.
2. "Talking about suicide is a bad idea and can be interpreted as encouragement" (p. 94). The WHO report suggests that because of social and cultural stigma around suicide, it becomes difficult for those who are living with suicidal ideation to know who to reach out to. Encouraging an individual to share may introduce the option to reflect on and reexamine their decision. This approach can lead to the prevention of an attempted suicide.
3. "Only people with mental disorders are suicidal" (p. 77). Although "suicidal behavior indicates deep unhappiness" (p. 77), it does not always indicate the comorbidity of a mental health disorder.
4. "Most suicides happen suddenly without warning" (p. 41). As indicated by the WHO report, most suicides are preceded by warning signs and symptoms. Knowing what to look for can make you a protective factor for a person contemplating suicide.
5. "Someone who is suicidal is determined to die" (p. 64). The WHO report suggests that most suicidal people are "often ambivalent about living or dying" (p. 64). There are also occasions of impulsivity, but those individuals may still hold uncertainty.
6. "People who talk about suicide do not mean to do it" (p. 21). The WHO report suggests that "a significant number of people contemplating suicide are experiencing anxiety, depression and hopelessness and may feel that there is no other option" (p. 21). Most likely, those people who are speaking about suicide are looking for someone to talk to and are reaching out for assistance.

Additional mental health advocacy organizations, such as the AAS, have also created materials to dispel suicide myths.

Suicide Nomenclature

To further our understanding of the individual living with suicidal behavior, we turn to the terms we use to talk about suicide. Having a common language supports continuity of care within the helping profession and across disciplines. Many agree that how suicidal behavior is labeled is essential (Hoff, Hallisey, & Hoff, 2009; National Suicide Prevention Lifeline, 2017a; WHO, 2014); however, there have been difficulties adopting universal nomenclature.

Next, you will find the most widely accepted terminology as well as language that is no longer used. The accepted and defined terms are suicidal behavior, suicide, suicidal ideation, suicide plan, suicide attempt, and suicide survivor. Although there are other more specific terms connected to assessment, such as levels of lethality (which are covered later), these terms are essential for documentation and for communicating about suicide with other professionals.

Recommended Terms

The following are recommended terms to use when describing the range of concepts related to suicide.

Suicidal behavior. *Suicidal behavior* is viewed as a range of activities linked to suicide thoughts and behaviors, including preparatory acts (National Suicide Prevention Lifeline, 2017a; U.S. Department of Health and Human Services [DHHS], Office of the Surgeon General [OSG], & National Action Alliance for Suicide Prevention [NAASP], 2012; WHO, 2014). The WHO (2014) has defined suicidal behavior as "a range of behaviors that include thinking about suicide (or ideation), planning for suicide, attempting suicide and suicide itself" (p. 18). Suicidal ideation is occasionally included under the umbrella of suicidal behavior in some sources, which is the case throughout this chapter.

Suicide. *Suicide* is understood as taking one's life with conscious intent. When a death by suicide is discovered, there is evidence of a conscious self-inflicted act. Suicide entails deliberate self-directed intent to die with the knowledge that death is irreversible (Centers for Disease Control and Prevention [CDC], 2011; Hoff et al., 2009; WHO, 2014).

Suicidal ideation. *Suicidal ideation* is having thoughts about killing oneself. These are self-reported passive or active thoughts of engaging in suicidal behavior (CDC, 2011; Goodfellow, Kolves, & de Leo, 2017; O'Carroll et al., 1996; DHHS, OSG, & NAASP, 2012).

Suicide plan. A *suicide plan* may include suicidal ideation, methods, location, and procurement of the means to kill oneself, and plan specificity connected to suicidal behavior. A suicide plan may also include a timeframe (CDC, 2011).

Suicide attempt. A *suicide attempt* has all elements of a suicide (holding within it suicidal ideation and suicidal plan), except the person does not die. Many researchers agree that a suicide attempt is carried out by a person with full intent to die (CDC, 2011). Suicide attempts, although intentional, may or may not result in injuries (O'Carroll et al., 1996).

Suicide survivor. A *suicide survivor* is a person or people who have a level of relation to a victim of suicide and who are bereaved by suicide, including family members, significant others, friends, acquaintances, peers, coworkers, counselors, first responders, and others (National Suicide Prevention Lifeline, 2017a; DHHS, OSG, & NAASP, 2012).

Terms to Avoid

Some terms are no longer recommended in speaking about suicide (i.e., suicidal threat and suicidal gesture). The CDC (2011) deemed the following terms unacceptable: "completed suicide, failed attempt, nonfatal suicide, parasuicide, successful suicide, suicidality" (p. 23). Suicidal threat and suicidal gesture—two contraindicated terms that have been used to describe episodes of nonfatal self-directed violence—are further described next.

Suicidal threat. A *suicidal threat* is saying or doing something that indicates a self-destructive desire. Hoff et al. (2009) used this term to describe people who threaten suicide or talk about it with a vague to specific plan, including past suicide attempts. This term is vague and can lead to complications in assessment and communication.

Suicidal gesture. *Suicidal gesture* refers to the behavioral form of a suicide threat. Like suicide threat, suicidal gesture is a highly subjective term with negative and dismissive connotations (Silverman, Berman, Sanddal, O'Carroll, & Joiner, 2007).

Often, the terms *self-injury* or *nonsuicidal self-injury* (NSSI) are confused with suicidal gesture. Some believe that those engaging in self-injurious behaviors have no intent to die but aim to give the appearance of a suicide attempt (Nock & Kessler, 2006). Some specialists see NSSI behavior as an act of emotional regulation, whereas others see it is a precursor to suicidal ideation and attempts (Grandclerc, De Labrouhe, Spodenkiewicz, Lachal, & Moro, 2016, pp. 1–2). Nock and Kessler (2006) suggested that it is important to highlight the difference between self-injurers with and without intent to die. After removing the terms suicidal threat and suicidal gesture and distinguishing suicidal behavior from NSSI, the CDC (2011) has recommended the terms "nonsuicidal self-directed violence" or "suicidal self-directed violence" (p. 23).

The use of contraindicated terms has created inconsistency and imprecision in suicide assessment and intervention. The fear is that with continued use, there will be a negative impact on the quality of care provided to clients living with suicidal behavior (Heilbron, Compton, Daniel, & Goldston, 2010). The CDC (2011) has advised against using these terms and has recommended that they be removed from clinical assessment reports (i.e., verbal or written), clinical practice, research, and clinical training and education. As a helping professional, it is strongly suggested that you advocate for proper terminology at your site and with your colleagues to increase precision and reduce stigma.

The Scope of Suicide: Prevalence, Risk Factors, and Warning Signs

Suicide Prevalence and Statistics

An examination of world and U.S. data on suicide reveals its strong prevalence in society. The WHO (2015, 2017c) has estimated that 800,000 people die from suicide globally each year. This equals approximately one death every 40 seconds. A large percentage of global suicides take place in low- and middle-income countries, with the most common methods of suicide being ingestion of pesticide, hanging, and the use of firearms. In high-income countries, there is a larger link to mental health diagnoses (WHO, 2017c).

Suicide rates have risen across age, gender, and race in the United States, and suicide has been cited as the 10th leading cause of death for all ages between 2008 and 2015 (CDC, 2017). Sources also indicate the rates of nonfatal suicide attempts. In 2015, it was estimated that there were 1,104,825 annual attempts in the United States. Suicide mortality in the United States increased 24% between 1999 and 2014 (Curtin, Warner, & Hedegaard, 2016). Despite a narrowing gender gap in suicide mortality, males still die from suicide more often than females in the United States. Although women are three times more likely than men to attempt suicide, four men die by suicide for every woman who dies by suicide (American Foundation for Suicide Prevention [AFSP], 2016).

A major element in the continuum of suicide is suicidal ideation, including suicidal plans. According to Substance Abuse and Mental Health Services Administration (2014) data, an "estimated 9.3 million adults (3.9%) age 18 or older had serious thoughts of suicide in the past year" (p. 29). Further research is needed to fully understand the impact of demographic variables, age, ecological factors, privilege and society, and co-occurring mental health and medical issues on the rate of suicide.

Societal and cultural narratives of suicide can severely affect one's desire to reach out, attend counseling, or engage in prevention programs, such as crisis hotlines. The WHO (2017c) reported that "few countries have included suicide prevention among their health priorities and only 28 countries report having a national suicide prevention strategy" (p. 1). As a counselor, it is important to recognize the need to work toward reducing stigma and to be an active participant in raising suicide awareness. Counselors should also increase their awareness about how living without certain privileges can affect mental health, and how mental health can affect suicidal ideation, plans, and attempts. Finally, counselors should be mindful of social justice advocacy when assisting diverse populations affected by suicide while creating prevention strategies.

Risk Factors for Suicidal Behavior

Risks factors for suicidal behavior have been discussed by many sources in the field (National Institute of Mental Health, 2017; National Suicide Prevention Lifeline, 2017b; DHHS, OSG, & NAASP, 2012). Risk factors are defined as the presence of a measurable demographic, trait, behavior, or situation (e.g., age, sex, psychiatric diagnosis, past suicide attempts). Risk factors are distal variables that positively correlate with suicide attempts and death by suicide (Hendin, Maltsberger, Lipschitz, Haas, & Kyle, 2001; Sommers-Flanagan & Sommers-Flanagan, 2015), but they cannot cause or predict suicidal behavior (National Suicide Prevention Lifeline, 2017b).

When examining general risk factors, consider the client's sociocultural context. Understanding the risk factors for different age and developmental groups is also important (e.g., bullying and cyberbullying in the adolescent population). The DHHS, OSG, and NAASP (2012) have identified certain groups as being at a higher risk for suicidal behaviors: American Indians/Alaska Natives; individuals in justice and child welfare settings; lesbian, gay, bisexual, transgender, and intersex (LGBTI) populations; members of the Armed Forces and veterans; men in midlife; and older men.

The AFSP (2017) created three domains of risk factors for suicidal behavior: (a) health factors, (b) environmental factors, and (c) historical factors. A compilation of several resources on risk factors organized under these three domains can be seen in Table 7.1.

Warning Signs of Suicidal Behavior

Distinct from risk factors, warning signs (a) are proximal, (b) imply imminent risk, and (c) are said to be particular to the individual's current state of being (Rudd et al., 2006). The AFSP (2017) created three domains of warning signs for suicidal behavior: (a) talk, (b) behavior, and (c) mood. A summary of risk factors organized under these domains can be seen in Table 7.2.

In addition, the AAS (n.d.) developed a mnemonic to assist with identifying the warning signs of suicidal behavior. Counselors may consider using the acronym IS PATH WARM: Ideation, Substance abuse, Purposelessness, Anxiety, Trapped, Hopelessness, Withdrawal, Anger, Recklessness, Mood changes (AAS, n.d.; Juhnke, Granello, & Lebrón-Striker, 2007).

Table 7.1 • Suicide Risk Factors

Domain	Risk Factors
Health factors	Mental health conditions (e.g., depression and depression characteristics, bipolar disorder, schizophrenia, certain personality disorders, conduct disorder, psychotic disorders, or psychotic symptoms in the context of any disorder); anxiety disorders; alcohol or other substance use disorders; major or chronic health condition or pain; lack of health care; genetic and biological factors
Environmental factors (social, community, relationships)	Stressful life events, which may include a death, divorce or discord, financial or job loss; prolonged stress factors, which may include harassment, bullying, relationship problems, and unemployment; lack of social support; access to lethal means, including firearms and drugs; exposure to another person's suicide or nonsuicidal death, or to graphic or sensationalized accounts of suicide; inappropriate media reporting; stigma associated with help-seeking behavior; having recently been released from prison or jail; cultural factors and religious beliefs that support suicide as a resolution; disaster, war, and conflict; stresses of acculturation and dislocation; discrimination; current trauma or abuse
Historical factors	Previous suicide attempts; family history of suicide attempts; individuals bereaved by suicide; history of trauma or abuse; family history of a mental disorder or substance abuse; individuals who engage in nonsuicidal self-injury

Note. Adapted from American Foundation for Suicide Prevention (2017); Hendin et al. (2001); National Institute of Mental Health (2017); National Suicide Prevention Lifeline (2017b); Rudd et al. (2006); U.S. Department of Health and Human Services, Office of the Surgeon General, and National Action Alliance for Suicide Prevention (2012); and World Health Organization (2014).

Connecting With and Working Alongside Clients Expressing Suicidal Behavior

The foundation of working with individuals living with suicidal behavior involves listening deeply, connecting compassionately, offering genuineness, and sharing mutual empathy. Accepting the perception of the client's current state will allow the counselor to foster a strong alliance with the client. Long ago, when I started learning about crisis intervention (as a crisis phone counselor), I was presented with the concept of *The Well*. The Well was introduced as a place where I would have a full connection with my client. That is, I would enter The Well with them to secure a fuller understanding of their crisis from their perspective. To achieve this outcome, I would need to genuinely enact the following: empathy and advanced empathy, unconditional positive regard, genuineness, warmth, attending, validation, trust, and an understanding that the client and their experience are unique to them. In The Well, it would just be the two of us, fully focused, sharing emphatically about the pain, and pushing away outside distractions. I really take the image of The Well to heart. I believe that to assist clients through crisis, I need to understand and share in their potentially scary, dark, and emotionally intimate issues. They also need to trust that I want to hear them and be there with them. It is from that deep moment of mutual connection that I can search for hope in their story.

Recently, a student in our counseling program stated that "sitting with someone is seeing them," and she is absolutely correct. I can only see that person if I am

Table 7.2 • Warning Signs of Suicidal Behavior

Domains	Acute and Expanded Warning Signs
Talk	Talking or writing about wanting to die, killing themselves, or death or dying; talking about being a burden to others; talking about having no reason for living or no sense of purpose in life; talking about feeling trapped (like there is no way out) or experiencing unbearable pain; talking about seeking revenge; saying goodbye to friends and family
Behavior	Looking and obtaining means to kill themselves: seeking access to pills, weapons, or other means (online or in person); acting reckless or engaging in risky activities, seemingly without thinking; increasing alcohol or drug use; withdrawing or isolating from friends, family, activities or society; agitation, aggression, sleep disturbance (too much or too little), or change in eating habits; visiting or calling people to say goodbye; giving away prized possessions; putting affairs in order; making a will
Mood (feelings and affect)	Hopelessness, rage, anger; feeling trapped, empty, vengeful; anxiety depression, loss of interest, irritability, humiliation; guilt, shame, dramatic shifts in mood; feeling unbearable pain (emotional pain or physical pain)

Note. Adapted from American Association of Suicidology (n.d.); American Foundation for Suicide Prevention (2017); National Institute of Mental Health (2017); National Suicide Prevention Lifeline (2017b); and Rudd et al. (2006).

truly there with them. Carl Rogers believed this too, along with many of the conditions in The Well. One aspect that stands out from his teachings is his personal learnings—*To Hear* and *To Be Heard*—from his text, *A Way of Being* (Rogers, 1980). In his personal learning, To Hear, Rogers described the satisfaction of hearing someone. When hearing deeply, he is put in touch with "the words, the thoughts, the feeling tones, the personal meaning, even the meaning that is below the conscious intent of the speaker" (Rogers, 1980, p. 8). Hearing a client can create grateful looks, release, a sense of freedom, and more openness to the process of change for the person struggling in crisis. In all, the person believes that you know what it is like to be them.

Rogers (1980) believed that being heard without judgment, diagnosis, appraisal, and evaluation can affect a person's state, allowing a person to relax and permitting them to express frightening feelings such as guilt, despair, and confusion, which then opens the door to reperceiving their world in a new way. My goal, as I hear my client and enter The Well with them, is to become a person different from the people they have experienced before who have misunderstood them. I want him or her to say, "He gets me!"

As you have been learning in this text, relational-cultural theory (RCT) focuses on much of the aforementioned, and it heavily "emphasizes the critical role of the counseling relationship and relational tools in healing" (Frey, 2013, p. 179). In addition, RCT focuses on the relationship rather than a client's autonomy as the cornerstone of growth (Duffey & Somody, 2011; Jordan, 2010). RCT is a natural modality for working with individuals with suicidal behavior; in fact, RCT discusses the notion of mutual empathy in the therapeutic relationship (Jordan, 2010). Mutual empathy involves clients' understanding of their impact on counselors. It is within that shared space and recognition of impact that a stronger bond can be created, allowing for change, growth, and development (Freedberg, 2007). This connection is vital, because clients living with suicidal behavior must have trust in the counselor to invest in the kind of hope that can prevent death. The client's pathway to making an empathic connection can also strengthen his or her ability to create supportive connections with others (Freedberg, 2007; Jordan, 2010). This aspect is important to create additional protective factors and a safety plan. The counselor ideally becomes one of many protective factors in the client's life.

Embracing the notion that your client is unique is important to all crisis work. It prevents assumptions. Multicultural and social justice competence is vital to gaining a richer understanding of the individual and allows for flexibility when working with diverse clients (Ratts, Singh, Nassar-McMillan, Butler, & McCullough, 2015). RCT embraces this sociocultural and contextual framework. RCT allows counselors to "explore how issues related to sex role socialization, power, dominance, marginalization, and subordination affect the mental health and relational development of all people" (Comstock et al., 2008, p. 279). Learning about diverse perspectives and values connected to suicidal behavior allows the counselor to continually foster mutual empathy and increase the quantity and quality of protective factors.

Using RCT as a theoretical framework, along with appropriate suicide assessment and intervention, can empower the client dealing with suicidal behavior. Suicide intervention requires the crisis counselor to assess the client's lethality and to determine whether the client requires hospitalization. RCT's emphasis on mutual engagement and empathy, authenticity, mutual empowerment, relational competence, and growth-fostering relationships (Jordan, 2000, 2010) is a strong foundation from which to build competence in connection, assessment, and intervention.

Suicide Assessment and Interventions That Foster Healing and Resiliency

Suicidal behaviors are a sign of extreme distress—not a harmless bid for attention—and should always be taken seriously (National Institute of Mental Health, 2017). The process of assessment and intervention is vital to instilling hope in those living with suicidal ideation and aids the counselor in forming a postsession plan that feels achievable and supportive for the client.

I have always believed that if I do not feel comfortable that my client will be safe when leaving the session, then I do not feel comfortable letting them leave. The rub is that clients can leave no matter what you say. For example, I was working with a client with suicidal ideation, and as we were going through the lethality assessment and intervention, I realized that she might not be safe leaving my office. As we discussed this possibility, she abruptly left my office and the building, and she ran down the road. I let out a word to myself that resembled "ship," and I swiftly headed to a colleague's office to consult. We decided to call the police to do a welfare check at the client's address. I also left a message on the client's voicemail. The client and I both recognized that her lethality level was high and that she might necessitate hospitalization. She decided against it.

One of the most difficult questions for new mental health professionals to ask a client is "Are you thinking about killing yourself?" It is an intimidating question, but it is fundamental to obtaining a clear understanding of where the client is. Words have a lot of power, and if the client is thinking about dying, then using the words "kill" or "die" is appropriate. Your goal in assessment is to match empathy with your client, and using phrases such as "hurting yourself" or "ending it" are vague, and they can be defined differently by the client, you, and other mental health professionals. Another potential misstep can happen after hearing "yes" to the question, "Are you thinking about killing yourself?" It is natural to want to go into a full lethality assessment immediately, but what the clinician could do instead is reflect the client's feeling and meaning:

> *Sam:* . . . It all just hurts so much (looking down with exhaustion in his voice).
> *Counselor:* Sam, you've been in a lot of pain for a very long time. Are you think-
> ing about killing yourself?
> *Sam:* (silence) Yeah. (pause) I just don't see a reason to be here anymore. No one
> cares. Every day it's so hard to get up, and there's no way things will get better.
> *Counselor:* Sam, it sounds like you're exhausted from feeling alone and know-
> ing that things aren't getting better. Right now, it feels like dying [or killing
> yourself] is the best option in your heart.
> *Sam:* Yes, (tearful) I just can't handle this anymore.
> *Counselor:* Sam, you just feel like things would feel easier if you weren't here.

Although the above dialogue may feel intimidating to say, it does two things. It (a) clarifies the seriousness of the client's suicidal ideation and (b) allows the client to experience understanding from the clinician. The former is important in beginning a suicide assessment, and the latter is foundational to building a strong relationship that can later be used to find hope with the client. In my experience, this genuine connection communicates "I care about you," "I'm concerned for you," or "I want to see you live." With continued dialogue, this approach will not plant thoughts of suicide in a client's head. Suicide is an intense behavior with preceding thought. If clients are not thinking about killing themselves, they will most likely just say "no" when you ask them. See Sidebar 7.1 for more information on working with suicidal clients.

Suicide Assessment

Suicide assessment includes (a) suicidal risk factors and (b) lethality assessment (Jacobs et al., 2003). Several interview assessments assist with identifying suicidal behavior risk, and most of them cover both areas. The Collaborative Assessment and Management of Suicidality (CAMS), developed by Jobes (2006), and the Chronic As-

Sidebar 7.1 • Working With Suicidal Clients

Suicide is one of the most common crisis situations encountered by counselors. There are many risk factors to consider when working with suicidal clients. Counselors are aware of the role of disconnection and use the counseling relationship to foster growth and connection. The relationship enhances a sense of safety, mutual empathy, and understanding. These aspects are important when working with suicidal clients for them to feel seen and accepted. When this occurs, the relationship begins to serve as a protective factor.

sessment of Suicide Events (CASE), developed by Shea (2002), are two formalized assessments. The CAMS uses the Suicide Status Form in a flexible and collaborative manner to assess and offer intervention. Collaboration occurs around five components: (a) collaborative assessment of suicidal risk, (b) collaborative treatment planning, (c) collaborative deconstruction of suicidogenic problems, (d) collaborative problem-focused interventions, and (e) collaborative development of reasons for living. The CASE allows four time periods to allow for a more practical interview and accurate assessment of ideation, planning, and intent. The interview explores presenting events, recent events (e.g., past 6–8 weeks), past events, and immediate events.

Douglas Jacobs (2007), in collaboration with the Suicide Prevention Resource Center, developed a suicide assessment protocol called the Suicide Assessment Five-step Evaluation and Triage (SAFE-T) on the basis of data and recommendations provided by the American Psychiatric Association (Jacobs et al., 2003). Although assessments support a more competent lethality assessment, "the ultimate determination of suicide risk is a clinical judgment" (Jacobs, 2007, p. 5).

In Step 1, the clinician should assess risk factors that may increase suicidal behavior in a client. Certain risk factors can be modified or lowered through intervention: specific psychiatric symptoms such as hopelessness, decreased self-esteem, aggression, and panic attacks. In addition, environmental factors such as access to firearms and other lethal means of suicide can be limited. Finally, social supports can be developed by working with family and friends or by discovering additional appropriate supports for the client. Step 2 addresses protective factors used to provide the client with both internal and external support. In spite of the presence of protective factors, a significant acute suicidal risk may be present. In Step 3, the clinician conducts a suicide inquiry by asking, "Are you thinking about killing yourself?" Step 4 includes assessing the lethality level of means and specificity of suicide plan. Finally, in Step 5, counselors document their assessment and recommendations.

Unquestionably, the higher lethality of means connected to a plan with specificity incurs a higher probability for suicidal risk. High-lethal methods are viewed as methods that have a high probability that an individual will die from suicide with little chance of them being saved. Examples of high-lethal means are shooting, hanging, jumping, sleeping pills, drowning, carbon monoxide poisoning, high dose of aspirin/Tylenol, car crash, antidepressants, and exposure to extreme cold (Jacobs et al., 2003). Low-lethal methods include wrist cutting, nonprescription drugs, and anti-anxiety medication. Certainly, the client's knowledge of means influences an assessment and determination of risk. For example, if a client believes that taking a low dose of aspirin with alcohol will kill them, then they would be assessed as high lethal, even if the means are low risk. In addition, the clinician should ask about plan specificity. Next, I offer examples of questions to assess lethality.

Suicide Assessment of Risk Lethality Questions

Suicidal ideation. The following questions can be asked to determine whether a client has suicidal ideation:
- "Are you thinking about killing yourself?"
- "How long have you been thinking about killing yourself?"
- "When is the last time you have thought about killing yourself?"
- "Have you thought about suicide in the past 2 months?"
- "Have you ever attempted suicide?"

Lethality of method and determining the means. The following questions can be asked to determine whether a client has a method and the means to commit suicide:

- "Have you thought about what you would use or do to kill yourself?"
- "What ways have you thought about dying?"
- "Do you know how to use the means?"

Availability and proximity of means. The following questions can be asked to determine whether a client has the means available to commit suicide:

- "Where are the means?"
- "Do you have access to the means and where?"
- "Do you have the ability and know where to acquire the means?"

Plan specificity. The following questions can be asked to determine whether a client has a specific plan to commit suicide:

- "Do you have a plan for killing yourself?"
- "Do you know when you would do it?"
- "Do you feel comfortable walking me through how you plan on killing yourself?"

After specificity is gathered in Step 3, the clinician must determine the level of lethality and recommended interventions and treatment on the basis of risk factors, protective factors, and formation of suicidal plan. Step 4 may range from creating a safety plan with the client to involuntary hospitalization. A safety plan is indicated when the client has hope and is not in imminent danger of dying. The National Suicide Prevention Lifeline suggests that there are buffers against suicidality to look for in assessment and intervention: immediate supports, social supports, planning for the future, engagement with a helper, ambivalence toward living or dying, core values and beliefs, and a sense of purpose (Joiner et al., 2007). Presence of these buffers can lower risk of suicidal behavior and can add preventative factors to a safety plan.

Safety Plans

Clients and counselors can co-create safety plans to increase investment and personal power for hope. Although some professionals may indicate that a safety plan is not required for low-risk lethality, it is wise to create one for all risk levels. Even at high-risk lethality, when involuntary hospitalization is required, assisting the client to find some preventative factors for after discharge (e.g., people who would be concerned about them) allows them to enter the next 72 hours with that seed planted as they receive additional support.

One goal of safety planning is to reduce the client's psychological, emotional, and behavioral isolation. After you are able to find a spark of hope in the client, you will find that a safety plan may open up more. Stanley and Brown (2012) suggested that safety plans comprise

> recognizing warning signs of an impending suicidal crisis; (b) employing internal coping strategies; (c) utilizing social contacts as a means of distraction from suicidal thoughts; (d) contacting family members or friends who may help to resolve the crisis; (e) contacting mental health professionals or agencies; and (f) reducing the potential use of lethal means. (p. 258)

Further explanation and examples of these components are as follows: (a) increased connection with relationships that are influencing negative emotions and suicidal ideation, suicidal ideation, substance use, and additional psychological, emotional, and behavioral triggers (as determined through a continued assessment); (b) watching or listening to nontriggering television, movies, or music, exercise, reading, and maintaining fulfilling hobbies (i.e., self-soothing without the assistance of another person); (c) spending time with understanding, positive, and supportive friends and family (e.g., who may not know about the client's suicidal behavior) and public activities that put the client among others where the incidence of triggering is minimized; (d) creating a list of safe and trusted family and friends with whom they can disclose their suicidal behavior for use if these components do or do not soothe; (e) crisis counselors, ongoing counseling with mental health professionals, physicians, and suicide or crisis prevention lines (i.e., local or national); and (f) client giving means to trusted individuals, locking up or storing away means for lower accessibility, and visually removing any means to reduce the potential for triggering.

A safety plan can begin in-session. There have been times when I have asked my clients to text or call someone whom we deemed trustworthy, supportive, and nonjudgmental to lay the groundwork for future communications and then to program suicide hotlines into their phones. I have usually said (after building mutual empathy), "I would feel more comfortable if we started your safety plan now, and if it's okay, I would like to help with that." It is important to remember that safety plans, although formulaic, should be as unique to each client as their suicidal behavior. Just because "dad" is a great resource for one client does not mean that he or other family members would be healthy supports. Instead of asking clients whether they have a family or friends that they feel comfortable talking to, you could ask, "Who in your life OR what one person in your life do you know who would be open and supportive to hearing about your struggle to live?" This type of phrasing reduces the potential of triggering the client, reduces a client's overwhelming feelings of finding multiple people, and allows the client to have power to determine who they find comfort with.

In addition, counselors should consider the client's already successful self-soothing behaviors, their socioeconomic status, and social-cultural behaviors when building the safety plan. Counselors can ask the client what they already do that relaxes them. Suggesting "going to the gym" to a client may not be indicated for a client who hates the gym or cannot afford a gym membership. Creating resources that are not in close proximity may be difficult for a client who does not have the means to get there. Checking your bias, morals, principles, and values at the door is vital. Counselors may deem family and spirituality as vital to their own lives, but if their client does not, then we would not suggest those as protective factors. See Sidebar 7.2 on listening to suicidal clients.

In today's age of technology, some agencies have worked to create smartphone applications and computer-administrated forms for safety planning (Boudreaux et al., 2017; Skovgaard Larsen, Frandsen, & Erlangsen, 2016). For example, the free smartphone application MYPLAN—available in Denmark and Norway—is a tool that allows users to create a personal safety plan containing strategies, actions, and support systems through the use of templates (Skovgaard Larsen et al., 2016). This trend seems skewed toward more technologically savvy generations, those who

Sidebar 7.2 • Listening to Suicidal Clients

When a client discloses that they are thinking about suicide, it is important to remain calm while also taking the statement seriously. In the moment a client decides to share his or her pain and thoughts of suicide, it directly reflects a plea for help. They are reaching out with the hope that someone will understand what they are experiencing. This is the moment to listen empathically, have compassion, and assess the lethality of their suicidal thoughts.

have the financial means to own a smartphone or computer, and individuals who have self-direction regarding creating and maintaining a safety plan. There is no empirical evidence that signed "no-harm" contracts are helpful in keeping clients alive, and these contracts may increase counselor liability issues (Lewis, 2007).

Finally, counselors should always document their assessment. At times, the crisis intake counselor may not continue working with a client, so using universal and accurate nomenclature and specifics in the assessment write-up will ensure a more accurate communication of severity and lethality. Sommers-Flanagan and Sommers-Flanagan (2015) suggested that documentation should include adequate historical information, with records documenting previous treatment (if possible), suicidal ideation and behaviors, consultation if used, a discussion of limits of confidentiality, any implemented suicide interventions, and a collaborative safety plan with safety resources.

Intervention

The assessment and intervention process should take you through to a strong treatment, so it is important to find methods that feel comfortable, are empirically supported, and are approved by your agency. Several crisis intervention models act as umbrella assessments and intervention tools for suicide screening. One example is the hybrid model of crisis intervention (James & Gilliland, 2013). The hybrid model follows the following seven tasks: (a) predispositioning/engaging/initiating contact, (b) exploring the problem, (c) providing support, (d) examining alternatives, (e) making plans, (f) obtaining commitment, and (g) following up.

Finally, in my experience, crisis assessment and intervention can take place in myriad environments, including crisis phone lines, agency counseling rooms, and make-shift areas after a disaster or a tragedy. It is important to be flexible with your environment, read the environment for safety and confidentiality, know the resources that are attached to the environment, and feel secure in how you use suicide assessment and intervention.

Suicide Prevention Strategies

Suicide is complex, with multiple factors and pathways leading to suicidal behavior (WHO, 2014, 2017c), and suicide prevention efforts require comprehensive coordination and collaboration through a broad, multifaceted approach. Generally, suicide is preventable if risk factors and warning signs are caught early, assessment and intervention are thorough, aftercare and follow-up are strong, and gate-keepers exist in the individual's life.

Prevention strategies can be approached in three ways: universal, selective, and indicated (WHO, 2014):

- *Universal* prevention strategies are designed to reach an entire population to maximize health and minimize suicide risk by removing barriers to care and increasing access to help. Strengthening protective processes such as social supports and altering the physical environment are universal protections. Examples include mental health policies; policies to reduce harmful use of alcohol; access to health care; responsible media reporting; and raising awareness about mental health, substance use disorders, and suicide.
- *Selective* prevention strategies target vulnerable groups within a population on the basis of characteristics such as age, sex, occupational status, or family history. Although individuals may not currently express suicidal behaviors, they may be exhibiting warning signs and have risk factors. Examples include interventions for identified vulnerable groups, gatekeeper training (e.g., ASIST [Applied Suicide Intervention Skills Training], QPR [Question, Persuade, and Refer]), and crisis phone and chatlines (e.g., National Suicide Prevention Hotline: 1-800-273-TALK; IMALIVE: 1-800-442-HOPE).
- *Indicated* prevention strategies target specific vulnerable individuals within the population who are displaying early signs of suicidal behavior or who have made a suicide attempt. Example strategies include direct assessment and intervention, follow-up, and community support.

The WHO (2017b) compiled a consortium of profession-specific prevention materials in "Preventing Suicide: A Resource Series." Finally, prevention includes advocacy; therefore, it becomes the mental health field's responsibility to educate and create gatekeepers and preventative measures to suicide. See Sidebar 7.3 on suicide prevention.

Counseling Interventions for Survivors

Approximately 6 million Americans became survivors of suicide in the past 25 years. For every suicide, an average of 147 people are affected, and 18 experience major life disruptions (AAS, 2014). Suicide also has the potential to affect societies, communities, and campuses (WHO, 2015). The loss of a loved one to suicide can be intense and can have impact of an unknown timeframe. Grief and loss are complex, painful, and unexpected (AAS, 2014). Common grief reactions to note

Sidebar 7.3 • Suicide Prevention

The World Health Organization (2014) has identified three prevention strategies for suicide: universal, selective, and indicated. These strategies could increase in popularity if counselors and students advocate for and apply them in their communities. Education and breaking the stigma around suicide are both ways that counselors and counseling students can make an impactful difference.

are shock, denial, pain, numbness, anger, shame, despair, disbelief, depression, stress, sadness, guilt, rejection, loneliness, abandonment, and anxiety (AAS, 2014). Grief counseling and suicide support groups are indicated for working with this population. It is also important for counselors to assess suicide survivors for traumatic features (Sanford, Cerel, McGann, & Maple, 2016). Finally, the AAS (https://suicidology.org/) offers a variety of resources and programs for suicide survivors, including a directory of survivors of suicide support groups, personal stories from survivors, additional booklets and information, and the Healing After Suicide annual conference.

Case Example and Applications for Hope and Healing

Anna, Age 32

Anna identifies as cisgender female, heterosexual, and Puerto Rican. She is currently living in Boston, Massachusetts, in a one-bedroom, one-bath brownstone basement apartment that she is renting. She lives alone and works as an electrical engineer.

Context Leading Up to the Counseling Session

Anna's boyfriend of 2 years broke up with her 4 days ago. Anna was under the solid impression that their relationship was just fine. They did not fight all week and had a nice late dinner before going to sleep at her apartment (her now ex-boyfriend has his own apartment with roommates). The next morning, he told her, "It's just not working out," and he has not been in contact with Anna since then. The first day following the breakup was incredibly difficult for her. She felt shocked, alone, worthless, sad, and confused, and she stayed in her apartment all day, barely eating. The second day, she tearfully called her friend, Michelle. Michelle and another friend, Allison, spent some of the day with her. They did the same on Day 3. The morning of Day 4, she called them again. They let her know that they could not spend time with her because they were going on an impromptu weekend trip with their boyfriends. After hanging up, Anna felt isolated and increasingly angry, sad, scared, and lonely: "I am unlovable," "I'll be alone forever," and "It's always my fault."

Anna's History

Anna experienced a breakup 3 years prior that was also traumatizing. At that time, she ingested a small amount of alcohol and some leftover hydrocodone painkillers, which had been prescribed to her after an injury. She believed this amount would kill her. Anna woke up the same day, just feeling "out of it." After she drank some coffee to feel more alert, she pushed down feelings and put herself into her work. No one knows about this incident.

Crisis Session

Anna arrives at your counseling agency, alone, as a walk-in crisis client. She sits in your office, quietly staring at her hands in her lap. After she becomes more comfortable, she tells you about her recent breakup. Anna is expressing the same beliefs about herself regarding never being loved and a "forever" state of loneliness. Her affect is congruent. She also believes no one wants to bother with her, including her "girlfriends." She thinks she drove them away as well. Anna has suicidal ideation. She has a Taurus .380 handgun on the table next to her bed. There are no bullets in the gun or in the apartment. Her now ex-boyfriend bought it for her after her apartment was broken into last year. She reported that she could get bullets from Walmart or the gun range where they know her. She thought about killing herself but did not have a plan for the next 48 hours. No one knows she has any suicidal ideation but you.

Suicide Assessment and Intervention

For Anna to feel comfortable telling you she wants to die, you first have to build trust. That is, you need to enter "The Well" with Anna. When entering this session, she believes no one is there for her. Even though her friends spent time with her, she felt like a burden to them and sees them as too exhausted to "bother with her," just like everyone else. Later in the session, you may discover that these people may or may not be protective factors, but that is not your current role. Your role is to enter Anna's shoes and reflect what she is feeling, to truly hear her so that she will feel heard, and to let her know that you are moved by her experience. After feeling more comfortable, Anna states, "It's too hard waking up to this pain. It's just too much." This statement is a warning sign that she may have suicidal ideation. You may feel a desire to ask, "Are you thinking about killing yourself?" after this statement. That is normal, and it should be in the back of your mind; however, offer one or two reflections first that directly connect to her pain in that moment and show your empathy.

> *Counselor:* The pain is just so overwhelming that you just want it to go away.
> *Anna:* It hurts so much. I can't go through all of this all over again.
> *Counselor:* Anna, I can really hear and see your pain as you are sitting here, and I know it feels unbearable.
> *Anna:* Yeah. (in a more sorrowful voice)
> *Counselor:* (silence) . . . Anna, are you thinking about killing yourself?

If Anna says, "yes," you may feel another desire to go straight to questions about means, methods, and plan. Take another pause and connect with her pain. You are the only other person who knows about her suicidal ideation. Reflecting her desire to die will not push her to die, and she is right in front of you and safe. This process is not linear, so you may find yourself going back and forth between assessment and reflection to make sure you and Anna are connected. Your goal after the lethality assessment is to find a grain of hope for her wanting to live. In addition, using "her words" (e.g., wanting to die, using a gun) will only strengthen the connection.

Should Anna connect with some hope, reflect that hope, and move toward discussing a mutually created safety plan. If hope is not there, then keep connecting and reflecting until you are sure that there is no hope and that she is going to die when she leaves. After that conclusion, you are potentially moving toward hospitalization. In this case example, Anna does have hope, and she is willing to create a safety plan with you. She has the potential for healing. An example of Anna's safety plan using Stanley and Brown's (2012) suggestions is shown in Appendix 7.1. See Table 7.1 for risk factors to suicidal behavior.

Future Directions and Emerging Research

Research on suicide warning signs, risk factors, assessment and intervention, and prevention efforts is an ongoing need. In addition, with the influx of social media and television and film influence on suicide, practitioners and researchers must be diligent when it comes to assisting in reducing stigma and the perceived glamorization of suicide (e.g., the television series *13 Reasons Why*) as well as creating and providing resources for those in need.

Social Media

The accessibility to an abundance of information on the Internet and the use of social media have a large impact on society, including the issue of suicide. The Internet is full of information on suicide awareness and prevention, but it also includes sites, forums, and blogs that discuss means, use, and attainment as well as sites that are pro-suicide. In a study by Biddle et al. (2016) on suicide content on the Internet, they discovered that pro-suicide sites (i.e., those that promote, encourage, or facilitate suicide) as well as graphic images of suicide and suicide methods, had increased through 2014, whereas prevention and support sites had reduced by nearly half since 2007. According to one study, youth who were exposed to or visited pro-suicide websites were seven times more likely to have suicidal ideation (Mitchell, Wells, Priebe, & Ybarra, 2014).

Social media is also a platform that can expose individuals to suicide behaviors. With anonymity comes an ability to be freer with emotions, thoughts, and concerns. In a study analyzing Twitter (i.e., 1,659,274 tweets) over a 3-month period, 37,717 (or about 2.3% of tweets) were identified as at risk for suicide, with these numbers being correlated with actual suicide rates (Jashinsky et al., 2014). This finding suggests that there is an opportunity to monitor and potentially support those experiencing suicidal behavior, either directly or through public health interventions. The same could be said for Instagram, Facebook, and other current and on-trend social media platforms. In addition, social media has the potential to provide an anonymous, accessible, and nonjudgmental medium to share experiences and to reach those who may typically be unreachable (Robinson et al., 2016). Counselors are encouraged to follow social media trends and become knowledgeable on what their clients are using. Despite some of the potential opportunities for outreach and prevention, there are downsides to intervening with those expressing suicidal behavior on social media. Robinson et al. (2016) suggested that ethical and clinical challenges include accurately assessing risk, issues relating to privacy and confidentiality, and the potential for contagion.

Several international studies have discovered upward trends of charcoal-burning (CB) suicides in East/Southeast Asian countries and helium suicides in the United Kingdom and Hong Kong (Chang, Cheng, Lee, & Yip, 2016; Chen, Yip, Lee, Gunnell, & Wu, 2015; Gunnell, Derges, Chang, & Biddle, 2015). Increases in online searches using CB-related keywords were discovered as well as an immediate and sustained increase in CB suicide after the suicide of South Korean celebrity Ahn Jae-Hwan in late 2008 (Chen et al., 2014; Cheng, Chang, Guo, & Yip, 2015). Popular culture, the Internet, and social media can influence suicidal behaviors, and this relationship should be explored further as it relates to warning signs and risk factors.

Prevention

An important part of prevention is recognizing the trends in suicide means and methods as well as at-risk groups. Certain at-risk groups still experience high rates of suicide. For example, groups such as U.S. males (ages 45–64), females (ages 10–14), and veterans have shown an increase in suicidality in recent years, and these trends warrant further attention (AFSP, 2016; Curtin et al., 2016). It is important to explore and address prevention for vulnerable groups that experience discrimination (e.g., refugees and migrants, indigenous peoples, LGBTI people, and prisoners), because these groups have higher rates of suicide (WHO, 2017a). Prevention also includes research, prevention campaigns, and restriction of means. Sareen et al. (2014, p. 259) suggested that there are three main strategies for advancement in knowledge of suicide risk factors and prevention:

1. Analysis of existing epidemiologic samples and clinical trial databases
2. Connecting networks and consortia of researchers to understanding the natural trajectory of suicidal behavior given the low base rate of suicide
3. Evaluation of current or new policies and programs through partnerships with policy makers and researchers

Suicide prevention campaigns that reduce stigma are also increasingly needed. Calear, Batterham, and Christensen (2014) found that stigma toward people who die by suicide and poor suicide literacy were significantly associated with reduced help-seeking behaviors and negative opinions regarding help seeking. There is a significant need to increase public knowledge and to reduce stigmas around help-seeking behavior. Reduction of access to high-lethality means and suicide method is also important. With firearms registering as the number one suicide method for males in the United States, there is an increased concern in this area.

Barber and Miller (2014) reported that some policies have been successful in reducing access to high-lethal means and methods. In the United Kingdom, where they experienced a high rate of suicide by inhalation of domestic gas, the rate of this method of suicide was decreased by replacing domestic gas with a novel nontoxic gas. In the United States, suicide barriers have been installed at popular jump sites (Barber & Miller, 2014). Prevention involves developing surveillance infrastructures after methods are discovered, counseling at-risk people and their families to temporarily make firearms inaccessible, and increasing awareness around the issue with the help of community leaders (Barber & Miller, 2014). Communication among researchers, mental health professionals, public policy makers, media, and the general public supports suicide prevention. Suicide prevention works best when all are involved and stigma is reduced. It is imperative to gain a solid understanding of ethical and sound practice while also developing a sociocultural understanding of your clients' connection to suicidal behavior.

References

American Association of Suicidology. (n.d.). *Warning signs of acute suicide risk.* Retrieved from http://www.suicidology.org/resources/warning-signs

American Association of Suicidology. (2014). *Survivors of suicide loss fact sheet.* Retrieved from https://c.ymcdn.com/sites/safestates.site-ym.com/resource/resmgr/SuicidePrevention/Survivors_of_Suicide_Loss_Fa.pdf

American Foundation for Suicide Prevention. (2016). *Suicide: 2016 facts and figures.* Retrieved from http://afsp.org/wp-content/uploads/2016/06/2016-National-Facts-Figures.pdf

American Foundation for Suicide Prevention. (2017). *Risk factors and warning signs.* Retrieved from https://afsp.org/about-suicide/risk-factors-and-warning-signs/

Barber, C. W., & Miller, M. J. (2014). Reducing a suicidal person's access to lethal means of suicide: A research agenda. *American Journal of Preventative Medicine, 47,* 264–272. https://doi.org/10.1016/j.amepre.2014.05.028

Biddle, L., Derges, J., Mars, B., Heron, J., Donovan, J. L., Potokar, J., . . . Gunnell, D. (2016). Suicide and the Internet: Changes in the accessibility of suicide-related information between 2007 and 2014. *Journal of Affective Disorders, 190,* 370–375. https://doi.org/10.1016/j.jad.2015.10.028

Boudreaux, E. D., Brown, G. K., Stanley, B., Sadasivam, R. S., Camargo, C. A., & Miller, I. W. (2017). Computer administered safety planning for individuals at risk for suicide: Development and usability testing. *Journal of Medical Internet Research, 19*(5), e149. https://doi.org/10.2196/jmir.6816

Calear, A. L., Batterham, P. J., & Christensen, H. (2014). Predictors of help-seeking for suicidal ideation in the community: Risks and opportunities for public suicide prevention campaigns. *Psychiatry Research, 219,* 525–530. https://doi.org/10.1016/j.psychres.2014.06.027

Centers for Disease Control and Prevention. (2011). *Self-directed violence surveillance: Uniform definitions and recommended data elements.* Retrieved from https://www.cdc.gov/violenceprevention/pdf/Self-Directed-Violence-a.pdf

Centers for Disease Control and Prevention. (2017). *Ten leading causes of death and injury.* Retrieved from https://www.cdc.gov/injury/wisqars/leadingcauses.html

Chang, S.-S., Cheng, Q., Lee, E. S. T., & Yip, P. S. F. (2016). Suicide by gassing in Hong Kong 2005–2013: Emerging trends and characteristics of suicide by helium inhalation. *Journal of Affective Disorders, 192,* 162–166. https://doi.org/10.1016/j.jad.2015.12.026

Chen, Y.-Y., Yip, P. S. F., Chan, C. H., Fu, K. W., Chang, S.-S., Lee, W. J., & Gunnell, D. (2014). The impact of a celebrity's suicide on the introduction and establishment of a new method of suicide in South Korea. *Archives of Suicide Research, 18,* 221–226. https://doi.org/10.1080/13811118.2013.824840

Chen, Y.-Y., Yip, P. S. F., Lee, C. K., Gunnell, D., & Wu, K. C. (2015). The diffusion of a new method of suicide: Charcoal-burning suicide in Hong Kong and Taiwan. *Social Psychiatry and Psychiatric Epidemiology, 50,* 227–236. https://doi.org/10.1007/s00127-014-0910-4

Cheng, Q., Chang, S.-S., Guo, Y., & Yip, P. S. F. (2015). Information accessibility of the charcoal burning suicide method in mainland China. *PLoS ONE, 10*(10), 1–15. https://doi.org/10.1371/journal.pone.0140686

Comstock, D. L., Hammer, T. R., Strentzsch, J., Cannon, K., Parsons, J., & Salazar, G., II. (2008). Relational-cultural theory: A framework for bridging relational, multicultural, and social justice competencies. *Journal of Counseling & Development, 86,* 279–287. https://doi.org/10.1002/j.1556-6678.2008.tb00510.x

Curtin, S. C., Warner, M., & Hedegaard, H. (2016, April). *Increase in suicide in the United States, 1999–2014* (NCHS Data Brief No. 241). Retrieved from https://www.cdc.gov/nchs/products/databriefs/db241.htm

Douglas, K. A., & Wachter Morris, C. A. (2015). Assessing counselors' self-efficacy in suicide assessment and intervention. *Counseling Outcome Research and Evaluation, 6,* 58–59. https://doi.org/10.1177/2150137814567471

Duffey, T., & Somody, C. (2011). The role of relational-cultural theory in mental health counseling. *Journal of Mental Health Counseling, 33,* 223–242. https://doi.org/10.17744/mehc.33.3.c10410226u275647

Freedberg, S. (2007). Re-examining empathy: A relational-feminist point of view. *Social Work, 52,* 251–259. https://doi.org/10.1093/sw/52.3.251

Frey, L. L. (2013). Relational-cultural therapy: Theory, research, and application to counseling competencies. *Professional Psychology: Research and Practice, 44,* 177–185. https://doi.org/10.1037/a0033121

Goodfellow, B., Kolves, K., & de Leo, D. (2017). Contemporary nomenclatures of suicidal behaviors: A systematic literature review. *Suicide and Life-Threatening Behavior, 48,* 353–366. https://doi.org/10.1111/sltb.12354

Gramaglia, C., Fetti, A., Bergamasco, P., Bert, F., Gattoni, E., Marangon, D., . . . Zeppegno, P. (2016). Clinical characteristics associated with suicide attempts in clinical settings: A comparison of suicidal and non-suicidal depressed inpatients. *Frontiers in Psychiatry, 7,* 1–6. https://doi.org/10/3389/fpsyt.2016/00109

Grandclerc, S., De Labrouhe, D., Spodenkiewicz, M., Lachal, J., & Moro, M. R. (2016). Relations between nonsuicidal self-injury and suicidal behavior in adolescence: A systematic review. *PLoS ONE, 11*(4), 1–15. https://doi.org/10.1371/journal.pone.0153760

Gunnell, D., Derges, J., Chang, S., & Biddle, L. (2015). Searching for suicide methods: Accessibility of information about helium as a method of suicide on the Internet. *Crisis, 36,* 325–331. https://doi.org/10.1027/0227-5910/a000326

Heilbron, N., Compton, J. S., Daniel, S. S., & Goldston, S. B. (2010). The problematic label of suicide gesture: Alternatives for clinical research and practice. *Professional Psychology: Research and Practice, 41,* 221–227. https://doi.org/10.1037/a00187712

Hendin, H., Maltsberger, J. T., Lipschitz, A., Haas, A. P., & Kyle, J. (2001). Recognizing and responding to a suicide crisis. *Annals of the New York Academy of Sciences, 932,* 169–187. https://doi.org/10.1111/j.1749-6632.2001.tb05805.x

Hoff, L. A., Hallisey, B. J., & Hoff, M. (2009). *People in crisis: Clinical and diversity perspectives* (6th ed.). New York, NY: Routledge.

Jacobs, D. (2007). *The Joint Commission: 2007 patient safety goals on suicide.* Retrieved from http://stopasuicide.org/assets/docs/JCAHO.pdf

Jacobs, D. G., Baldessarini, R. J., Conwell, Y., Fawcett, J. A., Horton, L., Meltzer, H., . . . Simon, R. I. (2003). *Practice guideline for the assessment and treatment of patients with suicidal behaviors.* Retrieved from https://psychiatryonline.org/pb/assets/raw/sitewide/practice_guidelines/guidelines/suicide.pdf

James, R. K., & Gilliland, B. E. (2013). *Crisis intervention strategies.* Belmont, CA: Cengage.

Jashinsky, J., Burton, S. H., Hanson, C. L., West, J., Giraud-Carrier, C., Barnes, M. D., & Argyle, T. (2014). Tracking suicide risk factors through Twitter in the US. *Crisis, 35,* 51–59. https://doi.org/10.1027/0227-5910/a000234

Jobes, D. A. (2006). *Managing suicidal risk: A collaborative approach.* New York, NY: Guilford Press.

Joiner, T., Kalafat, J., Draper, J., Stokes, H., Knudson, M., Berman, A. L., & McKeon, R. (2007). Establishing standards for the assessment of suicide risk among callers to the National Suicide Prevention Lifeline. *Suicide and Life-Threatening Behavior, 37,* 353–365. https://doi.org/10.1521/suli.2007.37.3.353

Jordan, J. V. (2000). The role of mutual empathy in relational-cultural therapy. *Journal of Clinical Psychology, 56,* 1005–1016. https://doi.org/10.1002/1097-4679(200008)56:8<1005::AID-JCLP2>3.0.CO;2-L

Jordan, J. V. (2010). *Relational–cultural therapy.* Washington, DC: American Psychological Association.

Juhnke, G. A., Granello, P. F., & Lebrón-Striker, M. A. (2007). *IS PATH WARM? A suicide assessment mnemonic for counselors* (ACAPCD-03). Retrieved from https://www.counseling.org/resources/library/ACA%20Digests/ACAPCD-03.pdf

Lewis, L. M. (2007). No-harm contracts: A review of what we know. *Suicide and Life-Threatening Behavior, 37,* 50–57. https://doi.org/10.1521/suli.2007.37.1.50

Mitchell, K. J., Wells, M., Priebe, G., & Ybarra, M. (2014). Exposure to websites that encourage self-harm and suicide: Prevalence rates and association with actual thoughts of self-harm and thoughts of suicide in the United States. *Journal of Adolescence, 37,* 1335–1344. https://doi.org/10.1016/j.adolescence.2014.09.011

Moskos, M. A., Achilles, J., & Gray, D. (2004). Adolescent suicide myths in the United States. *Crisis, 25,* 176–182. https://doi.org/10.1027/0227-5910.25.4.176

National Institute of Mental Health. (2017). *Suicide prevention.* Retrieved from https://www.nimh.nih.gov/health/topics/suicide-prevention/

National Suicide Prevention Lifeline. (2017a). *Mental health and suicide prevention glossary.* Retrieved from https://suicidepreventionlifeline.org/mental-health-suicide-prevention-glossary/

National Suicide Prevention Lifeline. (2017b). *We can all prevent suicide.* Retrieved from https://suicidepreventionlifeline.org/how-we-can-all-prevent-suicide/

Nock, M. K., & Kessler, R. C. (2006). Prevalence of and risk factors for suicide attempts versus suicide gestures: Analysis of the national comorbidity survey. *Journal of Abnormal Psychology, 115,* 616–623. https://doi.org/10.1037/0021-843x.115.3.616

O'Carroll, P. W., Berman, A. L., Maris, R. W., Moscicki, E. K., Tanney, B. L., & Silverman, M. M. (1996). Beyond the Tower of Babel: A nomenclature for suicidology. *Suicide and Life-Threatening Behavior, 26,* 237–252. https://doi.org/10.1007/0-306-47150-7_7

Ratts, M. J., Singh, A. A., Nassar-McMillan, S., Butler, S. K., & McCullough, J. R. (2015). *Multicultural and social justice counseling competencies.* Retrieved from https://www.counseling.org/docs/default-source/competencies/multicultural-and-social-justice-counseling-competencies.pdf?sfvrsn=20

Riethmayer, J. (2004). The impact of trauma: How best to help. *VISTAS Online, 23,* 219–228. Retrieved from http://www.counseling.org/docs/vistas/vistas_2004_23.pdf?sfvrsn=3

Robinson, J., Cox, G., Bailey, E., Hetrick, S., Rodrigues, M., Fisher, S., & Herrman, H. (2016). Social media and suicide prevention: A systematic review. *Early Intervention in Psychiatry, 10,* 103–121. https://doi.org/10.1111/eip.12229

Rogers, C. R. (1980). *A way of being.* New York, NY: Houghton Mifflin.

Rudd, M. D., Berman, A. L., Joiner, T. E., Nock, M. K., Silverman, M. M., Mandrusiak, M., . . . Witte, T. (2006). Warning signs for suicide: Theory, research, and clinical applications. *Suicide and Life-Threatening Behavior, 36,* 255–262. https://doi.org/10.1521/suli.2006.36.3.255

Sanford, R., Cerel, J., McGann, V., & Maple, M. (2016). Suicide loss survivors' experiences with therapy: Implications for clinical practice. *Community Mental Health Journal, 52,* 551–558. https://doi.org/10.1007/s10597-016-0006-6

Sareen, J., Isaak, C., Katz, L. Y., Bolton, J., Enns, M. W., & Stein, M. B. (2014). Promising strategies for advancement in knowledge of suicide risk factors and prevention. *American Journal of Preventive Medicine, 47,* 257–263. https://doi.org/10.1016/j.amepre.2014.05.041

Shea, S. (2002). *The practical art of suicide assessment: A guide for mental health professionals and substance abuse counselors.* Hoboken, NJ: Wiley.

Shneidman, E. S. (1998). Further reflections on suicide and psychache. *Suicide and Life-Threatening Behavior, 28,* 245–250. https://doi.org/10.1111/j.1943-278x.1998.tb00854.x

Shneidman, E. S. (1999). Perturbation and lethality: A psychological approach to assessment and intervention. In D. G. Jacobs (Ed.), *The Harvard Medical School guide to suicide assessment and intervention* (pp. 83–97). San Francisco, CA: Jossey-Bass.

Silverman, M. M., Berman, A. L., Sanddal, N. D., O'Carroll, P. W., & Joiner, T. E., Jr. (2007). Rebuilding the Tower of Babel: A revised nomenclature for the study of suicide and suicidal behaviors: Part 2: Suicide-related ideations, communications, and behaviors. *Suicide and Life-Threatening Behavior, 37,* 264–277. https://doi.org/10.1521/suli.2007.37.3.264

Skovgaard Larsen, J. L., Frandsen, H., & Erlangsen, A. (2016). MYPLAN—A mobile phone application for supporting people at risk of suicide. *Crisis, 37,* 236–240. https://doi.org/10.1027/0227-5910/a000371

Sommers-Flanagan, J., & Sommers-Flanagan, R. (2015). *Clinical interviewing* (5th ed.). Hoboken, NJ: Wiley.

Stanley, B., & Brown, G. K. (2012). Safety planning intervention: A brief intervention to mitigate suicide risk. *Cognitive and Behavioral Practice, 19,* 256–264. https://doi.org/10.1016/j.cbpra.2011.01.001

Substance Abuse and Mental Health Services Administration. (2014). *Results from the 2013 National Survey on Drug Use and Health: Mental health findings.* Retrieved from https://www.samhsa.gov/data/sites/default/files/NSDUHmhfr2013/NSDUHmhfr2013.pdf

U.S. Department of Health and Human Services, Office of the Surgeon General, & National Action Alliance for Suicide Prevention. (2012). *2012 national strategy for suicide prevention: Goals and objectives for action.* Washington, DC: Author. Retrieved from https://www.ncbi.nlm.nih.gov/books/NBK109917/

World Health Organization. (2014). *Preventing suicide: A global imperative.* Retrieved from http://apps.who.int/iris/bitstream/10665/131056/8/9789241564878_eng.pdf?ua=1&ua=1

World Health Organization (2015). *Questions and answers on suicide.* Retrieved from http://www.who.int/features/qa/24/en/

World Health Organization. (2017a). *Global Health Observatory (GHO) data: Suicide rates (per 100,000 population).* Retrieved from http://www.who.int/gho/mental_health/suicide_rates_male_female/en/

World Health Organization. (2017b). *Preventing suicide: A resource series.* Retrieved from http://www.who.int/mental_health/resources/preventingsuicide/en/

World Health Organization. (2017c). *Suicide: Key facts.* Retrieved from http://www.who.int/mediacentre/factsheets/fs398/en/

Appendix 7.1

Anna's Safety Plan

Recognizing warning signs of an impending suicidal crisis

- Desire to call her ex-boyfriend
- Seeing the gun her ex-boyfriend gave her on her side table
- Thinking "I am unlovable," "I'll be alone forever," and "It's always my fault"
- Feeling lonely, abandoned, worthless, and hopeless

Using internal coping strategies

- Watching *Antman* and *Guardians of the Galaxy* at home
- Listening to Tom Petty
- Cleaning out her closet to give clothes to Goodwill (something she wants to do but has been putting off)
- Going to her gym after she wakes up
- Using grounding techniques practiced in session

Using social contacts as a means of distraction from suicidal thoughts

- Spending time with her mother, Mel, whom she will tell about the break-up but not the suicidal ideation
- Yoga in the park or at the studio
- Bringing her dog to the dog park
- She is not ready to call Michelle and Allison.

Contacting family members or friends who may help to resolve the crisis

- She wants to reach out to her friend, Jay, who was her best friend before this most recent relationship. Jay sent Anna a "hello" message on Facebook Messenger last week. She feels comfortable telling her about the breakup, her suicidal ideation, and her safety plan. Jay lives in Boston.
- Her cousin Mel is a backup to Jay, and she feels comfortable telling her about the breakup, her suicidal ideation, and that she is seeking help. Mel lives in Hartford, Connecticut.
- She is not ready to call Michelle and Allison.

Contacting mental health professionals or agencies

- The agency where the crisis counselor who did the assessment works
- A local 24-hour emergency treatment facility
- A local suicide and crisis support line (programmed into her phone under a fake title before the session ended)
- A national suicide and crisis support line (programmed into her phone under a fake title before the session ended)

Reducing the potential use of lethal means

- Anna agrees to move the gun from her side table to the upper part of her closet where it can be locked up (she will have Jay or a crisis line on the phone when she does this).
- You both decide that she will not bring her gun to the gun range locker the next day because that could be triggering. She instead agrees to give it to her friend, Jay, the next day (if she feels scared in her apartment with-

out the gun, because of the past break-in, she feels comfortable staying with Jay).

- You also learn that she does not have any hydrocodone in the house, and she has only one bottle of wine that she does not plan on drinking (means and methods from past suicide attempt).

Anna's protective factors to be mindful of

- She has been spending the past 2 days with friends with the knowledge that she is not doing well.
- Anna voluntarily came into counseling.
- She has Jay, Mel, and her mom.
- She seemed relieved to know you care.
- She does have hope and imagines a world where she is not in pain but is living.
- She does not have bullets.
- She was able to restate the safety plan with what to do if she can't get a hold of her friend.

Potential threats to success

- Focusing on the breakups instead of present feelings of hopelessness and worthlessness
- Stacking suicide assessment questions without allowing space for the relationship and trust and assuming that her primary family or Michelle and Allison are protective factors
- Not pacing and taking your time

Multiple-Choice Questions

1. According to the text, first-time counselors working with suicide may
   a. Feel overly confident.
   b. Feel their skills are lacking.
   c. Feel they need to use only cognitive-behavior therapy (CBT).
   d. None of the above

2. Who is the father of contemporary suicidology?
   a. Edwin S. Shneidman
   b. Edward Smith
   c. Cameron Scott
   d. John Bowlby

3. The World Health Organization published _____ myths about suicide.
   a. 50
   b. 3
   c. 6
   d. 25

4. Suicidal behavior includes
   a. Planning for suicide.
   b. Suicide ideation.
   c. Suicide attempt.
   d. All of the above

5. Which best describes a suicide survivor?
   a. A person who attempted suicide but did not succeed
   b. A person who has connection to the person who committed suicide
   c. A group of people
   d. None of the above

6. The term "suicidal threat" should be an avoided term because
   a. No one can threaten suicide.
   b. It could be vague and complicate communication.
   c. It is only in medical journals.
   d. It is negative.

7. Those engaging in self-injury are suicidal.
   a. True, all of the time
   b. False, all of the time
   c. True, if the gesture is done with intent to die
   d. False, if the person is a child

8. Suicide was the _____ leading cause of death for all ages in the United States between 2008 and 2015.
   a. 1st
   b. 20th
   c. 10th
   d. 2nd

9. The American Foundation for Suicide Prevention (2017) has the following three domains of warning signs for suicidal behavior:
   a. Talking, affect, style.
   b. Talking, age, mood.
   c. Age, culture, religion.
   d. Talking, behavior, mood.

10. Suicide assessment can be broken down into two areas:
    a. Suicidal risk factors and lethality assessment.
    b. Risk and protective factors.
    c. Addiction and risk factors.
    d. Suicidal risk factors and risk factors.

11. According to the National Suicide Prevention Lifeline, _____ can buffer against suicide.
    a. Engagement with helper
    b. Immediate supports
    c. Financial security
    d. Both a and b

12. One umbrella assessment for suicide is called
    a. The efficient model.
    b. The umbrella assessment.
    c. The hybrid model of crisis intervention.
    d. None of the above

13. Suicide can be preventable if
    a. Warning signs are caught early.
    b. The person is put in outpatient treatment.
    c. Counselors learn all assessments.
    d. None of the above

14. For every suicide an average of _____ people are affected.
    a. 40
    b. 147
    c. 100
    d. 200

15. Pro-suicide sites have _____ since 2014, and prevention sites have _____ since 2007.
    a. Decreased, decreased
    b. Increased, increased
    c. Increased, decreased
    d. Increased, increased

Essay Questions

1. The author talked about how he was worried and scared that his clinical skills were lacking for working with a client who felt suicidal. Have you ever known someone or counseled someone who told you he or she felt suicidal? What was your reaction?

2. The author discussed myths about suicidal behavior provided by the World Health Organization. Did any of the myths surprise you?

3. The Well is a concept that allows the counselor and client to have a full connection while discussing the potential suicide. The concept encourages the counselor to fully share dark, emotionally intense client stories. As a counselor or student, how does this sound to you?

4. The author talks about how new counselors may find it difficult to ask, "Are you thinking about killing yourself?" Do you feel this question will be (or has been) hard for you to ask?

5. Creating a safety plan, even if a client's lethality is low, may be a great idea for helping a client have a way to cope if suicidal thoughts come up. The chapter lists items to help the client identify signs and to include in the plan. What specific items might you add? What are your feelings and thoughts about a safety plan?

CHAPTER 8

Violence, Abuse, and Neglect
Across the Life Span

Thelma Duffey and Shane Haberstroh

According to the Federal Bureau of Investigation (FBI; 2017), rates of violence have risen since 2010. In 2017, more than 5.6 million people experienced a violent crime. These incidences included sexual assault, domestic and interpersonal violence, and stranger violence. Data trends show that there has been an overall downturn of violent acts since 1993, but in the recent several years, violence has increased (FBI, 2017). Given the sheer numbers of people who experience violent acts, and the high rates of underreporting (FBI, 2017), counselors will encounter people who have experienced aggressive acts, fearful for their lives, targets of people with criminal and vicious intent.

In this chapter, we consider the impact of violence, abuse, and neglect on the lives of people throughout the life span, and we structure this chapter chronologically. Beginning with childhood adverse experiences, we look at the crisis experiences of many children and the developmental traumas that can arise from consistently neglectful and abusive care. We consider the means by which counselors can support children suffering these crises, and then we transition to some painful adolescent and adulthood experiences that uniquely challenge people who suffer at the hands of others. Finally, we conclude this chapter by describing the distinctive dynamics of neglect and abuse in older adulthood and the ways in which counselors can intervene. Neglect, abuse, and harassment bring formidable challenges to people who endure them, and counselors are well positioned to support and empower them on their journey to healing.

The Relational Foundation:
Childhood Abuse, Neglect, and Adverse Childhood Events (ACEs)

In the span of 30 minutes, everything changed, forever. Esteban woke early on a weekday morning during summer break. Seventh grade was right around the corner, and the late July days brought sunshine, warm breezes, and new freedoms. Esteban explored his new neighborhood, riding his bike through winding wooded trails and suburban landscapes. This new place was a far cry from the impoverished and dangerous neighborhood where he lived for years following his parent's divorce. When he was 5 years old, his parents told him they were divorcing and it "wasn't his fault," which felt extra confusing to hear. His parent's marriage was often punctuated with loud arguments and probable physical altercations. Esteban would hear yelling and crashes as he fell asleep each night, dreading alone time with his father.

When he and his father would be home alone, his dad would torment him like a cruel older sibling. His father hunted Esteban throughout house, welting and bruising him with his high-powered paint gun, and when catching him, he would pin him down and tickle him painfully until near suffocation. Suffering from a history of near-fatal asthma attacks requiring multiple hospitalizations, these moments terrified Esteban. The sadistic glee in his father's face etched into his memory. This was play time with his father.

A few months preceding the divorce, Esteban's father took him up to the roof and chased him around, pelting him with tar-soaked stones. One of Esteban's most vivid memories of his childhood was the image of a rock slamming into his right eye, exploding into a starburst of misery. As he dropped to his knees, he briefly saw the scared look on his father's face. Maybe this time he had gone too far. Esteban cried out with a wounded guttural wail, buried his head in his hands, and curled into himself for protection. His right eye was damaged for life. The memory of his father's face, shocked and scared, was strangely soothing to Esteban. Maybe he mattered a little bit.

Now, far away in his new home, life seemed full of new possibilities. His family felt stable. His stepfather was loving and supportive. Moreover, he was making new friends. One of the older teenage boys, J.R., began spending time with Esteban, which inspired a newfound kind of pride. On this sunny July morning, they met up at the fort they built together. As Esteban got off his bicycle, J.R. tackled Esteban from behind, slammed him to the ground, flipped him over, and pinned him down, knees on his shoulders. J.R. was 50 pounds heavier than Esteban and muscular. There was little hope for escape.

J.R. pulled a large hunting knife from his back pocket and pressed the tip to Esteban's throat. "Keep me from killing you," J.R. instructed as he applied increasing pressure on the knife. Esteban was shocked and terrified, and he pressed both hands against the blade, feeling the cold tip bear down with even more force. This was not playful teasing. J.R.'s face was red with rage. The knife began to penetrate his skin. The dawning awareness that he might die here fueled panicked resistance in Esteban. In an unexpected lull, J.R. stood up and said, "Congratulations, you passed the test. I wanted to see if you were really a man." Running to his bike, Esteban sped away. As he slowly walked his bike up his driveway, a grayness settled over everything. The rustle of leaves felt ominous, and the cold blue skies mocked his previously felt hope with indifference. See Sidebar 8.1 for information on assisting abused children.

ACEs

Nearly half of the U.S. population experienced at least one serious ACE (Centers for Disease Control and Prevention [CDC], 2019; Felitti et al., 1998). The CDC (2019) has defined *ACEs* as "all types of abuse, neglect, and other potentially traumatic experiences that occur to people under the age of 18" (para. 1). Examples of ACEs include (a) physical abuse, (b) sexual abuse, (c) having a family member incarcerated, (d) drug use and serious mental health problems among family members in the home, (e) parental separation and divorce, (f) domestic violence, and (g) food insecurity and deficiencies in basic nurturance (CDC, 2019). These experiences are born from spaces and relationships where the need for attached and secure connections are met with cruelty, indifference, and random violence.

The Origins of ACEs Research

In 1997, the CDC and Kaiser Permanente surveyed more than 9,000 people to explore the impact of these type of events on health and mortality (Felitti et al., 1998). This research was the inaugural ACEs study, and this team found that trauma and neglect during childhood led to significantly poorer health and increased mortality later in life. This landmark study paved the way for future research into the effects of ACEs, and numerous studies have attested to the fact that early trauma and neglect weave into people's physiological and psychological tapestry (to view the ACEs screening form and to learn more information, see https://acestoohigh.com/got-your-ace-score/).

Long-Term Psychological Effects of ACEs

Merrick et al. (2017) reported on the relationship between ACEs and incidences of depression, problematic drug and alcohol use, and suicide attempts later in life. They found a strong relationship between these factors. For example, they found that people who experienced one ACE were twice as likely to attempt suicide, and those who experienced six or more ACEs were 24 times more likely to attempt suicide. These trends held for depression and drug and alcohol use. For example, people experiencing six or more ACEs were approximately 4 times more likely to use drugs and nearly 3 times more likely to engage in problematic or heavy drinking (Merrick et al., 2017). These childhood and adolescent experiences of trauma and neglect seem to set the stage for how people relate to others, make choices, take risks, and care for themselves and others. The complexities of personal traumatic upbringing become more complex when we consider the impact

Sidebar 8.1 • Assisting Abused Children

> Children like Esteban struggle with abuse on several fronts, and they have a difficult time living with the traumatic fallout that can ensue. If you were Esteban's counselor when he was in middle school, what would you consider most vital to support Esteban?

of historical and cultural traumas with biological susceptibilities to addiction and mental health issues (National Institute on Drug Abuse, 2018). Therefore, a holistic method is needed to assess and provide counseling interventions for youth and adults who experienced serious adversity in their history. Beyond the 10 domains evaluated in the ACEs studies, we are keenly aware that bullying, racism, interpersonal violence, witnessing violence among other family members, accidents, and other traumatic injuries represent serious adverse events, and we honor the pain and grief associated with all forms of loss.

Developmental Trauma Disorder (DTD): A Proposal

To honor the reality of multiple childhood traumas and their profound effects on a child's quality of life, a team of researchers reviewed the copious studies available on childhood trauma (Spinazzola et al., 2005; van der Kolk, 2014). What they found was that many traumatized children often received diagnoses that reflected outward manifestations of their inner painful experiences. These children would be diagnosed with multiple disorders that often did not accurately reflect the truth of their histories. They were medicated and treated on the basis of labels such as oppositional defiant, mood dysregulation, and attention-related disorders (van der Kolk, 2014). van der Kolk (2014) contended that these behavioral diagnoses disregard the true experiences and issues that lie at the root of a child's pain— multiple and often complex traumas.

van der Kolk and colleagues at the National Child Traumatic Stress Network (2009) advocated for a new diagnostic category titled *developmental trauma disorder* (DTD). The proposed criteria for DTD included exposure to (a) multiple or chronic adverse events, (b) affective and physiological dysregulation, (c) self- and relational dysregulation, (d) experiences of some posttraumatic stress disorder (PTSD) symptoms, and (e) impairments in life domains (van der Kolk et al., 2009). This proposal was rejected by the American Psychiatric Association, and DTD was not included in the *Diagnostic and Statistical Manual of Mental Disorders* (5th ed.; *DSM-5*; American Psychiatric Association, 2013). The *DSM-5* work group reported that DTD research did not substantiate enough evidence related to this proposed diagnosis (van der Kolk, 2014) and that more studies were needed focusing on biological and genetic markers, predispositional factors, and the environmental causes of DTD (van der Kolk, 2014). As cited in van der Kolk (2014), the American Psychiatric Association rejected the DTD proposal because "the notion that early childhood adverse experiences lead to substantial disruptions is more clinical intuition than a research-based fact" (p. 148).

As counselors working with people referred to counseling for any number of reasons, our focus and compassion surrounding developmental traumas can help explain seemingly maladaptive behaviors and help us focus on underlying experiences. We can explore how relational and controlling images (Jordan, 2018) keep people from connection and authenticity, and then we can create the space to honor, grieve, and grow. People form their *relational images* from their experiences. These relational images can influence people's expectations for how others will treat them, and they can inform how people expect others will behave. *Controlling images*, however, are societal expectations based on cultural and social norms that can be oppressive. For example, some people expect women to be fragile and men to be strong. These expectations can be generalized to personal relationships, which can result in both men and women feeling unseen. As we bear witness to clients' stories, we see how our fundamental need for attachment can be twisted, dismissed, and torn through various forms of abuse and neglect.

Childhood Physical Abuse

Esteban never considered himself to be a person who was abused as a child until he was sitting in a presentation on abuse in high school. As the presenter shared stories of abuse, definitions, and looked on with compassion, Esteban felt a cold panic rise in him. He wanted to scream. He wanted to cry. He felt pasty and sweaty and desperately wanted to run out of the room. These powerful feelings were confusing and seemingly unconnected to any coherent thoughts. He just felt them, strongly, and did not know why in that moment. He had become adept at not feeling, and his recent explorations into smoking weed removed him more from a lonely reality. He distracted himself from the stories and worked furiously to keep his face stoic and blank. From news and social media sites, he learned of stories of horrendous abuses, torture, and sexual assaults. He heard rumors in school of students with rageful fathers who beat them regularly. This was not his life, but somehow this presentation was reorienting him in a dizzying way. Maybe he had been hurt. He skipped the rest of the day at school and got high in the woods alone. He still could not shake these feelings.

The Child Welfare Information Gateway (2019b) defined *physical abuse* as

> a nonaccidental physical injury to a child caused by a parent, caregiver, or other person responsible for a child and can include punching, beating, kicking, biting, shaking, throwing, stabbing, choking, hitting (with a hand, stick, strap, or other object), burning, or otherwise causing physical harm. (p. 3)

In 2017, approximately 674,000 children experienced abuse or neglect in the United States (U.S. Department of Health and Human Services [USDHHS], Administration for Children and Families [ACF], Administration on Children, Youth and Families [ACYF], & Children's Bureau [CB], 2019). The youngest suffer the most frequent abuse. In 2017, 70% of the children killed by their abusers were younger than 3 years old (USDHHS, ACF, ACYF, & CB, 2019). These children were innocent souls thrust into a world of violence and neglect. Their cries for comfort, connection, and nourishment were silenced through starvation and brutal torture. This abuse is happening today as you read this passage. A young child lives on the frayed edges of survival in a bitter merciless world where they are bound to savagery and death. There will be no one there to help them. We must do better to protect them. The effects of child physical abuse are well documented, and physically maltreated children experience the direct effects of their physical wounds as well as long-term physical, social, and psychological consequences (Child Welfare Information Gateway, 2019a) through no fault of their own.

Child Sexual Abuse (CSA)

The memories snapped Esteban awake. Flashes of J.R. and the knife. And then more memories. The images came in waves, and Esteban laid in bed frozen in his pain and alone. He told himself he would never tell anyone and tried to shake the thoughts from his head. The National Child Traumatic Stress Network (n.d.) defined *child sexual abuse* (CSA) as "any interaction between a child and an adult (or another child) in which the child is used for the sexual stimulation of the perpetrator or an observer. CSA can include both touching and non-touching behaviors" (para 1). This definition speaks to the dehumanizing effects of these violations.

According to reports of CSA to protective services, more than 63,000 children experienced sexual abuse in 2017, and most of the abuses were committed by someone the child knew (USDHHS, ACF, ACYF, & CB, 2019). Given the potential of underreporting CSA, these statistics may be modest approximations. Children and adolescents may share their story with friends (48%), adults (24%), and rarely (12%) the authorities (Lahtinen, Laitila, Korkman, & Ellonen, 2018). Like other forms of interpersonal developmental trauma, CSA can leave powerful controlling and relational images in people's minds, shaping their strategies (see Chapter 2) to stay safe in future relationships.

To explore the impact of CSA, Finkelhor and Browne (1985) developed the *traumagenic dynamics* model to highlight how CSA can shape a person's experience of themselves and the world. People may carry feelings of betrayal, powerlessness, traumatic sexuality, and self-blame throughout their life (Finkelhor & Browne, 1985). Researchers confirmed these factors as predictors of anxiety, depression, and low self-esteem among adults who experienced CSA (Cantón-Cortés, Cortés, & Cantón, 2012). These themes centered around how people respond to power, experience sexuality, and carry blame for experiences in which they were blameless. They shape the contours of relational connections, self-compassion, and safety. As Esteban remembered his experiences, he felt deep shame, especially because he continued to stay in contact with J.R. However, he avoided any circumstances in which they could be alone. Later in counseling, he would recount how that day felt like a turning point, in which the seeds of his depression began to sprout into the canopy of darkness that followed him throughout high school.

Childhood Emotional Abuse and Neglect

Emotional and psychological abuse can take many forms. Children who are emotionally abused live in situations in which they are regularly deprived of love and support (USDHHS, ACF, ACYF, & CB, 2019). They may be repeatedly demeaned, spurned, belittled, and criticized by caregivers (Child Welfare Information Gateway, 2019a, 2019b; Royse, 2016). These interpersonal and relational assaults leave no physical scars or bruises, and they can be difficult to prove to outside observers (Royse, 2016). What they do create are relational images that can lead people into condemned isolation (Jordan, 2018)—spaces where individuals protect themselves from the intentional assaults of not mattering. Children learn to negotiate their caregiver's repudiations of their worth, make sense of psychological manipulations, and endure the seclusion of chronic disconnection (Jordan, 2018; Royse, 2016). Emotional abuse in the home may also keep youth from disclosing other forms of CSA (Lahtinen et al., 2018), which may lead to carrying polytraumatic experiences throughout life. As children learn to function within in the pain of an emotionally abusive family, they may experience heightened daily anxieties in adulthood, suffer from more physical ailments, and experience poorer health (Weltz, Armeli, Ford, & Tennen, 2016).

Neglect of children differs in some ways from emotional abuse. The Child Welfare Information Gateway (2019b) defined *child neglect* as "the failure of a parent or other caregiver to provide for a child's basic needs" (p. 1.). Perhaps, the intentionality behind withholding care by caregivers may help differentiate emotional abuse from neglect. Neglectful parents may simply not care, be absorbed in their own addictions, or lack the resources to provide attention to their children. By contrast, emotionally abusive caregivers may be more active in their inflictions. Therefore, children can experience both emotional abuse and neglect. Examples of child neglect include the failure of parents to (a) attend to medical concerns, (b) provide basic necessities, (c) attend to psychological needs, and (d) ignore educational (including special educational) concerns (Child Welfare Information Gateway, 2019b). Parental neglect also includes allowing children to use alcohol or drugs in the household, and guardians may abandon their children by disappearing for periods of time while not providing adequate support and resources for their child's care and safety (Child Welfare Information Gateway, 2019b). Neglected children experience disconnections and live with the mental health repercussions of their relationally barren upbringings (Child Welfare Information Gateway, 2019a). See Sidebar 8.2 for information on dissociation and abuse.

Sexual Assault in Adulthood

The prevalence of sexual assaults, which involves egregious and unwanted acts of sexual violence, is astounding. Recent data show that every 92 seconds another American is assaulted (Rape, Abuse, and Incest National Network [RAINN], 2019b). These statistics, however, are understated because a majority of these assaults go unreported (U.S. Department of Justice, Office of Justice Programs, Bureau of Justice Statistics, 2017). Several factors contribute to this pattern of underreporting, with the effects of rape culture being a leading concern (Marshall University Women's Center, n.d.). This cultural travesty involves the normalization of violence against women, exacerbated by media accounts and popular culture (Marshall University Women's Center, n.d.). Perpetuated by societal objectification of women, misogynistic attitudes and language, and media portrayal of violence against women, this culture diminishes the perceived value of all women and makes women vulnerable to assaults on their rights and safety (Marshall University Women's Center, n.d.).

Sidebar 8.2 • Dissociation and Abuse

A prevalent concern with emotional abuse, neglect, and physical abuse is that a child or adult may feel unsafe or unable to connect with others following the trauma and may feel vulnerable with a counselor. In fact, a child may engage in several strategies of disconnection that create a safe distance from their counselor. A relationally attuned counselor respects these strategies and, in the words of relational-cultural theory, views them as strategies for survival. If you were the counselor, how would you honor these strategies while also supporting movement and connection in your relationship?

Rape Culture

As we discussed in Chapter 3, social forces, community mores, and unexamined assumptions for normative behaviors constrain people's worldviews. Recalling that Snell, Rosenwald, and Robey (1964) explained domestic violence as a healthy expression of sexuality and a cathartic experience for both partners, we see how narratives of power and control dismiss brutally painful experiences. When we examine our current culture, we challenge the boundaries of our own social norms, especially when it comes to advocating for people who have been sexually assaulted. Consider the definition of *rape culture* endorsed by the Marshall University Women's Center (n.d.):

> Rape Culture is an environment in which rape is prevalent and in which sexual violence against women is normalized and excused in the media and popular culture. Rape culture is perpetuated through the use of misogynistic language, the objectification of women's bodies, and the glamorization of sexual violence, thereby creating a society that disregards women's rights and safety. (para. 1)

One need only consider the recent Supreme Court hearings involving Justice Brett Kavanaugh (Berenson, 2019). Across the United States, families were fractured in their discussions on whether to believe Dr. Christine Blasey Ford or then–U.S. District Judge Brett Kavanaugh. When Dr. Ford testified about her experiences, she faced political and legal powers intent on dismantling the facts and veracity of her narrative. The courage it takes for a person who was assaulted to share their story requires that they revisit the traumatic moments etched in their memory, which are much more vivid than the mundane daily experiences few of us remember. This is a function of people's normal neurobiology (van der Kolk, 2014).

Unless it was a special occasion, or something happened to you that was memorable, you probably cannot recall what you had for lunch 7 years ago on this day. People's brains simply do not place heightened significance on remembering routine events, but individuals do often remember traumas as flashes of vivid imagery and associated bodily sensations (van der Kolk, 2014). This is a reason why testimony about sexual assault can feel formidable. People may not remember many specific details of events before the trauma because they were routine, and then their posttrauma memory formations may be affected by toxic cortisol levels and dissociation (van der Kolk, 2014). When others dismantle and negate a vivid and true experience of sexual assault because of vague ancillary details, people can experience a retraumatization and have their stories silenced through power-over dynamics. Consider how common rape myths can sustain dehumanizing worldviews that play out in relationships, courts of law, and society.

Another cultural myth is that men and boys do not experience sexual assault and abuse. Like Esteban, 17% of men, or one in every six, experienced this kind of abuse or assault before age 18 (1in6.org, 2019). Although rates vary among research studies, the effects of sexual abuse and assault for men are complicated by societal and gendered expectations for men and boys who similarly experience distress and trauma (Peterson, Voller, Polusny, & Murdoch, 2011). Gendered myths for men and boys center on (a) being able to stay tough and strong—that real men are not vulnerable; (b) that they may have enjoyed the act, especially if the perpetrator was female; (c) that their perpetrators were gay; and (d) that they will go on to perpetrate acts of sexual aggression themselves (1in6.org, 2019). The societal expectations for men can limit their help-seeking behavior and compound feelings of shame (Peterson et al., 2011). For a boy who was sexually abused, these messages can feel hurtful and lead to increased isolation, especially when gendered stereotypes keep them locked in isolation (for more resources on rape myths, see Marshall University Women's Center, n.d.).

Intimate Partner Sexual Violence

When committed in close relationships, sexual assault is known as *intimate partner sexual violence* (RAINN, 2019a). This form of aggression often accompanies other abuses, including emotional, physical, and psychological torment that often begins with controlling behaviors from a partner (RAINN, 2019a). At other times, perpetrators may be acquaintances or ex-partners (U.S. Department of Justice, Office of Justice Programs, Bureau of Justice Statistics, 2017). Finally, strangers account for another category of violent abusers (RAINN, 2019b; U.S. Department of Justice, Office of Justice Programs, Bureau of Justice Statistics, 2017).

In those cases in which perpetrators are known to those whom they violate and betray (RAINN, 2019b; U.S. Department of Justice, Office of Justice Programs, Bureau of Justice Statistics, 2017), a series of behaviors generally precede the violations. These behaviors include (a) restricting access to social supports, work, school, and family; (b) insulting their partner's worth and value; (c) reacting with jealousy when a partner leaves; (d) making physical threats and damaging property; and (e) controlling decision making related to major shared responsibilities and finances (RAINN, 2019a). These power-over (Jordan, 2018) behaviors include real threats to a person's physical and emotional safety and become even more complex when children are involved (see Chapter 10 for a discussion on interpersonal violence).

Older Adulthood

Older adulthood can carry memories of a lifetime, and as the last stage in Erikson's (1982) stages of development, it can also bring into sharper focus a sense of one's mortality. Retirement, the death of a loved one or the loss of close friends, and the transition out of familiar roles and social contexts all contribute to this reflection and period of reminiscence. Erikson described this reminiscence as particularly productive when conducted with others, and he viewed this period as an opportunity to reconcile life journeys, make peace with the past, and celebrate life's successes. However, when people feel a sense of failure at this stage—or when societal stressors, injustices, or microinvalidations arise that lead them to isolate and experience regrets—they may feel a particularly painful sense of loss, often accompanied by depression, bitterness, and despair (Goodcase & Love, 2017). Older adults experiencing mistreatment or self-neglect are at particular risk for isolation, depression, and feelings of despondency. Vulnerable and understudied, older adults can bring great wisdom, experience, and knowledge to their families and communities, and they can also be recipients of inhumane abuse and neglect.

Hannah is a 94-year-old woman with big bright eyes and a contagious smile. She entered my (Thelma's) office with her daughter Isabel (age 66). Hannah stared at me with an intent look and said, "We need help!" I soon learned the backstory on Hannah and Isabel's relationship, and the pain in both mother and daughter was palpable. "Isabel tries to be the boss of me," Hannah exclaimed, as Isabel looked on with frustration. Whereas Isabel had long attempted to convince Hannah to move to an independent living facility, Hannah resisted. "This is my home. I want to live here."

Although Hannah tried to do basic things around the house, Isabel worried when she would go down the sidewalk to get the mail or walk down the steps to the pool area. Isabel thought Hannah was stubborn and reckless, and Hannah thought Isabel was controlling and micromanaging. At one point, Hannah looked toward me and said, "Isabel is running my life! She is ruining it! She is mean to my caretaker, who is my friend, and she is driving my friends away." Isabel looked on with exasperation and cried, "I don't trust these caretakers and new 'friends.' Her jewelry is disappearing, I don't think Mom is being taken care of well. I don't think she has had a bath in days, and she is so stubborn, she just won't see how she is being manipulated. I don't think they are looking out for her in the way that she thinks they are."

Hannah continues, "I need Marissa [caretaker], and you have always tried to take my friends away. Why do you do that? Are you jealous of me? Billy [the gardener] said I am pretty, and I think he likes me. Who says I can't have another relationship? I may be older, but I am not dead." Isabel tries to bite her tongue, recalling the years she was estranged from her mother after she abandoned her and her siblings to be with another man. Hannah and Isabel are struggling with historical hurts, Hannah's life stage challenges, and the dynamics between them.

Life transitions to older age can be marked by a mixture of joyful memories, poignant experiences, ongoing losses, and—often—changes in health and physical strength. Several risk factors threaten a person's successful navigation of this important stage in life, making them exposed to neglect and abuse. In Hannah's case, Marissa and Billy both proved to be predators, and although Isabel was able to remove Billy as a threat, doing so with Marissa proved more challenging.

In spite of Isabel's pain over her mother's earlier treatment of her siblings and her, she loves her mother and wants to protect her. An avid reader, she is aware of the physical, sexual, emotional, and financial abuse that older adults can experience at the hands of unscrupulous caretakers, and she wants to protect Hannah from this treatment. The research indicates that family members who stay connected to these situations can help avert them from danger (DiNapoli, Scogin, Bryant, Sebastian, & Mundy, 2016; LaRocca & Scogin, 2015). Isabel feels impatient with Hannah but wants to do right by her. When Hannah's belongings began to disappear, and Isabel learned she was "giving" them to her caretaker, Isabel reported the situation.

As one would expect, Hannah became furious when she was forced to have a new caretaker and felt helpless to have agency over her own life. She barely spoke to Isabel, whom she blamed for the transition. Soon thereafter, though, Hannah's spirit lifted, much to Isabel's relief. What Isabel did not know was that Marissa continued to visit Hannah during those times she was alone, and Hannah felt consoled having her "friend" there. Before long, Isabel noticed that treasured family pieces were missing, the spending money Hannah had available to her for incidentals was depleted, and there were sudden withdrawals from Hannah's bank account. Isabel was able to ascertain that Marissa was responsible for these thefts, and Hannah became confused and felt betrayed by both.

Researchers speak to the financial exploitation inflicted on older adults. Theft, fraud, real estate and email scams, and shady investments are all means by which caretakers can take advantage of vulnerable older adults (Forman & McBride, 2010). Isabel paid Hannah's bills, but Hannah was a signatory on her account, making Marissa's manipulation possible. Isabel was perplexed by these financial abuses and Hannah's protectiveness of Marissa. Even more so, she was horrified by Hannah's continued poor hygiene and the ways in which both caretakers neglected her vulnerable mother. Moreover, she was hurt and frustrated by her mother's attempts to blame Isabel for these abuses.

Hannah, however, felt more competent than she was and, in her attempt to maintain her independence, placed herself at risk when she would walk down a pebbled path to the mailbox or when she would walk independently down the treacherous stairs leading to the pool area. She was self-neglectful in her grooming and, ultimately, in her nutrition. Although Hannah died following a brief illness unrelated to neglect or abuse, she did struggle in her attempts to live a full life with limitations that felt life taking. Hannah had a daughter that attended to her care, and even then, it was a challenge to navigate the independence versus safety and health factors involved in older adulthood. Imagine those situations in which family is not involved and in which compassionate care is not provided by caretakers and other medical staff. Crises and traumatic experiences in older adulthood can be particularly devastating, not only because of the vulnerability of those affected but also because of what these assaults ultimately represent. Our hope is that older adults will approach the end of their lives with self-respect and an awareness and appreciation of their ultimate mattering.

Challenges in Older Adulthood

Having purpose, taking part in opportunities for engagement, and enjoying social outlets are means through which older adults can continue to use their gifts and enjoy their ongoing well-being (DiNapoli et al., 2016; LaRocca & Scogin, 2015). These are also deterrents to experiencing self-neglect, which is a formidable threat to the welfare of older adults (MacLeod & Douthit, 2015). Research indicates that family involvement and social support are primary deterrents to neglect, abuse, and self-neglect (DiNapoli et al., 2016; LaRocca & Scogin, 2015). These deterrents were more easily seen in previous generations, when many families lived close to one another. Mobility is now such that families must be creative in supporting older family members who live at a distance. For example, Clyde, age 89, is an active and independent gentleman living alone hundreds of miles from his children. His world has narrowed in recent years, with the loss of his partner and beloved dogs; in addition, the volunteer work he did for decades in his town was eliminated as a need, and Clyde found himself "out of work." Working in the yard and tending to his house have become integral components of Clyde's daily life.

Clyde's children are concerned now that his social and civic life are limited, particularly because he lives alone. They do follow him on Facebook, knowing he regularly shares music or other posts he finds interesting. This connection helps them know he is okay. They have also made it a point to visit more, and when they do, they reminisce, listen to music, play with Clyde's new shelter puppy, and watch old movies together. Clyde, of course, delights in these visits, and he enjoys when his friend, Abe, occasionally visits as well. They sit on the outside patio area they jokingly refer to as "their office" and have a beer and discuss politics and life. Clyde is one of the lucky ones who has family support, adequate health, and a history he feels good about. Still, he remains vulnerable to the challenges of old age and the losses that accrue over time.

Risks and Vulnerabilities in Older Adulthood

Risks of Abuse

Older adults can suffer isolation and lack of medical care, access to grooming, and emotional support (Forman & McBride, 2010). For example, in reflecting on the case of Hannah, we can see that, fearing abandonment, some people in Hannah's position prefer to deny wrongdoing than lose the person to whom they most feel connected. Family abandonment and caretaker neglect and abuse are often cited as contributing to the emotional and physical pain inflicted on older adults (Forman & McBride, 2010).

Older adults also suffer physical and sexual abuse at the hands of caretakers and family members. Moreover, when they also suffer from dementia and other forms of cognitive decline, the potential for abuse increases. Clearly, in addition to the satisfaction that older adults can reach in life reflection, the final life stages in human development can also bring physical decline, loneliness, and a host of medical issues that can alienate them from the larger world and their own reality. For example, when people suffer from dementia or depression, or when they abuse substances, they become more vulnerable to abuses of all kinds (MacLeod & Douthit, 2015).

In a recent news article, a dementia patient in a Tennessee nursing home who fractured her knees in a fall was not seen by a doctor for 9 excruciatingly painful days, in spite of her continued pleas for help (Kelman, 2018). She fell lifting herself out of her bed with a nurse present. In spite of her cries of feeling "intense pain" and the considerable swelling and bruising she sustained, the facility did not conduct an X-ray for 5 days. It took 4 additional days of her crying "please, please, please" for her to be seen by a doctor, who then referred her for knee surgery (Kelman, 2018). She died in the hospital 1 month later.

Imagine the desperation, anguish, helplessness, and terror of falling out of your bed, injuring yourself to the point where you can barely stand it, and knowing you are being ignored by those entrusted with your care. You are at the final stage in your life, and this is how you experience your sense of mattering, this is the dignity afforded you, and this is the way you draw your final breath. Counselors can join other helping professionals and caretakers in being alert to potential abuses and neglect of this important yet vulnerable population. Although specific criteria for older adult abuse are still in development, connecting with our humanity can attune us to these dangers. We do not need a check sheet or other diagnostic criteria to recognize a person in pain, and we can advocate for swift attention and action should these situations arise.

Just as the appreciation for older adults varies from reverence to complete disregard across countries and nationalities, families vary in their respect for and support of older adults. A counselor's care, compassion, advocacy, and education of others can all promote dignity and humane regard for people who, in many cases, paved the way for our opportunities and privileges. Attending to the needs of older adults to prevent abuse and neglect is an important social justice consideration, which both honors the lives of our predecessors and contributes to the developing culture of dignity and respect (Lindner, Hartling, & Spalthoff, 2011).

Risks to Self-Neglect

Another challenge to older adults is their own lack of capacity to care for themselves and the self-neglect that can occur. Lee, Burnett, Xia, Smith, and Dyer (2018) referred to *self-neglect* as "an inability or unwillingness to provide for oneself the good or services to meet basic needs" (p. 223). Among the risk factors involved in self-neglect are impaired cognitive, physical, and emotional functioning; medical disorders, such as dementia and depression; and refusal of care (Dong, Simon, & Evans, 2012). Older adults with impaired areas in the brain can experience apathy and distractibility; they can also fail to keep targeted goals (Dyer, Goodwin, Pickens-Pace, Burnett, & Kelly, 2007; Lee et al., 2018). In addition, they may experience mood shifts, irritability, and impaired decision making and insight (Lee et al., 2018).

Reaching old age can be considered a blessing not available to everyone. Indeed, life brings hardships and premature deaths to people of all ages every day. In that context, being an older adult and living an expansive life is seen as a privilege by many. There are other cases, however, in which older adulthood brings unfathomable crises and potentials for abuses. Neglect, self-neglect, and abuse are all potential risks for older adults. When counselors are in positions to identify, intervene, and advocate for people experiencing these crises and traumas, they contribute to changes that support the humane treatment of a generation to whom we owe so much.

Reporting Abuse and Neglect With Vulnerable Populations

Counselors are mandated in all 50 states and U.S. territories to report child abuse and neglect when they suspect these activities have occurred in the present and past, and reports and relevant information are often shared among social service and legal personnel (Child Welfare Information Gateway, 2016; Henderson, 2013). Most of the 4.1 million referrals made in 2017 came from educational professionals (19.4%) and law enforcement employees (18.4%); mental health workers referred approximately 5.7% of the calls to Child Protective Services (CPS) nationwide (USDHHS, ACF, ACYF, & CB, 2019).

When deciding to make a report (Henderson, 2013), counselors should consider the child's safety and immediately provide resources for protection when necessary. In my (Shane's) experience as a counselor and supervisor, reporting abuse can feel stressful. When we are not sure whether to move forward with a report, we should remember that we (a) do not have to prove abuse, only suspect it, and (b) consult as necessary and document this consultation (Henderson, 2013). Often, we contact our state CPS agency and consult with them about the case and seek their guidance. When we decide to report, it is essential to have as much factual information as possible. We provide names, dates, and addresses, and we share whether the child is in immediate danger and any other information relevant to the report.

After we make the report, CPS will investigate to determine the scope and evidence to support the allegations and frequently will follow up with you after you make your report (Child Welfare Information Gateway, 2016). In some cases, the police will become involved for the protection of the child and investigation of laws broken. At other times, CPS can coordinate social services to help meet the needs of a family. We describe an example of this kind of response in Chapter 15.

To hear the details of child maltreatment while maintaining a therapeutic relationship with a client and family and while facing the fear of your client possibly being hurt in the future may ignite feelings of stress, fear, and uncertainty about your next steps. Again, we suggest that you consult with your team and state protective services; you should also learn about reporting procedures in your state, because many laws do vary. You will need to report within a prescribed timeframe by state law, so it is essential that you move with expediency when these suspicions arise (Child Welfare Information Gateway, 2016).

The National Center on Elder Abuse offers resources and information for reporting suspected abuse for older adults and other adult vulnerable populations. Unlike most reporting procedures and agencies for reporting child maltreatment, adult protective services "can differ from state to state and even from county to county in terms of definitions, client eligibility requirements and standards of practice" (National Center on Elder Abuse, n.d., para. 2). You can access state reporting procedures at http://www.napsa-now.org/get-help/help-in-your-area/. Like the procedures for reporting child abuse and maltreatment, we gather pertinent details, seek consultation, and document our process. For older adults and people with disabilities related to dementia, self-care and institutional abuse may be present and would be helpful details to provide to investigators.

Factors and Approaches That Foster Hope and Healing

Like Esteban, some children experience *polyvictimization*, described by David Finkelhor, director of Crimes Against Children Research Center, University of New Hampshire, as experiencing abuses of various kinds (Finkelhor, Turner, Hamby, & Ormrod, 2011). Whether inflicted once or by numerous methods and over time, violence can have reeling effects on children and individuals of all ages, including developing posttraumatic stress disorder (PTSD). Thankfully, devastating experiences of neglect and assault do not define a person, and connecting with even one empathic person can begin a trajectory of healing. The brain's neuroplasticity, coupled with strong connections and support systems, can make a powerfully positive difference in the lives of people who experience trauma.

After a serious suicide attempt and several near-fatal overdoses on cocaine, Esteban reached out for help. He had a few friends who had been to treatment and were involved in recovery. At his first Narcotics Anonymous meeting, Esteban felt an unexpected and profound relief. Yalom (1995) discussed the pivotal therapeutic benefits of universality. Hearing other people share similar struggles and pain while they support one another in a group setting can break the binds of isolation. Group work offers the potential for connections out of loneliness. Because the nature of childhood maltreatment strikes at the foundations of safety and secure connections, individual, group, and family approaches build on mutually empathic (Jordan, 2018) and secure relational foundations.

Early Childhood Programs

Lawson and Quinn (2013) reviewed and evaluated evidence-based models to work with maltreated children, and these approaches can be categorized as interventions that strengthen child-parent bonds, alleviate PTSD symptoms, and help children cope with the range of intense feelings and behaviors that emerge from their complex traumas. For preschoolers, Lawson and Quinn reviewed three approaches. In *child-parent psychotherapy,* the counselor and family work together to strengthen the relationships through play, developing and sharing trauma narratives, and addressing thoughts and reactions to current life stressors worsened by traumatic memories. Likewise, partners from the National Child Traumatic Stress Network developed the *attachment, self-regulation, and competency model.*

The attachment, self-regulation, and competency model is a flexible approach that focuses on building connections and attachments as well as skills to manage and identify emotions, reactions, and intrusive and frightening memories. Parents learn empathic and relational attunement skills to stay connected with their children during times of distress (Lawson & Quinn, 2013). Finally, the *intergenerational trauma treatment model* covers elements of the treatments mentioned earlier, and it also focuses on helping parents address their own trauma histories as well as their secondary trauma resulting from the realities of their child's suffering. The aim of this approach is to help caregivers be present with their children when difficult stories and feelings arise (Lawson & Quinn, 2013).

Programs for Middle School Children and Adolescents

In later childhood and adolescence, trauma-focused cognitive behavioral therapy (TF-CBT) remains a well-documented approach to help youth reconcile the traumas in their life, learn calming techniques, explore and reconceptualize cognitions related to theirs traumas, and share details of the events in a compassionate setting while learning to regulate their autonomic reactions (Lawson & Quinn, 2013). In Chapter 6, we provide an example of TF-CBT in action. Likewise, cognitive behavioral intervention for trauma in schools (CBITS; Jaycox, Langley, & Hoover, 2018) follows many of the principles covered in TF-CBT but uses a group format. School-based mental health professionals can deliver this program during the school day. Because of the high attrition in individual TF-CBT, CBITS demonstrates higher levels of attendance and program completion (Jaycox et al., 2018).

CBITS also harnesses the curative factors found in group work (Yalom & Lesczc, 2005). According to Jaycox et al. (2018), when designing group settings, it may be beneficial to create specialty groups (e.g., a gender-homogeneous group for those who have been sexually assaulted). Although the effects of child maltreatment can seem daunting, we can develop safe and secure bonds with youth in individual and group settings, work with parents to develop their capacity for mutual empathy, and provide destigmatizing psychoeducation to help relieve the stresses and burdens of traumas that children face routinely.

Approaches for Adults and Older Populations

As we have explored in previous chapters, many adults benefit from the many evidence-based approaches for crisis and trauma work, including cognitive processing therapy, eye movement desensitization and reprocessing, creative interventions, and mind-body approaches. As we have emphasized throughout the text, we intentionally develop mutual empathic and compassionate counseling relationships and recognize and respect a person's culture and context in our work. See Sidebar 8.3 for information on understanding dissociation.

There is federal assistance for counselors and programs to create services for victims of violence and crime. The Victims of Crime Act of 1984 (VOCA) funds agencies to deliver free services to people affected by all forms of violence. To help agencies consider applying for funding, Equal Justice USA provides a toolkit (https://ejusa.org/wp-content/uploads/EJUSA-VOCA-Toolkit-updated-Jan-2017.pdf). After the mass shooting in Sutherland Springs, Texas, we partnered with several regionally agencies and applied for VOCA funding. As a result, we were able to offer a wide range of free services for people of all ages suffering from the effects of violence. In Chapter 11, we outline our process for developing and establishing VOCA-funded services.

In responding to sexual assault, we can follow the crisis response approaches shared in Chapter 5. Chakaryan (2018) applied these principles in a model for responding to the crisis of a sexual assault. Specific adaptations of the basic crisis response approaches included (a) asking whether a person needs immediate medical attention and then providing information about what may happen in the emergency room, (b) providing information about forensic exams and important timeframes to follow, (c) assessing ongoing threats from the perpetrator and discussing the factors involved in restraining orders and police involvement, (d) determining whether a mandated report needs to occur (i.e., child, older adult, and people with a disability reporting as well as Title IX reporting requirements), and (e) determining relevant social resources for immediate and long-term support.

Case Example and Applications for Hope and Healing

Hannah and Isabel were able to come to an understanding that was marginally healing for them both. Their disconnection ran deep and spanned decades, yet their love for one another was strong. Although Isabel shared her feelings over her early childhood injuries and feelings of abandonment, this topic was not the focus of their family counseling. Instead, she engaged in individual work and was able to connect with those feelings and honor the young girl who assumed such a large responsibility at such an early age.

Part of Isabel's struggles with her mother in later life centered on her need to intervene and become involved in ways that Hannah did not want. Isabel was able to see how her involvement and care for others were lifelong patterns that

Sidebar 8.3 • Understanding Dissociation

People may dissociate during and after they have experienced deplorable traumas. A person in a dissociated state may appear catatonic or out of touch with reality. Relationally competent counselors recognize that when people dissociate, their brain is responding naturally to protect themselves from becoming overwhelmed.

came from caring for her younger sisters and her father. She saw how some of her actions could be considered controlling, yet she was able to honor her investment in the welfare of those she loved and understood she had been a scared little girl who wanted everyone to be safe. Hannah's health declined steadily soon after these sessions, but she maintained her spirited ways. She did not ever fully or consistently understand that her caretaker had manipulated and stolen from her and continued to long for their time together after the abuses were discovered. Hannah died at home following a short illness at 96 years of age, with Isabel by her side.

Future Directions and Emerging Research

Linda Hartling and Evelin Lindner have advocated for a world that embodies dignity and the cessation of humiliation through their work with the Human Dignity and Humiliation Studies (e.g., Lindner et al., 2011), which is discussed in detail in Chapter 15. Jeremy Richman and Jennifer Hensel are cofounders of the Avielle Foundation organized to study brain health through research and education on violence and compassion following the death of their 6-year-old daughter, Avielle, in the 2012 Sandy Hook Elementary School shootings. Both groups are dedicated to building global compassion and creating a world where violence is eradicated. In addition, the Human Connectome Project (http://www.humanconnectomeproject.org) engages in trailblazing research to map the brain and explore neural interconnectivity.

As this chapter reflects, abuse, violence, neglect, and harassment occur in the lives of people throughout the life span. For that reason, research that explores brain health and those practices that support building and sustaining communities of compassion seem salient. This research is timely and may offer new approaches in working with people who experience trauma—and those who perpetrate destructive and life-changing acts of violence.

References

American Psychiatric Association. (2013). *Diagnostic and statistical manual of mental disorders* (5th ed.). Arlington, VA: Author.

Berenson, T. (2019, June 28). Inside Brett Kavanaugh's first term on the Supreme Court. *TIME*. Retrieved from https://time.com/longform/brett-kavanaugh-supreme-court-first-term/

Cantón-Cortés, D., Cortés, M., & Cantón, J. (2012). The role of traumagenic dynamics on the psychological adjustment of survivors of child sexual abuse. *European Journal of Developmental Psychology, 9*(6), 1–16.

Centers for Disease Control and Prevention. (2019). *Preventing adverse childhood experiences.* Retrieved from https://www.cdc.gov/violenceprevention/childabuseandneglect/acestudy/aboutace.html

Chakaryan, H. (2018, July 10). Effective ways to approach sexual assault response. *Counseling Today.* Retrieved from https://ct.counseling.org/2018/07/effective-ways-to-approach-sexual-assault-response/

Child Welfare Information Gateway. (2016). *Cross-reporting among responders to child abuse and neglect.* Washington, DC: U.S. Department of Health and Human Services, Children's Bureau.

Child Welfare Information Gateway. (2019a). *Long-term consequences of child abuse and neglect.* Washington, DC: U.S. Department of Health and Human Services, Administration for Children and Families, Children's Bureau.

Child Welfare Information Gateway. (2019b). *What is child abuse and neglect? Recognizing the signs and symptoms.* Washington, DC: U.S. Department of Health and Human Services, Administration for Children and Families, Children's Bureau.

DiNapoli, E. A., Scogin, F., Bryant, A. N., Sebastian, S., & Mundy, M. J. (2016). Effect of individualized social activities on quality of life among older adults with mild to moderate cognitive impairment in a geriatric psychiatry facility. *Aging and Mental Health, 20,* 262–270. https://doi.org/10.1080/13607863.2015.1008990

Dong, X., Simon, M. A., & Evans, D. (2012). Elder self-neglect and hospitalization: Findings from the Chicago Health and Aging Project. *Journal of the American Geriatrics Society, 60,* 202–209. https://doi.org/10.1111/j.1532-5415.2011.03821.x

Dyer, C. B., Goodwin, J. S., Pickens-Pace, S., Burnett, J., & Kelly, P. A. (2007). Self-neglect among the elderly: A model based on more than 500 patients seen by a geriatric medicine team. *American Journal of Public Health, 97,* 1671–1676. https://doi.org/10.2105/AJPH.2006.097113

Erikson, E. H . (1982). *The life cycle completed.* New York, NY: Norton.

Federal Bureau of Investigation. (2017). *Crime in the United States, 2016.* Washington, DC: Author.

Felitti, V. J., Anda, R. F., Nordenberg, D., Williamson, D. F., Spitz, A. M., Edwards, V., . . . Marks, J. S. (1998). Relationship of childhood abuse and household dysfunction to many of the leading causes of death in adults: The Adverse Childhood Experiences (ACE) study. *American Journal of Preventive Medicine, 14,* 245–258.

Finkelhor, D., & Browne, A. (1985). The traumatic impact of child sexual abuse: A conceptualization. *American Journal of Orthopsychiatry, 55,* 530–541.

Finkelhor, D., Turner, H., Hamby, S., & Ormrod, R. (2011, October). Polyvictimization: Children's exposure to multiple types of violence, crime, and abuse. *Juvenile Justice Bulletin.* Retrieved from https://www.ncjrs.gov/pdffiles1/ojjdp/235504.pdf

Forman, J. M., & McBride, R. G. (2010). Counselors' role in preventing abuse of older adults: Clinical, ethical, and legal considerations. *Adultspan Journal, 9,* 4–13. https://doi.org/10.1002/j.2161-0029.2010.tb00067.x

Goodcase, E., & Love, H. (2017). From despair to integrity: Using narrative therapy for older individuals in Erikson's last stage of identity development. *Clinical Social Work Journal, 45,* 354–363. https://doi.org/10.1007/s10615-016-0601-6

Henderson, K. (2013). Mandated reporting of child abuse: Considerations and guidelines for mental health counselors. *Journal of Mental Health Counseling, 35,* 296–309.

Jaycox, L. H., Langley, A. K., & Hoover, S. (2018). *Cognitive behavioral intervention for trauma in schools (CBITS)* (2nd ed.). Santa Monica, CA: RAND Corporation.

Jordan, J. V. (2018). *Relational–cultural therapy* (2nd ed.). Washington, DC: American Psychological Association.

Kelman, B. (2018, August 1). New patients barred at Knoxville nursing home after woman with broken knees left in agony for 9 days. *Knox News.* Retrieved from https://www.knoxnews.com/story/news/2018/07/30/knoxville-elder-abuse-nursing-home-westmoreland/866232002/

Lahtinen, H., Laitila, A., Korkman, J., & Ellonen, N. (2018). Children's disclosures of sexual abuse in a population-based sample. *Child Abuse and Neglect, 76,* 84–94.

LaRocca, M. A., & Scogin, F. R. (2015). The effect of social support on quality of life in older adults receiving cognitive behavioral therapy. *Clinical Gerontologist, 38,* 131–148. https://doi.org/10.1080/07317115.2014.990598

Lawson, D. M., & Quinn, J. (2013). Complex trauma in children and adolescents: Evidence-based practice in clinical settings. *Journal of Clinical Psychology, 69,* 497–509. https://doi.org/10.1002/jclp.21990

Lee, J. L., Burnett, J., Xia, R., Smith, S. M., & Dyer, C. B. (2018). Feasibility of intervention in elder self-neglecters: Setting the stage for future research. *Journal of Elder Abuse and Neglect, 30,* 223–235. https://doi.org/10.1080/08946566.2018.1450172

Lindner, E., Hartling, L., & Spalthoff, U. (2011). Human dignity and humiliation studies: A global network advancing dignity through dialogue. *Policy Futures in Education, 9*(1), 66–73. https://doi.org/10.2304/pfie.2011.9.1.66

MacLeod, M. Z., & Douthit, K. Z. (2015). Etiology and management of elder self-neglect. *Adultspan Journal, 14,* 11–23. https://doi.org/10.1002/j.2161-0029.2015.00033.x

Marshall University Women's Center. (n.d.). *Rape culture.* Retrieved from https://www.marshall.edu/wcenter/sexual-assault/rape-culture/

Merrick, M. T., Ports, K. A., Ford, D. C., Afifi, T. O., Gershoff, E. T., & Grogan-Kaylor, A. (2017). Unpacking the impact of adverse childhood experiences on adult mental health. *Child Abuse and Neglect, 69,* 10–19.

National Center on Elder Abuse. (n.d.). *Adult protective services, what you must know.* Retrieved from https://ncea.acl.gov/NCEA/media/Publications/APS-Fact-Sheet.pdf

National Child Traumatic Stress Network. (n.d.). *Sexual abuse.* Retrieved from https://www.nctsn.org/what-is-child-trauma/trauma-types/sexual-abuse

National Institute on Drug Abuse. (2018). *Comorbidity: Substance use disorders and other mental illnesses.* Retrieved from https://www.drugabuse.gov/publications/drugfacts/comorbidity-substance-use-disorders-other-mental-illnesses

1in6.org. (2019). *Myths and facts about male sexual abuse and assault.* Retrieved from https://1in6.org/get-information/myths/

Peterson, Z. D., Voller, E. K., Polusny, A. A., & Murdoch, M. (2011). Prevalence and consequences of adult sexual assault of men: Review of empirical findings and state of the literature. *Clinical Psychology Review, 31,* 1–24.

Rape, Abuse, and Incest National Network. (2019a). *Intimate partner sexual violence.* Retrieved from https://rainn.org/articles/intimate-partner-sexual-violence

Rape, Abuse, and Incest National Network. (2019b). *Sexual assault.* Retrieved July from https://www.rainn.org/articles/sexual-assault

Royse, D. (2016). *Emotional abuse of children: Essential information.* New York, NY: Routledge.

Snell, J. E., Rosenwald, R. J., & Robey, A. (1964). The wifebeater's wife: A study of family interaction. *Archives of General Psychiatry, 11,* 107–112. https://doi.org/10.1001/archpsyc.1964.01720260001001

Spinazzola, J., Ford, J. D., Zucker, M., van der Kolk, B. A., Silva, S., Smith, S. F., & Blaustein, M. (2005). Survey evaluates complex trauma exposure, outcome, and intervention among children and adolescents. *Psychiatric Annals, 35,* 433–439.

U.S. Department of Health and Human Services, Administration for Children and Families, Administration on Children, Youth and Families, & Children's Bureau. (2019). *Child maltreatment 2017.* Retrieved from https://www.acf.hhs.gov/sites/default/files/cb/cm2017.pdf

U.S. Department of Justice, Office of Justice Programs, Bureau of Justice Statistics. (2017). *National crime victimization survey, 2010–2016.* Washington, DC: Author.

van der Kolk, B. A. (2014). *The body keeps the score: Brain, mind, and body in the healing of trauma.* New York, NY: Viking.

van der Kolk, B. A., Pynoos, R. S., Cicchetti, D., Cloitre, M., D'Andrea, W., Ford, J. D., . . . Teicher, M. (2009, February 1). *Proposal to include a developmental trauma disorder diagnosis for children and adolescents in DSM-V.* Retrieved from http://www.traumacenter.org/announcements/DTD_papers_Oct_09.pdf

Victims of Crime Act of 1984, H.R. 6403. Retrieved from https://www.congress.gov/bill/98th-congress/house-bill/6403

Weltz, S. M., Armeli, S., Ford, J. D., & Tennen, H. (2016). A daily process examination of the relationship between childhood trauma and stress-reactivity. *Child Abuse and Neglect, 60,* 1–9.

Yalom, I. D. (1995). *The theory and practice of group psychotherapy* (4th ed.). New York, NY: Basic Books.

Yalom, I., & Lesczc, M. (2005). *The theory and practice of group psychotherapy* (5th ed.). New York, NY: Basic Books.

Multiple-Choice Questions

1. According to the chapter, why may counselors want to be aware of using the word "victim"?
   a. The word may imply weakness
   b. This is a term only used by lawyers
   c. A counselor is trained not to use this word
   d. None of the above

2. How many definitions exists for child sexual abuse (CSA)?
   a. 5
   b. Around 100
   c. Numerous, because they differ from state to state
   d. 1, the federal definition

3. All CSA involves direct touch.
   a. False, but other forms are not as bad
   b. True, because this is nationally agreed on
   c. False, some acts include non-touch
   d. True, because otherwise it is a different form of abuse

4. Using a relationally attuned lens in your conceptualization, what is (are) a potentially protective factor(s) for a child?
   a. Support and family
   b. Family and chaotic environment
   c. Invalidating peers, because this builds character
   d. Learning autonomy early on

5. There is one CSA assessment used by all professions called the
   a. CSA national assessment.
   b. Abuse assessment.
   c. Sexual childhood abuse assessment.
   d. None of the above

6. According to the text, a close counseling process with a child who experienced trauma may include
   a. Fun.
   b. Neurofeedback.
   c. Moving in and out of connection.
   d. None of the above

7. Polyvictimization involves
   a. More than one child.
   b. More than one type of abuse.
   c. More than one kind of race and culture.
   d. All of the above

8. Emotional abuse is often found alongside _____ abuse.
   a. Most other forms of
   b. Sexual
   c. Physical
   d. Psychological

9. There are _____ types of child maltreatment.
   a. 2
   b. 20
   c. 4
   d. 7

10. What type of trauma is passed down through the cycle of abuse?
    a. Ecological
    b. Generational
    c. Addiction
    d. Only complex PTSD

11. What kind of parenting can confuse a child?
    a. Perfect
    b. Quality
    c. Inconsistent
    d. None of the above

12. Which is not a form of older adult abuse?
    a. Neglect
    b. Financial exploitation
    c. Disconnection
    d. Self-neglect

13. According to the text, which can be a sign of sexual abuse in older adults?
    a. Bruises
    b. Sleeping
    c. Friendship
    d. Eating

14. When did PTSD begin to be located in the "trauma and stressor-related disorders" and not the "anxiety disorders" category in the *DSM*?
    a. 2007
    b. 2000
    c. 2018
    d. 2013

15. Around _____ of people experience a traumatic event during their lifetime.
    a. 40%
    b. 20%
    c. 70%
    d. 90%

Essay Questions

1. Sexual abuse is often formally reported more often than emotional abuse. The text states this could be due to a lack of self-reporting. As a relationally ethical and engaged counselor, how would you empower your adult client to report abuse while still respecting their ambivalence about making a report?

2. Older adults experience several anticipated losses as they advance in age. Some older adults are victimized by caretakers and may be vulnerable to protect themselves. How can counselors support their older clients and advocate for their safety?

3. Many people experience trauma at some point during their life. As a counselor or counselor-in-training, how do you envision yourself using therapies such as cognitive processing therapy (CPT) or eye movement desensitization and reprocessing (EMDR)?

4. Prolonged exposure therapy asks clients to stay with their trauma in the present moment and emotionally connect with their experiences. What do you see as the pros and cons to this intervention?

5. Research varies on the effect of child sexual abuse (CSA) on a child's development. What are some ways in which a relationally engaged counselor may work with adults who suffered abuse in childhood?

CHAPTER 9

Developmental, Transitional, and Situational Crises Throughout the Life Span

Shane Haberstroh, Katherine A. Feather, and Madelyn Duffey

As we explored in previous chapters, catastrophic events arise in the lives of people every day. Counselors trained in trauma-informed approaches and equipped with basic disaster mental health and crisis counseling tools can work to provide compassionate care and connect people with needed resources. Other times, people seek counseling when situations exceed their trusted and familiar ways of coping and living life (James & Gilliland, 2017). Throughout the life span, people experience many stressors that invade their lives with toxic stress and uncertainty but do not rise to the threshold for a posttraumatic stress disorder (PTSD) diagnosis.

Chronic mental or physical issues, disorienting life events, expected and unexpected losses, developmental and identity transitions, new situations, and illnesses and role stressors can wear down people's capacity to cope. Expected life transitions may feel bittersweet, and unexpected events can shake individuals deeply. As people mature, families, friends, and communities also grow and change, and not all change is growth oriented. Sometimes groups, people, and loved ones seem to devolve into chaos. However, although crises and transitions can leave people shaken, they can also serve as a point of reflection and beginning of personal growth.

The Relational Foundation: Integrative Perspectives

People do not develop well in isolation, disenfranchisement, and disconnection (Jordan, 2018). Attuned counselors emphasize a relational core at the heart of human development. When clients encounter troubling times, the quality of their relationships can either mitigate their pain or exacerbate their situations, and the therapeutic relationship can serve as a strong and reliable alliance. In fact, voluminous research supports the power of the counseling relationship (Wampold & Imel, 2015), reporting that the quality of the relationship, as experienced by clients, is the most powerful predictor of growth (Wampold & Imel, 2015). Research indicates that the healing relational qualities in counseling supersede technical approaches and serve as the foundation for many manualized treatments (Wampold & Imel, 2015). Given the primacy of our therapeutic connections, our relational intentionality and clarity shape the experience of the counseling relationship and process for us and our clients.

Integrative Considerations

When working with people who face new life roles, stressful life events, and abrupt planned and unplanned changes, counselors integrate relational principles and practices, grief models, trauma work, and crisis counseling approaches to conceptualize losses in context and to harness shared creativity to inspire some practical solutions. Within this chapter, we explore relational processes, integrative frameworks, and practices that guide our understanding of life crises and transitions.

Relational Process

The experience of *mutual empathy* (Jordan, 2018) demonstrates our understanding of a person in their context. Knowing you really matter to another human being can break the bonds of exclusion and private suffering. As we discussed in Chapter 3, microinvalidations accentuate differences and further alienate people from one another. As counselors, we may partner with people who have more social privilege than we do. Alternatively, we may work with others whose social location mirrors ours, and we may also connect with people who endure a life of scarcity and oppression. As counselors, our ethical principles place our clients' welfare first (American Counseling Association, 2014), and we should invest the energy to understand a person's world and pain as they experience it.

A Life and Identity in Context

Destabilizing life events occur within work, family, and broader social contexts. Within all social strata and systems, constellations of power, privilege, oppression, and rejection exist and cause distress and isolation. By example, many people commit suicide who seem successful (Centers for Disease Control and Prevention [CDC], 2018), and numerous deaths by suicide seemingly have no clear precursor. Moreover, a significant number of people commit suicide when faced with life crises and relational strife (CDC, 2018). These statistics speak to the miseries people experience, how seeming success does not protect individuals from the deepest pain, and how shame and the pains of life can seem unsurmountable. In other words, a person's pain, confusion, and anxieties make sense in their context.

Perspectives on Loss

Theories of grief chart life experiences during and after losses. When conceptualizing chronic and transitional life stresses, we consider how people move between the sharp anguish of their loss and living a new and unknown life. The dual process model (Stroebe & Schut, 2010) of grief work highlights the untidiness of change. Individuals may find themselves feeling sorrow one moment, hope in the next, and confusion in between. This process normalizes and validates the seemingly chaotic feelings around transitions and stressors and stands in contrast to messages people receive that urge them to move on or get over their situation and feelings. These messages ignore the fact that people's losses are part of their stories. People often live with pangs of loss while charting a new life framed by their memories and experiences. See Sidebar 9.1 for more information on the grief process.

Mobilizing Resources

A life crisis is a new territory where people can feel lost and alone. People can be stretched beyond the strategies and relationships that sustained and comforted them through many other life experiences. Given that crises upend familiar ways of being in the world, prepared counselors can help clients chart a new life course and explore valuable information and connections within the community. As counselors, we stay abreast of community resources and network with partners in the community who offer specialized services. We develop resources and explore groups that provide financial planning, employment support, medical practice, and legal issues. For example, when we worked to develop the Sutherland Springs coordinated response grant after the mass shooting, we partnered with multiple agencies, law enforcement, legal services, schools, and social service agencies to support people dealing with their trauma but also the exacerbated and interrelated stress that emerged. When we develop community partnerships and share accurate and helpful information for clients, we can help customize their map to navigate the stresses and confusions of this new territory.

Crises of Identity Development

Developmental transitions, growing self-awareness, social pressures, and stressful events can strike the heart of people's identity. As people learn about who they are, their awareness is influenced by societal expectations, their demographic and cultural backgrounds, and interactions with the world. Developmental crises occur throughout life, and many traditional developmental theories often describe human growth in a linear or task-oriented manner. From these perspectives, identity crises may result from failing to meet developmental milestones, unsuccessful self-individuation, or dissolution of ego strength (Jordan, 2018).

The notion that people's identity is multifaceted and a convergence of many factors (Gemignani & Hernández-Albújar, 2019) highlights that their sense of who

Sidebar 9.1 • Grief Process

The grief process used to be viewed as a linear process, and people were believed to move through each step before they could get to the next. Although grief can follow this process, current literature talks about how grief is different for everyone and does not always follow a certain path. Have you ever experienced grief or a big change? Did you ever feel like you took two steps forward and one back?

they are grows from an intersection of roles, cultural influences, power positions, earned and unearned privileges, and their own unique histories. Although an intersectional identity speaks to a person's diversity and uniqueness, we are acutely aware that many people experience subtle and overt forms of racism, bullying, oppression, and stigmatization, especially when they appear different or experience shame in their social circles.

People's multiple identities are vibrant expressions of their whole personhood. Intersecting identities or intersectionality signifies the interrelated nature of social classifications such as race, ethnicity, class, nationality, gender, sexual orientation, religion, age, and disability as they apply to an individual or group, as well as how people with privileged and stigmatized identities experience these interconnecting systems (Ching, Lee, Chen, So, & Williams, 2018). Counselors help clients recognize, as well as label, everyday psychological distress stemming from systemic, rather than personal, flaws and encourage clients to embrace their connection with others to build resilience against oppression (Ching et al., 2018).

Ultimately, the work of counselors is to appreciate clients' multifaceted intersections and contexts; integrate our knowledge into crisis response care; and work to dismantle forms of oppression at the individual, community, and societal level. All of the transitions and situations we highlight in this chapter speak to life and role stressors that entangle themselves in role expectations and personal and social identities, potentially leading to feelings of isolation and chronic anguish.

Childhood and Developmental Stressors in a Family Context

"I'm afraid the thing that is broken in me is also broken in him," Rick said as he told the story of his 10-year-old son, Jacob, who was being bullied at school. Jacob's parents felt helpless as they watched their son withdraw into himself after being sent to the office repeatedly for throwing his classwork in the garbage in frustration. "It's like he has crumpled in on himself," his mom, Jeanne, shared. "Maybe it's us? Maybe he can sense somehow what's going on. He won't tell us anything." As they spoke more about their circumstances, they shared a story of multiple and compounded life crises. As they watched their son wither, met with school administrators who responded with legalese instead of compassion, and felt their own emptiness and fears blossom, they had to also navigate several personal and familial losses. A week after they decided to separate, Jeanne's physician referred her to an oncologist.

Considering this situation from a relational perspective, we consider Jacob's social context. We explore how he may be experiencing power abuses at school. We discover his experiences with peer and teacher relationships. We validate that when he reaches out to his parents, even in the smallest ways, he is showing relational resilience. We also move from the idea that something is broken within Jacob and Rick to exploring disconnections, power in context, and isolation as our primary focus.

Watching a child suffer is heartbreaking. It can leave us feeling lonely, frustrated, and powerless. Recent data from the National Center for Education Statistics (2019) indicated that nearly 7 million children receive special education services in the United States. These numbers do not account for the estimated 20% of young children who also suffer from a mental health issue such as depression or anxiety. Frequently, children who struggle with mental health issues do not receive adequate services (Whitney & Peterson, 2019). As schools continue to budget to deliver adequate programming, families and children may miss much needed services and begin to lose hope.

The cumulative impact of early adverse childhood experiences often leads traumatized children to be diagnosed with multiple and often inaccurate diagnoses. Researchers at the National Child Traumatic Stress Network conducted several studies (van der Kolk, 2014) related to the impact of multiple childhood traumatic stresses. They concluded that a vast majority of children in their studies experienced multiple traumas, and many of them did not reach the threshold for PTSD for any one event (van der Kolk, 2014).

A team of researchers and clinicians sought to include developmental trauma disorder (DTD) in the *Diagnostic and Statistical Manual of Mental Disorders* (5th ed.; *DSM-5*; American Psychiatric Association, 2013); however, the *DSM* review team rejected the proposal for inclusion (van der Kolk, 2014). The move to include DTD as a diagnostic category represents an epistemological shift in the view of trauma-related disorders to a social malady rather than a dysfunction within a person. That is, DTD would be drastically reduced by the elimination of social contexts that foster child abuse, assault, chronic maltreatment, poverty, bullying, and the many faces of neglect. Developmental traumas can influence a person's growth by limiting their experience of nurturing relationships and growth-oriented relational bonds (D. J. Siegel, 2012).

Parenting Children With Disabilities: A New "Normal"

The added demands of raising a child with a disability is a source of significant stress and can shift the foundation of the whole family (Dabrowska & Pisula, 2010; Guralnick, Neville, Hammond, & Connor, 2008). As parents learn that they will not be raising a neurotypical child, they may experience stress adapting to their new and unexpected roles. Such adjustments include coping with disappointment, guilt, uncertainty, and grief (Neely, Amatea, Echevarria-Doan, & Tannen, 2012; Sheehan & Guerin, 2018). It is important to note that painful feelings can decrease with time, but grief can be triggered by both internal and external factors. Triggers are often related to developmental milestones (e.g., starting school, graduation). These situations resurrect feelings of loss that occurred when their child was first diagnosed. When these milestones occur, caregivers may be faced with the difference between their imagined or hoped for future while facing the realities of loving a child with a different ability.

Many parents strive to create supportive and nurturing environments for their family and child, but many are never told how. The joys and challenges of parenting a child with a different ability can be stressful because of the complex needs of the child and caregivers. Families who receive little instruction on how to best meet their responsibilities face an increased risk for psychosocial distress and physical health problems (Resch, Benz, & Elliott, 2012). Fortunately, counselors can work with parents through these times, sharing the burdens and helping the family learn practical strategies for living (Hohlfeld, Harty, & Engel, 2018). However, before addressing psychoeducation and skills training, we build trusting relationships with the parents (Sheehan & Guerin, 2018). Counselors play a dynamic role in supporting parents of children with different abilities and promoting greater life satisfaction. Some helpful recommendations for counselors working with this population are presented next.

Parent Education

Caregivers understand their child's physical, social, developmental, and family history better than anyone else and are respected and valuable partners in the counseling process. Counselors offer information specific to parenting a child with specific needs as well as the accurate facts about disability, validate and normalize the adjustment process, and offer linkages to resources in the community. Counselors appreciate how language can disempower and humanize the child and their family. For example, counselors need to avoid disempowering terminology, "Your autistic, handicapped child," and instead use more empowering language (i.e., use the child's name; say "people with disabilities, different abilities"; or ask how people wish to identify themselves), honoring the idea that a disability is only one aspect of a person's identity. Finally, we educate and support parents, helping them develop their assertive communication and advocacy skills, which may serve them in many situations (e.g., pre-K–12 school systems, medical practices, and within their community).

Skills Training

Early intervention and skills training set the foundation to build on a child's potentials for developmental, social, and functional growth (Hohlfeld et al., 2018). We teach parents techniques and skills and connect them with helping specialists in their community. For example, Stepping Stones Triple P (Positive Parenting Program) is a leading prevention program that supports parents with children with disabilities by providing skills and principles to help parents cope with behavioral and emotional upheavals (Ruane & Carr, 2019). This program also educates parents on how to (a) adopt an assertive approach to discipline, (b) adapt to the reality of their child's disability, (c) establish realistic expectations about the development of their child, (d) link children in in a shared community, and (e) practice effective self-care (Ruane & Carr, 2019). For an exhaustive summary of marriage, couples, and family counseling interventions for autism spectrum disorder (ASD), see Feather (2016).

Parent Environmental and Social Support

Counselors share resources and connect parents with services in the community and tailor social services for children. Parents who join with social supports reported higher levels of well-being, and they appreciated the tools and shared resources provided by people facing common concerns (Hohlfeld et al., 2018). Parental well-being and family adaptation is tied to social connections, in which individuals in the network offer emotional support and provide experiences and solutions about various problems (Guralnick et al., 2008; Resch et al., 2012). I (Katherine) have found through my conversations and research with mothers of children with ASD that they often treasured the connections with others who understood their situation. These mothers felt relieved because they were no longer alone and could express their experiences with another parent. See Sidebar 9.2 for more information on parent education.

Parent Well-Being

When people manage the many routine stresses of parenthood, coupled with the unique stressors facing parents of a child with disability, wellness may dwindle because of the nature of these circumstances. Given that these stresses may settle into a family's life permanently, the chronic stress can take its toll. Isolation may increase as a function of their many roles and responsibilities. Parents' needs for nurturance, self-compassion, and connection may not be met because of the sundry associated tasks (Dabrowska & Pisula, 2010). Parents who share in a community of support gain access to helpful information and services and often experience higher levels of overall well-being (Resch et al., 2012). Therefore, counselors develop resources and information to reduce distress and increase parent well-being. Practical efforts and social connections reduce systemic distress and can support the family and child as they navigate developmental milestones and potential behavioral issues; these connections also provide parents with meaningful support (Guralnick et al., 2008).

Additional Stressors During Parenthood

Adjusting to Parenthood

Nguyen always wanted to be a mother. Her husband, Eric, was less enthusiastic about the prospect of parenthood. Although Eric was open to the idea of having a child, he could not imagine having one anytime soon. He worried about undertaking the responsibility of a new life and the lifestyle changes that come with children. After discussing the possibility of adding to their family for 2 years, Nguyen and Eric decided to move forward. Pregnancy proved difficult, but the couple conceived through in vitro fertilization. Despite Eric's initial hesitancy, he was an attentive partner, and the two prepared for the arrival of their new baby, Amelia, as a team. He and Nguyen decided that she would stay home until Amelia began primary school.

Although Nguyen expected a difficult labor, and acknowledged hers as being painful, she described her labor as otherwise uneventful. After dreaming of being

Sidebar 9.2 • Parent Education

Throughout this chapter, we include resources for individuals wanting more information about parent education and parent well-being. Creative outlets may also help families express their experiences and strengthen their connections with each other. Some examples of these activities include dancing, gymnastics, team sports, music, and painting. These outlets could connect a child with other children through creative expression, and the parent could also connect with other parents sharing similar experiences.

a mother for years, Nguyen was hopeful that she would find joy in her new role. Much to her surprise, although there were moments of joy in new parenthood, and she loved Amelia fiercely, she struggled considerably. Nguyen had difficulty breastfeeding and felt criticized when she decided to stop. Lack of sleep severely affected her mood and lucidity. Eric also struggled with sleep, and the two began to argue frequently. Nguyen also realized that she was quicker to anger with her friends, and she often felt overwhelmed by small tasks. Little things she used to take for granted, such as time alone and moments of silence, seemed like part of her past. A meticulous researcher and planner, Nguyen expected many of these struggles. What caught her off guard most was a powerful sense of loss, anger, and isolation. Nguyen had fought to be a mother, so why did she still dream of her old life? Every life stage can bring a mixture of feelings, and parenthood is no exception. Becoming a parent is a massive transition in many people's lives. This was the case for Nguyen. Even though she desperately wanted and loved her child, adjusting to motherhood was turbulent.

Parents who eagerly anticipate the birth of their newborn may feel a mixed sense of joy and loss after the baby's arrival. These sentiments are not always societally understood, and new parents can feel pressured, and even judged, when they communicate frustration and discomfort. New parents accustomed to pleasing others or presenting well in public may hide these struggles. Relational-cultural theory describes this form of hiding as antithetic to authenticity (Jordan, 2018). In relational-cultural theory terms, authenticity relates to being able to represent oneself fully and freely (Jordan, 2018). Therefore, hiding, which is opposite to authenticity, may create a crisis of meaning and belonging for new parents. New parents like Nguyen may love their babies deeply and also profoundly miss their friends, activities, and—as Nguyen indicated—"the quiet stillness" she once took for granted.

Like Nguyen, new parents may feel shame over their developmentally appropriate, yet socially invalidated, emotions, and they may keep these feelings to themselves. Doing so increases their chances of isolation. In addition, financial stressors may also exacerbate parents' adjustment to parenthood. Although parents may be overjoyed by a recent birth, they may also feel particularly stressed and conflicted when economic challenges arise. In some families, a tenuous medical history may prompt parental concerns with the anticipated birth of a child, and they may feel alarmed and fearful over their child's future physical or emotional health. In those cases in which the pregnancy was not expected, the prospect of parenthood can be perplexing. For parents who suffer a traumatic childbirth, these adjustments can be particularly challenging.

Traumatic Childbirth

Caroline and her husband, Stewart, celebrated their eighth wedding anniversary by painting a nursery in preparation for the birth of their first child. The couple met as student athletes in college, and after years of building their careers and nurturing their relationship, they yearned to begin growing their family. Caroline had cut off communication with her mother 3 years before her son's, Caleb's, birth, following decades of verbal and emotional abuse. More than anything, Caroline wanted to create a loving and happy home. She was excited but anxious about giving birth, especially after the doctor informed her that the child would be large.

Five weeks before her scheduled due date, Stewart rushed Caroline, who was in severe pain, to the hospital. Caroline experienced several serious complications during labor, including hemorrhaging and maternal sepsis. Shortly after giving birth, she began experiencing frightening panic attacks. Multiple factors added to Caroline's postpartum distress. She was estranged from her mother and grieved maternal support and guidance. As an athlete, Caroline prided herself on her physical strength and ability to control her body. Her birth experience, and the ensuing physical and emotional trauma, was chaotic and frightening. Caroline felt disconnected, disempowered, and betrayed by her body. The anxiety and panic attacks made it hard for Caroline to be the mother she had envisioned herself to be, and she felt lost coping with the trauma of delivery. Although experiences like Caroline's are not unique, they are sometimes obfuscated by happier narratives of "successful" childbirth. If both mother and child made it through delivery, shouldn't everyone feel relieved and fortunate? See Sidebar 9.3 for more information on disconnection after childbirth.

Pregnancy and childbirth can lead to several mental health concerns (Chartier et al., 2015). These concerns are particularly salient when parents view the birth as having been physically or emotionally traumatic (Inglis, Sharman, & Reed, 2016). Studies have shown that 1%–6% of women develop PTSD after giving birth (Alcorn, O'Donovan, Patrick, Creedy, & Devilly, 2010). The perception of negative emotions and distress during childbirth and obstetrical emergencies are among the highest predicting factors for a mother to develop PTSD (Anderson, Melvaer, Videbech, Lamont, & Joergensen, 2012). Because perceived distress is inherently subjective, it is important for counselors and other medical and mental health professionals to listen to a mother recount her own experience during childbirth rather than projecting their own beliefs, opinions, or values on her. It is important that counselors recognize how lonely, isolating, and confusing these experiences can be and respond to their clients in ways that foster connection, help them make sense of their confusion, and let them know they are not alone in the experience.

Nguyen and Caroline's stories differ in several respects, yet they share salient commonalities. Both women were overjoyed at the prospect of parenting, and they dearly loved their babies. Both were financially secure and, by both accounts, knew their privilege in being parents of healthy children. However, this awareness only increased their loneliness, panic, and feelings of guilt.

Even when people seem to "have it all," no one is immune to the stress and the small and large crises that life transitions bring. Counselors attuned to these dynamics recognize the varied cultural, familial, and logistical expectations new

Sidebar 9.3 • Disconnection After Childbirth

Caroline felt a sense of disconnection from her body after giving birth. Social media depicts how wonderful being a mother is, and although this may be true, the process of becoming a mother is a different journey for every woman. Feeling disconnected from her body, Caroline may benefit from a loving-kindness meditation or slow-moving exercises when she feels ready. These activities could include tai chi or yoga. What are your thoughts on this?

parents may have placed on themselves and the real challenges that can come with life-changing transitions, such as new parenthood. Counselors can create a space where clients can share their genuine feelings and experiences, and they can support them as they navigate these adjustments. They can also guide new parents in finding ways to connect with the people and activities they enjoy and to develop their self-compassion. Transitions can be critical times in the lives of many people, and self-compassion can counter.

Stress and Loss in the Workplace

Sexual Harassment

Sexual harassment is a major concern for people in the workplace and within school and university settings. Although this term was coined to describe male treatment of women, it now encompasses both genders in its application (R. Siegel, 2012) and includes unwanted verbal and sexual advances in the workplace. Sexual harassment can be a confusing experience for subordinates or people with less power. It can occur in the workplace, at university settings, and in any setting where there is a power differential. It is viewed by the U.S. government as a form of discrimination and stands in direct violation of Title VII of the Civil Rights Act of 1964 (U.S. Equal Employment Opportunity Commission [EEOC], 2019b).

The EEOC (2019a) has posited that any

> unwelcome sexual advances, requests for sexual favors, and other verbal or physical conduct of a sexual nature constitute sexual harassment when this conduct explicitly or implicitly affects an individual's employment, unreasonably interferes with an individual's work performance, or creates an intimidating, hostile, or offensive work environment. (para. 2)

This policy acknowledges the full range of dynamics that can constitute harassment, and it stipulates that the means by which harassment occurs can be both direct and indirect. Complaints can be filed by any person who is affected by the behaviors, even if he or she is not directly harassed (EEOC, 2019a).

Quid pro quo is one common example of harassment (Mellon, 2013). For example, a supervisor might say, "you will have this opportunity if you give me this form of sexual gratification." It can also be communicated as "you will not have this raise if you do not do that for me." The EEOC (2019a) is clear, however, that it is not necessary for these two conditions to be present for harassment to exist. Sexual harassment can be a deeply isolating and confusing experience. Counselors working with clients who undergo this violation can offer education, support, and advocacy.

Job Loss

Growing up, Richard always knew he wanted to make a comfortable living, although he never had a clear vision of how to do so. There were not many opportunities in his neighborhood, and his parents juggled multiple unsatisfying jobs to make ends meet. Richard's big break came when his uncle helped him get a job as a bell hop in an independent boutique hotel he worked at across town. Richard found that he enjoyed working with hotel guests. The guests loved Richard, and management took note. Over the next 26 years, Richard worked in several different departments within the hotel. He was eventually promoted to management. Richard considered getting a degree in hospitality management now that he was more financially secure but felt that it was too late for him to go back to school. The hotel had become Richard's second home, and the staff like his second family. Two days after Christmas, Richard received word that the hotel was closing. At age 45, Richard had only been on one job interview, which he secured through family. He was terrified at the thought of not being hired or having to take a lower position because he did not have a degree. Most of all, Richard was heartbroken at the thought of leaving the place, and the people, that he had grown to love.

Job loss is often pervasive and adversely affects personal and physical well-being. Specifically, job loss negatively affects life satisfaction, mental health, and life domains (i.e., financial and relationship strain, poorer health and quality of life, diminished identity and self-esteem; Synard & Gazzola, 2019). Research illustrates the link between unemployment and mental health concerns, such as depression, somatization, anxiety, and substance use (Bluestein, Kozan, & Connors-Kellgren, 2013). We also note there are positive effects of job loss, which include personal growth following adversity, greater self-awareness, new career paths and exploration, and improved relationships (Waters & Strauss, 2016). According to Bluestein et al. (2013), there is an emotional continuum of job loss: On one end, individuals can experience unemployment as "the bottom falling out" (i.e., distraught, traumatized, angry), and on the other end, there is a mixed response to unemployment, characterized by a sense of loss but opportunities for growth. The ways in which people cope with job loss and unemployment are complex because of individual (e.g., psychological protective and risk factors), social (e.g., proximal relational resources, one's intersecting identity), economic (e.g., financial resources), and political (e.g., policies, governmental support) factors, which have a profound impact and shape the experiences of unemployed people (Bluestein et al., 2013).

After the shock of a job loss, we help people develop positive daily routines (i.e., cognitive and behavioral adaptation responses to the loss), and we explore past coping and resilience strategies (Synard & Gazzola, 2019). Also, we nurture and explore a person's strengths and curiosity in their new and potentially unstable life (Synard & Gazzola, 2019). We may consider reframing unemployment and encourage supportive and realistic optimism during periods of joblessness to lessen some of the stress (Bluestein et al., 2013). The change process can be enhanced through a counselor's positivity; however, a mutually empathic relationship, and true compassionate understanding, creates a partnership where we can consider new opportunities that may unfold over time (Synard & Gazzola, 2019). Most important when it comes to unemployment, we coordinate community-based services and assist with unemployment benefits, which may buffer financial hardship and, ultimately, psychological stress (Bluestein et al., 2013). We also explore the many career counseling tools available to us and our clients to help gain clarity on values, strengths, and potential pathways for new training or job opportunities (https://www.onetonline.org/).

Physical Challenges and Rehabilitation

Adults and children differ in development and maturity, and people in all age groups may face other developmental and medical issues. Young children, people living with developmental disabilities, and those with medical needs may be more susceptible during sudden destabilizations. Notably, people with a disability are more likely to experience sexual assaults. For example, about 50% of young boys and girls who are deaf report being sexually assaulted, and these numbers are drastically higher than those of their nondeaf counterparts (Center on Victimization and Safety, 2015). Counselors seek to especially address any physical, structural, or social needs to consistency and linkages to medical and specialized services when needed (American Red Cross, 2012).

Disabling conditions and chronic illness affect the lives of about 53 million adults who experience physical, sensory, psychiatric, or cognitive disabilities (CDC, 2018; Courtney-Long et al., 2015). Individuals with disabling conditions and chronic illness face physical and psychological crises, increased stress, experiences of loss and grief, as well as changes to their body image and self-concept; they also experience stigma and uncertainty in their life (Livneh & Antonak, 2005). Adjustment to a disability is an essential part of the rehabilitation counseling process (Stuntzner, 2017).

The process of adjustment is nonlinear, with possible setbacks, new medical issues, and increased distress when adverse events occur. Through these ups and down, counselors foster compassion and encourage self-compassion for people enduring these difficult times (Stuntzner, 2017). Strategies to strengthen self-compassion can include meditation (e.g., loving-kindness) as well as practicing compassion and self-compassion (for an overview of the eclectic theoretical counseling approach, see Stuntzner, 2017). As people negotiate their new identities and debilitating experiences, they may benefit from counseling relationships focused on gaining new and realistic perspectives of their situations (Livneh, 2015). Livneh and Antonak (2005) summarized comprehensive interventions developed for clients with chronic illness and disabling conditions. They recommended that counselors should (a) assist with the exploration of the personal meaning of their condition (i.e., processing feelings of loss and grief), (b) provide relevant medical information (i.e., prognosis; functional and vocational implications), (c) encourage supportive family and group services (i.e., educational, psychotherapeutic, coping skills training groups), and (d) teach adaptive coping strategies for community functioning (i.e., assertiveness; interpersonal, decision-making, and stigma management skills).

Transitions and Stressors in Later Adulthood

Empty Nest

A bustling household becomes eerily quiet when the seemingly endless school days, rushing to extracurricular activities, celebratory moments, and holidays end and a new exciting chapter begins in a family's life. When children leave home for the world of work or even college, parents have to start their new chapter and may experience *empty nest syndrome*. The empty nest phenomenon is a time of crisis when the absence of their child creates a vacuum of interactions, responsibilities, and routines. Empty nesters may even feel directionless, lonely, and lost as they adjust to life without being a steady caregiver. Stresses related to marital discord may materialize when children leave the home because the parent-child relationship often served as a buffer between the couple (Gold, 2013). Apart from the children, a life together as a couple can seem foreign, as changing parental roles may lead to an intense renegotiation of the marriage (Gold, 2013).

Filling the relational void when children leave home while coping with the prevailing feelings of loss and identity may inform the counseling process. Counselors consider how grief and the loss related to a parent's identity lead to redefinitions of roles and interests. Counselors partner with empty nesters to engage in self-discovery and consider new friendships outside of the child-rearing role. Connecting parents to a support group can link parents with others to feel validated, supported, and connected. If there is marital discord present with empty-nest couples, the couple works to develop a new partner-focused versus child-focused marriage (for a summary of eight tasks of a couples' counselor when working with empty nesters, see Gold, 2013). Counselors facilitate reconnection through developing shared meaning (i.e., rituals, roles, goals, and symbols) and intimacy, so couples can continue on the new journey together (Beaty, 2016).

Retirement

As the CDC (2017) reported, Americans who work full time spend one third of their day in the workplace 5 days a week. Because people spend a considerable amount of time in the world of work, their career becomes a part of their identity and self-concept (Froidevaux, Hirschi, & Wang, 2016). The loss of the work role can bring new identities and roles as a person transitions from work life to retirement. In retirement, the loss of income, social contact, status, daily structure, and purposeful activity can create a social and vocational vacuum (Damman, Henkens, & Kalmign, 2015). One of the major life transitions in late adult life is retirement. However, there are inconsistent findings when it comes to retirement and adjustment. Some studies have reported lower life satisfaction and happiness, greater depression and loneliness, lower activity levels, partial identity disruption, and even death anxiety for retirees, whereas other studies have reported that people look forward to retirement and have overall satisfaction with retirement (Osborne, 2012; Wang, Henkens, & van Solinge, 2011).

The disengagement from work life may involve adjusting to the loss of the work role and the development of the meaningful postretirement lifestyle (Osborne, 2012). When it comes to developing a postretirement lifestyle, counselors assist people with establishing meaningful activities, interests, and recreations that replace the void of work (Osborne, 2012). As a person prepares for retirement, Froidevaux et al. (2016) recommended retirees face questions about how to still feel useful through mattering and meaning, reflecting on how they will continue to make a difference in the world. Wang et al. (2011) suggested connecting retirees to social and emotional resources to support their adjustment.

Factors, Approaches, and Interventions That Foster Healing and Resiliency

As we discussed in this chapter, working with people who contend with major and often chronic crisis situations involves nurturing social connections in the counseling process and within the communities where people live. Incorporating tenets of crisis counseling models, we become knowledgeable about community resources, and we link people with supportive contexts and people who share similar struggles. We recognize the toll that the life crises take as well as how isolation and dismissiveness can deepen a person's misery. By contrast, counselors can fully engage with and appreciate what these events mean to people in their context and work together to strengthen relational and social bonds. We also provide tangible resources, links to community supports, and a commitment to working with people throughout tumultuous times.

Amarah was referred to me (Katherine) by her primary care physician, who shared concern about Amarah's stress and overall well-being. Amarah recently confirmed that her son, Sam, was diagnosed with ASD, and she was living in a world where that diagnosis made some sense, but she was filled with deep sadness and fear for her son's future. Amarah shared that, since receiving the diagnosis, she and her wife have distanced themselves from each other. Amarah stated, "Our marriage has really taken a turn for the worse."

In our first meeting, Amarah shared, "I feel so terrible. I love my son so much, but I can't shake these thoughts and even feelings that I wish he did not have autism. I hate it. and I love him so, so much." Amarah imagined how her beautiful son would face future tormentors and would struggle with communicating his experiences. She felt hopeless, angry, alone, and tired. She could not see how she would have the strength to "do this every day for the rest of our lives."

The importance of nurturing relational resilience and cultivating social connections with Amarah could help break her from the loneliness borne from her stressful and isolating context. I also considered how Amarah felt the sharp pangs of grief for herself and her family—that, because of some twist of medical fate, the bright and exciting future she envisioned for her son and family seemed tarnished with the specter of this new unknown territory. She did not know where to turn. We spent time exploring her feelings of loss and considered resources that could provide some immediate relief and support. In our conversations, we validated her grief and explored permission to care for herself and her family, asking for help when she needed it. We began planning for her first support group meeting. Amarah felt a mix of trepidation, relief, and excitement to attend the meeting.

Future Directions and Emerging Research

In Chapter 15, we discuss the work of the Human Dignity and Humiliation Studies organization as a framework for social action and compassionate change. Given that many people lack access to mental health and social support, future directions for social change include enhancing our social service delivery system. A movement exists toward integrated mental health, addiction, and physical care (Ratzliff, 2016). However, these models are deeply embedded in the medical traditions and can be driven by diagnoses and the provision of short-term solutions. Moving toward the future, we encourage the expansion of integrated systems to include readily available and well-funded counseling and social services that promote dignity and long-term relationships within the community. The current integrated care models may be the first step, and efforts to advocate for the work of counselors to fully serve people regardless of income, diagnoses, and social status are needed.

References

Alcorn, K. L., O'Donovan, A., Patrick, J. C., Creedy, D., & Devilly, G. L. (2010). A prospective longitudinal study of the prevalence of post-traumatic stress disorder resulting from childbirth events. *Psychological Medicine, 40,* 1849–1859.

American Counseling Association. (2014). *ACA code of ethics.* Alexandria, VA: Author.

American Psychiatric Association. (2013). *Diagnostic and statistical manual of mental disorders* (5th ed.). Arlington, VA: Author.

American Red Cross. (2012). *Disaster mental health handbook: Disaster services.* Washington, DC: Author.

Anderson, L. B., Melvaer, L. B., Videbech, P., Lamont, R. F., & Joergensen, J. S. (2012). Risk factors for developing post-traumatic stress disorder following childbirth: A systemic review. *Acta Obstetricia et Gynecologica Scandinavica, 91,* 1261–1272.

Beaty, J. (2016, October 28). *How to rescue your marriage from empty nest syndrome.* Retrieved from https://www.gottman.com/blog/rescue-marriage-empty-nest-syndrome/

Bluestein, D. L., Kozan, S., & Connors-Kellgren, A. (2013). Unemployment and underemployment: A narrative analysis about loss. *Journal of Vocational Behavior, 82,* 256–265.

Center on Victimization and Safety. (2015, November 12). *Measuring capacity to serve survivors with disabilities: Performance indicators.* Retrieved from https://www.endabusepwd.org/publications/performance-indicators/

Centers for Disease Control and Prevention. (2017, February 2). *Workplace health promotion: How CDC supports a healthy, competitive workforce.* Retrieved from https://www.cdc.gov/chronicdisease/resources/publications/aag/workplace-health.htm

Centers for Disease Control and Prevention. (2018, June 7). *Suicide rates rising across the U.S.* [Press release]. Retrieved from https://www.cdc.gov/media/releases/2018/p0607-suicide-prevention.html

Chartier, M. J., Attawar, D., Volk, J. S., Cooper, M., Quddus, F., & McCarthy, J. (2015). Postpartum mental health promotion: Perspectives from mothers and home visitors. *Public Health Nursing, 32,* 671–679.

Ching, T. H. W., Lee, S. Y., Chen, J., So, R. P., & Williams, M. T. (2018). A model of intersectional stress and trauma in Asian American sexual and gender minorities. *Psychology of Violence, 8,* 657–668. https://doi.org/10.1037/vio0000204

Courtney-Long, E., Carroll, D., Zhang, Q., Stevens, A., Griffin-Blake, S., Armour, B., & Campbell, V. (2015). Prevalence of disability and disability type among adults—United States, 2013. *Morbidity and Mortality Weekly Report, 64,* 777–783. https://doi.org/10.15585/mmwr.MM6429a2

Dabrowska, A., & Pisula, E. (2010). Parenting stress and coping styles in mothers and fathers of pre-school children with autism and Down syndrome. *Journal of Intellectual Disability Research, 54,* 266–280. https://doi.org/10.1111/j.1365-2788.2010.01258.x

Damman, M., Henkens, K., & Kalmign, M. (2015). Missing work after retirement: The role of life histories in the retirement adjustment process. *The Gerontologist, 55,* 802–813.

Feather, K. A. (2016). Low functioning to high functioning autism: A prescriptive model for counselors working with children across the spectrum. *VISTAS Online.* Retrieved from https://www.counseling.org/knowledge-center/vistas/by-subject2/vistas-children/docs/default-source/vistas/article_11d2bf24f16116603abcacff0000bee5e7

Froidevaux, A., Hirschi, A., & Wang, M. (2016). The role of mattering as an over-looked key challenge in retirement planning and adjustment. *Journal of Vocational Behavior, 94,* 57–69. https://doi.org/10.1016/j.jvb.2016.02.016

Gemignani, M., & Hernández-Albújar, Y. (2019). Critical reflexivity and intersectionality in human rights: Toward relational and process-based conceptualizations and practices in psychology. *European Psychologist, 24*(2), 136–145.

Gold, J. M. (2013). Supporting later-in-life intimate relationships: The role of the couples' counselor. *The Family Journal: Counseling and Therapy for Couples and Families, 21,* 351–357.

Guralnick, M., Neville, B., Hammond, M., & Connor, R. (2008). Continuity and change from full-inclusion early childhood programs through the early elementary period. *Journal of Early Intervention, 30,* 237–250. https://doi.org/10.1177/1053815108317962

Hohlfeld, A., Harty, M., & Engel, M. (2018). Parents of children with disabilities: A systematic review of parenting interventions and self-efficacy. *African Journal of Disability, 7,* 437–437. https://doi.org/10.4102/ajod.v7i0.437

Inglis, C., Sharman, R., & Reed, R. (2016). Paternal mental health following perceived traumatic childbirth. *Midwifery, 41,* 125–131.

James, R. K., & Gilliland, B. E. (2017). *Crisis intervention strategies* (8th ed.). Boston, MA: Cengage Learning.

Jordan, J. V. (2018). *Relational–cultural therapy* (2nd ed.). Washington, DC: American Psychological Association.

Livneh, H. (2015). Quality of life and coping with chronic illness and disability: A temporal perspective. *Rehabilitation Counseling Bulletin, 59,* 67–83.

Livneh, H., & Antonak, R. F. (2005). Psychosocial adaptation to chronic illness and disability: A primer for counselors. *Journal of Counseling & Development, 83,* 12–20.

Mellon, R. (2013). On the motivation of quid pro quo sexual harassment in men: Relation to masculine gender role stress. *Journal of Applied Social Psychology, 43,* 2287–2296. https://doi.org/10.1111/jasp.12178

National Center for Education Statistics. (2019, May). *Children and youth with disabilities.* Retrieved from https://nces.ed.gov/programs/coe/indicator_cgg.asp

Neely, J., Amatea, E. S., Echevarria-Doan, S., & Tannen, T. (2012). Working with families living with autism: Potential contributions of marriage and family therapists. *Journal of Marital And Family Therapy, 38,* 211–226.

Osborne, J. W. (2012). Psychological effects of the transition to retirement. *Canadian Journal of Counselling and Psychotherapy, 46*(1), 45–58.

Ratzliff, A. (2016). *Integrated care: Creating effective mental and primary health care teams.* New York, NY: Wiley.

Resch, J. A., Benz, M. R., & Elliott, T. R. (2012). Evaluating a dynamic process model of well-being for parents of children with disabilities: A multi-method analysis. *Rehabilitation Psychology, 57,* 61–72.

Ruane, A., & Carr, A. (2019). Systematic review and meta-analysis of Stepping Stones Triple P for parents of children with disabilities. *Family Process, 58*(1), 232–246. https://doi.org/10.1111/famp.12352

Sheehan, P., & Guerin, S. (2018). Exploring the range of emotional response experienced when parenting a child with an intellectual disability: The role of dual process. *British Journal of Learning Disabilities, 46*(2), 109–117. https://doi.org/10.1111/bld.12221

Siegel, D. J. (2012). *The developing mind: How relationships and the brain interact to shape who we are* (2nd ed.). New York, NY: Guilford Press.

Siegel, R. (2012). A short history of sexual harassment. In C. A. MacKinnon & R. B. Siegel (Eds.), *Directions in sexual harassment law* (pp. 1–39). New Haven, CT: Yale University Press.

Stroebe, M., & Schut, H. (2010). The dual process model of coping with bereavement: A decade on. *OMEGA—Journal of Death and Dying, 61,* 273–289.

Stuntzner, S. (2017). Compassion and self-compassion: Conceptualization of and application to adjustment to disability. *Journal of Applied Rehabilitation Counseling, 48,* 15–25.

Synard, J., & Gazzola, N. (2019). Moving towards positive well-being in the face of adversity: What explains individual variations of well-being following job loss? *International Journal for the Advancement of Counselling, 41,* 415–435. https://doi.org/10.1007/s10447-018-9359-6

U.S. Equal Employment Opportunity Commission. (2019a). *Facts about sexual harassment.* Retrieved from https://www.eeoc.gov/eeoc/publications/fs-sex.cfm

U.S. Equal Employment Opportunity Commission. (2019b). *Title VII of the Civil Rights Act of 1964.* Retrieved from https://www.eeoc.gov/laws/statutes/titlevii.cfm

van der Kolk, B. (2014). *The body keeps the score: Brain, mind, and body in the healing of trauma.* New York, NY: Viking.

Wampold, B. E., & Imel, Z. E. (2015). *The great psychotherapy debate: The research evidence for what works in psychotherapy* (2nd ed.). New York, NY: Routledge.

Wang, M., Henkens, K., & van Solinge, H. (2011). Retirement adjustment: A review of theoretical and empirical advancements. *American Psychologist, 66,* 204–213.

Waters, L., & Strauss, G. (2016). Finding growth during unemployment: A qualitative examination of distress and positive transformation. *International Journal of Wellbeing, 6*(11), 117–141.

Whitney, D. G., & Peterson, M. D. (2019). US national and state-level prevalence of mental health disorders and disparities of mental health care use in children. *JAMA Pediatrics, 4,* 389–391.

Resources

Americans With Disabilities Act (ADA) Amendments Act of 2008, Pub. L. No. 110-325, 122 Stat. 3553

The following website provides information about the ADA Amendments Act:

https://www.congress.gov/110/plaws/publ325/PLAW-110publ325.pdf

Crisis Text Line (Text 741741 for free, 24/7)

This hotline by text connects people in crisis to supportive crisis counselors.

http://www.crisistextline.org/who-we-are/

Individuals With Disabilities Education Act (IDEA), Pub. L. No. 108-446, 108th Congress

The following website provides information about the IDEA:

http://www.gpo.gov/fdsys/pkg/PLAW-108publ446/html/PLAW-108publ446.htm

National Dissemination Center for Children with Disabilities
This center provides information on children with disabilities for families, educators, and professionals. Phone: 1-800-695-0285

https://www.parentcenterhub.org/nichcy-gone/

O-Net Online
This site provides resources for job and occupational information and direction.

https://www.onetonline.org/

PACER Center
This organization of parent groups provides information on education and advocacy for children with disabilities. Phone: 1-888-248-0822

https://www.pacer.org/

Trevor Project
This national organization provides life-affirming crisis intervention and suicide prevention services to LGBTQ+ people younger than 25 years old.

http://www.thetrevorproject.org/

U.S. Department of Education
This site provides numerous resources and research for parents of children with disabilities.

https://www2.ed.gov/parents/needs/speced/list.jhtml

Multiple-Choice Questions

1. According to Wampold and Imel (2015), _____ is the most powerful predictor of growth.
   a. Theoretical orientation
   b. Quality of relationship
   c. Evidence-based interventions
   d. All of the above

2. All suicide deaths have a clear precursor.
   a. False, if the suicide is the second attempt
   b. False, because many deaths by suicide involved no identified precursor
   c. True, the precursor is a mental illness
   d. True, the precursor is a substance use disorder

3. The _____ model of grief work highlights the untidiness of change (Stroebe & Schut, 2010).
   a. Grief
   b. Dual process
   c. Untidy change
   d. Changing

4. Human development is influenced by
   a. Cultural influences.
   b. Unearned privileges.
   c. Unique histories.
   d. All of the above

5. According to Chartier et al. (2015), pregnancy and childbirth can
   a. Lead to perfect happiness.
   b. Create an array of societal issues.
   c. Make counseling difficult.
   d. Lead to several mental health concerns.

6. How many women develop PTSD after giving birth?
   a. 40%–70%
   b. 1%–6%
   c. 10%–11%
   d. 80%–90%

7. An estimated _____ of young children suffer from a mental health issue such as anxiety or depression.
   a. 10%
   b. 50%
   c. 20%
   d. None of the above

8. When a family must adjust to the role of a child with a developmental disorder, they may experience
   a. Nothing different than a normal family.
   b. Guilt.
   c. Uncertainty.
   d. Both b and c

9. An important concept for counselors to consider is avoid using _____ terminology.
   a. Disempowering
   b. Empowering
   c. Correct
   d. Bureaucratic

10. What percentage of young children who are deaf are reportedly sexually assaulted?
    a. 30%
    b. 50%
    c. 20%
    d. 70%

11. Adjusting to a chronic illness or disabling condition follows a _____ trajectory.
    a. Nonlinear
    b. Linear
    c. Certain five-step process
    d. None of the above

12. Which action can help clients who develop a chronic illness or disabling condition?
    a. Exploring personal meaning
    b. Encouraging family support
    c. Teaching adaptive coping strategies
    d. All of the above

13. According to Gold (2013), when a child leaves home for college or work, what might a married couple experience?
    a. No change
    b. Marital issues
    c. Confusion
    d. Only stress

14. Research depicts a correlation between job loss and concerns of
    a. Depression.
    b. Anxiety.
    c. Somatization.
    d. All of the above

15. Retirees may face _____, whereas other research studies have reported the opposite.
    a. Greater depression
    b. Partial identity disruption
    c. Psychosis
    d. Both a and b

Essay Questions

1. Think about the case of Nguyen. Have you ever known someone who struggled with motherhood and felt guilty about it? How would you work with Nguyen if you were her counselor?

2. If parents have a child with a disability, much time could be spent helping the child cope, live, and function. How could you, as the counselor, best support a parent from feeling isolated?

3. Life brings about a lot of change. The change may feel welcome to some, and it may feel traumatic to others. When reading this chapter, were there any of the vignettes that resonated for you? If so, why?

4. Job loss can be a devasting experience. Not only can it potentially exacerbate mental health concerns, it can also create a loss of identity. Have you known a peer or client who experienced a job loss? How did you respond to them?

5. Older adults tend to retire at some point. This can be both a rewarding experience and a traumatic change all at once. How could you best support an older adult client preparing to retire?

CHAPTER 10

Crisis and Trauma Counseling
With Couples and Families

Thelma Duffey, Barbara Herlihy, J. Claire Gregory,
and Meredith Klipple

Myriad crises arise in families, and, in this chapter, we seek to communicate the complexity of these challenges. In keeping with the spirit of this text, we underscore the role of the counseling relationship as a vital component of growth, and we emphasize an awareness of power dynamics, advocacy, and culture in this important work. We also discuss some common crises and traumatic events that arise in the lives of couples and families. Although we are not able to capture the full range of critical incidences and traumatic events experienced by families, we do offer a brief introduction to challenges involved in some common family crisis experiences, such as domestic violence, infidelity, incest, divorce, suicide, addiction, and chronic and terminal illness. Using relational-cultural theory (RCT) as a framework, we posit that, for us to have an impact in our role as counselors, we must first be affected by the experiences and the stories that our clients share (Jordan, 2018). Refer to Chapters 1 and 2 for a more thorough review of RCT.

We use brief snapshots via case examples in several family dynamics later in this chapter to illustrate family crises. Our goal is not to share tidy solutions to these stories, because the context of the situations and resolutions are more complex than the scope of this chapter allows. Rather, we invite you to connect with these vignettes and to your own responses to these experiences. Consider your own reactions to the vignettes, and reflect on how you would respond authentically, empathically, and in connection with your clients should these situations arise. We recognize and value creative strategies and interventions as useful components to our work, and we posit that our shared creativity and the therapeutic relationship remain our greatest resources as we navigate the connections and disconnections that invariably arise in couple and family counseling (Duffey, Haberstroh, & Trepal, 2016). Chapter 5 of this text includes theories and interventions on crisis counseling, and Chapter 6 offers theories and interventions on trauma counseling. Chapter 7 focuses exclusively on suicide, and Chapter 8 addresses sexual, emotional, and physical violence. Each of these chapters provides related information that can be applied to couple and family counseling.

No discussion on couples and family counseling would be complete without considering some of its inherent ethical challenges. We frame this chapter using relational ethics (described in Chapter 1) as a guide, and we invite you to consider your own ethical decision-making process when working with couples and families in crisis. We consider the contributions of family systems theory (Lucero, Jones, & Hunsaker, 2018), which usually guides the work of counselors in working with couples and families. We also share some of our concerns about the ethical implications of applying family systems concepts such as circular causality, intergenerational family processes, and the functionality of symptoms to some common family dynamics.

Connections and Disconnections in Families

As human beings, we are hardwired to desire connection with others and to feel a sense of belonging in our groups. Research attests to the joy, contentment, and purpose that people feel when they are part of a supportive group, team, tribe, or community (Gershgoren et al., 2016; Ind, Iglesias, & Schultz, 2013). Indeed, some of our deepest connections can be found within our family systems. These are the people whose proximity positions them to see and experience us in our various forms as we grow. These are also the relationships to which, in an ideal world, we can turn when we are most vulnerable.

Family are often the people whose understanding we want—whose acceptance and lack of judgment are like salve to our pain. Moreover, although some families enjoy this kind of support and mutuality to varying degrees, families are also a place where deep pain, injury, and harm can coexist. Some families foster abuse, neglect, and betrayal. Many endure the pain of loss or illness of another family member or carry the weight of knowing our loved ones hurt when we are ill. Families are human systems, at times home to love and connection and at other times to despair and disconnection. Crises and traumatic events occur within family systems and intimate relationships, and when these occur, these powerfully affect the fiber of our worlds.

Domestic Violence

Imagine you are sitting comfortably in your living room, watching television and eating your favorite snack, when all of a sudden, your partner enters the room and begins yelling at you, calling you names, and accusing you of wrongdoings you do not understand. Imagine your loved one screaming obscenities, punching walls, and telling you just how worthless you are. Be with that for a moment. Imagine that person conjures up every insecurity you have and throws them in your face. Then imagine that, incited by rage, the person begins to throw objects at the wall, at a mirror, at you. What is that image like for you?

Domestic violence, also known as intimate partner violence (IPV), occurs all too frequently within the United States. Name calling, chastising, throwing objects, hitting walls, hitting a partner, and sexual coercion are but a few examples of these terrorizing acts. IPV is both complex and terrifying. Power, control, insecurities, impulse control, and failure to manage emotions and stress are core features of IPV (Brown, McGriff, & Speedlin, 2018). In these cases, a person (or people) imposes dominance over a partner, child, or other family member and creates chaos and mayhem. This form of violence is not only abusive in a literal sense, but it also cuts at the fundamental layer of the recipient's sense of being. It can destroy a person's sense of trust and threaten a person's ability to sustain trust in others. After all, "If someone who is supposed to love me can act this way, what can I expect from others who don't?" People who experience IPV not only suffer the injuries of the abuse but they also suffer a profound sense of betrayal.

Kate, a 40-year-old fashion model, was married to a man who alternated between seeming adoration and emotional abuse and who ultimately resorted to physical violence. Her once loving husband, Bill, ran the gamut from proclaiming his love to pulling her hair and dragging her across the floor, calling her deplorable names as he did so. Bill punched holes in walls, screamed profanities at Kate, and would then recoil in despair, begging Kate not to leave him. Bill sought an emergency appointment for couples counseling during Christmas week, asking the counselor to please see them as he was at risk of losing the most amazing woman he ever met. Kate and Bill are in the throes of IPV.

IPV is described by the World Health Organization (2010) as "behavior within an intimate relationship that causes physical, sexual or psychological harm, including acts of physical aggression, sexual coercion, psychological abuse and controlling behaviors" (p. 11). Although both men and women experience IPV in their relationships, women are subjected to IPV at disproportionately higher rates than men. They are also at a higher risk for sustaining injury and even death (Black et al., 2011). In addition, gay, lesbian, and bisexual individuals experience proportionately greater instances of IPV than their dominant heterosexual counterparts (Walters, Chen, & Breidig, 2013). Psychological or physical aggression inflicted by an intimate partner can create a wound so profound it leaves the receiving partner in shock, bewildered, and sometimes immobilized, distorting a person's perception of worth, sense of control, and logistical options.

IPV also injures a person's sense of mattering in the world and place of belonging at home and in larger contexts. "You bring this out in me" are fighting words in IPV, designed to shift responsibility for the traumatizing behaviors to the partner. Spouses blamed for "making me act this way" may not always believe this to be true, but they often question themselves. They may also carry some of the societal fallout that comes when others pass judgment on how they should manage the situation. Anyone who has been part of an IPV relationship knows just how difficult it is to sort through these myriad feelings.

Counselors working with IPV recognize the crises these experiences bring and the often traumatic consequences to such violations. The family systems theory tradition of couples counseling calls for counselors to consider the *circular causality* in conflicted situations, in which one aspect of the system affects the other (Barnwell & Stone, 2016). This concept has been criticized, and we believe justly so, for its potential to blame the victim or hold the victim responsible for the abuse along with the perpetrator. The family systems concepts of first- and second-order change, however, may be helpful in working with couples who experience IPV. In the case of Kate and Bill, described earlier, first-order change would involve Bill learning new and nonviolent ways to communicate with Kate but continuing to believe he holds the power in the relationship and finding other ways to make her stay. Changes of this sort do not ultimately support lasting change. Second-order change, however, would require that Bill and Kate develop a relationship founded on mutual respect and shared decision making, and RCT provides a pathway for creating this type of change.

Feminist theories and RCT conceptualize IPV dynamics by considering who holds the most power in the relationship. They also consider how social and cultural contexts influence the couple dynamics and how these contexts can be introduced and navigated to empower the relationship, support the person with less power, and bring awareness to both parties (Hurless & Cottone, 2018). These models also consider the relational histories (images) of the couple and how these may influence their perceptions of what caring relationships look like (Jordan, 2018). In addition, counselors use their position to advocate for each person's safety while navigating the disconnections and relational expectations or images each carries (Brown et al., 2018). Counselors attend to building connection while helping both individuals and the couple engage in the challenging work of mutual understanding and eliminating IPV behaviors. Counselors are clear in articulating that abuse is never acceptable, and they clearly identify the accountability factors that must be in place for IPV to cease and for couples to move toward shared honor and respect.

In working with couples like Kate and Bill, relationally engaged counselors would consider variables such as the context of the situation, identifying who holds the power in the relationship and in the larger culture, how power is negotiated, a shift from victim blaming to advocacy, and societal variables (Brown et al., 2018). They recognize a person's right to be free of injury within a relationship and use a direct yet relational frame for conceptualizing abuse. Relationally competent counselors use the power of the relationship to support injured clients while offering a valuable connection to the perpetrating partner. Although recognizing that multiple contexts exist in a dynamic, and there are times when mutual aggression and abuse exist, these counselors do not engage in the traditional "every person plays a role in this" response that family theory can promote. Rather, they use the principles of advocacy and social justice as baselines for their work (Maghsoudi, 2019).

There are various methods for providing counseling to couples experiencing IPV. Individual counseling is the historically preferred method of treatment because of the perceived risk of increased violence following conjoint counseling and concerns about victim shaming (Rowe, Doss, Hsueh, Libet, & Mitchell, 2011). Others see conjoint counseling as beneficial for IPV because, together, the couple and counselor can navigate the often turbulent and volatile terrain characteristic of domestic violence (Antunes-Alves & Stefano, 2014; Hurless & Cottone, 2018). IPV advocates to educate the public on domestic safety and to research ways to eradicate IPV (Brown et al., 2016). Counselors support clients in developing emotional regulation skills, effective communication patterns, and compassion for self and others, recognizing that sociopolitical, environmental, fiscal, and entrenched patterns contribute to the preponderance of assaults committed every day.

Infidelity

Few experiences can pierce a person's soul more than learning that one's spouse is having an affair. To imagine that one's partner is intimately involved with another person is excruciating for most people, and when this fear proves to be true, it can trigger intense and traumatic grief reactions. The injured spouse and any children who may be aware of the circumstances often become immersed in shock, despair, disbelief, and a profound sense of abandonment. Infidelity creates crisis points in marriages, and families are often thrust into an orbit of personal agony and, at times, public scrutiny.

Brandon was in a 14-year marriage when he learned about his wife Candace's affair with a coworker. Both Brandon and Candace come from tight-knit Hispanic families and consider Catholicism as an important part of their lives. Brandon and Candace are the first in their families to suffer this kind of crisis, and the affair has affected all those who love them. Brandon's family loves Candace, and they want to support them both in sustaining the marriage. Candace's family also loves Brandon deeply, and they are stunned to hear of this news.

Brandon, humiliated, scared, and eager to "fix things," has sought counseling. At first, Candace vehemently denied the affair and angrily assured Brian that his imagination was getting the best of him. Brandon wanted to believe her, and he tried to do so, until she and the person with whom she was having an affair traveled publicly, and with others, to an out-of-town event—a public display that created gossip and talk within their small community.

Whereas Brandon was again shocked, and now enraged, by the confirmation of the affair, Candace vacillated between expressing her love for him and her desire to stay in the marriage and becoming angry, sullen, withdrawn, and resentful of Brandon for caging her in. Brandon, a man of faith, deeply wanted to trust that God would find a way to bring them together. He also suffered immeasurable grief and wondered how he had failed in his marriage. His trust was shattered, and his sense of personhood and masculinity were offended by his wife's actions. He could not imagine what it would take for the family to recover.

The traditional systems approach offers some important considerations when working with Brandon and Candace. For example, it is important for their counselor to recognize that multiple systems are affected by the situation—not just Brandon and Candace but also both of their families of origin and even the larger community to which they belong. At the same time, we hope the counselor will remain aware of some of the potential pitfalls of the systemic approach. For example, the systems approach assumes that symptoms (in this case, Candace's infidelity) are an expression of how the family system functions and are serving a purpose for the family. This method could inadvertently suggest that Brandon is partially responsible for the infidelity, which could further victimize him and convolute the crisis. See Sidebar 10.1 for information on counseling clients who are experiencing infidelity.

Sidebar 10.1 • Counseling Clients Experiencing Infidelity

In the vignette regarding Brandon, his faith played an important role in how he felt about his marriage. Infidelity, and other upsetting actions in romantic relationships, may feel especially destructive and painful to a person who holds faith as a high priority. Moreover, a relational-cultural theory (RCT) counselor would consider the context of this marriage and explore how the infidelity may affect a person's belief system.

Relationally competent counselors, however, would look at power dynamics within the couple relationship and the experiences of connection-disconnection-reconnection. RCT would consider whether chronic disconnections exist, leading to experiences of condemned isolation. As members of the couple would attempt to represent themselves fully and accurately in the sessions, RCT counselors would support and encourage respectful, authentic dialogue, recognizing the many disconnections that can exist.

While maintaining professionalism, RCT counselors would reject assuming a neutral or protective distance in counseling because that would invite disconnection (Jordan, 2018). It could also potentially disconnect counselors from the reality of the crisis, the emotions of the couple, and their own empathic feelings. This distance could cause clients to feel unsupported and disconnected within the therapeutic relationship and could ultimately exacerbate their feelings of shame and isolation. Being with clients like Brandon and Candace, who are in the throes of infidelity, calls us to bring our compassion, care, and clarity to the relationship and to use our own trusted connections and resources to support us in our work.

Furthermore, relationally competent counselors bring forth their authenticity and presence in counseling. We recognize the complexity of human dynamics and our own unique responses to painful stories. We recognize the potency of shame, injury, anger, and confusion evoked by infidelity. Regardless of how worthy people feel they are, it is natural to feel less than others when a spouse has an affair. Moreover, in those instances in which the offending partner refuses to attend counseling and the other partner remains in counseling, continued work can involve restoring a sense of dignity and self-compassion as he or she decides on what to do next.

Incest

Discovering incest within a family is another devastating dynamic that counselors encounter. Children have an inherent right to believe that the people entrusted with their care—those who, by all accounts, are there to support and love them—will have their best interest at heart. When this trust is violated by sexual abuse, the damage can be profound. Chloe was 8 years old when her father first sexually assaulted her. Chloe was terrified, and feeling absolutely alone, she lived with this abuse for several years. Chloe's family was prominent in a thriving community, and her father was widely admired. Chloe, fearing for her safety and struggling with the reality of the abuse, kept this secret long after the abuse ended. Chloe was, unfortunately, one of too many children wounded by childhood incest.

The discovery of incest within the family clearly is a time of chaos and crisis. Children are vulnerable, and caregivers do not always support or believe them when they disclose abuse. In fact, some families retreat to secrecy or denial because they fear litigation or public shame, and because they do not truly trust that counseling can help (Katz & Hamama, 2017). When children disclose the abuse to one parent, and that parent either does not believe the child or denies the child's reality, the child suffers not only the abuse of the perpetrating parent but also the betrayal of both parents. The betrayal is exacerbated by the strong attachment that some children feel with their perpetrating parent. Perpetrators of family incest often "groom" a child to prepare them for incest (Pettersen, 2013). They invest in creating a distinctive bond with the child, perhaps bringing special gifts, sharing personal information more appropriately shared with an adult, estranging them from other people, and building a secret society of sorts between the two. This perceived closeness can elicit a sense of confusion and protectiveness within the child toward the abusing person. Over time, children try to make sense of what is happening and can come to believe the perpetrator's reality at the expense of their own. Moreover, if they do see the abuse for what it is, they may feel emotionally torn between desiring the familiar attachment and detesting the abuse.

Research indicates that children often experience multiple traumas of sexual abuse before reaching out for help (Katz & Hamama, 2017). In fact, sexual abuse can be repetitive and prolonged. Furthermore, given the developmentally vulnerable age of the child, sexual abuse can deeply affect the child's future relationships. For example, when Chloe became an adult, she sought counseling. At that time, she described growing into a young woman who desired connection but could not sustain a romantic relationship. She did not easily connect with her peers, and she used her keen mind to engage in intellectual pursuits devoid of intimacy.

Some children like Chloe are abused by their fathers, whereas other children are sexually abused by their mothers, siblings, grandparents, extended family members, neighbors, and other members of the community. These violations not only severely injure the child but also disrupt the family unit itself. For example, a perpetrating parent may be removed from the family home. This removal could be considered a welcomed relief; however, the emotional connection between a perpetrating parent and child can be complex and convoluted, creating mixed feelings about the separation for the child and assorted feelings of anger and distress for other family members.

In those cases in which one sibling abuses another sibling, families must consider whether the perpetrating sibling will be removed from the home and, if so, where he or she will be placed. When a grandparent or older family member is perpetrating the abuse, multigenerational factors may come into play because other members of the family may come forward with stories of their own experiences. There are also those cases in which perpetrating family members were also abused. Moreover, nonoffending caregivers may have also been abused as children, and their own child's experience triggers memories long suppressed.

Working with family incest can involve individual counseling for the child and psychoeducation or family counseling. Providing emotional support to caregivers may help children adjust psychologically (van Toldeo & Seymour, 2016). Counselors can help nonoffending caregivers heal from potential vicarious trauma, and they can encourage consistent and nurturing care and protection for the children. Counselors can also help families examine any multigenerational patterns of abuse while using the power of the therapeutic relationship to support family healing. For example, family systems theory can frame our understanding of intergenerational family patterns in those cases in which perpetrators were themselves victims when they were children.

Divorce

"Are you getting a divorce?" These are the words that haunt many a parent attempting to explain the fallout of a failed marriage to a child. The words "it's not your fault, this is on us," albeit true, can feel shallow and insufficient to children

213

who see their lives as depending on the sustained family unit as they know it. This perception can be particularly strong in those cases in which they have asked about potential divorce before and have been reassured otherwise. Divorce is a crisis that over the past several decades has come to affect more and more families. According to the National Center for Health Statistics, Centers for Disease Control and Prevention (2017), yearly rates of divorce ranged from 3.1 to 4.0 in 1,000 per total population. There were 787,251 divorces within the United States in 2017.

Divorce can be a tumultuous time in the lives of family members and, depending on the circumstances, traumatic to at least some of its members (van der Wal, Finkenauer, & Visser, 2019). High-profile divorces; family disruptions due to abuse, neglect, infidelity, and financial problems; as well as other issues are crisis points for some families. Moreover, whereas some families regroup during these times and seek support, others are simply too preoccupied with logistical issues, emotional distress, and other factors, which can overwhelm parents and ultimately leave children feeling especially vulnerable and alone.

Supportive counseling services and psychoeducation related to the mediation and divorce process are useful resources for family members undergoing high-conflict divorce. At the same time, not all families successfully resolve these issues in spite of these interventions (Barnwell & Stone, 2016). These patterns of behavior increase stress and can create traumatic environments for those involved. Furthermore, families with high-conflict patterns generally engage in legal custody battles that potentially wreak havoc on at least some of its members, particularly the children (van der Wal et al., 2019).

Although divorce can create a crisis within the family, the way that both spouses manage the divorce and treat one another in the process directly affects how children view relationships and respond to their own relationships (Barnwell & Stone, 2016). Given the generally high-stress nature of divorce, using RCT principles—such as counselor authenticity, honoring of disconnections while fostering connection, and moving toward a power-with position—can help couples and their children cope with these often chaotic times more authentically and can enhance the potential for each person's healing and growth toward connection.

Suicide of a Family Member

The Wilson family came in for counseling following the attempted suicide of their son, Alex. Alex was extremely bright and friendly, and as one of eight children, Alex distinguished himself by being particularly studious and well mannered. In a boisterous family environment, Alex's sweet disposition was welcome relief from the chaos that permeated his home. Alex's older brother Joe was in prison for attempted murder, and the family's pain surrounding his incarceration was devastating. Alex's response was to study harder and support his mother, who was particularly affected by Joe's imprisonment.

In the haze of his family's confusion and grief, Alex found solace and hope in his academic achievement, despite being bullied and called names at school. Joe had always been a protective figure in Alex's life, and without Joe, Alex felt deeply alone. The Wilsons' pride in Alex's achievement was a counterpoint to their grief and humiliation. Alex shouldered the weight of both his high self-expectations and the hopes of his family. In his desperation to succeed, he cheated on a math quiz. When he was caught, his world crashed down around him. Humiliated and ashamed, he swallowed a handful of his sister's anti-anxiety medicine when he was home alone.

Suicide is often described as a permanent solution to a temporary problem. People can become overwhelmed by situational crises and stressors and cannot see a way out. Although strong connections between family members may serve as protective factors against suicidal behaviors, this outcome is not always the case. Sometimes, beloved family members succumb to suicide while surrounded by people who love them. This loss is devastating to those who are left to make sense of the tragedy. They often question their own words and actions and wonder what they missed and how they could have done things differently.

If connection is a protective factor for suicidal behavior, one could say that an absence of connection in key relationships may place a person at higher risk for suicide. Approximately 47,000 individuals in the United States lost their lives to suicide in 2017 (Centers for Disease Control and Prevention, 2018). Current statistics show suicide to be the second leading cause of death for people within the 10–34 age group and the fourth leading cause of death for people ranging in age from 35 to 54 (Centers for Disease Control and Prevention, 2018; Hanschmidt, Lehnig, Riedel-Heller, & Kersting, 2016). Chapter 7 provides an extensive review of suicide.

Death by suicide destabilizes the family in profound ways, and it alters the way family members live their daily lives. Surviving children assume various roles following a suicide, such as caretaker, peacemaker, or rebel, and whereas some seek closeness, others withdraw. Still others escape into substances and other self-destructive behaviors. Some children feel a need to talk about the loss, whereas others do not. Sometimes they wish they could talk to their parents but do not want to burden them, so they keep their feelings, fears, and pain inside (Dickens, 2014; Duffey, 2007). Counselors can guide parents in understanding the diversity of ways that children grieve and the developmental factors that influence their children's grief. Chapter 9 provides detailed information on these factors and the grief process of children.

Parents whose children commit suicide experience a unique form of grief that is complex and often clouded with guilt, remorse, and despair. In Chapter 1, we discussed the death of a young man, David, and the devastating impact of that loss on his family and community. David had been bullied at school and online, and his parents had taken every step they knew to protect him. After his death, news of the bullying spread, and the community rose in horror. David's parents have tried to honor him by educating others on the devastating and life-threatening impact of bullying, and they have worked with lawmakers to institute antibullying legislation. It is profoundly difficult to find meaning in a child's death by suicide, but parents do find purpose. In this case, David's parents believed that if one child can be saved by these efforts, they will be living out their purpose. Establishing David's Legacy is one way that David's family found to honor his memory and give voice to the legacy he left.

Childhood Illness and Death

Kyle was 12 years old when he was first diagnosed with brain cancer. Bright-eyed and full of life, Kyle was the only boy in the family and was big brother to his two doting sisters. Kyle's family was in the military, and when his diagnosis was confirmed, his family relocated for easy access to the best medical treatment the military could provide. Both parents had strong religious beliefs, and their faith sustained them through much of Kyle's illness. Kyle and I (Thelma) would have long talks about his faith, his fears, and his hopes. We would talk about computers, life, and the Spurs (a basketball team in San Antonio). At one point when Kyle's illness had progressed and there was little hope, he let me know he wished he could do God's work. I remember saying something like "I know God better by knowing you." He looked up at me at just the moment I said this—a powerfully humbling moment for me.

Kyle's mother and father were in high school when he was born, and they left school to work full time to support their family. Their lives have not been necessarily easy, but they have lived a life of "family and country first" values. Bewildered, beaten down, and yet holding onto hope, Kyle's family is living a crisis suffered and experienced by so many others.

The terror parents face when learning that their child has a chronic or terminal illness is unspeakable. It often creates anticipation that the worst situation they could imagine may materialize. The palliative care literature refers to this as *anticipatory grief* (Al-Gamal & Long, 2010). At the same time that parents want to have hope and fight with all they have to keep their child alive, often other parts of them can creep in. These are the parts that grieve and try to cope with the impending loss of their beloved child. Although their hopes and dreams for their child and family flash before their eyes, anticipatory grief can become a ticking clock.

Families undergo devastating stress during a child's diagnosis of a chronic or terminal illness. Dynamics in play before the diagnosis are often exacerbated, and parents' responses will vary depending on their own personalities and life histories. Single parents must navigate attending to their child—and, in some cases, to their other children—while maintaining a job, traveling for medical care, juggling exorbitant financial costs, and dealing with their own emotions. Sibling reactions run the gamut. Some become protective of parents and their brothers and sisters, assuming a caretaking role, whereas others become quiet and distant. Fear is often a part of their reality, and some feel guilt for past discord and bargain that they will do better if given a chance. Still others go into denial and detach from their feelings and their family. Few escape the devastation of a child's death should that come to pass. See Sidebar 10.2 for information on counseling families facing a terminal illness.

Addiction and Mental Health: A Family Perspective

When Faith first came to counseling, she was depressed, detached, and could barely speak. I (Thelma) soon learned of Faith's history of drug addiction and her hope to escape the clutches of a drug fixation to heroin. Brilliant and funny, Faith could charm almost anyone. However, it was her authenticity and stark honesty that were her distinguishing features. Deeply committed to counseling and her own recovery, she would

Sidebar 10.2 • Counseling Families Facing a Terminal Illness

Imagine learning your clients' child was recently diagnosed with a terminal illness. As you sit with your clients, what would you imagine their initial needs to be in counseling? How would you support a client facing this tragedy?

bring journals, poems, and her own music to sessions, and she would share her hopes, frustrations, and fear that she would not stay sober. Faith had lost everything during her drug use, and she valiantly fought to get it back—a career, the love of family and friends, and a chance to live a life of meaning with a profound love.

Addiction is a disease of disconnection (Duffey, 2005; Haberstroh, 2005)—disconnection from the family, a spouse, children, a job, and from one's self. Addiction creates the illusion that drugs truly are a best friend or, in some cases, a supportive relative. With the rise of addictions increasing to an estimated 1 in 12 Americans (U.S. Department of Health and Human Services, 2018), addiction has become an epidemic. Moreover, process addictions of all kinds exist, with culture, systems, biology, and genetics as factors.

Families with addiction experience heartbreak of many kinds. Some feel shame, guilt, and regret; at other times, they feel resentment, anger, and embarrassment. They blame themselves and each other, and many feel isolated and alone. While leading monthly groups for families and clients at an inpatient treatment center, my (Claire's) goal was to help family members develop empathy for one another and see each other's point of view. It was critical to foster a safe environment, knowing that few people in the room could truly feel safe in their daily worlds. Creating and maintaining safety is challenging for families entrenched in addiction, long after treatment ends. For more information on counseling clients with addiction, see Chapter 9. See Sidebar 10.3 for information on recognizing addiction.

Case Example and Applications for Hope and Healing

One evening while Amy was on a walk with her neighbor, she stopped for a moment and said, "Hmmm. I am feeling a little short of breath." Dr. Rishabh—Amy's neighbor, friend, doctor, and chief of staff for geriatrics at a local teaching hospital—responded with "I need you to come to my office first thing in the morning." This encounter began what turned out to be a deadly turn of events for Amy and the greatest nightmare of Amy's family's life.

Amy, a vibrant, life-loving woman, was diagnosed at age 83 with a heart condition. Dr. Rishabh and another cardiologist agreed that the condition would require major surgery. This diagnosis came as a surprise to Amy and her family, given that earlier that year she had been given a clean bill of health. The A+ report card on her health had been a point of celebration for Amy and her husband, Fred, who did not take their good health and good fortune for granted. Recognizing their blessings, they often marveled that waking up every day to a life well lived and with each other was a gift. They also appreciated their community and church, and they viewed their long-established medical team as contributing to the comfort of their lives.

Therefore, Fred was concerned when earlier that year Amy decided to transfer her care to Dr. Rishabh's office, which was across town and connected to a large

Sidebar 10.3 • Recognizing Addiction

Addiction does not discriminate. Although genetics, family dynamics, mental health, culture, and other factors contribute to addiction, we cannot generalize the demographics of an addicted person. As a counselor, how do you recognize signs of addiction in your clients?

teaching hospital unfamiliar to them both. For context, Amy had grown up in a small town where family doctors made house visits and took special care of the community, and Dr. Rishabh's actions and demeanor elicited those memories and engendered that trust. Amy would often say, "Dr. Rishabh is an excellent gerontologist. She is my friend, and she cares about me."

It did come as a surprise to Fred and Amy when Dr. Rishabh and the cardiologist told them she needed major surgery. However, when they both assured her and her family that a triple bypass surgery was common practice these days, particularly given what they described as Amy's *vitality*, their fears were allayed. When Amy and the family brought up concerns about her age, their response was almost dismissive. "Don't worry. You'll be fine," Dr. Rishabh said, adding, "and you'll have the heart of a 25-year-old."

Clearly, Amy did not expect to have the heart of a 25-year-old; however, she did trust Dr. Rishabh, and her doctor's assurances carried tremendous power. Dr. Rishabh had taken a personal interest in Amy since the first day they met at a neighborhood gathering several months back, and they had enjoyed a friendly relationship. There was no talk of dual relationships or cautionary disclaimers when Dr. Rishabh became her primary care physician, and conflicts did not arise until Amy's medical condition required the kind of attention and follow-through that Dr. Rishabh did not consistently or adequately provide.

As counselors, we are cautioned to avoid dual relationships and encouraged to communicate in our informed consent any potential threats to our client's safety. Dr. Rishabh was a gerontology specialist who practiced under a separate ethical code than counselors. Like the *ACA Code of Ethics* (American Counseling Association [ACA], 2014), the American Medical Association's (2016) *Principles of Medical Ethics* and the Gerontological Society of America's (2002) *Code of Ethics* have provisions regarding dual relationships and patient harm. Amy, of course, had no context for understanding the power dynamics of their relationship and the negligent practice that came into play when Amy failed to recover as expected from her surgery, and how confusing these dual roles would come to be during a time of crisis.

For example, during those days after Amy's surgery when she was home and physically struggling, Dr. Rishabh would walk over with a bowl of soup and tell her to continue doing her breathing exercises—again, assuring her she would be just fine—and to be patient. However, during those times when Amy would take yet another emergency trip to the hospital where she was admitted into the intensive care unit, Dr. Rishabh would repeatedly schedule times to meet with her, but then she repeatedly no-showed, often without advising Amy on the change of plans, leaving Amy to say, "I guess Dr. Rishabh is not coming tonight."

Amy's family witnessed their beloved matriarch endure 4 months of her doctor's overconfident assurances and her own deeply disappointing trips back to the intensive care unit. Amy's family felt helpless in their attempts to secure answers, and they felt angry at Dr. Rishabh's disregard during such a critical time. They felt helpless in knowing Amy never once complained about her pain, treatment, or condition, yet she suffered so. Although they were generally capable and articulate, they felt inept in navigating the medical system within this teaching hospital, and their grief was compounded by the unanswered questions surrounding Amy's condition. It was not until after her death that they learned the surgery itself caused damage, and she did not recover from these complications. Moreover, in addition to grieving their momentous loss, they felt hurt and anger in recalling that several evenings before her death, Amy quietly acknowledged, "I do not *feel* abandoned, but I *am* being abandoned [by Dr. Rishabh]."

Envisioning Yourself as Amy's Family

We ask you to place yourself in this family's position and to imagine that your deeply beloved parent, grandparent, or spouse had been functioning exceedingly well, and then, following a recent symptom and diagnostic procedure, she is advised by her new doctor and cardiac team that major surgery is necessary. She trusts this doctor/friend implicitly, and although you ask about more conservative treatment because of potential age-related risks, your concerns are dismissed. Days after the surgery, on the day before she is expected to return home, something goes terribly wrong.

For months, you see her go in and out of the hospital with alarming symptoms no one can explain. Teams of 10–15 residents, students, and doctors enter her room every day and leave without answers, and her own doctor/friend who coordinated the team is shockingly uninvolved. Then, 2 days before she is scheduled to be released again, she has an episode late at night, and when the nurses do not respond to the alarm, you run up and down the halls screaming for assistance. You run back in to see your loved one, and the last words you hear her speak are "Help me!" The next day, the team of doctors who responded to the emergency by performing another procedure on Amy call you into a room to let you know she did not survive. Amy's doctor/friend, who is present at that point, matter-of-factly states, "I'm sorry. She is in a better place, and this happens with people her age." Knowing that you, other members of the family, and Amy herself had raised concerns about her age—and these concerns were categorically dismissed by Dr. Rishabh and the team before the surgery—made this comment particularly devastating. van der Kolk (2014) has spoken to the medical trauma that family members experience in cases such as Amy's, and counselors recognize the impact of these traumas on the family.

Envisioning Yourself as the Counselor

After you have taken the time to imagine yourself in Amy's family's place and are able to connect with the various systemic dynamics, we ask you to step back and figuratively switch gears. Imagine you are the counselor, and Fred and the children have sought your help. Amy was vibrant, healthy, and involved in life, hosting Christmas dinner and other events months before the surgery, and now she is gone. Furthermore, they have learned that the surgery, which ultimately took her life, was not medically necessary, in that other less invasive alternatives were not presented as options. Consider the impact of this shocking loss on them, and how you would support them in this time. What contextual, systemic, and logistical factors would you need to consider? What impact might this experience have on their trust in authority figures, and what would they need from you as their counselor, given their experience? We ask you to consider how you would imagine this family responding to a neutral or hierarchical relationship between you and them, as is often typical of many traditional therapies. Finally, we ask you to consider how you would see yourself helping them grieve and acclimate to life in a world without their beloved Amy.

A Relational-Cultural Response

When counselors work with people in crisis, who they are *with* their clients is as important as what they do. In addition, counselors consider any power dynamics that could exacerbate the impact of the crisis, and they reflect on how they can use their power well. RCT would refer to this process as sharing "power-with" another person. Counselors would also consider what relational images the family brings to the counseling session. For example, counselors working with Amy's family could consider the "power-over" relationship that Dr. Rishabh ultimately had with Amy and her family and the impact of Dr. Rishabh's management of her dual roles in their relationship. Amy's family grieved their loss and what they saw as a premature and overreactive medical intervention, as well as the inhumane treatment of their wife, mother, and grandmother. A counselor working with Amy's family can support them in their grief while also considering how the relational images created in the experience with Dr. Rishabh and others on the medical team could potentially color the counseling experience and relationship.

Counselors living in rural areas or communities where dual roles may be especially common are cautioned to recognize the power of carrying coexisting personal and professional roles. When a professional has a personal relationship with a client or patient, the onus is on the professional to protect the relationship and maintain the standard of professional care, and all helping professions are bound by the principle of "do no harm" (ACA, 2014). Relationally competent counselors are aware that people in crisis need relationships they can trust, and they strive to create authentic and empowering connections with them. They recognize the challenge of caring for a loved one in their suffering and of fighting alongside them for their lives. They understand that when the fight is unsuccessful and the medical treatment questionable or traumatic, a family's grief can become what van der Kolk (2014) described as a medical trauma. Seeing a loved one in such a vulnerable position experience betrayal, indifference, and neglect can be exceptionally hurtful, and working through these feelings can take time.

The Healing

Families such as Amy's who are experiencing crisis situations and tragedies need the space, time, care, and connection that can support them in their healing. Amy's family came to recognize that caring for their loved one can also deeply connect them with their genuine beliefs on what is important in life, who they want to be, and how they want to ultimately love and show love. Processes such as these are not seamless. For example, at the onset of the loss, some members of Amy's family grieved by withdrawing, striking out, and boycotting events, such as the viewing, that were not planned to their liking. Others grieved in disbelief of the loss and held on to one another for comfort. Like most families, they experienced some disconnections, and the family Amy so effortlessly supported and enjoyed seemed fractured and lost. Working through those disconnections was not always easy, and not all the rifts mended.

Still, in time, Fred and the children began to heal, and they did so together. Amy left behind a legacy of faith, love, joy, and laughter; and her children, in particular, used her example to navigate their grief. Prayer became an integral part of their lives, and they came together to read some of her favorite scriptures on her birthday. They were each intentional in describing her legacy, and one child remarked, "I'm not the most patient person, but knowing just how patient and loving Mom was makes me want to be better." Another child talked about how courageous their mother was and how she found joy in the little things. "I want to be like Mom in that way," she said. Fred acknowledges living life as best he can, and laments, "She was the best thing that ever happened to me, and I feel so lost without her. I guess I'm greedy. My life was perfect with her in it." Fred adds, "I just miss her—particularly when the sun begins to set. But sometimes I'll take out this old letter [a love note from Amy], and I'll think to myself, 'What a life! What a wife!' And then I feel grateful."

Future Directions and Emerging Research

Couples and families in crisis need the support and professionalism of their counselors. They need to trust their counselors, and they need their counselors to understand the impact of their use of power on them. Developmental relational counseling is a model that looks at the role of power, the degree of clarity and balance with which people respond to life situations, a person's awareness of the impact of their behaviors and actions, and their compassion and clarity in relation to others (Duffey & Haberstroh, 2012). Exploring client perceptions of the therapeutic relationship using developmental relational counseling could be useful to counselors.

In addition, research is needed to explore crisis and trauma dynamics in nontraditional families, such as lesbian, gay, bisexual, transgender, and questioning (LGBTQ) families; multicultural families; or families with incarcerated members. The needs of other vulnerable groups, such as families in poverty or families with members with disabilities, are also salient. Moreover, researching the needs of families with economic privilege who suffer relational, systemic, and institutional crises is also warranted. Given the rise in school shootings in affluent areas, suicides following bullying experiences in higher socioeconomic school districts, and the pain families experience as a result of domestic violence and other abuses, attention to the needs of all demographic populations is critical.

References

Al-Gamal, E., & Long, T. (2010). Anticipatory grieving among parents living with a child with cancer. *Journal of Advanced Nursing, 66*, 1980–1990.

American Counseling Association. (2014). *ACA code of ethics.* Alexandria, VA: Author.

American Medical Association. (2016). *AMA principles of medical ethics.* Retrieved from https://www.ama-assn.org/delivering-care/ama-principles-medical-ethics

Antunes-Alves, S., & Stefano, J. (2014). Intimate partner violence: Making the case for joint couple treatment. *The Family Journal, 22*, 62–68. https://doi.org/10.1177/1066480713505056

Barnwell, B. J., & Stone, M. H. (2016). Treating high divorce conflict. *Universal Journal of Psychology, 4*, 109–115. https://doi.org/10.13189/ujp.2016.040206

Black, M. C., Basile, K. C., Breiding, M. J., Smith, S. G., Walters, M. L., Merrick, M. T., . . . Stevens, M. R. (2011). *The National Intimate Partner and Sexual Violence Survey (NISVS): 2010 summary report.* Atlanta, GA: National Center for Injury Prevention and Control, Centers for Disease Control and Prevention.

Brown, S., McGriff, K., & Speedlin, S. (2018). Using relational-cultural theory to negotiate relational rebuilding in survivors of intimate partner violence. *Journal of Creativity in Mental Health, 13,* 136–147. https://doi.org/10.1080/15401383.2017.1355289

Center for Disease Control and Prevention. (2018, June 7). *Suicide rates rising across the U.S.* [Press release]. Retrieved from https://www.cdc.gov/media/releases/2018/p0607-suicide-prevention.html

Dickens, N. (2014). Prevalence of complicated grief and posttraumatic stress disorder in children and adolescents following sibling death. *The Family Journal, 22,* 119–126. https://doi.org/10.1177/1066480713505066

Duffey, T. (2005). The relational impact of addiction across the lifespan. In D. Comstock (Ed.), *Diversity and development: Critical contexts that shape our lives and relationships* (pp. 299–318). Belmont, CA: Brooks/Cole.

Duffey, T. (2007). Promoting relational competencies in counselor education through creativity and relational-cultural theory. *Journal of Creativity in Mental Health, 2,* 47–59. https://doi.org/10.1300/J456v02n01_05

Duffey, T., & Haberstroh, S. (2012). Developmental relational counseling: A model for self-understanding in relation to others. *Journal of Creativity in Mental Health, 7,* 262–271. https://doi.org/10.1080/15401383.2012.711709

Duffey, T., Haberstroh, S., & Trepal, H. (2016). Creative approaches in counseling and psychotherapy. In D. Capuzzi & M. D. Stauffer (Eds.), *Counseling and psychotherapy: Theories and interventions* (pp. 445–468). Alexandria, VA: American Counseling Association.

Gerontological Society of America. (2002). *Code of ethics.* Retrieved from https://www.geron.org/code-of-ethics

Gershgoren, L., Basevitch, I., Filho, E., Gershgoren, A., Brill, Y. S., Schinke, R. J., & Tenenbaum, G. (2016). Expertise in soccer teams: A thematic inquiry into the role of shared mental models within team chemistry. *Psychology of Sport and Exercise, 24,* 128–139. https://doi.org/10.1016/j.psychsport.2015.12.002

Haberstroh, S. (2005). Facing the music: Creative and experiential group strategies for working with addiction related grief and loss. *Journal of Creativity in Mental Health, 1*(3–4), 41–55. https://doi.org/10.1300/J456v01n03_03

Hanschmidt, F., Lehnig, F., Riedel-Heller, S. G., & Kersting, A. (2016). The stigma of suicide survivorship and related consequences—A systematic review. *PLoS ONE, 11*(9), e0162688. https://doi.org/10.1371/journal.pone.0162688

Hurless, N., & Cottone, R. (2018). Considerations of conjoint couples therapy in cases of intimate partner violence. *The Family Journal, 26,* 324–329. https://doi.org/10.1177/1066480718795708

Ind, N., Iglesias, O., & Schultz, M. (2013). Building brands together: Emergence and outcomes of co-creation. *California Management Review, 55*(3), 5–26. https://doi.org/10.1525/cmr.2013.55.3.5

Jordan, J. V. (2018). *Relational–cultural therapy* (2nd ed.). Washington, DC: American Psychological Association.

Katz, C., & Hamama, L. (2017). From my own brother in my own home: Children's experiences and perceptions following alleged sibling incest. *Journal of Interpersonal Violence, 32,* 3648–3668. https://doi.org/10.1177/0886260515600876

Lucero, R., Jones, A., & Hunsaker, J. (2018). Using internal family systems theory in the treatment of combat veterans with post-traumatic stress disorder and their families. *Contemporary Family Therapy, 40,* 266–275. https://doi.org/10.1007/s10591-017-9424-z

Maghsoudi, M. (2019). Addressing counselor stigma in working with female intimate partner violence survivors. *Journal of Professional Counseling: Practice, Theory and Research, 45,* 33–44. https://doi.org/10.1080/15566382.2019.1603015

National Center for Health Statistics, Centers for Disease Control and Prevention. (2017). *National marriage and divorce rate trends 2000–2016.* Retrieved from https://www.cdc.gov/nchs/data/dvs/national_marriage_divorce_rates_00-16.pdf

Pettersen, K. T. (2013). A study of shame from sexual abuse within the context of a Norwegian incest center. *Journal of Child Sexual Abuse, 22,* 677–694. https://doi.org/10.1080/10538712.2013.811139

Rowe, L. S., Doss, B. D., Hsueh, A. C., Libet, J., & Mitchell, A. E. (2011). Coexisting difficulties and couple therapy outcomes: Psychopathology and intimate partner violence. *Journal of Family Psychology, 25,* 455–458. https://doi.org/10.1037/a0023696

U.S. Department of Health and Human Services. (2018). *Results from the 2017 National Survey on Drug Use and Health: Summary of national findings.* Retrieved from https://www.thenationalcouncil.org/capitol-connector/2018/09/samhsa-releases-national-survey-on-drug-use-and-health/

van der Kolk, B. (2014). *The body keeps the score: Brain, mind, and body in the healing of trauma.* New York, NY: Viking.

van der Wal, R. C., Finkenauer, C., & Visser, M. M. (2019). Reconciling mixed findings on children's adjustment following high-conflict divorce. *Journal of Child and Family Studies, 28,* 468–478. https://doi.org/10.1007/s10826-018-1277-z

van Toledo, A., & Seymour, F. (2016). Caregiver needs following disclosure of child sexual abuse. *Journal of Child Sexual Abuse, 25,* 403–414. https://doi.org/10.1080/10538712.2016.1156206

Walters, M. L., Chen, J., & Breidig, M. J. (2013). *The National Intimate Partner and Sexual Violence Survey: 2010 findings on victimization by sexual orientation.* Atlanta, GA: National Center for Injury Prevention and Control, Centers for Disease Control and Prevention.

World Health Organization. (2010). *Preventing intimate partner and sexual violence against women: Taking action and generating evidence.* Retrieved from https://www.who.int/violence_injury_prevention/publications/violence/9789241564007_eng.pdf

Multiple-Choice Questions

1. Which is a core relational feature of intimate partner violence (IPV)?
    a. Power
    b. Unethical morals
    c. Mental health issues
    d. None of the above

2. _____ out of 10 women experience IPV.
    a. Ten
    b. One
    c. Three
    d. Five

3. What is one thing relational-cultural theory (RCT) counselors consider when working with IPV?
   a. Diagnosis of both partner
   b. Power dynamics
   c. Cognitive-behavior therapy (CBT) techniques
   d. The one at fault

4. Children often experience _____ trauma(s) before reaching out to an authority figure.
   a. Two
   b. One
   c. Multiple
   d. 10–15

5. Which can be a great protective factor against suicide?
   a. Money
   b. Education
   c. Shelter
   d. Family relationships

6. How many people in the United States lost their lives to suicide in 2016?
   a. 500
   b. 10,000
   c. 45,000
   d. 75,000

7. One thing RCT counselors work on with families who experience suicide is
   a. REBT worksheets.
   b. DBT homework.
   c. Pushing past the grief.
   d. Letting the family grieve.

8. Anticipatory grief includes mourning, coping, and planning for a loved one's future death.
   a. False, because the person has not yet passed
   b. True, if the person is only an adult
   c. True, for all ages
   d. False, it does not include planning

9. The developmental relational counseling (DRC) model explores
   a. The role of power.
   b. Medical outcomes.
   c. Dissociation.
   d. None of the above

10. People can become addicted to
    a. Work.
    b. Alcohol and drugs.
    c. Shopping.
    d. All of the above

11. What is the goal of using a creative intervention in an addiction treatment group process using RCT?
    a. Releasing anger
    b. Mutual empathy
    c. Resolving past family traumas
    d. Supporting an internal locus of control

12. In this chapter, counselors living in rural areas are urged to be aware of
    a. Therapeutic rapport.
    b. Dual roles.
    c. Floods.
    d. Research.

13. Systemic thinking—in particular, circular causality—can be misused by
    a. Blaming the victim.
    b. Approaching change with only a few family members.
    c. Recognizing the role of intergenerational trauma.
    d. Appreciating how member's roles influence family change.

14. Family members can experience the effects from an addiction as much as the addicted person.
    a. True, if the family is dysfunctional
    b. True, all the time
    c. False, because it is not a family issue
    d. False, the addicted person feels the effects more

15. How many Americans struggle with addiction?
    a. 1 in 20
    b. 1 in 50
    c. 1 in 12
    d. 1 in 3

Essay Questions

1. What is your reaction to the vignette about Kate and Bill? Intimate partner violence (IPV) may feel confusing and anxiety provoking. Have you ever worked with a client who has expressed being in an unstable relationship? How did you respond?

2. Relationally competent counselors work to authentically connect with clients, and as counselors, our needs and experience cannot interfere with the work of our clients. How do you respond when your clients bring up concerns you also find challenging?

3. Just as mental health issues can be stigmatized in society, suicide can also carry a stigma. How do you view suicide? If you have a family member or client struggling with thoughts of suicide, how would (or did) you respond?

4. Consider the case in which you are working with family members whose loved one dies by suicide. How do you respond?

5. Homeostasis within a family system involves attempting to maintain balance. How have you experienced homeostasis? Can you think of times when your family or community tried to maintain homeostasis?

CHAPTER 11

Responding to Community Violence and Community Trauma

Thelma Duffey, Shane Haberstroh, and Deb Del Vecchio-Scully

Communities in crisis share many commonalities. For one, life as they have known it will never be the same. Two, their shared tragedy binds them in ways most members of the community would never have imagined. These trauma-bonds create an interconnectedness and shared experience unlike any other. Floods, earthquakes, tornadoes, and other natural disasters ravage communities with an unimaginable intensity, leaving people homeless and with an indescribable wreckage. Terroristic acts of violence, mass shootings, and other violently abusive acts bring horror and disbelief to communities whose fiber is often torn by the rampage. These events create chaos, strain community infrastructures, and require significant resources to manage the immediate damage and to support longer term recovery efforts. Whether the crisis is a result of a natural disaster, a mass shooting, terroristic attack, or the brutal assaults of hazing and other sadistic rituals, communities in crises are flooded with pain. They deserve the attention, focus, and care of well-trained and informed counselors committed to compassionate action.

This chapter addresses relationally based counseling interventions in communities following a collective crisis or trauma and some distinguishing features that characterize them. Collectively, we have participated in outreach efforts either through direct services or consultation following the 9/11 terrorist crisis in New York, Hurricanes Sandy and Katrina, the Sandy Hook Elementary School (Newtown, CT) shooting, the Marjorie Stoneman Douglas (MSD) High School (Parkland, FL) shooting, the Pulse nightclub shooting in Orlando (FL), and the mass shooting at a church in Sutherland Springs (TX). We detail some of our own recent experiences and provide some organizational and conceptual strategies we found useful.

We also emphasize that community needs are distinctive across settings and require support individualized to the community. Moreover, we suggest that supporting communities in crisis begins with a sense of humility and a desire to listen, learn, and respond to community needs rather than assuming we know what they are.

Natural Disasters

Throughout history, people have sought to predict, control, and explain the devastation natural disasters can bring. The raw power of a natural disaster can level a community in minutes, erasing all that was familiar and leaving the survivors stunned by the magnitude of their loss. Recent examples of natural disasters that triggered communal traumatic reactions include the California wildfires of 2018, which were the worst reported in history; Hurricanes Katrina and Sandy; the 2013 Moore, Oklahoma, tornado; and the 2013 Prescott, Arizona, wildfire, which killed 19 firefighters. Although the scope and destruction of natural disasters vary, similar general processes may underscore most disaster events. Wukich (2016) summarized these processes as "prevention, mitigation, preparedness, response and recovery" (p. 230). Before natural disasters strike, communities and agencies can focus on prevention, mitigation, and preparedness efforts, which could include developing response protocols, buttressing physical structures, and educating people about how to respond to disasters. The refinement of response and recovery protocols develops from experience, reflection, and strategic collaboration among disaster response agencies (Federal Emergency Management Agency [FEMA], 2016), and community interventions follow a timeline of recovery lasting years for some disaster events (see Figure 11.1)

FEMA Guidelines

FEMA published several resources to assist communities with disaster planning and recovery. The National Disaster Recovery Framework (FEMA, 2016) overviews this continuum of disaster planning and disaster recovery. FEMA's (2006) disaster planning model follows seven core principles to follow when developing disaster response plans and designing community recovery efforts:

1. Individual and family empowerment,
2. Leadership and local primacy,
3. Predisaster recovery planning,
4. Engaged partnerships and inclusiveness,
5. Unity of effort,
6. Timeliness and flexibility,
7. Resilience and sustainability, and
8. Psychological and emotional recovery (p. 5).

These principles set a tone for transparency, local empowerment, and respect for families, and they support the psychosocial recovery of individuals and the community. Counselors often serve communities coping with anxiety, fear, and grief during these crises. The FEMA Community Recovery Management Toolkit is available as a resource (http://www.fema.gov/national-disaster-recovery-framework/community-recovery-management-toolkit). This resource offers specific

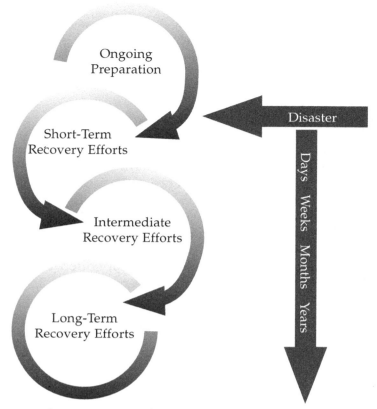

Figure 11.1 • The Disaster Planning and Responsiveness Timeline

recommendations for planning and disaster relief and provides the framework for counselors to work with clients experiencing distress.

Communal Trauma and Grief

Natural disasters and the sheer uncontrollable force of nature can evoke persistent hypervigilance and traumatic grief reactions in survivors. Victims and survivors grieve for the unimaginable loss of their loved ones and pets and reel from the destruction and loss of their homes and property while coping with a personal worldview that may now be radically different. They also experience what Arendt and Alesch (2015) have referred to as *experiential incongruence.*

Experiential incongruence occurs when disasters strike unexpectedly, out of context, or with incomprehensible magnitude (Arendt & Alesch, 2015). For example, experiencing 3 weeks of subzero weather in south Florida would be out of context for its residents, and the weather conditions would receive considerable media attention. The same cold spell in Greenland would be less newsworthy. Incongruence challenges worldviews and can destabilize a person's sense of safety and security. Experiential incongruence can also complicate reactions to disasters and other traumatic events (Arendt & Alesch, 2015). According to the American Red Cross (2019), this challenge may be especially true for children. See Sidebar 11.1 for information on addressing communal loss.

229

Sidebar 11.1 • Communal Loss

Just as with other types of grief and loss, the communal loss experience varies across and within communities. How do counselors respect the unique experience of clients while supporting community in their healing?

People respond to disasters with a host of physical and emotional reactions. Some people find it difficult to concentrate, sleep, or garner energy. Although several people's conditions improve in the short term (American Red Cross, 2019), other people isolate and continue to experience challenges in sleeping, eating, and in the affect regulation. In these instances, it is important that counselors avoid pathologizing their experiences. Rather, counselors provide an accepting space for clients to move through their grief at their own pace and understand that healing has its own timeframe. Counselors also recognize that behaviors that may appear maladaptive are actually strategies for survival. If supported, these strategies can transform into relational bonds that have the power to transcend the original trauma bond (Del Vecchio-Scully, 2018).

Aware of these dynamics, counselors assist people during all phases in the aftermath of disaster. They provide on-the-ground support immediately after a disaster and work with clients as they process their losses in longer term settings. The American Red Cross provides guidance to help responders, counselors, parents, and communities prepare for disasters and to navigate the aftermath of a crisis. Finally, when counselors approach disaster response systemically, they can appreciate that powerful traditions still drive many interactions, despite shattered infrastructures.

When Hurricane Katrina struck in 2005, more than 1,500 people died (FEMA, 2006), thousands more were displaced, and the damage to the New Orleans area was severe. In the aftermath, more than 10,000 people found their way to San Antonio, Texas (Reybold, Konopasky, Trepal, & Haberstroh, 2015). Many braved horrific situations and dangerous conditions on their journey. A local recently decommissioned Air Force base served as the focal point for the disaster recovery efforts and became a temporary home to thousands of displaced people. We (Thelma and Shane) volunteered with other members in our department to provide relief services for the evacuees. As we entered the facility, we were struck by the sheer magnitude of loss and uncertainty about how we could really be of any help. The need was high, and most social service agencies had only begun to establish themselves in this ocean of humanity. One local mental health group coordinating some of the intervention services asked us to walk around and identify people who seemed especially lost or in need of assistance. That first day, we helped people find their way to the restroom, looked for lost pets, and listened. Eventually, the triage systems came online, companies staffed cubicles with social workers and counselors, and the agency and professional hierarchies took root.

Communities are social systems composed of overt and unspoken interpersonal, economic, and cultural expectations. When disaster strikes, recovery efforts can infuse structure, support, and resources in the ensuing vacuum. Without compassionate and informed first responders and law enforcement strategies, the site of a natural disaster can breed opportunities for illegal and violent behavior. Violence spawned from a natural disaster can be real, and people can become targets of violence in the aftermath of an extreme natural event.

Community Violence

From small communities to large cities and nations, violence pervades the fabric of society. According to the Bureau of Justice Statistics (BJS, 2016), just more than 1 million people older than age 12 suffered from physical violence in 2014. Nearly 16,000 people died from murder in 2015, and just more than 9,600 of them (Federal Bureau of Investigation, 2015) were killed with a firearm. Homicide by firearm is the most common cause of violent death in the United States, killing roughly as many people who die in car accidents.

When a person is murdered, the effects ripple through a community. The effects of these losses can range from the devastation felt by close friends and family to widespread reactions when many people experience unexpected violence. Most people (68%) who have experienced a violent crime have developed social and economic problems (BJS, 2014). Thus, the toll that violence takes on a community can be profound, and the recovery process following a communal trauma must address long-term goals. Barron (2013) conducted a needs assessment of the Sandy Hook community and concluded, "We must adequately brace the support structures in the community that support the children in the community: Families, First Responders, Health Care Providers, Educators, Clergy, Arts and Recreation" (p. 11). Although the trends in violence seem to be decreasing, only about half of the victims report these acts to the police (BJS, 2014). These data suggest that many people suffer privately and perhaps alone.

Global Crises: War and Immigration

In recent years, hundreds of thousands of people have fled from the horrors of war. As we write this chapter, news reports detail the horrors of chemical warfare in Syria and a growing crisis on the southern border of the United States. Hundreds of thousands of people have died in that conflict, and hundreds of thousands of people are displaced, rejected, and suffering profoundly across the globe. It is not surprising then that many immigrants suffer from posttraumatic stress disorder (PTSD), anxiety, and profound traumatic grief (Graef-Calliess, 2017). They yearn for a home that may not exist anymore, struggle to find employment and connection in new cultures, and mourn their many losses (Villalba, 2009; Williams, 2003; Yakushko, Watson, & Thompson, 2008). These stressors are real, pervasive, and not easy to fix (Cárdenas, Taylor, & Adelman, 1993; Graef-Calliess, 2017). Counselors honor the pain, hear the losses, and work with immigrant clients to address the grief, trauma, and current situations (Nilsson, Schale, & Khamphakdy-Brown, 2011).

Given the chance, immigrants want to lead successful and productive lives in their host country. They benefit from guidance and resources to help them begin anew in a strange and sometimes intolerant community (Duffey & Haberstroh, 2018; Yakushko et al., 2008). Practical strategies, concrete suggestions, and training opportunities can provide some hope for people suffering from the horror, grief, and loss of war. Understanding these stories of loss from a relational framework provides counselors with conceptualization strategies to understand how forced disconnections, traumatic loss, and the intrusion of the media and others into a wounded community can make things worse. See Sidebar 11.2 for information on counseling immigrants.

The Relational Foundation for Responding to Community Violence and Trauma

From a relational perspective, disasters and violence forcibly separate people from others, shatter a sense of safety, and limit much needed access to resources. These abrupt disconnections from existing supports, comforting relationships, and familiar routines can shock people into isolation. The fracturing among communal trauma survivors often causes debilitating survivor guilt. At other times, people may not know how to speak to one another about their shared trauma. Avoidance, fatigue, and outright denial can freeze productive communication. Other community members may respond to these events with a desire to put the event behind them and move forward, and they may resent people who want to reflect on and discuss their common loss. The ways in which people relate to one another throughout the course of coping with a community trauma will characterize how, and the degree to which, they heal. When counselors live in a community ravaged by violence, their work becomes even more challenging. This work is further complicated when counselors are survivors themselves. The Sandy Hook community is small, and it is common for residents to have multiple roles in the community. Counselors practicing in Newtown had multiple relationships to the deceased and the survivors.

Counselors Living in Traumatized Communities: Connecting in Shared Trauma

Horrific violence, such as the shootings at Sandy Hook Elementary School, MSD High School, Sutherland Springs Church, and others affect local counselors deeply, and they share in a traumatic reality (Tosone, Bauwens, & Glassman, 2016). Communal trauma survivors are unique in their needs compared with other types of trauma survivors. Each communal trauma has its own characteristics and culture. Survivors are affected by media coverage, the criminal aspect and investigation, and perhaps the loss of body functions or body parts, as seen in the Boston Marathon bombings. Many experience the loss of homes and personal belongings in the aftermath of a natural disaster, such as Hurricanes Katrina and Sandy. To

Sidebar 11.2 • Counseling Immigrants

Some immigrants may suffer from posttraumatic stress disorder along with other social-cultural concerns, such as biases toward their native culture. They may also experience acculturation distress as they attempt to adapt to their new environment. In addition, immigrants may feel alone and worry about their homeland. Counselors can help support immigrants by offering understanding and acceptance for them to process their fears. What other factors may you need to consider when working with immigrants?

competently work with communal trauma survivors, we must understand and acknowledge cultural concerns, educate ourselves on the medical aspects of survivor injuries, and attend to our own reactions to the event(s).

When, as counselors, we experience first-hand trauma exposure, by virtue of residing within the affected community, we may serve the traumatized community while attending to our own psychological wounds (Tosone, Nuttman-Shwartz, & Stephens, 2012). We experience our own traumatic process and need support to share the horrors we hear and see. As we listen to stories about people we know and psychological places they visit, we can potentially develop our own trauma reactions.

Existential Trauma

Counselors hear stories that hit close to home in almost every way. When counselors and clients connect in times of destruction, chaos, and horrific loss, we share in what is termed an *existential trauma* (Grand, 2013). There are times when we both struggle to find meaning and purpose in a circumstance that alters the moral fabric of a community. Acknowledging this existential trauma fosters the therapeutic bond with community members who reach out for counseling. When a shared and shattered reality is the tapestry for counseling work, we connect with our humanity; respect our need for wellness; and work through our own trauma with peers, counselors, and supervisors. There are times when our trauma reactions can be multifaceted, heart wrenching, and haunting to us throughout our work and personal life. Seeking support, recognizing when we do not have the resources to give our clients, and sharing healing experiences with others are vital to our health and well-being.

Shared Trauma

The nature of a counselor's job is to share the burden of trauma, to help shoulder pain and confusion, and to provide compassion and strategies for healing. When counselors live in a shared traumatic space with clients, they experience what is called a *primary trauma* (Saakvitne, 2002). This trauma can be exacerbated when communities are overrun by the media, preventing access to travel and connection with others. This happened at the Sandy Hook Elementary School and the MSD High School shootings. Likewise, during the Boston Marathon bombings, the search for the perpetrators required that the city of Boston and surrounding suburbs close schools, businesses, and public transportation, extending the traumatization beyond the initial event. Counselors experiencing primary trauma experienced their own gut-wrenching feelings, worried for their loved ones, feared for their own safety, and struggled to make sense of a new terrible reality. As counselors live in their communities, they hear stories of others' losses, and as they work closely with those in pain, they hear the intimate details of many losses. These stories clearly shape the hearts and minds of professional helpers.

Secondary and Vicarious Traumas

The effects of shared trauma on a counselor's family, friends, and religious community can permeate these relationships and possibly erode once strong connections (Tosone et al., 2012). While dealing with a primary trauma, counselors may experience secondary traumatic effects that arise from a horrific communal event, such as the shootings at Sandy Hook Elementary School, the Orlando Pulse nightclub, the Denver theatre, MSD High School, and Sutherland Springs Baptist church. Secondary traumatization can happen in small and large groups and can occur among colleagues when one individual is more affected than another, among social groups, and within the community at large. Staff members at both Sandy Hook Elementary School and MSD High School described being triggered in staff meetings when listening to peers and affected by the reactions of others. Although the trauma-bond among school staff tends to be strong, the differences in their experiences—a direct witness, a gunshot survivor, or a staff member who sheltered in place—fracture the trauma-bond and lead to resentment and rupturing of the relationship (Del Vecchio-Scully, 2019).

Hearing others' stories can open wounds, reinvigorate intrusive images, and deepen hopelessness. As counselors, we are not immune to the stories from our personal friends, colleagues, and social networks. These stories hit home and can reopen our pain. Finally, as counselors, we hear the private details of our clients' losses. Our imagination can be flooded with horrific images and intimate information. Caring about clients, and really hearing their losses, opens counselors to vicarious traumatization. When, as counselors, we bear clients' traumatic stories and share a common traumatic reality (Figley, 1995; McCann & Pearlman, 1990), we can be retraumatized and lose our way in this vicarious trauma. See Sidebar 11.3 for information on counselor self-care when assisting traumatized communities.

The Journey of Healing

How, then, do counselors begin this journey of healing with survivors? We believe it begins with a personal awareness that can be mirrored by those with whom we are connected and with an honest evaluation of our clinical competence. This work requires a commitment to enhancing our skills and training. It requires that we attend to our own wounds, personal experiences, and reactions to the communal trauma as well as the perpetrators, victims, and survivors. It calls for us to remain connected to others and to allow our relationships to support our own health and resilience. Healing following a communal trauma is complex and requires strength and courage far beyond what most individuals can imagine. Counseling communal trauma survivors requires clinical expertise in complex trauma, traumatic grief, and sound methods of caring for each other and one's soul beyond traditional self-care. Professional helpers, depending on the relationship to the event itself, will experience a wide range of emotional reactions and will be personally and professionally affected.

Sidebar 11.3 • Counselor Self-Care in Traumatized Communities

Counselors in a traumatized community experience their own traumas, which can be complicated when they hear the experiences of those in their immediate world. Counselors need a social support system themselves. They may find people outside their community to debrief about their experiences as a traumatized member of the community and a helper to others. How would you seek social support and create personal parameters to give yourself moments of peace and respite if you were to experience communal trauma?

In my (Deb's) experience in working with survivors of the September 11th terrorist attack, as well as the Sandy Hook Elementary School and MSD High School shootings, I noticed that communal trauma wounds were influenced by the type of event (natural disaster vs. violence or sudden unexpected loss), the physical and emotional proximity of the event, and the degree of impact. As a result, the scope of reactions can best be considered as a continuum from mild with low personal impact to severe with high personal impact. For example, whereas Hurricane Sandy deeply affected anyone living on the shoreline with loss of home and personal possessions, others experienced only severe weather. Although I was unable to work for a week because of widespread power outages, I was fortunate to escape unscathed from the storm. As counselors deal with power outages, lack of resources, family trauma, and their own feelings and shock, they venture out into the destruction, chaos, and pain, remembering to nurture themselves and others and apply all they have learned to help hurting communities.

Working With Communities in Crisis, Trauma, and Loss

Traumatic Grief

Not all traumatic events leave people with enduring grief, but all trauma contains elements of loss. When the loss is particularly unexpected, violent, tragic, or unexplained, traumatic grief can occur. Grief is considered a normal and healthy response to loss. However, when the symptoms of grief are overwhelming and disrupt normal daily functioning for an extended period, people may experience *complicated grief* (Duffey, 2014; Neimeyer, 2012). People experience this kind of grief as a persistent and heightened state of bereavement. They may not be able to stop thinking about the circumstances of the loss, or they may be at odds with making sense of its enormity. They are challenged in making the loss fit into their lives. The traumatic event seems so incongruent and so foreign that an awareness of absence becomes a primary characteristic of a complicated grief reaction (Shear, Frank, Houck, & Reynolds, 2005). Although survivors of communal trauma share similarities, there are differences in how they process the experience and in their available external and internal resources.

Communal Neurobiological Responses to Trauma and Neuroception

As we discussed in Chapter 4, a person's autonomic nervous system springs into action during a traumatic event. Adaptive neurological responses happen automatically, and within milliseconds, the brain activates nervous system functions to help people avoid danger. A person's heart rate increases, muscles tense, and stress hormones flood their system. These responses are commonly known as the fight, flight, or freeze response (van der Kolk, 2014), and they equip people to escape dangerous situations. Although these functions help people escape threats, they also can persist, characterizing some of the experiences of PTSD. Activation of the autonomic nervous system, triggered by memories and associations, may lead people to avoid addressing their trauma, remain hypervigilant, and suffer from insomnia and sleep problems (van der Kolk, 2014).

Conversely, other key brain structures deactivate to adapt to a threat. Usually, nontraumatic memories are routed through Broca's area of the brain, which is responsible for language processing. During a traumatic event, Broca's area essentially deactivates. This means that people experience traumatic memories in sensory form. Rather than remembering a traumatic event in words, they feel the bodily sensations of the trauma. The sounds, smells, tastes, and images remain as memories. Trauma survivors often struggle to provide a coherent verbal recall of the event, and they can grow increasingly anxious, hyperaroused, and dissociative if prompted to try. Simply thinking or attempting to talk about a traumatic event can activate and trigger the limbic brain. Further talking about it is unlikely to calm it. When discussing trauma, many people feel visceral feelings of hypervigilance and hyperarousal (Marich, 2014).

Porges (2004) discussed how these neurobiological processes operate within social contexts. When a person is in a state of distress, these autonomic systems engage, and they show anguish and fear through subtle and obvious physiological effects. In social situations, people read these reactions subconsciously as their brain scans for danger and safety. Subtle changes in a person's face indicating distress generate autonomic reactions in those around them. Porges described this process as *neuroception,* and he explained stress contagion within traumatized communities. Facilitated through mirror neurons, neuroception can keep communities feeling on edge and explain people's social vulnerability to traumatic triggers. Interventions that foster emotional relief and healing connections can soften the edges of shared anxiety.

Thus, effective treatment of complex trauma and traumatic grief requires specialized training and expertise in whole-brain, bottom-up treatment approaches. These include eye movement desensitization and reprocessing (Shapiro & Maxfield, 2002); brainspotting (Grand, 2013); mindfulness-based approaches; neurofeedback and biofeedback (Hodgdon et al., 2016; van der Kolk et al., 2016); somatic-based approaches, including somatic experiencing (Levine, 2005); emotional freedom techniques (Feinstein & Feinstein, 2010); and treatment based on the neurosequential model of therapeutics (Perry, 2006).

Timing and Type of Interventions

The immediate response to a community-based tragedy or natural disaster is referred to as *disaster mental health* (American Red Cross, 2019). Psychological first aid is considered the gold-standard model of response during this phase, and it consists of primary needs assessment of basic and mental health needs, promoting stabilization and coping, and targeted interventions (American Red Cross, 2019; Rudow, 2012). Victim services may vary from state to state, and for events that occur outside of the United States, the Office of Justice for Victims of Overseas Terrorism, U.S. Department of Justice, provides services and support to victims traveling abroad. These agencies are tasked with providing direct support to affected individuals, and it is important for counselors to be acquainted with the scope and types of services and methods to access victim services.

After the immediate disaster and basic community needs are assessed and stabilized, the intermediate phase begins (Del Vecchio-Scully & Glaser, 2018). It is in this phase that the creation of organized strategies and plans for individual and community recovery begin to take place. This involves identifying affected individuals and groups, targeting services, building resources, enhancing clinical capacity of existing organizations, and instituting trauma-informed training.

Factors, Approaches, and Interventions That Foster Healing and Resiliency

Creating the Newtown Recovery and Resiliency Team (NRRT)

The NRRT was formed with funding from a 7-million-dollar U.S. Department of Justice (2013) grant to address consequence management secondary to the Sandy Hook Elementary School shooting. Led by two licensed professional counselors, this was the first U.S. Department of Justice grant of its kind to address the mental health needs of an entire community following a school shooting. The team consisted of a community outreach liaison, clinical recovery leader/trauma specialist, project manager, and three part-time care coordinators.

The grant offered basic directives, and the team was challenged to create a project plan, goals, policies, and services while establishing best practices for a highly affected community. The initial task began with a comprehensive assessment of the community's needs based on these characteristics. Reflecting on my (Deb's) experience as the NRRT Clinical Recovery Leader, I see several principles as vital when establishing a communal trauma recovery team. For one, the team must be educated and operate from a trauma-informed lens. The physical structure should be designed, when possible, to support trauma survivors' privacy and concerns. Safety is a primary concern among trauma survivors, and the Substance Abuse and Mental Health Services Administration (2009) has recommended safe physical environments with culturally familiar decorations, child-friendly spaces, a handicapped entrance and means of egress, handicapped bathrooms, private entrances, and well-lit parking areas with lockable doors.

Privacy is another major concern, requiring visible efforts to enhance confidentiality with secure, confidential, and double-locked client files and white noise machines and soundproofing. Furthermore, a long-term sustainability strategic plan is vital to not only engender trust in the community but also secure ongoing services beyond initial funding. When creating a recovery team, the members must have a high tolerance for public scrutiny, aggressive reactions, and others' inability to acknowledge the value of members' efforts and contributions. Team members must be educated in emotional tolerance to avoid taking such criticisms personally. Fostering team cohesion, mutual support, and self-care is vital to prevent vicarious traumatization (Chandra et al., 2011).

A large part of the Sandy Hook work involved meeting with individuals and families to listen to their stories, identify their needs, and match them with therapeutic supports. The team developed a comprehensive resource list of therapists, therapeutic services, and resources to aid in this process. As the NRRT Clinical Recovery Leader, I (Deb) was tasked with working with some of the most highly affected groups, and I was embedded in the Sandy Hook Elementary School as a staff support clinician.

Communal trauma recovery is complex and requires multiple types of counseling and social-emotional activities. We found that most needed the therapeutic support of a primary trauma-informed therapist and additional supplemental support of other interventions, including trauma-sensitive yoga, exercise, expressive art therapies (art, music, play, drama), and equine-assisted therapy, as well as meditation and mindfulness classes. Families who were directly affected by the Sandy Hook Elementary School shooting received comfort dogs, which were widely used in the schools to assist children when they returned to school following the shooting.

Although trauma is experienced individually, a traumatized community heals collectively. The NRRT worked to form partnerships with community and religious leaders as well as communal trauma experts, and we collaborated to provide community programs and services. One collaboration provided psychoeducation and support for Sandy Hook therapists, education leaders, and the Sandy Hook Elementary School staff and families.

The NRRT: Ongoing Recovery Support

Clearly, organizing an effort such as this is complex and requires a community. I (Deb) reached out to then–American Counseling Association President Thelma Duffey and sought her support in Newtown. She organized a team from the University of Texas at San Antonio (UTSA), and together we created a program for clinicians, survivors, faculty who were present at the shooting, faculty new to the community, staff, the school leadership, and the city's first selectman. This began a collaboration between UTSA and the NRRT that continued beyond the work in Newtown. Later, when this group led efforts to support the Sutherland Springs community following the shooting in their neighboring community, I (Deb) provided support and consultation to them. Soon thereafter, UTSA became part of a larger coalition created by the Texas Governor's Office, which continues to meet and offer services to Sutherland Springs and the surrounding community.

The Sutherland Springs Shooting: It Takes a Village

The shootings at the First Baptist Church of Sutherland Springs involved a massacre of exponential proportions while in a space where most people would expect to feel most safe. Children, parents, grandparents, aunts, uncles, and cousins were all beloved members of a small community that enjoyed the calm and tranquil beauty of this Central Texas town. As a community, Sutherland Springs was characterized by self-sufficiency, privacy, and congeniality. Following the shooting, national media and others descended on the area, while Sutherland Springs and the surrounding communities attempted to assess needs and care for their own.

Recognizing the importance of remaining respectful to the expressed needs of the community, we (Thelma and Shane) joined other nearby groups in a collaboration organized in part by the Texas Governor's Office, which resulted in the formation of the Collaborated Response Team of South Texas. Given the diverse efforts and skills needed and available, one of the goals of the group was to, in providing support, optimize the skills and training of those involved. UTSA's goal was to establish a center easily accessible to community members, and, with the unparalleled partnership of the Children's Bereavement Center of South Texas (CBCST), we established a centrally located crisis clinic we called Paloma Place.

Quickly, our collective attention was drawn to (a) meeting with the community to learn more about how we could help, (b) building the infrastructure for this service, (c) collaborating with many sectors of the city and region through the Collaborated Response Team of South Texas, (d) navigating the UTSA administrative and legal offices, (e) successfully working with the CBCST to secure our center and create a structure, (f) identifying personnel to lead the effort onsite, (g) working with the CBCST during the development and groundbreaking stages of its opening, and (h) participating in ongoing events, including regular meetings with the Texas Governor's Office and members of the Collaborated Response Team of South Texas.

As part of this work, and a grant secured by the U.S. Department of Justice, UTSA doctoral students serve clients in individual, group, and family crisis counseling, neurofeedback services, creative and expressive counseling, and older adult counseling. Recognizing the complexity of trauma, these services were designed to continue as long as services are needed.

Counseling Strategies

In the aftermath of a communal trauma, community-wide education on all aspects of trauma is needed. Education may include common communal reactions, treatment options, and access to treatment; available resources; and, in the event of a weather-related disaster or an event that disrupts housing, access to financial support, temporary housing, medical care, and activities of daily living needs. Public psychoeducation should be delivered as early as possible, repeatedly, and through a variety of delivery methods, including technology: automated phone calls, text messages, email communication, and media alerts. Collaborating with religious leaders is helpful in delivering information to individuals without access to technology.

Sensitivity to the needs of the community, as well as recognizing the fracturing between and among groups that can arise, is vital. For example, the burden of survivor guilt was a recurrent theme among survivors in Newtown. Navigating through the complexities of altered relationships, immeasurable grief, and guilt was among the bigger challenges the community faced. In response, we provided workshops, programs, resources, public forums, and panel discussions to clinicians, leaders, and residents of the Newtown community (Del Vecchio-Scully & Glaser, 2018). Furthermore, we strived to provide ongoing communication, because doing so is essential to the well-being of survivors tasked with managing the personal and psychological consequences of the traumatic event while also seeking services and resources for themselves and their families.

In another community response to tragedy, Orlando Pulse Shooting Survivor Counselors responded to the MSD High School community. Soon after the shooting, a group of these counselors formed Professionals United for Parkland (PU4P) to identify and meet the short- and long-term needs related to the mental health and well-being of South Florida. The group provided education for the general community and area professionals, clinical training, clinical services, support for clinicians, and more. This nonpolitical group works alongside other local organizations to ensure that they identify gaps in current services and that the needs of the community are adequately addressed (PU4P, 2018). As part of the coordination, they created a database of trauma-informed clinicians; sponsor, facilitate, and promote clinical trauma and grief training; assess the mental health needs of the community; and provide support (consultation, supervision, therapy, support groups) for mental health professionals in collaboration with other organizations with similar missions.

Similarly, the shootings at Sandy Hook Elementary School inspired several families to form nonprofit foundations in their children's names. Some initiatives focused on their children's interests, whereas others sought to further the understanding of the brain and its connection to the factors that lead to mass violence. For example, the Avielle Foundation, which was formed in memory of Avielle Richman, strives to prevent violence and to build compassion through neuroscience research, community engagement, and education. The foundation is also dedicated to community engagement and education initiatives that empower youth, parents, teachers, health care providers, law enforcement, and the everyday citizen to advocate for brain health in themselves and others (Avielle Foundation, 2019).

Community interventions also encourage connection and creativity. For example, the Avielle Foundation's Brainstorming public events bring renowned speakers to Newtown and activities such as the Ragnar Relay, in which community members form teams, train for months in advance, and run in a 26.4-mile relay. These initiatives bring many groups together, fostering new friendships. The initial strategies for survival of isolation and disconnection in the early months and years following the shooting are transforming into relational bonds that transcend the original trauma bond. This is the power of healing in relationships and in community.

Case Example and Applications for Hope and Healing

The Newtown community suffered devastating losses following the school shooting on December 14, 2014. Through the U.S. Department of Justice grant, systems were set in place to support the community via the office of the NRRT. Herein we describe a collaborative event involving a psychoeducational and relationally based retreat designed to foster increased hope and healing within the community. The retreat included Newtown teachers, noncertified staff and their families, counselors in the community, school district leadership (principal, assistant principals, superintendent), and the town's first selectman.

Tragedies such as these can bring people together or tear them apart. Sometimes, they do both. In this case, community members continued in their valiant efforts to find a pathway following the devastation, and the NRRT and UTSA collaboration was yet another support for them. Timing is an integral factor in how people process information, and there are times when information gleaned early on in a tragedy cannot be integrated into awareness. For this reason, the team reintroduced information that may have been previously challenging to process, introduced new information that could potentially help them make sense of their experiences and make shifts in their healing, and created a forum for everyone to share in the material and experience and to come together for a meal.

Disconnection is one of the casualties of communal trauma, and isolation is a frequent experience. Creating contexts that promote connection, compassion, and empathy was integral to the goal of the retreat. In addition, through large- and small-group presentations and discussions, participants were encouraged to learn and practice (a) self-care tools for managing and discharging stress, (b) the difference between trauma and grief reactions, (c) emotional self-regulation skills, (d) the brain's reaction to trauma and traumatic grief, and (e) the ways in which a person's personality style may affect his or her needs during a crisis and influence how the trauma is processed. We also provided concurrent support programs for spouses or significant others, as well as babysitting services.

To stand before a large group that experienced one of the most horrific tragedies in U.S. history was sobering. We recognized how we could not know their experiences, and we could not imagine awaking to this new reality. What we could connect with, however, was our sincere desire to help in whatever way we could and to provide information and shared time that could hopefully be of support. Our efforts were well received, and we discussed topics such as cultural contexts of trauma, trauma and the brain, descriptions of shared trauma, vicarious and secondary trauma, and differences between trauma (PTSD) and traumatic grief.

Given the relational challenges that communal trauma engenders, participants seemed to be curious about how it is that people respond so differently to trauma. "Why is it that my neighbor will barely speak to me now? I miss her company so much." "How is it that one person wants to shut down all discussion on the tragedy, while others so badly need to talk?" We used a tool called the Enneagram Personality Typology to illustrate a perspective on how people respond to crises and traumatic events (Webb, 2013). Recognizing that some decisions that were made were not personal, but rather a result of a hard-wired response based on how a person's personality responds to crises, diluted some painful feelings and brought context to the complexity of communal pain.

To conclude the event with a shared meal, where people sat and shared space with one another, and with us, was simply beautiful. It brought home the reality that we all need one another, and traumas may be too big for any of us to bear alone. It also illuminated the differences in how people process their experiences. There are times when we need others as well as times when we need to be alone. Yet, through it all, at various intervals in the process, we need each other. Moreover, we need the self-compassion to know that our path cannot be rushed or silenced.

Future Directions and Emerging Research

A common theme in this chapter and throughout this text is the importance of community. When communities are traumatized, the ripple effect of pain and wounding has large reaching effects. People often hurt in isolation, yet there is much potential for healing through community. Trauma is disconnecting by its nature, as people attempt to live with great loss. Research focusing on how counselors can respect and honor these disconnections while also creating and supporting opportunities for healing through community may be a salient aspect for future research.

References

American Red Cross. (2019). *Emotional responses*. Retrieved from http://www.redcross.org/find-help/disaster-recovery/recovering-emotionally

Arendt, L. A., & Alesch, D. J. (2015). *Long-term community recovery from natural disasters*. Boca Raton, FL: CRC Press.

Avielle Foundation. (2019). *Mission and vision*. Retrieved from https://avielle-foundation.org/about-the-foundation/welcome-message/

Barron, J. (2013, October 25). Almost a year after massacre, Newtown begins razing Sandy Hook school. *The New York Times*. Retrieved from https://www.nytimes.com/2013/10/26/nyregion/almost-a-year-after-massacre-newtown-begins-razing-sandy-hook.html?searchResultPosition=1

Bureau of Justice Statistics. (2014, September 23). *Socio-emotional impact of violent crime.* Retrieved from https://www.bjs.gov/index.cfm?ty=pbdetail&iid=5114

Bureau of Justice Statistics. (2016). *Criminal victimization, 2015.* Retrieved from https://www.bjs.gov/content/pub/pdf/cv15_sum.pdf

Cárdenas, J., Taylor, L., & Adelman, H. S. (1993). Transition support for immigrant students. *Journal of Multicultural Counseling and Development, 21,* 203–210. https://doi.org/10.1002/j.2161-1912.1993.tb00231.x

Chandra, A., Lara-Cinisomo, S., Jaycox, L., Tanielian, T., Han, B., Burns, R., & Ruder, T. (2011). Views from the homefront: The experiences of youth and spouses from military families. *Rand Health Quarterly, 1*(1), 12.

Del Vecchio-Scully, D. (2018, August 3). *Communal trauma: A journey of hope and healing.* Presentation at the Florida Counseling Association, Florida Atlantic University, Boca Raton, FL.

Del Vecchio-Scully, D. (2019, January 7). *A journey of hope and healing: Anniversary reactions, trauma, and mourning.* Oral presentation at Professional Development Day, Marjory Stoneman Douglas Staff, Coral Springs, FL.

Del Vecchio-Scully, D., & Glaser, M. (2018). Disaster recovery in Newtown: The intermediate stage. In J. M. Webber & J. B. Mascari (Eds.), *Disaster mental health counseling: A guide to preparing and responding* (4th ed., pp. 233–252). Alexandria, VA: American Counseling Association.

Duffey, T. (2014). Divorce and other loss issues in family therapy. In D. Capuzzi & M. Stauffer (Eds.), *Foundations of couples, marriage, and family counseling* (pp. 449–478). Hoboken, NJ: Wiley.

Duffey, T., & Haberstroh, S. (2018). Current issues and trends in the counseling profession. In S. C. Nassar & S. G. Niles (Eds.), *Orientation to professional counseling: Past, present, and future trends* (pp. 311–340). Alexandria, VA: American Counseling Association.

Federal Bureau of Investigation. (2015). *2015 crime in the United States.* Retrieved from https://ucr.fbi.gov/crime-in-the-u.s/2015/crime-in-the-u.s.-2015/offenses-known-to-law-enforcement/murder

Federal Emergency Management Agency. (2006, April). *Summary report on building performance: Hurricane Katrina 2005.* Retrieved from https://www.fema.gov/media-library-data/20130726-1446-20490-0294/548_SumRprt0329fnl.pdf

Federal Emergency Management Agency. (2016). *Publication 1.* Retrieved from https://www.fema.gov/pub1

Feinstein, D., & Feinstein, D. (2010). Rapid treatment of PTSD: Why psychological exposure with acupoint tapping may be effective. *Psychotherapy: Theory, Research, Practice, Training, 47,* 385–402. https://doi.org/10.1037/a0021171

Figley, C. R. (1995). Compassion fatigue as secondary traumatic stress disorder: An overview. In C. R. Figley (Ed.), *Compassion fatigue: Coping with secondary traumatic stress disorder in those who treat the traumatized* (Brunner/Mazel psychological stress series, No. 23, pp. 1–20). Philadelphia, PA: Brunner/Mazel.

Graef-Calliess, I. (2017). Working with traumatized immigrants with a PTSD diagnosis. *European Psychiatry, 41,* S17. https://doi.org/10.1016/j.eurpsy.2017.01.105

Grand, D. (2013). *Brainspotting: The revolutionary new therapy for rapid and effective change.* Boulder, CO: Sounds True.

Hodgdon, H., Gapen, M., Musicaro, R., Suvak, M., Hamlin, E., & Spinazzola, J. (2016). A randomized controlled study of neurofeedback for chronic PTSD. *PLoS ONE, 11*(12), e0166752. https://doi.org/10.1371/journal.pone.0166752

Levine, P. (2005). *Somatic experiencing: Resilience, regulation, and self.* Unpublished manuscript.

Marich, J. (2014). *Trauma made simple.* Eau Claire, WI: PESI.

McCann, I. L., & Pearlman, L. A. (1990). Vicarious traumatization: A framework for understanding the psychological effects of working with victims. *Journal of Traumatic Stress, 3,* 131–149. https://doi.org/10.1007/BF00975140

Neimeyer, R. A. (2012). *Techniques of grief therapy creative practices for counseling the bereaved.* New York, NY: Routledge.

Nilsson, J. E., Schale, C. L., & Khamphakdy-Brown, S. (2011). Facilitating trainees' multicultural development and social justice advocacy through a refugee/immigrant mental health program. *Journal of Counseling & Development, 89,* 413–422. https://doi.org/10.1002/j.1556-6676.2011.tb02838.x

Perry, B. D. (2006). Applying principles of neurodevelopment to clinical work with maltreated and traumatized children: The neurosequential model of therapeutics. In N. B. Webb (Ed.), *Social work practice with children and families: Working with traumatized youth in child welfare* (pp. 27–52). New York, NY: Guilford Press.

Porges, S. W. (2004). Neuroception: A subconscious system for detecting threats and safety. *ZERO TO THREE Journal, 24*(5), 19–24. Retrieved from https://pdfs.semanticscholar.org/44e4/004fb363b42a17b92035971fe097ae29cccb.pdf

Professionals United for Parkland. (2018). *Mission statement: What drives us.* Retrieved from http://www.pu4p.org/about-us/mission-statement/

Reybold, L. E., Konopasky, A., Trepal, H., & Haberstroh, S. (2015). Negotiating the practitioner-faculty dialectic: How counselor educators responded to Hurricane Katrina. *Innovative Higher Education, 40,* 229–245. https://doi.org/10.1007/s10755-014-9307-2

Rudow, H. (2012, November 16). Sandy's aftermath: Counselors weigh in on how to help. *Counseling Today.* Retrieved from https://ct.counseling.org/2012/11/

Saakvitne, K. W. (2002). Shared trauma: The therapist's increased vulnerability. *Psychoanalytic Dialogues, 12,* 443–449. https://doi.org/10.1080/10481881209348678

Shapiro, F., & Maxfield, L. (2002). Eye movement desensitization and reprocessing (EMDR): Information processing in the treatment of trauma. *Journal of Clinical Psychology, 58,* 933–946. https://doi.org/10.1002/jclp.10068

Shear, K., Frank, E., Houck, P. R., & Reynolds, C. F. (2005). Treatment of complicated grief: A randomized controlled trial. *Journal of the American Medical Association, 293,* 2601–2608. https://doi.org/10.1001/jama.293.21.2601

Substance Abuse and Mental Health Services Administration. (2009). *Practice guidelines: Core elements in responding to mental health crises.* Retrieved from https://store.samhsa.gov/system/files/sma09-4427.pdf

Tosone, C., Bauwens, J., & Glassman, M. (2016). The shared traumatic and professional posttraumatic growth inventory. *Research on Social Work Practice, 26,* 286–294. https://doi.org/10.1177/1049731514549814

Tosone, C., Nuttman-Shwartz, O., & Stephens, T. (2012). Shared trauma: When the professional is personal. *Clinical Social Work Journal, 40,* 231–239. https://doi.org/10.1007/s10615-012-0395-0

U.S. Department of Justice. (2013, September 27). *Attorney general Eric Holder announces funding for school resource officers in Newtown, Conn.* Retrieved from https://www.justice.gov/opa/pr/attorney-general-eric-holder-announces-funding-school-resource-officers-newtown-conn

van der Kolk, B. (2014). *The body keeps the score: Brain, mind, and body in the healing of trauma.* New York, NY: Viking.

van der Kolk, B., Hodgdon, H., Gapen, M., Musicaro, R., Suvak, M., . . . Spinazzola, J. (2016). A randomized controlled study of neurofeedback for chronic PTSD. *PLoS ONE, 11*(12), e0166752. https://doi.org/10.1371/journal.pone.0166752

Villalba, J. A. (2009). Addressing immigrant and refugee issues in multicultural counselor education. *Journal of Professional Counseling: Practice, Theory and Research, 37*, 1–12. https://doi.org/10.1080/15566382.2009.12033851

Webb, K. (2013). *Principles of the Enneagram* (2nd ed.). London, England: Jessica Kingsley.

Williams, C. (2003). Developing community involvement: Contrasting local and regional participatory cultures in Britain and their implications for policy. *Regional Studies, 37*, 531–541. https://doi.org/10.1080/0034340032000089086

Wukich, C. (2016). Government social media messages across disaster phases. *Journal of Contingencies and Crisis Management, 24*, 230–243. https://doi.org/10.1111/1468-5973.12119

Yakushko, O., Watson, M., & Thompson, S. (2008). Stress and coping in the lives of recent immigrants and refugees: Considerations for counseling. *International Journal for the Advancement of Counselling, 30*, 167–178. https://doi.org/1007/s10447-008-9054-0

Multiple-Choice Questions

1. Wukich (2016) summarized a natural disaster event to include
   a. Prevention, mitigation, and rebuilding.
   b. Preparing and rebuilding.
   c. Prevention, mitigation, preparedness, response, and recovery.
   d. Preparing, waiting, and responding.

2. Which emergency agency published resources to assist communities with disaster planning?
   a. Federal Emergency Management Agency (FEMA)
   b. FEMMA
   c. State-mandated disaster planning
   d. Federal-published disaster plan

3. Counselors mainly serve communities during _____ and _____
   a. Recovery, evacuation.
   b. The disaster, before the disaster.
   c. Response, evacuation.
   d. Response, recovery efforts.

4. After a natural disaster, Arendt and Alesch (2015) stated that people experience
   a. Experiential incongruence.
   b. Crisis.
   c. Communal grief.
   d. None of the above

5. People respond to a natural disasters by finding it hard to
   a. Concentrate.
   b. Have energy.
   c. Sleep.
   d. All of the above

6. Communal trauma is devastating to
   a. Members of a community.
   b. People in other communities.
   c. Counselors working with trauma.
   d. All of the above

7. What percentage of people who experience a violent crime tend to develop social and economic issues?
   a. 10%
   b. 80%
   c. 68%
   d. 1%

8. Trauma can be intensified when communities are bombarded by media.
   a. False, this does not affect trauma
   b. True, only when the community is in a small city
   c. False, media helps trauma symptoms
   d. True, this can make it hard for connection with others

9. According to the chapter, communal trauma may make counselors more open to
   a. Vicarious trauma.
   b. Travel.
   c. Biases.
   d. Empathy.

10. Complicated grief refers to
    a. Numerous relationships.
    b. A heighted state of bereavement.
    c. Overwhelming grief.
    d. Both b and c

11. Which area of the brain deactivates during a traumatic event?
    a. Prefrontal cortex
    b. Occipital lobe
    c. Broca's area
    d. Sensorimotor strip

12. Porges (2004) described _____ as the ability to detect subtle changes in a person's face.
    a. Wisdom
    b. Neuroception
    c. A sixth sense
    d. Disconnection

13. Which is considered the gold standard for response after a trauma?
    a. Mental first aid (MFA)
    b. Psychological first aid (PFA)
    c. First aid response (FAR)
    d. None of the above

14. Communal trauma requires multiple types of counseling, including supplemental interventions of
    a. Nutritional therapy.
    b. Equine-assisted therapy.
    c. Dance therapy.
    d. Both b and c

15. Community tragedies always brings people together.
    a. False, it can bring people together and tear them apart
    b. False, it always tears people apart
    c. True, because people always want to help
    d. True, if the tragedy is in the United States

Essay Questions

1. Natural disasters can destroy whole communities in a matter of minutes. Have you ever experienced a natural disaster? If so, how did your community respond?

2. Communal trauma may involve a collective experience of grief. The trauma may be a natural disaster different from the norm (e.g., cold spell in Florida). If you were a counselor responding to the need for crisis counselors, what would be your approach in securing counselors?

3. Think about the personal experiences of the authors when they offered support to people who experienced Hurricane Katrina. What would it feel like for you to see thousands of people without a home? How could your community best support evacuees?

4. According to the authors, trauma may be difficult for clients or people to process, and talking may trigger feelings of hypervigilance. The authors also mention mindfulness-based approaches and biofeedback as interventions. What are your thoughts about these alternative treatments?

5. Creative thinking can help bring people together and support communities. For example, the Newtown Recovery and Resiliency Team (NRRT) and the University of Texas at San Antonio (UTSA) collaborated to help a community after a school shooting. Who would you collaborate with to help support a community? How could you creatively support a community?

CHAPTER 12

Counseling Military Members and Families

Erin Kern Popejoy

Independent. Strong. Guarded. Autonomous. These are descriptors often attributed to military service members. In fact, the Army took this portrayal a step further and used it as part of their recruitment campaign in the early 2000s. With the slogan "An Army of One," the Army targeted younger recruits and their ideals of individualism and independence (Dao, 2001). Interestingly, the military system is known to function best as a collective society built on strong group cohesion and ideals of selflessness (Hall, 2016). Perhaps as a tribute to a more cohesive environment, they modified the former campaign slogan to "Army Strong" (Burns, 2006).

The Relational Foundation of the Military

Although it may be easy to pigeonhole those who are trained in a "warrior" culture to be cold, unyielding, and completely self-reliant, to do so would be an egregious error. Military culture is complex and unique, and counselors must have insight into the specific actions, rituals, and values of the military to establish a broad understanding of its culture (Burk, 2008; Hall, 2011). Military cultural norms are, in fact, founded in relationship, connectedness, and trust (Burk, 2008).

Framing common military issues—such as emotional compartmentalization, the importance of connection with comrades, the challenges of hierarchy and authoritarian structure, and Western cultural expectations of heroism—within a relational-cultural framework can bring a great deal of insight to both service members and their families. Additionally, many service members marry partners quickly and at a young age. Clinicians using a relational approach are able to explore relational images, competence, and confidence with their clients, helping to strengthen marriages and endorse healthy relational skills (Miller, 1987).

Collectivism

Group cohesion and a collectivist mind-set are paramount for success in combat and are, therefore, an inescapable necessity within military culture (Burk, 2008; Hall, 2011, 2016). When service members enter their initial training, they are placed in situations that facilitate the development of a "bond that transcends all others, even the marriage and family bonds we forge in civilian life" (Tick, 2005, p. 141). Soldiers are trained to rely on each other and work as a team to achieve their goals; without this dynamic, combat would turn to chaos, and risk for fatalities would increase. Training is more than simply being able to work together and includes the knowledge that any one service member would give his or her life to protect the group. This is, in part, why many service members struggle with returning from combat. While in combat, members of the military know exactly who they can trust and to what extent. This sense of security and connection is powerful and is different from what most people experience within the civilian world. Leaving the military culture behind can be a great loss for some and can leave service members feeling unsure about whom they can trust (Junger, 2016).

Hierarchy

The value of group cohesion in the military is reflected in part through the "rigid hierarchical system based on dominance and subordination" (Hall, 2011, p. 11), which is designed to promote superlative functioning of the military system. Consequently, the expectations for obedience and respect for authority are high (Hall, 2016). Higher ranking members may choose to use their authority collaboratively with their lower ranking colleagues in situations in which there is no immediate threat. However, during combat situations, when defiance could cost lives, there is no room for disobedience or disrespect. Despite the power differential inherent in hierarchy, trust and cohesion remain a critical component of these relationships.

Masks and Compartmentalization

If trust and connection create room for a successful and safe mission, the Masks—a term coined by Mary Wertsch (2001)—are methods by which service members disconnect from others. The strict enforcement of hierarchy and focus on successfully completing the mission often result in service members keeping personal challenges to themselves. The ability to compartmentalize is necessary because personal issues may distract from the mission and, in the worst cases, can put service members and those serving with them at risk. The Masks of the military system, according to Wertsch, include secrecy, stoicism, and denial.

Secrecy within a military context involves the separation of work and home life and involves keeping problems in each area from overflowing into other areas of life. For example, service members experiencing stressors in their marriage may choose not to bring that information into their workspace. Unfortunately, service members are also shown to have low levels of help seeking for mental health care or other problems (Blais & Renshaw, 2013; Eaton et al., 2008). As a result, it is not uncommon for these individuals to try to handle challenges on their own, even when they may not be equipped to do so. This form of secrecy can also permeate the family system at times, creating distance between spouses who then feel that they are unable to share their full selves with each other (Slep, Foran, Heyman, & Snarr, 2011).

Acts of *stoicism,* such as maintaining an outward appearance of stability at all times, are another critical component to combat survival. Stoicism can foster trust in surrounding service members and provide reassurance to those who are facing stressors. Military rituals and ceremonies may help to support stoicism among service members and their families through "[controlling or masking] anxieties and ignorance [and affirming] solidarity with one another" (Burk, 2008, p. 1247). Although a military member's outward appearance may be calm, the stress of constantly preparing for change can induce emotional havoc for service members and their families (Hall, 2011). Before deployments, family members may find that the service member develops an intense focus on preparation and readiness but is unable to discuss the possibility of death or injury. This refusal is not necessarily denial of the possibility but represents the mind-set the service member must have to perform successfully; exploring the possibility of death could allow for crippling fear and anxiety that may take focus away from the mission, thereby putting lives at risk (Hall, 2016).

Denial moves military members a step further from stoicism and involves hiding fear and anxiety from others and from him- or herself. This mask involves the complete rejection of stressors that could become problematic during combat to allow for full focus on the mission at hand (Hall, 2016). However, when military members continue to use denial as a coping mechanism after it is safe to explore the stressors, problems can arise for both service members and their families.

Deployments are a common source of stress for families, during which they may use masks of secrecy, stoicism, and denial. Deployments occur for different purposes (e.g., combat, peacekeeping, training) and often have varying levels of risk associated with them. The purpose of the deployment is likely to influence the family's distress levels and the service member's comfort with the deployment (Sheppard, Malatras, & Israel, 2010). Additionally, deployments vary in their duration depending on military branch, purpose, and ongoing conflicts. For example, during the most recent conflicts in Iraq and Afghanistan, the deployments (i.e., deployment, sustainment, and redeployment phases) typically ranged from 6 to 18 months, which are some of the longest deployments the U.S. military has seen since World War II (Hall, 2016; Sheppard et al., 2010).

The Deployment Cycle

All counselors working with military families need to have an understanding of the deployment cycle and its meaning to and impact on families. The cycle can be conceptualized in various ways but is most often sectioned into five distinct phases: predeployment, deployment, sustainment, redeployment, and postdeployment (Padden & Agazio, 2013; Pincus, House, Christensen, & Adler, 2001). *Predeployment* is the time during which (a) the service member is notified of an impending deployment, (b) the service member is training for the deployment, and (c) the family is preparing for the separation. This time is often busy for everyone involved because of the various issues that need attention (Padden & Agazio, 2013).

In lay terms, what is typically referred to as a "deployment" actually spans three discrete phases of time. *Deployment* is characterized as the first month of physical absence, in which the family and the service member adjust to their new roles and routines. *Sustainment* is the period of time during which family and the service member have adjusted to their new lifestyles and expectations. Sustainment lasts until the final month of the deployment, called *redeployment,* during which service members and families prepare for the service member's return home (Padden & Agazio, 2013). After the service member has returned, the *postdeployment* stage begins. During postdeployment, which lasts 3–6 months, the service member reintegrates into the family. During this stage, the routines, roles, and responsibilities established during sustainment are often renegotiated (Padden & Agazio, 2013). See Sidebar 12.1 for information on creating connections before a deployment.

Reentry Into Civilian Life

Ease of reentry into civilian life depends on many interconnected factors. People serving as reservists or National Guard members may have an easier time transitioning into a fully civilian lifestyle because they already live as a civilian part of the time, and they may have an established civilian identity in conjunction with their military status (Hall, 2016). While serving, active-duty members can choose to live on a military post or off post within the surrounding civilian community. This may have a small degree of impact on reintegrating into the civilian world, because those who live off post must manage certain life skills such as paying rent or a mortgage and utility bills. There may also be a slightly higher degree of interaction with civilian neighbors than for those who live on post simply because of environmental proximity. Reentry to civilian life is often due to one of the following primary factors: (a) redeployment and postdeployment and (b) separation or retirement.

Redeployment and Postdeployment

During redeployment stage, a service member prepares to return home from a deployed status. This transition may be anxiety provoking for many service members, because they wonder how their families and home lives have changed without them while they were away. Spouses and partners have continued to live their lives during this time, and most have taken on many of the roles that the service member filled. Children have grown over the months that the service member

Sidebar 12.1 • Creating Connection Before Deployment

Consider the value of being connected to loved ones, particularly to those who live far away. We often rely on technology to keep us connected and up to date on each other's lives. However, deployed service members do not always have access to technology, and those who do may be permitted to only use technology sparingly. Strengthening connectedness before deployment, particularly with partners and children, is important. How might working toward connections help families through the deployment process? Brainstorm some ideas to help foster this attachment and connection in military families.

was away. There may be a sense of disconnection or detachment from family and friends as service members try to renegotiate their place within the system (Faber, Willerton, Clymer, MacDermid, & Weiss, 2008; Pincus et al., 2001). Even if the individual is remaining in service, returning home can be a difficult adjustment, particularly if the deployment was to a combat zone or in an environment that posed a high threat of injury or death (Faber et al., 2008; Pincus et al., 2001).

Postdeployment begins after the service member returns home. This occasion can be joyful but does not come without challenges. At this point, relationships may need to be redefined and reestablished. Spouses or partners must negotiate which roles and responsibilities they will take on or give up, and both may have trouble taking each other into account as they live their daily lives. Service members may have grown accustomed to having their freedom in an environment free of civilian tasks (e.g., paying bills, cooking, caring for children), and partners at home have become used to taking care of the household and other responsibilities on their own (Blaise, 2006). This period is often a time of ambiguous presence, during which the service member is physically present but psychologically absent (Faber et al., 2008). He or she may feel pressure to immediately fall back into predeployment roles, without considering that the family system has changed in their absence.

Spouses sometimes report feeling irritated with the service member, feeling as though they are in the way and having a desire to maintain their own personal space even after roles are renegotiated (Pincus et al., 2001). However, spouses also express irritation that the returning service member wants to spend time with other returning troops rather than spending free time at home. For the nondeployed partner who has had to take on everything while the service member was gone, this need to keep a strong connection to other service members can feel like an additional abandonment. Hall (2016) reported that service members may benefit emotionally from processing combat experiences with individuals with whom they served. Spouses often need help to understand that this connection and time spent with other returning military members may help their service member heal and readjust faster than if they tried to ignore their experiences (Hall, 2016).

Separation or Retirement

Separation or retirement from the military is the end of a military service member's career. At this point, they no longer serve the military and fully reenter the civilian world. This reentry can be experienced in a variety of ways, most commonly through involuntary separation, voluntary separation, or retirement.

Involuntary Separation

If the service member did not want to leave service but was required to do so because of a medical reason or injury (physical or psychological) or because of disciplinary actions, the separation can be particularly difficult. These separations often happen quickly and may cause the service member to feel lost or without direction (Smith, 2015). Medical discharges, especially, can leave service members angry and upset that they are not being allowed to serve despite a strong desire to do so. These individuals may voice a longing to be with their military family, and some carry a great deal of hurt and anger, feeling that the discharge is a betrayal by the military (Devine, 2008). Additionally, some separations are due to disciplinary actions resulting in a general or dishonorable discharge, limiting or eliminating postservice benefits such as medical coverage for military-related disability or educational funding (Hall, 2016). The experience of involuntary separation can be traumatic, leaving some individuals struggling to find meaning and purpose in a civilian community.

Voluntary Separation

Voluntary separation occurs if a service member chooses to leave service before being eligible for retirement. Different branches of the military require different terms of service, and contracts vary in length (Hall, 2016). However, most military personnel are eligible to retire after 20 years of service. Given that not all service members enter the military to make it a lifetime career, many will separate from service after several years for various reasons. Some marry and want to settle in one place. Others have children and do not want to continue with frequent relocations, whereas still others entered the service with the purpose of serving a few years to acquire the means to pay for higher education (Henderson, 2006).

Although separation is voluntary in these cases, transition can still be a challenge for service members. They must leave their military family, and they may not stay in the immediate area (Hall, 2016). Individuals may return home to their family of origin, to the area where they grew up, or to an entirely new place, either alone or with a family of their own. In any of these cases, it is not uncommon for service members to feel disconnected, alienated, and misunderstood by their civilian counterparts (Demers, 2011).

It can be difficult for service members to connect with non–military affiliated civilians. There is a shared understanding of lifestyle and experience among military members and a strong "other" mentality regarding civilians (Demers, 2011; Hall, 2016). Military service members know and understand their culture and have often come to expect that civilians will not have a full comprehension of these experiences. Additionally, after being in a combat zone or areas of destitution, priorities and perceptions of what matter are inevitably altered. It is not uncommon for a military service member to become irritated or angry at a civilian for complaining about something they see as trivial. As a result, some service members may choose to limit their social interaction to those whom they are already close with.

I once worked with a client I will call Jacob, who served in the Air Force for 8 years and deployed to Iraq once and Afghanistan twice. Jacob voluntarily separated from service and moved to a city where he had few friends and no family. It was a challenge to find a meaningful career opportunity—potential employers told him that he had excellent experience, but his lack of a college degree was an obstacle. When Jacob applied for a part-time job at the local mall, he was met with resistance because managers were concerned he may not be able to take direction from coworkers who were much younger than him. Jacob was left stuck, with nothing to keep him busy and no friends or family in his geographical area. This was an awful feeling for someone who was used to a daily mission and purpose.

In response, Jacob filled his days with online video games—which gave him a renewed sense of meaning and connected him with a virtual friend group. In a sense, the missions in the game mimicked the military. However, Jacob still spiraled into a heavy depression. Jacob's case reflects established research that military members may often feel a strong loss of identity after separation, even when they chose to leave (Demers, 2011).

Military service and lifestyle are ingrained in service members from the first day in basic training, and its loss can leave a service member feeling aimless and chaotic. In response, service members may seek out career opportunities that are closely affiliated with military service, such as government contracting or first-responder services (e.g., police, fire department, emergency medical technician) because they are knowledgeable about the field and are trained to operate in emergency situations. Although these types of environments can feel familiar and comfortable for prior service members, they can take time to transition into, and they are certainly not the only choice. Many service members choose to build completely new and different career paths for themselves, creatively using the skills they acquired while in service.

Retirement

Retirement within the military often occurs much earlier than retirement within the civilian world (U.S. Senate, Committee on Armed Services, 2014). Individuals who retire from military service face many of the same challenges encountered by those who separate. People who enter the military at 18 years old and serve 20 years are only 38 years old by the time they can retire, leaving them with the opportunity to enter into a completely new career if they wish. However, many individuals who retire do so with a sense of achievement and completion (Taylor, Schultz, Spiegel, Morrison, & Greene, 2007). These individuals have served their full time within the military, and although they may miss components of their time in service, retirement often marks a time of transition. Some service members, though, may resist retirement because they have not reached a certain rank or because they do not want to leave their unit behind. The decision to retire may result in a sense of not having completed their larger mission (Taylor et al., 2007).

Suicide and Substance Use

At any point during reintegration to the civilian world, suicide risk may be elevated (Pease, Billera, & Gerard, 2016). The process of reintegration may be chaotic and isolating, which can overwhelm the service member and leave them feeling extremely disconnected from others. This disconnection may feel insurmountable, which can lead to the possibility for suicidality. Use and abuse of substances are common to numb chronic physical pain from injuries as well as feelings of fear, depression, and posttraumatic stress or other trauma symptoms (Wilk et al., 2010). Substance use issues may cause conflict with family and friends, and the service member may believe that their loved ones are better off without them.

Losing a Family Member

There has been a heavy focus on trauma and posttraumatic stress disorder (PTSD) during wartime. However, research has not given the same attention to issues of grief and loss, which are inherent to many of the military population's experiences. The military lifestyle is one of constant transition, which means loss occurs frequently. One of the most traumatizing losses facing the military can be that of a family when their service member does not return from combat.

Grieving the death of a parent, child, or sibling who dies in combat may produce feelings of ambiguous loss for those who are left behind. Ambiguous loss defies resolution or closure, and it often results in a prolonged state of confusion about the loss (Boss, 2016). With the increased use of improvised explosive devices and firearms that can do a great deal of damage to the body, it is possible that family members will not have the opportunity to view the deceased's body after their return home. Viewing the body can be an act of closure, and without this ritual, individuals may find themselves stuck in a state of waiting for the service member to return home alive and safe (Lieberman, Compton, Van Horn, & Ghosh Ippen, 2003). Some individuals report hope that the deceased was not actually their relative but was misidentified because of the extent of damage to the body. Similarly, for those service members who are captured by enemy forces, their family may continue to hold out hope that they will return someday.

Children may also experience unique challenges when facing the death of a parent while in combat. Young children may exhibit jealousy or resentment toward other youth whose military parent returned safely, and they may show heightened concern for the safety and well-being of the remaining parent (Kaplow, Layne, Saltzman, Cozza, & Pynoos, 2013). Young children may also struggle to understand the permanence of death and express a desire for the deceased parent to come home. Older children and adolescents may develop intense separation anxiety mitigated by reunification fantasies, which has the potential to lead to suicidal ideation (Kaplow et al., 2013). The death of a spouse or parent not only brings immediate grief for individuals but also has long-lasting ramifications for the family unit. The loss of a military service member means that the family may lose their military identity when they must move away from the support of their military community (Holmes, Rauch, & Cozza, 2013).

The Effect of Traumatic Injuries

Combat stress "is not a by-product or side effect that can be sanitized away" (p. 13) but is inherent to combat (Nash, 2007). Unfortunately, the aftermath of such trauma can severely disrupt service members' lives and the lives of those around them. Traumatic injuries include PTSD and moral injuries. Added traumas that may or may not occur during combat, but can occur at any time during military service, include military sexual trauma (MST) and domestic violence.

PTSD

In most incidences of trauma, survivors take a passive role as the trauma event is imposed on them. However, military service members play a uniquely active part in their own trauma (Van Winkle & Safer, 2011). This active role is thought to account for elevated arousal symptoms such as anger, aggression, and hostility. Although PTSD does not automatically result in violent behaviors, it is linked to higher rates of interpersonal aggression thought to be due to these elevated arousal symptoms (Van Winkle & Safer, 2011). Additionally, it is not uncommon for service members to abuse substances in an attempt to self-medicate and escape reminders of trauma (Wilk et al., 2010), which can result in lowered inhibitions and increased aggression toward others (Martin et al., 2010; Slep et al., 2011). With combat stress at the heart of war, "it is hard for warriors to not perceive stress symptoms of any kind as evidence of personal weakness and failure" (Nash, 2007,

p. 17), because this is at the core of their identity and what they have been called on to do. See Sidebar 12.2 for information on a controversial treatment for PTSD.

Living with a service member who has PTSD can be challenging. The symptoms, which consist of avoidance behaviors, negative mood and cognitions, hyperarousal and reactivity, and intrusive thoughts and memories, can transform a loved one into someone unrecognizable (American Psychiatric Association, 2013). In these situations, family members are at risk for developing secondary traumatic stress, a reaction to indirect exposure to traumatic events that have happened to the service member (Renshaw et al., 2011; Yambo et al., 2016). The service member's symptoms may also reduce individual functioning in certain situations, thereby

Sidebar 12.2 • A Controversial Treatment

Posttraumatic stress disorder (PTSD) is prevalent in conversations related to military populations. According to Dr. John Krystal, who heads the Neuroscience Division at the U.S. Department of Veterans Affairs National Center for PTSD, only one in three combat veterans are effectively treated (Phillips, 2018). Recent research has explored novel therapeutics, including MDMA. Medical-grade MDMA is almost completely pure, with none of the potentially toxic fillers found in the street version commonly known as Ecstasy or Molly. The effects of MDMA include reduction of the "fight, flight, or freeze" fear response and augmented feelings of safety, trust, and relaxation—an ideal state for exploring and reexamining traumatic memories (Sessa, 2017). Here's how it is proposed to work:

After several sessions of traditional counseling, MDMA is administered in office by a licensed professional. After taking the drug, the client lays down in a quiet, relaxing environment, with both a male and a female counselor present. Sessions will typically last a minimum of 5 hours (Sessa, 2017). The client is not allowed to leave the office until the substance effects have subsided—some offices will keep the client overnight. Other practices will allow clients to leave with a significant other. In following sessions, clients process through insights and emotions evoked during the MDMA session (Phillips, 2018). The client will take MDMA an additional 2–3 times, approximately 1 month apart, with traditional therapy sessions in between.

Initial trial results appear extremely effective, with most clients no longer meeting the criteria for PTSD after receiving treatment (Phillips, 2018). MDMA-assisted psychotherapy recently entered Phase 3 clinical trials, and if safety and efficacy results are replicated, it may be approved by the Food and Drug Administration for legal use by 2021.

This new and controversial treatment has many considerations. Discuss your own thoughts and feelings about the use of MDMA to aid in treating PTSD. What questions do you have? What are the potential benefits? Drawbacks? Think critically and challenge one another as you explore this possibility.

restricting functioning for the entire family. For example, the service member may experience paranoia and be highly reactive in large crowds because of high levels of anxiety. This behavior can result in the entire family avoiding crowded restaurants, movie theatres, shopping centers, or concerts. Conversely, the family may choose to engage in such outings without the service member, possibly furthering a sense of disconnection and isolation.

Moral Injury

Different from PTSD, *moral injury* is a more recently recognized concept. Moral injury is trauma that occurs when a service member must go against a deeply embedded moral belief or ideal, usually because of military orders or the environmental context (Litz et al., 2009; Shay, 2014). The military system symbolizes a highly ethical code of conduct, and during times of warfare, killing and violence are normal, acceptable, and expected behaviors. However, modern conflicts have been rife with ambiguity that can require unanticipated moral decisions from service members (Litz et al., 2009).

For example, children are sometimes used as weapons or a method of distraction during wartime conflict. When military convoys spot someone in their path, they may be unsure whether that person poses a threat. The child may be trying to signal them to stop for any number of benign reasons, strapped with explosives, or creating a distraction so that the convoy can be ambushed. Not knowing which of these situations is presenting, troops may yell at the child to move out of the way because stopping on an open road could be a major threat to safety. If the child does not move, the service members are faced with the option to shoot or to run the child over. Although this may make sense in the moment, service members often find themselves ruminating over these situations after they are removed from combat. They may feel intense guilt or shame, and they often replay the scene in their head wondering what could have been done differently.

Although PTSD and traumatic brain injuries have the potential to be horrific, researchers believe that moral injury is the crippling force that drives some service members to criminal actions, uncontrollable aggression, and suicidality (Shay, 2014). Moral injury is believed to "impair and sometimes destroy the capacity for trust. When social trust is destroyed, it is replaced by the settled expectancy of harm, exploitation, and humiliation from others" (Shay, 2014, p. 186). With these expectations, the individual can choose to always be on the attack, withdraw and isolate, or create deceptions and distractions in the attempt to keep themselves safe. These options create a difficult situation for those who are living with the service member, because families may bear the brunt of the resulting behaviors.

MST

Sexual harassment and assault have been present in the military for centuries but have recently gained public recognition in the news media during the recent conflicts in Iraq and Afghanistan. The Pentagon estimated that 26,000 experienced MST in 2012 (Farris, Schell, & Tanielian, 2013). Data collected from unrestricted reports of MST in 2012 showed that 78% of incidents involved a service member survivor, and 84% involved a service member perpetrator. Of the perpetrators, 25% were in the survivor's chain of command (Farris et al., 2013). The military system creates a uniquely oppressive context for sexual trauma survivors in which (a) the assault occurs where the survivor lives and works, and where they will continue to have to live and work, usually with ongoing contact with the perpetrator; and (b) the survivor may feel unable to speak out about the assault because the perpetrator may be in a position of power over them and also because reporting the assault could damage the group cohesion necessary for successful unit functioning (Anderson & Suris, 2013). The challenging environment in which the MST survivor often lives may leave them feeling isolated and unable to reach out for help, creating complex responses to the original trauma.

Symptoms of PTSD have been found to be nine times more likely to manifest in female service members who are victims of MST than of female service members who do not have a history of sexual trauma (Street & Stafford, 2014). Additionally, sexual trauma during military service is known to heighten the risk of suicide attempt and completion (Kimerling, Makin-Byrd, Louzon, Ignacio, & McCarthy, 2016). Although MST reports are significantly higher among women, those men who report are twice as likely to complete a suicide attempt (Kimerling et al., 2016). The Veterans Health Administration has taken numerous steps to provide support and care for service members who have experienced MST, and the U.S. Department of Defense has established a zero-tolerance policy around sexual assault within the military (Farris et al., 2013; Kimerling et al., 2016). Unfortunately, the stigma around MST, and the fear of retribution by survivors, frequently prevents individuals from reporting and, subsequently, seeking help.

Family members of those who have suffered MST are affected by the trauma as well. PTSD symptoms may be apparent to both partners and children, and suicidality is known to have a devastating effect on the family. Additionally, physical touch and sexual intimacy may be difficult for these service members, creating barriers within their relationships. Because partners may become frustrated with the absence of physical intimacy, it can lead to other issues within the relationship, such as resentment, emotional disconnection, and infidelity.

Domestic Violence

In 2014, 16,287 reports of military spouse abuse were made, and 7,464 of these—less than half—were determined to be substantiated (U.S. Department of Defense, Family Advocacy Program, 2015). Of the substantiated abuse reports, 65% of the perpetrators were men. Additionally, nine of the 11 reported fatalities due to domestic violence were perpetrated by men on active-duty service. Two of these nine perpetrators had prior charges of abuse (U.S. Department of Defense, Family Advocacy Program, 2015). Most reports and research data reflect a higher level of male-perpetrated violence (Klostermann, Mignone, Kelley, Musson, & Bohall, 2011), but women certainly perpetrate against male partners as well, engaging in both physical and verbal or emotional abuse. Additionally, there appears to be a lack of research around the experience of domestic violence among gay and lesbian military couples.

The military system offers a unique context for domestic violence. The cultural values of hypermasculinity, aggression, group cohesion, hierarchy, and authoritarianism may converge to create a perfect storm when they are used abusively (Kern, 2017). Military training necessarily prepares service members to be comfortable with violence and killing and harnesses aggression and anger to be used within combat. Within the military lifestyle, though, work and home often converge, and this aggression and violence may permeate the family system (Hall, 2011; Kern, 2017). Additionally, the arousal symptoms of PTSD, crippling mistrust due to moral injury, and inhibitions lowered by substance abuse—often used to avoid trauma memories—can augment the risk of domestic violence.

The U.S. Department of Defense has pushed efforts to recognize and reduce incidences of domestic violence by establishing the Family Advocacy Program and other interventions and support systems (U.S. Department of Defense, Family Advocacy Program, 2015; U.S. Department of Defense, Task Force on Domestic Violence, 2003). However, the context for abuse is so deeply embedded within the necessary military training and structure that it is extremely challenging to eradicate this issue (Hall, 2016). Additionally, the military has invested a great deal of time and money into their service members, and the system operates in a way that protects perpetrators (Kern, 2017). Similar to MST, domestic violence frequently goes unreported because of perceived (and sometimes real) lack of support (Kern, 2017).

Counseling Strategies

Cognitive-Behavioral Therapy (CBT)

The most consistent approach to working with the military population is some form of CBT (Everson & Figley, 2011). This is due, in part, to the empirical evidence that suggests the effectiveness of CBT with trauma, depression, anxiety, and a variety of other challenges (Dass-Brailsford, 2007). The structure and strength-based nature of CBT is attractive to service members, who are often partial to straightforward and directive approaches. However, there is a risk that this type of approach may cause the counselor to miss important factors, such as failing to place marital and other important family relationships within a relational framework or glossing over issues of spirituality (Figley & Nash, 2007). Clinicians must make efforts to address these issues as they present and be sure that they are meeting the service member when they are in the process of healing.

Some clinicians have found that a combination of eye movement desensitization and reprocessing (EMDR) therapy with CBT has been particularly helpful for trauma processing (Foa, Davidson, Frances, & Ross, 1999). The ability to use EMDR in combat situations, directly after the trauma event, may significantly reduce PTSD symptoms and trauma effect (Wesson & Gould, 2009). However, it can be challenging to find time and space to conduct such an early intervention on the front lines, particularly when it is deeply embedded in military training to quickly compartmentalize traumatic events with the purpose of staying focused on the present situation (Wesson & Gould, 2009).

Solution-Focused Brief Therapy

Solution-focused brief therapy is another commonly used approach with service members, in part because of its structured nature and focus on client strength and resilience; it also emphasizes solution-oriented behaviors, which require the service member and family to remain in the present moment (Tews-Kozlowski, 2012).

The brief nature of this approach is ideal for situations in which service members and their families need to take action and make changes quickly (Hall, 2016). Military service members may have a limited number of sessions because of insurance restrictions or as a result of trainings or relocations.

Relational-Cultural Theory (RCT)

War reporter and author Sebastian Junger (2016) detailed the innate human yearning for connection and belonging in his book, *Tribe*. Although he overviewed many different tribal groups, he focused particularly on the military unit and the paramount role that connection and cohesion play in the function and emotional well-being of this group. Foci such as these allow RCT to be used effectively with military populations.

Although many counseling theories underpin the need for autonomy and individuation to develop personal growth, RCT theorists postulate that growth and wellness are cultivated through *growth-fostering relationships*—those connections that allow for mutual authenticity, empathy, and collaboration (Miller, 1987). It is through these relationships that individuals gain awareness of self and others and further develop their relational competence and confidence. Many service members have come from an environment where they are connected with those who have served next to them but may feel an innate disconnection from the civilian population, believing civilians cannot genuinely understand their experiences (Junger, 2016).

The emphasis RCT theorists put on issues of power dynamics, the importance of context, the central relational paradox, the inevitability of disconnection, and the necessity of connection are all relevant to the effective functioning of the military unit and also to the emotional wellness of the individuals within (Miller, 1987).

Power

Military service members live in a culture where both *power-over* others and *power-with* others exist simultaneously (Hall, 2016). Military orders come down the chain of hierarchy, and power is used over subordinates to create quick and effective changes without mutuality or collaboration. This is frequently seen in combat and life-and-death situations, in which commands are given and acted on without question (Hall, 2016). This is necessary for the safety of troops and effective combat missions. However, there are also frequent acts of collaborative power, or power-with acts, in which change is accomplished through collaboration and mutual decision making. This may occur when split-second decisions do not need to be made, and higher ranking officials are able to take the time to discuss options within the military unit.

Counselors must have a firm understanding of how and when these types of power are necessary, because this will clarify the client's relationships with other service members. Additionally, counselors may benefit from drawing parallels into family dynamics—because military families often become mini-units of their own. However, family units are different from military units, and power-over strategies often result in disconnection and relationship violations (Jordan, 1991, 2010). Helping clients to engage collaboratively with their families may reduce relational stress at home and encourage growth-fostering family relationships.

Connection and Disconnection

It is not uncommon for service members to feel isolated, particularly after separating from service. However, some may report feelings of isolation while serving—perhaps after returning from combat or after a diagnosis of PTSD or other mental health disorder. Service members may try to hide parts of their military identity from others, believing that it will result in rejection or disapproval. This is done in an attempt at furthering connection, but the inauthenticity instead drives disconnection (Jordan, 2010; Miller, 1988). This is a central theme of RCT, coined the *central relational paradox*: Individuals desire connection and will hide parts of themselves that they believe are unacceptable in an attempt to avoid rejection (consider the masks of secrecy, stoicism, and denial). However, connection is created through authentic relationship, and the act of hiding creates a disconnect (Jordan, 2010; Miller, 1988). Chronic disconnection results in isolation, which may be accompanied by feelings of shame, worthlessness, and a loss of empathy for one's self. See Sidebar 12.3 for information on the necessity of authentic relationships.

Rather than pathologizing and labeling symptoms, relationally competent counselors normalize and validate individuals' responses to the environment and stimuli to which they have been exposed (Jordan, 2010). Some service members may react negatively to an initial diagnosis—particularly PTSD—because of the negative stigma of weakness that accompanies mental health disorders within the military (Kim, Britt, Klocko, Riviere, & Adler, 2011). Framing the disorder, or symptoms of the disorder, as an adaptive human reaction may help the service member reduce feelings of shame. Taking a nonpathologizing approach may decrease feelings of isolation and increase self-empathy, thereby facilitating authenticity and increased perception of *relational competence*—the belief that one is able to engage competently in and bring value to various relationships (Jordan, 2010).

Sidebar 12.3 • The Necessity of Authentic Relationship

Humans are a social species, designed to co-regulate within small groups. Sebastian Junger (2016), author of *Tribe*, explored historical and current tribal communities to examine cultural norms of loyalty and belonging as well as their perspectives on combat and those who experienced it. He found that groups who welcomed soldiers back into the fold of the community, offering care and support, saw minimal, if any, symptoms of posttraumatic stress. Moving from the close-knit tribal community of a military unit, back into traditional Westernized society with its focus on autonomy and individual strength, may then play a part in the development and prolonging of posttraumatic stress in U.S. service members. Discuss how our highly individualized society might be detrimental for returning service members, and what relational systems could be implemented for a better transition.

Resources for Service Members and Their Families

There are a multitude of resources for the military population at the local, regional, and national levels. Resources will differ depending on region, but several national services are listed below:

- Family advocacy programming was established within each branch of the military in 1981 to address domestic violence issues. Programs are in place at each military post to support families through issues of marital stress, domestic abuse, and substance abuse. They offer education and awareness programming as well as seminars and workshops, new-parent support programs, counseling services, and public awareness campaigns. Contact information for various family advocacy programs will depend on location.
- Give an Hour was founded in 2005, and it helps to provide no-cost mental health counseling to military service members and their families. This nonprofit organization recruits licensed mental health professionals to provide at least 1 hour per week of free services to the military community. A fundamental belief of this nonprofit organization is giving back, and they ask that clients also donate their time within their own communities when they are able. Website: https://giveanhour.org/
- Military OneSource provides an overview of military life for the military community, along with policy and procedure updates from the U.S. Department of Defense. Their website includes numerous blogs and publications on the military lifestyle, which can be useful for new military families. Additionally, they offer references for counseling and medical services based on the area in which the service member is living. Website: http://www.militaryonesource.mil/
- U.S. Department of Veterans Affairs hospitals exist throughout the country and provide mental health counseling, psychiatric services, medical services, housing-related assistance, and some educational services. They also provide vocational rehabilitation services for service members who are seeking out new career opportunities. Website: https://www.va.gov/
- The Wounded Warrior Project connects wounded service members and provides free programs and services that help to bridge gaps in government care. The project's mission is to honor and empower wounded warriors through their services and to create well-adjusted and well-rounded service members. The Wounded Warrior Project also helps to connect families and caregivers of wounded warriors in an effort to provide support to the entire family system. Website: https://www.woundedwarriorproject.org/

Fostering Healing and Resilience

A common military saying, originated in the 1980s film *Heartbreak Ridge* (Eastwood, 1986) and unofficially adopted by the Marine Corps, is "improvise, adapt, and overcome" (Allard, 2009). So much of military life is centered on transitions—into the military, out of the military, deployments, personal and professional role changes, relocations, and much more—and constantly adapting to new environments. Within this adaptation is resiliency, a characteristic found among the vast majority of military personnel and their families. These individuals and families are often resilient to change, accepting what comes to them in stride with grace and flexibility (Asbury & Martin, 2012).

This resilience, though, is not an intrinsic toughness held as an individual characteristic. Instead, it comes through the authentic connections and support found within growth-fostering relationships—a concept known as *relational resilience* within RCT (Hartling, 2008). RCT theorists propose that all relationships are defined by the social and cultural environments in which they are formed (Hartling, 2008). The sociocultural environment of the military emphasizes the need for cohesion, trust, courage, loyalty, and strength. Therefore, it is likely that these values are imbued in each relationship formed within the military community, creating further resilience. Families and individuals are often well supported in their various transitions, and systems are in place to attempt to prevent isolation and withdrawal (Hall, 2016). Families are often connected with individuals in the service member's unit when they transition to a new post, and they may have friends or family from a previous post nearby.

However, some military values may work to impede relational resilience. Walker (2008) noted that cultural contexts in which there are hierarches of dominant-subordinate systems of power may subvert opportunities to create growth-fostering relationships. Out of necessity for combat effectiveness and safety, the military must maintain their strict rank hierarchy. Additionally, implicit values such as secrecy, stoicism, and denial—perpetuated by stigma around help seeking and again reinforced by combat necessity (Wertsch, 2001)—can further diminish opportunity for relational resilience. In such instances, this resilience may be found in relationships among same-ranking individuals or within family units. Relational resilience can also be created within the therapeutic relationship. However, resilience, even with strong relationship and support, does not come without loss, trauma, or grief (Asbury & Martin, 2012; Hall, 2016). Honoring these difficult and often painful components of experience is likely to be a key factor in working toward healing for this population.

Trauma events, such as those described earlier in this chapter, have a significant neurological impact on the brain and body. Individuals meeting even partial criteria for PTSD demonstrate elevated heart rate, elevated blood pressure, and high levels of skin conductance when exposed to reminders of their trauma event (van der Kolk, 2000). Autonomic processes such as these are responsible for the fight, flight, or freeze phenomenon (Siegel, 2010).

Early neuroimaging research has demonstrated that individuals who are exposed to vivid narratives of their trauma experience depressed activity in the left inferior hemisphere of the brain (Rauch et al., 1996). This part of the brain—commonly known as *Broca's area*—is responsible for speech production and language comprehension. Verbal communication is reduced during exposure to trauma narratives while right-brain activity increases, particularly in the areas responsible for emotional arousal (Homeyer & Sweeney, 2011; Rauch et al., 1996). This function of the nervous system therefore creates a challenge for verbalizing traumatic experiences before they are integrated across both brain hemispheres.

Sand tray therapy is a nonverbal and expressive technique in which the sand tray and miniature figures are the primary mode of communication. The client can project the traumatic event onto the miniature figures, creating a safe method to process through the event without becoming severely overwhelmed or distressed (Homeyer & Sweeney, 2011). This safety is a result of several distinct sand tray properties: (a) The use of miniatures creates a therapeutic detachment through symbolism of the event; (b) clients can play out various scenarios and take control of situations that they were unable to control during the trauma event; (c) the client can project difficult or overwhelming emotions through the miniature, instead of having to verbalize these feelings; and (d) this projection allows clients to express anger or sadness in a safe way, through the miniatures (Homeyer & Sweeney, 2011). These components of sand tray therapy are particularly salient for military personnel and their families, given the cultural stigma around seeking mental health care within the military. Service members cannot express intense anger toward those who are hierarchically above them, and natural trauma responses, such as fear or lack of control, may be interpreted as weakness (Kern & Perryman, 2016).

Sand tray therapy can implemented within any theoretical model. It works well with relational approaches that address both intra- and interpersonal factors, as described in the following case example.

Case Example and Applications for Hope and Healing

Imagine: You are in a hostile foreign country, thousands of miles from the familiarity and comfort of home. There is only heat, sand, and the constant threat of danger. You are a medic with the Marine Corps, deployed to Iraq during Operation Iraqi Freedom. Your purpose—what you have devoted your life to—is to heal the wounded and to save lives in combat. You and several of your men are gathering reconnaissance data for an area not too far from your forward operating base. You see a Humvee in the distance, one of your own, and welcome the sight of men returning safely. Suddenly you see a bright flash, and, soon after, a loud explosion rings in your ears. The Humvee is engulfed in flames, and the men around you begin jumping to action. Before you realize, you are running toward the Humvee, only thinking about the ability to save those inside. There is a gunnery sergeant screaming orders over your left shoulder, telling you to stop. He's yelling that the area needs to be cleared before you can go in. You ignore him, your focus solely on treating the wounded. You reach the battered Humvee and realize the doors are sealed shut from the heat. A team of men pries them off, only to find casualties inside; the impact of the explosion knocked the bolts securing the seats loose, allowing the bodies inside to be thrown around mercilessly. There is no saving them.

This was Michael's experience. He is a Marine corpsman, now separated from service, who presented to counseling with symptoms of PTSD. When we began using sand tray therapy in session to process his trauma, this was the first scene he chose to place in the sand. He created a literal map of the area—piling sand up into ridges, digging trenches, and drawing lines to show who was where, and when. He chose a goose with its wings spread to protect its young as a figure representative of himself, and a large, ugly monster to take the spot of the screaming gunnery sergeant. After the scene was created, he described the event in detail—his words choked through tears as he shared the experience of being unable to protect his men and the trauma of being told that he was disobeying orders and would be written up while trying to save others.

After Michael's scene was created and he had processed through his original narrative, I asked him what various pieces might say if they could speak. He touched the goose and simply said, "I'm sorry." We began to slowly rotate the tray to give Michael different perspectives of the scene he had created. He stopped me several times to rearrange figurines so that they were the appropriate distances from each other, to reflect the scene as he remembered it. He also mentioned, that as the goose and explosion figurines rotated away from him, he began to feel more anxious and protective over them until they rotated back around toward him again.

Finally, I asked Michael whether he would like to make any changes to the scene. He looked at it thoughtfully and removed the monster representing the gunnery sergeant, replacing him with a treasure chest he found on the figurine shelf. He was quiet for a moment and then explained that he did not want to remember that part of the event because it distracted from the loss of his brothers. Instead he chose to put that part of the memory in the treasure chest, silencing him and ridding himself of the fear and doubt that came from that part of the trauma memory. He said, "Now that it's quiet, I can take care of my men properly." When asked how he could take care of them, he responded, "I can know that I did everything I could to help them. And I can say goodbye."

Michael continued to process other parts of this scene in future sessions, eventually moving on to other trauma events that occurred during his time in combat. The ability to distance himself from the trauma event using sand tray figurines was helpful to his storytelling process, and the opportunity to restory by changing components of his scene allowed him to begin moving out of the shame and guilt that surrounded the event.

Future Directions and Emerging Research

There has been a recent push for neurofeedback as a valid treatment option for service members who suffer from military-related trauma (Fragedakis & Toriello, 2014). Prolonged amounts of time are spent in states of hyperarousal as part of their training and in combat. This excessive responsiveness can lead to chronic maladaptive functioning in the autonomic and central nervous systems (Brosschot, Gerin, & Thayer, 2006). Neurofeedback technology provides clinicians the opportunity to study patterns of brain waves and to explore functioning of the central nervous system. At the same time, the service member can be trained to alter the electrical activity in their brain to appropriately correspond with neurochemical activity, creating an effect much like medication (Fragedakis & Toriello, 2014). Neurofeedback may be attractive to service members because of a common mistrust of medication (often stemming from the stigma of mental health issues and help seeking within military culture; Burk, 2008) as well as its structured training components—a format familiar to those who have served.

Animal therapies, particularly equine therapy, have also been suggested for use with service members. However, there appears to be a lack of current research—but a great deal of anecdotal stories—around equine therapy with the military population. Equine therapy uses the body as a tool for communication, to which the horse then responds. This modality of therapy emphasizes insight and emotional expression along with establishing trust and developing healthy relationships (Kirby, 2016). Equine therapy approaches are believed to be effective with nonmilitary populations, such as clients who struggle with disordered eating (Lac, Marble, & Boie, 2013), youth who have experienced trauma (McCullough, Risley-Curtiss, & Rorke, 2015), and adults who have been exposed to secondary trauma (Park & Arbaut, 2013). Equine therapy with military populations, specifically used in treating PTSD symptoms, has been tested through a pilot study conducted by the Equine Assisted Growth and Learning Association (2013) and another study led by Johnson et al. (2018). Results of these studies were positive, but more exploration is needed before the approach can be considered empirically validated.

Although the military system may appear to be founded in individual strength and resilience, it truly is a culture based in relationship (Hall, 2016; Junger, 2016). The cohesive nature of the military unit facilitates success both in and out of combat. This cohesion supports families and individuals during times of stress and transition, and it points to the power created within relational resilience. There are, however, experiences that service members may try to hide, both in general interpersonal interaction and within counseling, out of fear that they will be misunderstood or judged. A relational approach allows practitioners to honor these strategies of disconnection, normalize a variety of experiences, and build on the variety of connections that are an intrinsic piece of military life.

References

Allard, S. (2009). Adapt and overcome: A psychological battle. *Marine Corps Gazette, 93*(10), 87–91.

American Psychiatric Association. (2013). *Diagnostic and statistical manual of mental disorders* (5th ed.). Arlington, VA: Author.

Anderson, E. H., & Suris, A. (2013). Military sexual trauma. In B. A. Moore & J. E. Barnett (Eds.), *Military psychologists desk reference* (pp. 264–268). New York, NY: Oxford University Press.

Asbury, E. T., & Martin, D. (2012). Military deployment and the spouse left behind. *The Family Journal, 20,* 45–50. https://doi.org/10.1177/1066480711429433

Blais, R. K., & Renshaw, K. D. (2013). Stigma and demographic correlates of help-seeking intention in returning service members. *Journal of Traumatic Stress, 26,* 77–85. https://doi.org/10.1002/jts.21772

Blaise, K. (2006). *The heart of a soldier: A true story of love, war, and sacrifice.* New York, NY: Gotham Books.

Boss, P. (2016). The context and process of theory development: The story of ambiguous loss. *Journal of Family Theory and Review, 8,* 269–286. https://doi.org/10.1111/jftr.12152

Brosschot, J. F., Gerin, W., & Thayer, J. F. (2006). The preservative cognition hypothesis: A review of worry, prolonged stress-related physiological activation, and health. *Journal of Psychosomatic Research, 60,* 113–124. https://doi.org/10.1016/j.jpsychores.2005.06.074

Burk, J. (2008). Military culture. In L. Kurtz (Ed.), *Encyclopedia of violence, peace, and conflict* (2nd ed., pp. 1242–1255). San Diego, CA: Elsevier.

Burns, R. (2006, October 9). Army launching 'Army Strong' ad campaign. *AP News.* Retrieved from https://apnews.com/d68c986d6c73e6d3bdf65a6fe98439aa

Dao, J. (2001, January 10). Ads now seek recruits for 'An Army of One.' *The New York Times.* Retrieved from https://www.nytimes.com/2001/01/10/us/ads-now-seek-recruits-for-an-army-of-one.html

Dass-Brailsford, P. (2007). *A practical approach to trauma: Empowering interventions.* Thousand Oaks, CA: Sage.

Demers, A. (2011). When veterans return: The role of community in reintegration. *Journal of Loss and Trauma, 16,* 160–179. https://doi.org/10.1080/15325024.2010.519281

Devine, C. (2008, May 10). Walking wounded. *The Herald,* p. 7.

Eastwood, C. (Producer & Director). (1986). *Heartbreak ridge* [Motion picture]. United States: Warner Brothers.

Eaton, K. M., Hoge, C. W., Messer, S. C., Whitt, A. A., Cabrera, O. A., McGurk, D., . . . Castro, C. A. (2008). Prevalence of mental health problems, treatment need, and barriers to care among primary care–seeking spouses of military service members involved in Iraq and Afghanistan deployments. *Military Medicine, 173,* 1051–1056. https://doi.org/10.7205/milmed.173.11.1051

Equine Assisted Growth and Learning Association. (2013). *Equine Assisted Veteran Services (EAVS): December 2013 report.* Retrieved from https://static1.squarespace.com/static/5c45a4323c3a53c04e20d850/t/5c4afd00758d4695fce737cc/1548418307055/eavs-report-2013.pdf

Everson, R. B., & Figley, C. R. (Eds.). (2011). *Families under fire: Systemic therapy with military families.* New York, NY: Routledge.

Faber, A. J., Willerton, E., Clymer, S. R., MacDermid, S. M., & Weiss, H. M. (2008). Ambiguous absence, ambiguous presence: A qualitative study of military reserve families in wartime. *Journal of Family Psychology, 2,* 222–230. https://doi.org/10.1037/0893-3200.22.2.222

Farris, C., Schell, T. L., & Tanielian, T. (2013, Summer). Enemy within: Military sexual assault inflicts physical, psychological, financial pain. *RAND Review, 37*(1). Retrieved from https://www.rand.org/pubs/corporate_pubs/CP22-2013-06.html

Figley, C. R., & Nash, W. P. (Eds.). (2007). *Combat stress injury: Theory, research, and management.* New York, NY: Routledge.

Foa, E. B., Davidson, J. R. T., Frances, A., & Ross, M. A. (1999). Expert consensus treatment guidelines for post-traumatic stress disorder: A guide for patients and families. *Journal of Clinical Psychiatry, 60,* 69–96.

Fragedakis, T. M., & Toriello, P. (2014). The development and experience of combat-related PTSD: A demand for neurofeedback as an effective form of treatment. *Journal of Counseling & Development, 92,* 481–488. https://doi.org/10.1002/j.1556-6676.2014.00174.x

Hall, L. (2011). The importance of understanding military culture. *Social Work in Health Care, 50,* 4–18. https://doi.org/10.1080/00981389.2010.513914

Hall, L. (2016). *Counseling military families: What mental health professionals need to know* (2nd ed.). New York, NY: Taylor & Francis.

Hartling, L. (2008). Strengthening resilience in a risky world: It's all about relationships. *Women and Therapy, 31*(2–4), 51–70. https://doi.org/10.1080/02703140802145870

Henderson, K. (2006). *While they're at war: The true story of American families on the homefront.* New York, NY: Houghton Mifflin.

Holmes, A. K., Rauch, P. K., & Cozza, S. J. (2013). When a parent is injured or killed in combat. *The Future of Children, 23*(2), 143–162.

Homeyer, L. E., & Sweeney, D. S. (2011). *Sandtray: A practical manual* (2nd ed.). New York, NY: Routledge.

Johnson, R. A., Albright, D. L., Marzolf, J. R., Bibbo, J. L., Yaglom, H. D., Crowder, S. M., . . . Harms, N. (2018). Effects of therapeutic horseback riding on post-traumatic stress disorder in military veterans. *Military Medical Research, 5*(1), 3. https://doi.org/10.1186/s40779-018-0149-6

Jordan, J. V. (1991). The movement of mutuality and power. *Work in Progress, No. 53.* Wellesley, MA: Stone Center Working Paper Series.

Jordan, J. V. (2010). *Relational–cultural therapy.* Washington, DC: American Psychological Association.

Junger, S. (2016). *Tribe.* New York, NY: Hachette Book Group.

Kaplow, J. B., Layne, C. M., Saltzman, W. R., Cozza, S. J., & Pynoos, R. S. (2013). Using multidimensional grief theory to explore the effects of deployment, reintegration, and death on military youth and families. *Clinical Child and Family Psychology Review, 16,* 322–340. https://doi.org/10.1007/s10567-013-0143-1

Kern, E. (2017). Systemic barriers faced by women attempting to leave abusive military marriages. *Journal of Counseling & Development, 95,* 354–364. https://doi.org/10.1002/j.1556-6676.2014.00000.x

Kern, E., & Perryman, K. (2016). Leaving it in the sand: Creatively processing military combat trauma as a means of reducing risk of interpersonal violence. *Journal of Creativity in Mental Health, 3,* 446–457. https://doi.org/10.1080/15401383.2016.1172995

Kim, P. Y., Britt, T. W., Klocko, R. P., Riviere, L. A., & Adler, A. B. (2011). Stigma, negative attitudes about treatment, and utilization of mental health care among soldiers. *Military Psychology, 23*(1), 65–81. https://doi.org/10.1080/08995605.2011.534415

Kimerling, R., Makin-Byrd, K., Louzon, S., Ignacio, R. V., & McCarthy, J. F. (2016). Military sexual trauma and suicide mortality. *American Journal of Preventative Medicine, 50,* 684–691. https://doi.org/10.1016/j.amepre.2015.10.019

Kirby, M. (2016). *An introduction to equine assisted psychotherapy: Principles, theory, and practice of the Equine Psychotherapy Institute model.* Bloomington, IN: Balboa Press.

Klostermann, K., Mignone, T., Kelley, M. L., Musson, S., & Bohall, G. (2011). Intimate partner violence in the military: Treatment considerations. *Aggression and Violent Behavior, 7,* 53–58. https://doi.org/10.1016/j.avb.2011.09.004

Lac, V., Marble, E., & Boie, I. (2013). Equine assisted therapy as a creative relational approach to treating clients with eating disorders. *Journal of Creativity in Mental Health, 8*(4), 483–498. https://doi.org/10.1080/15401383.2013.852451

Lieberman, A. F., Compton, N. C., Van Horn, P., & Ghosh Ippen, C. (2003). *Losing a parent to death in the early years: Guidelines for the treatment of traumatic bereavement in infancy and early childhood.* Washington, DC: ZERO TO THREE.

Litz, B. T., Stein, N., Delaney, E., Lebowitz, L., Nash, W. P., Silva, C., & Maguen, S. (2009). Moral injury and moral repair in war veterans: A preliminary model and intervention strategy. *Clinical Psychology Review, 29,* 695–706. https://doi.org/10.1016/j.cpr.2009.07.003

Martin, S. L., Gibbs, D. A., Johnson, R. E., Sullivan, K., Clinton-Sherrod, M., Walters, J. L. H., . . . Rentz, E. D. (2010). Substance use by soldiers who abuse their spouses. *Violence Against Women, 16,* 1295–1310. https://doi.org/10.1177/1077801210387038

McCullough, L., Risley-Curtiss, C., & Rorke, J. (2015). Equine facilitated psychotherapy: A pilot study of effect on posttraumatic stress symptoms in maltreated youth. *Journal of Infant, Child, and Adolescent Psychotherapy, 14*(2), 158–173. https://doi.org/10.1080/15289168.2015.1021658

Miller, J. B. (1987). *Toward a new psychology of women* (2nd ed.). Boston, MA: Beacon Press.

Miller, J. B. (1988). Connections, disconnections, and violations. *Work in Progress No. 33.* Wellesley, MA: Stone Center Working Paper Series.

Nash, W. P. (2007). The stressors of war. In C. R. Figley & W. P. Nash (Eds.), *Combat stress injury: Theory, research, and management* (pp. 11–32). New York, NY: Taylor & Francis.

Padden, D., & Agazio, J. (2013). Caring for military families across the deployment cycle. *Journal of Emergency Nursing, 39,* 562–569. https://doi.org/10.1016/j.jen.2013.08.004

Park, H.-S., & Arbaut, K. (2013, July). *Effectiveness of equine-assisted psychotherapy in reducing secondary trauma among professionals.* Paper presented at the 121st Annual Convention of the American Psychological Association, Honolulu, HI.

Pease, J. L., Billera, M., & Gerard, G. (2016). Military culture and transition to civilian life: Suicide risk and other considerations. *Social Work, 61*(1), 83–86. https://doi.org/10.1093/sw/swv050

Phillips, D. (2018, May 1). A drug from the dance floor may soon help ease veterans' PTSD. *The New York Times,* p. A12.

Pincus, S. H., House, R., Christensen, J., & Adler, L. E. (2001). The emotional cycle of deployment: A military family perspective. *U.S. Army Medical Department Journal, 415*(6), 15–23.

Rauch, S. L., van der Kolk, B. A., Fisler, R. E., Alpert, N. M., Orr, S. P., Savage, C. R., . . . Pitman, R. K. (1996). A symptom provocation study of posttraumatic stress disorder using positron emission tomography and script-driven imagery. *Archives of General Psychiatry, 53,* 380–387. https://doi.org/10.1001/archpsyc.1996.01830050014003

Renshaw, K. D., Allen, E. S., Rhoades, G. K., Blais, R. K., Markman, H. J., & Stanley, S. M. (2011). Distress in spouses of service members with symptoms of combat-related PTSD: Secondary traumatic stress or general psychological distress? *Journal of Family Psychology, 25,* 461–469. https://doi.org/10.1037/a0023994

Sessa, B. (2017). MDMA and PTSD treatment: "PTSD: From novel pathophysiology to innovative therapeutics." *Neuroscience Letters, 649,* 176–180. https://doi.org/10.1016/j.neulet.2016.07.004

Shay, J. (2014). Moral injury. *Psychoanalytic Psychology, 31*(2), 182–191. https://doi.org/10.1037/a0036090

Sheppard, S. C., Malatras, J. W., & Israel, A. C. (2010). The impact of deployment on U.S. military families. *American Psychologist, 65,* 599–609. https://doi.org/10.1037/a0020332

Siegel, D. J. (2010). *Mindsight: The new science of personal transformation.* New York, NY: Bantam Books.

Slep, A. M. S., Foran, H. M., Heyman, R. E., & Snarr, J. D. (2011). Risk factors for clinically significant intimate partner violence among active-duty members. *Journal of Marriage and Family, 73*(2), 486–501.

Smith, D. L. (2015). *Transitioning from the military to civilian employment: A qualitative phenomenological study on involuntarily separating U.S. Army soldiers* (Doctoral dissertation). Available from ProQuest Dissertations and Theses database. (UMI No. 3745483)

Street, A., & Stafford, J. (2014). *Military sexual trauma: Issues in caring for veterans.* Retrieved from https://www.ptsd.va.gov/professional/treat/type/sexual_trauma_military.asp

Taylor, M. A., Schultz, K. S., Spiegel, P. E., Morrison, R. F., & Greene, J. (2007). Occupational attachment and met expectations as predictors of retirement adjustment of Naval officers. *Journal of Applied Social Psychology, 37,* 1697–1725. https://doi.org/10.1111/j.1559-1816.2007.00234.x

Tews-Kozlowski, R. (2012). Solution-focused therapy with military couples. In B. Moore (Ed.), *Handbook of counseling military couples* (pp. 53–87). New York, NY: Routledge.

Tick, E. (2005). *War and the soul: Healing our nation's veterans from post-traumatic stress disorder.* Wheaton, IL: Quest Books.

U.S. Department of Defense, Family Advocacy Program. (2015, August 28). *Child abuse/neglect and domestic abuse data.* Retrieved from http://www.bwjp.org/assets/documents/pdfs/fy14-fap-data-package.pdf

U.S. Department of Defense, Task Force on Domestic Violence. (2003). *Defense Task Force on Domestic Violence: Third year report 2003.* Retrieved from http://www.ncdsv.org/images/Year3Report2003.pdf

U.S. Senate, Committee on Armed Services. (2014). *Recent changes to the U.S. military retirement system.* Washington, DC: U.S. Government Printing Office.

van der Kolk, B. (2000). Posttraumatic stress disorder and the nature of trauma. *Dialogues in Clinical Neuroscience, 2*(1), 7–22.

Van Winkle, E. P., & Safer, M. A. (2011). Killing versus witnessing in combat trauma and reports of PTSD symptoms and domestic violence. *Journal of Traumatic Stress, 24*(1), 107–110. https://doi.org/10.1002/jts.20614

Walker, M. (2008). When racism gets personal: Toward relational healing. *Women and Therapy, 31*(2–4), 71–85. https://doi.org/10.1080/02703140802145938

Wertsch, M. (2001). *Military brats: Legacies of childhood inside the fortress.* St Louis, MO: Brightwell.

Wesson, M., & Gould, M. (2009). Intervening early with EMDR on military operations: A case study. *Journal of EMDR Practice and Research, 3*(2), 91–97.

Wilk, J. E., Bliese, P. D., Kim, P. Y., Thomas, J. L., McGurk, D., & Hoge, C. (2010). Relationship of combat experiences to alcohol misuse among U.S. soldiers returning from the Iraq war. *Drug and Alcohol Dependence, 108*, 115–121. https://doi.org/10.1016/j.drugalcdep.2009.12.003

Yambo, T. W., Johnson, M. E., Delaney, K. R., Hamilton, R., Miller, A. M., & York, J. A. (2016). Experiences of military spouses of veterans with combat-related post-traumatic stress disorder. *Journal of Nursing Scholarship, 48*, 543–551. https://doi.org/10.1111/jnu.12237

Multiple-Choice Questions

1. What are the stages of deployment (in order)?
   a. Predeployment, deployment, redeployment, sustainment, postdeployment
   b. Predeployment, deployment, sustainment, redeployment, postdeployment
   c. Predeployment, deployment, postdeployment, sustainment, redeployment
   d. Deployment, sustainment, postdeployment, predeployment, redeployment

2. What are the "Masks" of the military system?
   a. Moral injury, PTSD, and trauma
   b. Collectivism, hierarchy, and retirement
   c. Secrecy, stoicism, and denial
   d. Warrior, parent, and spouse

3. The death of a loved one in combat could result in this type of loss:
   a. Ambiguous
   b. Concrete
   c. Ambivalent
   d. Hierarchical

4. When a family member returns from combat with PTSD symptoms, other family members may be at risk for developing
   a. Moral injury.
   b. Group cohesion.
   c. Substance use.
   d. Secondary traumatic stress.

5. According to some researchers, this type of injury can destroy the ability to trust and cultivate expectations for harm and exploitation.
   a. Spiritual injury
   b. PTSD
   c. Moral injury
   d. Traumatic brain injury (TBI)

6. Female service members who have experienced military sexual trauma (MST) are how many more times likely to develop symptoms of PTSD?
   a. Two
   b. Seven
   c. Nine
   d. Twelve

7. What is the most consistent approach to working with military populations?
   a. Biofeedback
   b. Neurofeedback
   c. Solution-focused brief therapy (SFBT)
   d. Cognitive-behavioral therapy (CBT)

8. Which counseling approach is often used for those who need to take action and make changes quickly?
   a. Solution-focused brief therapy (SFBT)
   b. Cognitive-behavioral therapy (CBT)
   c. Relational-cultural theory (RCT)
   d. Equine therapy

9. When military members try to implement military strategies into their family units, they may use a power-over approach that can result in
   a. Connection and respect for authority.
   b. Obedience and group cohesion.
   c. Disconnection and relationship violations.
   d. Relational resilience and mutual empathy.

10. Taking a nonpathologizing approach, such as RCT, may help develop an increased perception of
    a. Power-over techniques.
    b. Relational competence.
    c. The central relational paradox.
    d. Isolation and alienation.

11. Reaching out to loved ones while in distress represents which RCT concept?
    a. The central relational paradox
    b. Mutual empathy
    c. Power-with techniques
    d. Relational resilience

12. Why is talk therapy not always a good choice for individuals who have not yet integrated their trauma events?
    a. Because the part of the brain responsible for verbalization essentially shuts down when trying to access trauma memories
    b. Because these clients are often resistant and don't like to talk about their trauma
    c. Because the right-brain hemisphere shuts down when accessing the trauma memories
    d. Because these clients prefer to use expressive arts techniques in counseling

13. The most recent deployments to Iraq and Afghanistan were some of the longest since World War II. How long did they last?
    a. 3–6 months
    b. 6–12 months
    c. 6–18 months
    d. 18–24 months

14. After reentry to the civilian community, it is common for service members to have the following feelings.
    a. Accepted, understood, connected to others
    b. Resilience, fear, exhaustion
    c. Disconnected, alienated, misunderstood
    d. None of the above

15. It is not uncommon for service members to view combat stress or traumatic injuries as a
    a. Fabrication.
    b. Weakness.
    c. Normal response to an intense stressor.
    d. A badge of honor.

Essay Questions

1. What were your initial biases about military service members before reading this chapter? How might those biases affect your work with this population?

2. Describe the presence of grief and loss within the military lifestyle.

3. How are traumatic events in the military community experienced differently than they might be in the civilian community?

4. Discuss the importance of connectedness and cohesion, not only to military functioning but also to the mental well-being of the service members and their families.

5. How do the key concepts of relational-cultural theory coincide with military cultural values and attitudes? Where are there discrepancies? What are some parallels?

CHAPTER 13

Crisis Intervention and Prevention in K–12 Schools

Brenda Jones, Elias Zambrano, and Shane Haberstroh

Schools are social contexts where young people seek to find their place in a community of peers and adjust to ever-increasing responsibilities. Natural stresses abound. Students face heartbreaks, interpersonal conflicts, disappointments, and performance anxieties. Many youth shoulder the added weights of traumatic stresses and significant or chronic losses as they navigate death of a family member, addiction at home, abuse and neglect, and social rejection in the school setting (Reinbergs & Fefer, 2018). Some may suffer quietly, others may act out, and some students maintain a productive disposition unable to outperform their feelings of loneliness and shame. Losses, crises, and traumas complicate and exacerbate the developmental and academic stresses that students navigate. Examples of crises and trauma in schools include bullying; school shootings; natural or accidental death of a student, teacher, or principal; death by suicide; physical and sexual abuse; neglect; substance abuse; family violence; sexual orientation or gender identity; natural disasters; ineffective relationships; wars or threats of war; and cultural issues and historical trauma. Facing these alone only makes matters worse, and it appears that empathy and compassion may be waning among youth.

A major study of more than 13,000 people showed that college-age students were less likely to show empathic concern or engage in perspective taking (Konrath, O'Brien, & Hsing, 2011). This finding is profound because relational resilience reflects the courage to reach out when in pain or disconnection (Jordan, 2017). When a student reaches out into an empathic vacuum or is met with ridicule or dismissiveness, life can seem hopeless. Social disconnections can lead to abject misery, risky behaviors, violence, and suicide (Boullier & Blair, 2018). The rising mental health problems in schools (Horowitz & Graf, 2019) speak to the need to support school counselors, staff, and administrators to create compassionate learning spaces.

As a social microcosm, the school culture reflects the values of the communities it serves. Social-economic status, levels of neighborhood violence, and community mores contribute to the school ethos (Löfving-Gupta, Lindblad, Stickley, Schwab-Stone, & Ruchkin, 2015). Strong connections between schools and families can buffer some social strife and offer hope for communities and schools in need. The Compassionate Schools Project (https://www.compassionschools.org/program/) is one such endeavor that focuses on holistic wellness and students' capacities to care for others and develop their own personal awareness. A compassionate school—focused on developing growth-promoting relationships, mind-body wellness, and resources to respond to inevitable crises—will be equipped to meet students and families when tragedies strike.

The Toll of Violence

Parents and other caretakers send their children to school each day with the hope that their children will enjoy positive learning and social experiences. However, statistics show growing incidences of violent acts performed at school, and even one school shooting, suicide, or story of a child suffering at the hands of a bully is one too many (Kress, Haiyasoso, Zoldan, Headley, & Trepal, 2018). Moreover, nearly 47% of children have experienced an adverse childhood event during their lifetime, and nearly 20% live with mental health issues (Boullier & Blair, 2018). Although school shootings and natural disasters are not a daily occurrence, life with traumatic stress can be. When school- or district-wide disasters strike, the chaos can destabilize safe environments and produce traumatic stress reactions.

Acts of violence in schools carry a heavy cost, and the traumatizing nature of such acts presents risks for students' mental health concerns. These include heightened levels of anxiety, posttraumatic stress, acute stress disorder, complex trauma, secondary trauma stress, mood changes, prolonged grief, and depression (Beland & Kim, 2016; Hinduja & Patchin, 2017; Holland & Neimeyer, 2011; Johanneson, Lundin, Hultman, Frojd, & Michel, 2011; Kristensen, Weisaeth, & Heir, 2012; Turunen & Punamaki, 2016; Wilson, n.d.). Additionally, violence in or related to the school environment affects students' cognitive, social, and emotional development; learning potential; and school attendance; as well as their engagement in career development (Banks, 2006, 2016; Pérez, Abrams, López-Martínez, & Asmundson, 2012; Zima et al., 2000). Therefore, it remains imperative that school personnel continue to obtain the knowledge and skills necessary to respond to and intervene when these acts of violence do occur. Equally necessary, schools must remain steadfast in working with students, school staff, and the community to build preventive capabilities before these violent occurrences.

In anticipation of a crisis, schools ideally create a thorough and collaborative crisis plan that allows the various personnel to understand potential risks and to implement a plan of action should a crisis occur (Brown, 2018). When crises arise at school, administrators must make quick decisions, often at the spur of the moment, to organize and manage those to stabilize and secure the campus and community. Without a well-vetted safety plan, a tumultuous situation can devolve into even more chaos. A comprehensive safety plan includes several key aspects.

The U.S. Department of Education (USDOE, 2013) offers comprehensive planning services through the Readiness and Emergency Management for Schools website. Crisis planning in school settings is a major undertaking and involves buy-in from all levels, clear channels of communication, and investment from the community and administration. Key elements of developing a safety plan (USDOE, 2013) include (a) creating a planning team to identify and rank potential threats and (b) outlining strategies and resources to address potential crises. After the plan is developed, the team provides regular ongoing training to staff and evaluates the plan on a regular basis. Planning teams consider practical elements such as identifying evacuation procedures, establishing annexes to provide physical safety, and developing communication strategies to mitigate the spread of misinformation (USDOE, 2013).

The Relational Foundation for Crisis Intervention and Prevention in K–12 Schools

School personnel should create environments to help students thrive using "developmental, strength-based, contextually-focused, and wellness perspectives" (Duffey & Somody, 2011, p. 223). Engaged school professionals understand and respond with anticipatory empathy to the varied crises and traumatic experiences experienced by their students. From this spirit, they respect that interpersonal conflicts and experiences of bullying, rejection, or humiliation can create miserable situations for students, especially when their pain is ignored or dismissed.

When responding to students in distress, counselors consider the contextual factors that affect students' ability to fully participate in the school community. These concerns may arise from troubling relational situations with peers, parents, or school personnel (Kress et al., 2018). An emphasis on growth-fostering relationships is an important relational-cultural theory (RCT) tenet inherent in the work of professional school counselors (Kress et al., 2018). Effective school counselors invest in relationships that empower students to develop accurate perceptions of themselves and their worth as well as the interpersonal skills that support meaningful connections with others (American Counseling Association [ACA], 2014; American School Counselor Association [ASCA], 2016; Gysbers & Henderson, 2012). See Sidebar 13.1 for information on supporting students.

Understanding the link between establishing healthy relationships and professional counseling emerges central for counseling efficacy (Duffey & Somody, 2011; Kress et al., 2018; Miller, 1986, 2003). RCT suggests that youth may engage in inauthenticity to survive a system that does not embrace or allow it (Duffey & Somody,

Sidebar 13.1 • Supporting Students

Teachers, counselors, parents, and school staff may view a child's concerns from different perspectives. Sometimes a teacher may blame a parent for a situation, or a parent may blame the school environment. Instead of blaming others, what could a counselor do to empower and support their students while creating a supportive atmosphere for all individuals involved?

2011; Kress et al., 2018; Miller, 1986, 2003). Bullying and school shootings are formidable events that threaten students' physical and emotional safety. When a school community faces violence and loss, healing grows when the people involved, and those outside the system, support one another in the immediate aftermath and maintain ongoing connection (Kress et al., 2018). This support can be especially poignant for students who experience complicated grief and posttraumatic stress reactions long after a crisis event occurs. School counselors anticipate that some students may experience prolonged or delayed reactions and respond with anticipatory empathy and nurture the relational resilience (Jordan, 2017) that students show when they reach out long after people say they should be over their loss.

Bullying

Bullying, which can erupt from unequal balances of power and influence, remains a prevalent form of violence on school campuses. Nearly one third of all students ages 12–18 reported having been bullied at school or on school buses (National Center for Education Statistics [NCES], n.d.). Bullying encompasses a variety of forms. Individual bullying occurs when one individual or a group bullies another person. Pack bullying, or bullying carried out by groups, is prominent in high schools and tends to last longer than bullying done by individuals. Bullying takes place in person or online as well as through emails, chat rooms, social networking services, text messages, instant messages, website postings, blogs, or a combination of these mediums.

According to Waasdorp, Pas, Zablotsky, and Bradshaw (2017), *physical bullying* includes physical abuse, threats of physical harm, and attempts to force individuals to act in ways against their judgment and values. *Emotional bullying*, most prevalent overall, includes attempts to demean, ostracize, or minimize others. *Relational bullying*, most prevalent among girls, involves the manipulation of social status or reputation. Bullies generally target particular youth who appear different because of sexual orientation; gender identity; religion; disabilities; and racial, ethnic, or immigration status (NCES, n.d.; Waasdorp et al., 2017). Victims of bullying and bystanders (individuals who witnessed the bullying event) experience low self-esteem, trust issues, lack of assertiveness, aggression, anger, and isolation (NCES, n.d.), which may last for many years following the bullying incidences.

School Shootings and Other Violent Acts

Shocking and startling headlines continue to plague the United States—"Thirteen lost their lives in one high school in Colorado; one killed and eight injured in another"; "Two students killed in a high school in New Mexico"; "A teacher and four students murdered with 10 others injured during a shooting spree in a small rural middle school"; "Twenty students and six adults killed at an elementary school in Connecticut"; "Two students killed at a high school in Arizona"; "Seventeen killed at a mass shooting at a high school in Florida." Although these headlines are concerning, a larger question is, "What is the motivation behind these shootings?" Research shows that 71% of school shooting offenders experienced depression and suicidal thoughts and made suicidal threats, gestures, or attempts before committing the offense (Langman, 2015; Vossekuil, Fein, Reddy, Borum & Modzeleski, 2002).

Two studies by Gerard, Whitfield, Porter, and Browne (2016) and Wike and Fraser (2009) found that 54% of youth who bully had been victims of bullying, abuse, or neglect and had a history of violence. Vossekuil et al. (2002) also contended that students who bully experienced or perceived rejection from individuals or organizations (Wike & Fraser, 2009). Langman (2015) identified three broad typologies of school shooters. Although there were shooters who suffered from traumatic backgrounds, other perpetrators had relatively supportive upbringings, and some exhibited schizophrenic and delusional thinking. Drug and alcohol use appeared to be a common thread that underscored many school shooters' histories. These startling statistics underscore the importance of mental health counseling in the public school systems and interventions to reduce access to lethal means for students at risk of harming others.

Prevention and Intervention

Professional school counselors address crisis and trauma events through evidence-based prevention and intervention programs. Comprehensive school counseling services support the *domains* of academic, career, personal, and social development (ASCA, 2016; Gysbers & Henderson, 2012; Texas Education Agency [TEA], 2018). These general services are available for all students, although some pupils may need additional and targeted program resources. School counselors provide interventions and support through (a) the guidance curriculum, (b) individual student planning, (c) responsive services, and (d) system support components (Gysbers & Henderson, 2012; TEA, 2018).

Briefly described, the *guidance curricula* help students acquire growth-supportive, age-appropriate competencies. Small to large groups support shared acquisition of these competencies. *Individual planning* focuses on individual students' goal setting and planning in major life and academic domains. *Responsive services* target students whose personal concerns and problems may affect their development. Through this modality, students receive direct individual or group counseling, and counselors partner with and support caregivers and invested professionals in students' lives. This responsive services team addressed any preventive, remedial, or crisis intervention issues in a student's life. *System support services* focus on the enhancing processes and systems that support students' success at institutional and district levels (ASCA, 2016; Gysbers & Henderson, 2012; TEA, 2018). Students receive a host of prevention and intervention activities through this program framework.

Prevention

Guidance and Classroom Activities

Students receive skills training to develop a repertoire of skills and knowledge to help them cope during potential crises and stressful situations. These involve developing communication and problem-solving skills to build and sustain relationships (i.e., using assertiveness skills, conflict resolution skills, and coping strategies to respond to peer pressure related to substance abuse, bullying, or other violent acts; TEA, 2018). Many counselors deliver age-level interactions focused on helping youth gain personal awareness and develop strategies to relate well with others in the school context.

Small Groups

Youth who experienced losses or abuse or those who struggle with mental health issues can find more intimate and tailored support in small group settings. In all these interactions, caring relationships seem to be the most powerful ingredient for helping pupils develop empathy, self-worth, and empowerment through authentic connections with others (Duffey & Somody, 2011; Miller, 1986, 2003). As students learn effective strategies and important information about their situations, they may begin to feel less alone and recognize that the counseling staff is a ready resource when crises and school stressors occur.

Intervention

Through individual and group counseling, students may begin to experience authentic relationships and develop mind-sets and skills necessary to address the stresses and problems in their lives. School counselors develop consultative relationships with parents, teachers, and support staff who can advocate for students as they make sense of traumatic incidents. In situations in which students experience a traumatic event and would benefit from ongoing care, approaches such as Cognitive Behavioral Intervention for Trauma in Schools provide psychoeducational modules, individual counseling, and skills training to mitigate the effects of trauma. Likewise, the Coalition for Grieving Students offers school personnel strategies to work compassionately and authentically with students who experienced loss.

Creative and Cognitive School Counseling Approaches

Children and adolescents often respond well to creativity in counseling, and counselors use creative modalities to connect with them in developmentally and culturally appropriate ways (Duffey & Somody, 2011; Gladding, 2015; Vernon & Schimmel, 2019). Creative and novel modalities provide a platform for culturally sensitive expressions that move students toward genuine authenticity and connections with others (Duffey & Somody, 2011; Gladding, 2015; Vernon & Schimmel, 2019). This stimulates engagement in counseling and promotes connections and change (Jacobs & Schimmel, 2013). Creative mediums (e.g., art, music, and poetry) heighten client personal awareness and encourage students to find their voices and explore novel ways to resolve concerns.

The cognitive aspects of rational emotive behavior therapy, motivational interviewing, and cognitive-behavioral therapy may help students explore and identify thought patterns and choices that lead to distress. Many students' presenting problems appear to be centered on all-consuming, and sometimes paralyzing, thoughts. Students enter counseling with patterns of communication with others and inner dialogues that may lead to isolation from other people. Some youth may feel lost and alone and may not be clear on any one specific stressor that seems problematic. By gently exploring beliefs and developing effective skills, students may find their voice, ask for the kinds of connections they need to thrive, and learn that they truly matter to a mutually empathic school counselor.

Multicultural Concerns

Children and adolescents belong to various systems—families, schools, peers, and communities. Because they are dependent in many ways on these systems, alliances and connections with these systems make significant differences in students' lives

(Vernon & Schimmel, 2019). Children develop worldviews from the influences of culture and socialization (ASCA, 2016; Arredondo, 1999; Sue & Sue, 2019). They share diverse values, beliefs, gender, gender identity expressions, abilities and disabilities, age, sexual orientation, culture, race, ethnicity, religion, social class, economic status, lived experiences, and other influences. An enduring level of respect for the cultural complexities reflected in each client serves as a guiding principle. See Sidebar 13.2 for information on creating respectful environments for children.

Counselors uphold an ethical and professional responsibility to develop multicultural competence and to be sensitive to the many nuances of client diversity (ACA, 2014; ASCA, 2016; Arredondo, 1999; Sue, Arredondo, & McDavis, 1992; Sue & Sue, 2019). Counselors attend to their own cultural attitudes, conditioning, and experiences that affect counselor-client relationships. Additionally, school counselors understand that multicultural awareness and experiences with diversity inform students' development. Counselors plan prevention and intervention activities with these ideas in mind (Pledge, 2004; Vernon & Schimmel, 2019).

Ethics and Legal Issues

State laws, school board policies, and standards of behavior expected of counselors in the community guide a school counselor's work. These standards support a school counselor's awareness of when to make appropriate referrals to medical, legal, and other counseling services (ASCA, 2016). Counseling relationships with minors require that counselors consider the specialized ethical obligations of confidentiality, parental consent, and counselor competencies needed for working with minors.

Confidentiality

Ethically, minors should be able to expect confidentiality in many instances; however, parents and guardians hold certain legal rights that limit confidentiality. Consequently, professional school counselors may find it challenging at times to ensure absolute privacy while working with other people and groups vested in a youth's well-being. The *ACA Code of Ethics* (ACA, 2014) require "that counselors protect the confidential information of prospective and current clients. Counselors disclose information only with appropriate consent or with sound legal or ethical justification" (B.1.c). Counselors also

> Recognize their primary ethical obligation for confidentiality is to the students but balance that obligation with an understanding of parents'/guardians' legal and inherent rights to be the guiding voice in their children's lives. School counselors understand the need to balance students' ethical rights to make choices, their capacity to give consent or assent, and parental or familial legal rights and responsibilities to make decisions on their child's behalf. (A.2.f)

Sidebar 13.2 • Respectful Environments for Children

Children come from diverse cultures and backgrounds. The school environment may be the first time a child interacts with someone different from them. If you were a school counselor, how could you implement a safe and respectful place for all children?

ACA (2014) and ASCA (2016) highlight exceptions to confidentiality. The general requirement that counselors keep information confidential does not apply when disclosure occurs to protect clients or identified others from serious and foreseeable harm or when legal requirements demand that confidential information must be revealed. Counselors consult with other professionals when in doubt about these exceptions (B.2.a and A.9.a–d). Although ethics and legal information can be complex, the ASCA ethical code contends that these concepts must be explained in developmentally appropriate terms through multiple methods such as student handbooks, school counselor department websites, school counseling brochures, classroom curriculum, and/or verbal notification to individual students (A.2.c).

Parental Consent

ASCA (2016) asserts that professional school counselors inform parents of the mission of the school counseling program and foci on relevant academic, career, and social-emotional domains. ASCA further emphasizes that parents and guardians become educated on the confidential nature of the school counseling relationship. Collaboration with parents is integral, and the confidentiality of counseling work is respected in accordance with the student's best interests (B.1.e–g). Additionally, ASCA highlights that "even though attempts are made to obtain informed consent, it is not always possible. When needed, school counselors make counseling decisions on students' behalf that promote students' welfare" (A.2.c).

Factors, Approaches, and Interventions That Foster Healing and Resiliency

Two sample cases are presented next that describe work with students using the RCT lens. The first case describes a head counselor's leadership while using a school-wide approach in meeting a campus need that minimized threats to students' development. The second case describes a systemic city-wide approach focused on intervention and prevention.

Case Example Illustrating Applications for Hope and Healing

Times of crisis present a clear and salient need for campus administration to consult and collaborate with professional school counselors. Crises appear to be inevitable on a school campus, and advanced preparation remains the best plan for managing them. Without this preparation, educators face highly charged emotions in the midst of severe time pressures.

At approximately 2 p.m. on a school day, the school principal informed my (Brenda's) staff and me of a student who collapsed at school and whom first responders rushed to the hospital. We were on standby because the student's condition, after attempts of medical stabilization, seemed grim. About an hour later, the student died, and the counseling staff immediately followed our critical incident plan and assisted the campus in navigating the loss of a beloved student.

Death on Campus and the Need for Relational Responsiveness

Death of an individual on campus leaves a void, even for those who never met the deceased. Some students may experience emotions evoked from previous losses. Handling a death on campus can be a daunting task. It presents challenges to most counselors and engenders fear and sadness in teachers and administrators. Because of their lack of training in this area, some teachers and administrators may appear uncomfortable assisting students with intense, but normal, emotional responses to death (e.g., crying, shock, anger, and numbness). Nevertheless, when a campus faces a traumatic situation, a team approach involving all school personnel remains crucial to develop strength-based, contextually focused, and wellness-centered perspectives (Duffey & Somody, 2011). Many theoretical approaches support the idea that most individuals possess the innate potential to cope with death. RCT posits that individuals' natural growth evolves through growth-fostering connections with others and offers a paradigm to support growth (Duffey & Somody, 2011; Kress et al., 2018; Miller, 1986, 2003).

First Steps

The principal and I prepared for an emergency meeting with the faculty and staff immediately after school. Before that meeting, we contacted the director of guidance and requested that additional district counselors be placed on standby. We prepared critical incident folders for these visiting counselors that contained name tags, a copy of the campus bell schedule, a map of the campus, a list of assigned rooms by class periods used for counseling, the approximate timeframe for counselors to meet with grieving students, a lunch and break schedule, and a sign-in sheet for grieving students.

Communicating With the School Community

By 4 p.m., I addressed 200 faculty, staff, and administration about this death that appeared to present a huge emotional impact on our campus. Our goal was to calmly support the professionals responsible for the 3,000+ student body who may experience and respond with intense feelings to this traumatic event. We let them know the relevance of their role in identifying students who might display immense grief. Recognizing that their own emotions and experiences could help or hinder the situation, we gave the faculty and staff a list of helpful responses for use with grieving students and unhelpful responses to avoid. Afterward, we collaborated in developing a memo prepared for all teachers to read to students in their first-period classes on the next school day. This memo included helpful hints for teachers and acquainted them with details on how to assist grieving students and teachers. Additionally, it informed them of counseling resources. See Sidebar 13.3 on supporting students during a school crisis.

Ongoing Responsiveness

Late that evening, we covered tables and wall areas with butcher paper and provided colored markers so students could express their grief nonverbally, with counselors facilitating. Finally, we reviewed the posters before presenting them as condolences to the family.

Steps to Provide Responsive Counseling Services

The following steps should be taken when providing responsive counseling services:

- First, seek accurate information from the campus principal before reacting and releasing. The principal confirms the facts of the incident by contacting the school superintendent and the public relation/communication director.
- If applicable, take the deceased student's sibling(s) to a private office (e.g., the principal's or counseling office) to receive the news preferably from a family member.
- Guide the family in giving the news of the death in a simple, direct, honest, factual, and supportive manner. Expect the sibling's reaction to range from shock and silence to traumatic screaming.
- Answer only those questions that can be answered and allow the family time to not only emote but also express their feelings and reactions. Designate school counselors to remain with the family until the family goes home. Give community agency referrals if needed.
- Make plans to respond to other individuals in the deceased student's immediate circle (i.e., contact the deceased student's former schools so that they might get prepared to respond to family members or other students on their campus[es]). Contact the counseling office where the deceased student's siblings attended as well.
- Designate rooms that will be used for visiting counselors; check-ins; counseling; and breakfast, snack, and lunch breaks.
- Assign a counselor to the deceased student's classes all day the next day so that the counselor can respond quickly to those in need. Make plans to receive students in need of grief counseling. Establishing growth-fostering relationships remains crucial. Meet the diverse needs of students by offering individual sessions or homogeneous and heterogeneous groups in which mutual empathy occurs.
- Inform the principal that a substitute teacher might be needed for grief-stricken individuals who experienced close relations with the deceased (e.g., teachers, coaches, and school nurses).
- Make plans to escort students and teachers in need of grief counseling to the counseling center.
- Assign counselors to visit clubs and organizations that the deceased student participated in and respond to their needs.

- Because of the potential for high emotions, assign a counselor to be with the grieving family members when they arrive on campus to secure the student's property from all lockers (those in classroom hallways and possibly those in the gymnasium).
- Make arrangements for grieving students who experienced immense grief to be picked up by parents.
- After receiving clearance from the principal, superintendent, or communications director, prepare to respond to television reporters. In responding to a death on campus, the principal may be more comfortable when a counselor serves as the campus spokesperson.
- Ask the administrative staff to contribute by providing lunch for additional counselors who arrived on campus to assist. Also ask administrators to remain available to assist, as the needs arise, with clerical or administrative details.
- Make plans to allow students to respond to this loss in a cultural, religious, or spiritual context. This may be comforting and reassuring to some individuals.
- On the day that the counselors implement a crisis plan response and after informing all classes of the student's death, ask the principal to do a moment of silence announcement at the end of the day or the following day.
- Make plans (with the help of central office counseling staff) to debrief teachers, principals, and counselors (in like groups) at the end of the day that the counselor implemented the all-day response to this crisis. Also, be aware that monitoring the campus's emotional climate should occur days after the death until the campus appears fully stabilized.

Case Example Illustrating the Impact of System-Wide Prevention

When a person dies by suicide after living with the torment of bullying, we are left with feelings of deep sadness and many questions. As counselors we look for ways to honor the lives of people who suffered so much and seek to make a difference in the lives of those who feel isolated, alone, and hurting. This investment underscored the ACA Impact Project, a program that emerged from ACA President Duffey's national Anti-Bullying and Interpersonal Violence Presidential Initiative 2015–2016 (Duffey, 2015).

Many activities across the United States surfaced to address the spirit of the Impact Project. Among them was a week-long community effort I (Elias) organized. School district–level program leaders of school counseling programs in the larger San Antonio, Texas, metropolitan area met regularly to discuss support strategies for continual improvement of their districts' school counseling programs. These leaders quickly embraced the idea of a city-wide effort to address the national antibullying and interpersonal violence campaign that was underway. The group adopted the principle of a "schoolwide foundation [that] provided students and staff with the supports and skills to develop and foster appropriate behaviors and healthy emotional adjustment" (USDOE, 2000, p. 7) as a framework for organizing their venture. Subcommittees structured a planned week-long campaign titled "Take the Challenge: Build Cool, Caring, and Inclusive Communities." Furthermore, this group aligned all planned activities to the Texas state guidance curriculum (TEA, 2018).

Subcommittees worked to address various tasks for a successful initiative. One member sent letters to all area school superintendents inviting district participation. Using activities aligned with the Texas model for comprehensive school counseling programs' (TEA, 2018) guidance curriculum, activities were created for each day of the designated week; members then sent prepared packets to area schools through each district's department of school counseling. Packets included instructions for procedures to follow, steps to use in debriefing activities daily with students, and worksheets needed for recommended activities. A brief description of each day's activities follows:

Monday Activity: Drumming Up Diversity

The week's kick-off activity emphasized cross-cultural effectiveness by encouraging students' understanding and appreciation of differences and similarities among one another to support an inclusive community. The committee provided various developmentally appropriate activities designed to help students gain insight and awareness of self and others. Motivational readings on cross-cultural effectiveness for morning announcement time, using the school's drumline during passing periods to highlight the morning's reading, and providing experiential activities as lunch time activities helped students get to know others.

Tuesday Activity: Career Interest Dress Day: Be Uniquely U!

We designed the activity for the second day to support students' self-confidence and to help them build personal empowerment against harmful behaviors. The committee provided an adaptable activity that addressed developmental differences in classroom guidance sessions. Additionally, the committee asked schools to encourage students to dress in clothing reflective of their current career interests—with a special emphasis on the word *current*—to highlight the fact that many students may not yet know where their interests lie. We offered activity instructions and materials for a puzzle used for the classroom guidance session. In this activity, the instruction called for students to answer questions such as "What is self-confidence?" "What do self-confident people look like? Sound like?" and "What are the benefits of self-confidence?" Facilitators allowed time for students to share responses with each other, expressing their thoughts about self-confidence in relation to interpersonal violence. Exercises such as these can offer students opportunities to explore the nuances of self-confidence.

Wednesday Activity: Pairing Up Against Put-Downs

Students demonstrated positive interpersonal skills by linking with others in support of safe and inclusive communities. The recommended age-appropriate activities underscored the idea of students standing together against bullying and interpersonal violence in support of peers who felt excluded or alone. Sample activities included reading motivational quotes throughout the day, structured classroom activities to give and receive positive affirmations to and from peers, and a fun dress day to wear matched crazy socks with friends or to dress identically with others.

Thursday Activity: Harmonious Heroes

Day 4 called attention to the importance of building healthy relationships with others by exploring personal and unique interests, aspirations, and goals. Learning more about each other discourages stereotypical thinking, teasing, and harassment. We addressed the importance of building harmonious school climates—safe climates that say "no" to bullying behaviors—and encouraged students to become change agents, or *heroes*, who support harmonious cultures. The committee suggested activities such as writing essays addressing how harmony can affect students' schools, their communities, and the world. Students also explored the concept of heroes, writing or drawing images about how they could become campus culture heroes. Given the negativity that can arise around cultural differences, another activity invited students to discover a list of countries represented by the student body in their school. Students created and displayed a flag for each representative country in a place of prominence. One other sample activity instructed students to create a paper doll chain and to uniquely decorate each figure to represent the diversity found in their school and community.

Friday Activity: Commitment Day

The culminating event for the week provided an opportunity for students to commit to actions that contribute to safe, caring, and inclusive communities. The committee provided two versions of student commitment pledge forms—one for elementary school students and one for secondary school students—and recommended that the signing of forms be given school-wide attention to demonstrate the community effort. Schools were encouraged to formally announce this activity over a school-wide speaker system and to provide these forms with requests for participation in classrooms. The committee recommended school campuses use campus-wide venues (e.g., rallies in cafeterias, gymnasiums, or auditoriums) to sign the commitment form.

Project Results

Fourteen school districts participated in this modified curriculum at their campuses. One district used the packet as planned, whereas others adjusted activities to accommodate other previously scheduled functions. Many incorporated activities within existing school programs, such as advisory periods, athletic rallies, band performances, or art contests. One district celebrated the spirit of the project and its culminating event at its community performing arts center, sending invitations to students, parents, and faculty across all grade levels to attend.

These activities fostered an opportunity for students to experience balance, authentic communication, connectedness, belonging, support, and validation through positive relationships while navigating and coping with this trauma experience (Duffey & Somody, 2011; Kress et al., 2018; Miller, 1986, 2003). The unfolding of this endeavor demonstrated a level of appreciation and trust in the counseling staff who invested in creating and supporting this project to help the school community address the many crises students face on campus and in their communities. Crises do arise in schools, and when we take proactive approaches, we can send a message of hope and healing.

Future Directions and Emerging Research

Although the U.S. Department of Justice reported that overall school violence rates have decreased between 1992 and 2014, 841,000 students experienced nonfatal violent acts at school in 2016 (Zhang, Musu-Gillette, & Oudekerk, 2016). Moreover, mass school shootings are on the rise, with school shootings in the past 19 years outnumbering all shootings during the 20th century (Katsiyannis & Whitford, 2018). Researchers are exploring the ways that schools can enhance safety, engage in prevention programming, and intervene with students who are distressed or at risk for committing violent acts (Katsiyannis & Whitford, 2018; Price, Khubchandani, Payton, & Thompson, 2016). In a study examining perceptions of 350 high school principals related to the factors influencing violence in schools, they reported that minimal parental monitoring of those who may commit violence, inadequate mental health services in the schools, and easy access to firearms were their top concerns (Price et al., 2016). Future directions in research and practice could speak to augmenting school-parent connections, supporting school counselors as mental health professionals in school settings, and helping families limit easy access to lethal weapons.

References

American Counseling Association. (2014). *ACA code of ethics.* Alexandria, VA: Author.

American School Counselor Association. (2016). *The ASCA national model: A framework for school counseling programs* (2nd ed.). Alexandria, VA: Author.

Arredondo, P. (1999). Multicultural counseling competencies as a tool to address oppression and racism. *Journal of Counseling & Development, 78,* 71–85. https://doi.org/10.1002/j.1556-6676.1999.tb02427.x

Banks, A. (2006). Relational therapy for trauma. *Journal of Trauma Practice, 5,* 25–47. https://doi.org/10.1300/J189v05n01_03

Banks, A. (2016). *Wired to connect.* New York, NY: Tarcher/Penguin.

Beland, L., & Kim, D. (2016). The effect of high school shootings on schools and student performance. *Educational Evaluation and Policy Analysis, 38,* 113–126. https://doi.org/10.3102/0162373715590683

Boullier, M., & Blair, M. (2018). Adverse childhood experiences. *Paediatrics and Child Health, 28,* 132–137. https://doi.org/10.1016/j.paed.2017.12.008

Brown, C. (2018). The role of leadership in surviving a school shooting. *Journal of Cases in Educational Leadership, 21*(2), 3–14. https://doi.org/10.1177/1555458917735357

Duffey, T. (2015, July). From the president: The synergy to make things happen. *Counseling Today.* Retrieved from https://ct.counseling.org/2015/07/

Duffey, T., & Somody, C. (2011). The role of relational-cultural theory in mental health counseling. *Journal of Mental Health Counseling, 22,* 223–242. https://doi.org/10.17744/mehc.33.3.c10410226u275647

Gerard, F. J., Whitfield, K. C., Porter, L. E., & Browne, K. D. (2016). Offender and offense characteristics of school shooting incidents. *Journal of Investigative Psychology and Offender Profiling, 13,* 22–36. https://doi.org/10.1002/jip.1439

Gladding, S. T. (2015). *Groups: A counseling specialty* (7th ed.). New York, NY: Pearson.

Gysbers, N. C., & Henderson, P. (2012). *Developing and managing your school guidance and counseling program* (5th ed.). Alexandria, VA: American Counseling Association.

Hinduja, S., & Patchin, J. W. (2017). Cultivating youth resilience to prevent bullying and cyberbullying victimization. *Child Abuse and Neglect, 73,* 51–62. https://doi.org/10.1016/j.chiabu.2017.09.010

Holland, J. M., & Neimeyer, R. A. (2011). Separation and traumatic distress in prolonged grief: The role of cause of death and relationship to the deceased. *Journal of Psychopathology and Behavioral Assessment, 33,* 254–263. https://doi.org/10.1007/s10862-010-9214-5

Horowitz, J. M., & Graf, N. (2019, February 20). *Most U.S. teens see anxiety and depression as a major problem among their peers.* Retrieved from https://www.pewsocialtrends.org/2019/02/20/most-u-s-teens-see-anxiety-and-depression-as-a-major-problem-among-their-peers/

Jacobs, E., & Schimmel, C. J. (2013). *Impact therapy: The courage to counsel.* Morgantown, WV: Impact Therapy Associates.

Johanneson, K., Lundin, T., Hultman, C., Frojd, T., & Michel, P. O. (2011). Prolonged grief among traumatically bereaved relatives exposed and not exposed to a tsunami. *Journal of Traumatic Stress, 24,* 456–464. https://doi.org/10.1002/jts.20668

Jordan, J. V. (2017). Relational-cultural theory: The power of connection to transform our lives. *The Journal of Humanistic Counseling, 53,* 228–243. https://doi.org/10.1002/johc.12055

Katsiyannis, A., & Whitford, D. (2018). Historical examination of United States intentional mass school shootings in the 20th and 21st centuries: Implications for students, schools, and society. *Journal of Child and Family Studies, 27,* 2562–2573.

Konrath, S. H., O'Brien, E. H., & Hsing, C. (2011). Changes in dispositional empathy in American college students over time: A meta-analysis. *Personality and Social Psychology Review, 15,* 180–198. https://doi.org/10.1177/1088868310377395

Kress, V. E., Haiyasoso, M., Zoldan, C. A., Headley, J. A., & Trepal, H. (2018). The use of relational-cultural theory in counseling clients who have traumatic stress disorders. *Journal of Counseling & Development, 96,* 106–114. https://doi.org/10.1002/jcad.12182

Kristensen, P., Weisaeth, L., & Heir, T. (2012). Bereavement and mental health after sudden and violent losses: A review. *Psychiatry, 75,* 76–97. https://doi.org/10.1521/psyc.2012.75.1.76

Langman, P. F. (2015). *School shooters: Understanding high school, college, and adult perpetrators.* Lanham, MD: Rowman & Littlefield.

Löfving-Gupta, S., Lindblad, F., Stickley, A., Schwab-Stone, M., & Ruchkin, V. (2015). Community violence exposure and severe posttraumatic stress in suburban American youth: Risk and protective factors. *Social Psychiatry and Psychiatric Epidemiology, 50,* 539–547. https://doi.org/10.1007/s00127-014-0965-2

Miller, J. B. (1986). What do you mean by relationships? *Work in Progress, No. 22.* Wellesley, MA: Stone Center Working Paper Series.

Miller, J. B. (2003). *Introducing relational-cultural theory: A new model of psychological development.* Retrieved from https://pdfs.semanticscholar.org/a925/f8b0c-58699c9414bc4350bcd6bd4e44adf31.pdf

National Center for Education Statistics. (n.d.). *Facts about school bullies and bullying behaviors.* Retrieved from http://www.bullyingstatistics.org/content/school-bullying.html

Pérez, L. G., Abrams, M. P., López-Martínez, A. E., & Asmundson, G. J. (2012). Trauma exposure and health: The role of depressive hyperarousal symptoms. *Journal of Traumatic Stress, 25,* 641–648. https://doi.org/10.1002/jts.21762

Pledge, D. S. (2004). *Counseling adolescents and children: Developing your clinical style.* Belmont, CA: Brooks/Cole.

Price, J., Khubchandani, H., Payton, J., & Thompson, E. (2016). Reducing the risks of firearm violence in high schools: Principals' perceptions and practices. *Journal of Community Health, 41*, 234–243.

Reinbergs, E., & Fefer, S. (2018). Addressing trauma in schools: Multitiered service delivery options for practitioners. *Psychology in the Schools, 55*, 250–263. https://doi.org/10.1002/pits.22105

Sue, D. W., Arredondo, P., & McDavis, R. (1992). Multicultural counseling competencies and standards. *Journal of Counseling & Development, 70*, 477–486. https://doi.org/10/1002/j.1556-6676.1992.tb01642.x

Sue, D. W., & Sue, D. (2019). *Counseling the culturally diverse: Theory and practice* (8th ed.). Hoboken, NJ: Wiley.

Texas Education Agency. (2018). *The Texas model for comprehensive school counseling programs* (5th ed.). Austin, TX: Texas Counseling Association.

Turunen, T., & Punamaki, R. L. (2016). Professionally led peer support group process after the school shooting in Finland: Organization, group work, and recovery phases. *Journal of Death and Dying, 42*(1), 42–69. https://doi.org/10.1177/0030222815575700

U.S. Department of Education. (2000, April). *Safeguarding our children: An action guide.* Retrieved from https://www2.ed.gov/admins/lead/safety/actguide/action_guide.pdf

U.S. Department of Education. (2013, June). *Guide for developing high-quality school emergency operations plans.* Retrieved from https://rems.ed.gov/docs/REMS_K-12_Guide_508.pdf

Vernon, A., & Schimmel, C. J. (2019). *Counseling children and adolescents* (5th ed.). San Diego, CA: Cognella Academic Publishing.

Vossekuil, B., Fein, R. A., Reddy, M., Borum, R., & Modzeleski, W. (2002). *The final report and findings of the Safe School Initiative: Implications for the prevention of school attacks in the United States.* Washington, DC: U.S. Secret Service.

Waasdorp, T. E., Pas, E. T., Zablotsky, B., & Bradshaw, C. P. (2017). Ten-year trend in bullying related attitudes among 4th to 12th graders. *Pediatrics, 139*(6), 1–8. https://doi.org/10.1542/peds.2016-2615

Wike, T. L., & Fraser, M. W. (2009). School shootings: Making sense of the senseless. *Aggression and Violent Behavior, 14*, 162–169. https://doi.org/10.1016/j.avb.2009.01.005

Wilson, K. (n.d.). *Trauma narrative.* Retrieved from http://www.mc.vanderbilt.edu/coe/tfcbt/workbook/Trauma%20Narrative/Trauma%20Narrative%20Goals%20and%20Process.pdf

Zhang, A., Musu-Gillette, L., & Oudekerk, B. A. (2016, May). *Indicators of school crime and safety: 2015* (NCES 2016-079/NCJ 249758). Retrieved from https://nces.ed.gov/pubs2016/2016079.pdf

Zima, B. T., Bussing, R., Freeman, S., Yang, X., Belin, T. R., & Forness, S. R. (2000). Behavioral problems, academic skill delays, and school failure among school-aged children in foster care: Their relationships to placement characteristics. *Journal of Child and Family Studies, 9*, 87–103. https://doi.org/10.1023/a:1009415800475

Multiple-Choice Questions

1. A recent major study showed that more than 13,000 college-aged students were _____ to show empathic concern than previous generations.
   a. Not at all likely
   b. More likely
   c. Equally likely
   d. Less likely

2. Around _____ of children have experienced an adverse childhood event during their lifetime.
   a. 47%
   b. 20%
   c. 10%
   d. 60%

3. Acts of violence in schools can put students at risk for developing
   a. Secondary trauma stress.
   b. Mood changes.
   c. Depression.
   d. All of the above

4. Which is a key element of a school safety plan according to the U.S. Department of Education?
   a. Rank potential threats
   b. Set goals
   c. Make sure the government knows about the plan
   d. None of the above

5. According to this chapter, which relational-cultural theory (RCT) tenet is important for professional school counselors to consider?
   a. Cognitive dissonance
   b. Fault thinking patterns
   c. Growth-fostering relationships
   d. Pushing students to heal after a crisis

6. According to the National Center for Education Statistics, almost _____ of students are bullied.
   a. 33%
   b. 75%
   c. 5%
   d. 10%

7. Bullying has three different types, which are
   a. Physical, emotional, and relational.
   b. Physical, psychological, and family.
   c. Emotional, relational, and family.
   d. None of the above

8. What percentage of school shootings were from offenders who experienced depression and suicidal thoughts?
   a. 10%
   b. 20%
   c. 71%
   d. 60%

9. Which is a commonality among school shooters?
   a. Drug and alcohol use
   b. Geographic location
   c. Supportive family
   d. All of the above

10. The American School Counselor Association's (2016) ethics state that limits of confidentiality must be
    a. Explained through creative modalities.
    b. Updated.
    c. Exclusively explained to the parents.
    d. Explained in a developmentally appropriate manner.

11. What is a counselor's first step in providing services after a death of a student?
    a. Make a plan
    b. Designate rooms for visiting counselors
    c. Seek accurate information from the principal
    d. Ask the administrative staff to contribute to providing lunch

12. Responsive services include
    a. Targeting students whose personal concerns may affect healthy development.
    b. Helping students to acquire growth-supportive competencies.
    c. Preparation and then responding to only the needs of the parents.
    d. None of the above

13. Counselors establish _____ relationships with parents to help support students after a traumatic event at the school.
    a. Real
    b. Consultative
    c. Counseling
    d. Direct

14. After a traumatic school event, music and poetry may help students to find their voices and
    a. Replace math and science.
    b. Increase personal awareness.
    c. Explore novel methods for working through their concerns.
    d. Both b and c

15. A national American Counseling Association antibullying initiative created by President Duffey in 2015 was called
    a. The Impact Project.
    b. The Kindness Project.
    c. Antibully Initiative.
    d. None of the above

Essay Questions

1. Think back to your school environment. Did this feel like a safe time for you, or did it feel daunting and unsafe? What do you remember about the teachers you liked and didn't like? What were the crisis response preparations your schools used?

2. As a school counselor or school staff member, how might you encourage students to be authentic and help them be aware of bullying in a school system that may not embrace authenticity? How do you help them in connecting to their true self?

3. Movies about school environments can be funny (*Mean Girls*) and sometimes emotionally intense (*13 Reasons Why*). How could you, as the counselor, spread awareness about movie media and its depiction of the school environment?

4. What are your thoughts about the Impact Project? How do you see this potentially creating change in the school system?

5. Do you envision cyberbullying becoming worse or better over the next decade? What about other types of bullying?

CHAPTER 14

Crisis Intervention and Prevention in Higher Education

Nathaniel Ivers

For many students, college and university campuses may be viewed as bastions against many of the ills and plights common to society—places where enlightenment and transcendence occur unabated. Although such a vision of higher education as sanctuaries nestled among manicured campuses appears idyllic and ideal, it does not recognize many realities faced by many students, staff, faculty, and administrators in these settings. For other students, they may have little time to enjoy campus communities and resources as they balance full-time work; family obligations; and the stresses of class attendance, homework, and the inevitable life stressors. These stressors are prevalent in college populations. In a recent study of more than 53,000 presenting concerns at college counseling centers, Pérez-Rojas et al. (2017) found that students listed their top concerns as anxiety, depression, stress, family issues, academic performance, relationship problems, self-esteem, adjustment, and sleep problems. Students, faculty, and staff at colleges and universities navigate these academic and vocational transitions and stresses while often facing incidents of bullying, sexual harassment, sexual assault, and physical violence.

Higher Education Settings and Contexts

There are more than 4,500 college and university communities in the United States (National Center for Education Statistics, 2019) and nearly 20 million students enrolled in these institutions in the fall of 2019. Given the unique campus contexts, student demographics, and institutional supports available in higher education settings, students, faculty, and staff may enjoy ready access to prevention resources and campus climates supportive of mental health needs. Other higher education systems may be woefully underfunded and unable to support their community during times of routine stresses and crises (Katz & Davison, 2014). For example, students attending community colleges had access to fewer mental health services when compared with peers at 4-year universities (Katz & Davison, 2014). They also presented with more pressing mental health concerns, such as schizophrenia, bipolar disorder, and substance use disorders (Katz & Davison, 2014), and reported lower frequencies of professional care for these concerns. Given that community college populations represent people who are first-generation students, are single parents, and have limited social economic resources, these students could benefit from extra support and targeted services from counselors and professionals in local communities (Kalkbrenner, Brown, Carlisle, & Carlisle, 2019). As you consider working with students in higher education settings, it is important to assess the availability of on-campus resources with a recognition that the programs may be limited. In this chapter, I explore crises and traumas in these myriad higher education contexts. I also discuss preventative measures and interventions that may be used to address these concerns.

Relational Foundations for Work in Higher Education Settings

I frame these crises and traumas experienced on college and university campuses from a relational-cultural lens. In Chapter 2, Jordan and Duffey provide a thorough and clear overview of the core principles of relational-cultural theory (RCT). I highlight a few principles salient to college and university campuses. RCT discusses the importance of authentic connection, recognizing that relationships continuously shift between connection and disconnection. College students, especially those in their first year of college and those who recently transferred colleges, can be particularly susceptible to feelings of disconnection as they attempt to create new friendships and social networks in their new setting. This sense of disconnection may contribute to loneliness, homesickness, and isolation.

Bullying in Higher Education

A common image of bullying is that of elementary school children on a playground at recess being harassed, intimated, or physically attacked by one or more of their peers. However, bullying can happen at all ages and in every setting where people interact, including higher education settings. On college and university campuses, bullying takes many forms and can cause a great distress for those who are targets of such intimidation, harm, or coercion.

The Many Forms of Bullying on Campus

Bullying may occur between and among students, professors, staff, and administrators. It can rise on an individual level, such as when an administrator intimidates or coerces a faculty member, or it can occur on an organizational level, such as when faculty members within a department intimidate, harm, or attempt to coerce members of another department. Bullying can occur between individuals sharing similar levels of power and prestige (e.g., assistant professor to assistant professor, sophomore student to sophomore student, department chair to department chair) as well as between individuals in which a clear power differential exists (e.g., professor to student; wealthy, popular student to poor, unpopular student). See Sidebar 14.1 for information on bullying in higher education.

Bullying can take many diverse forms, including overt and covert bullying; direct and indirect bullying; on-ground and online bullying; and physical, psychological, and social bullying. *Overt bullying* can be physical, verbal, or social, such as hitting, kicking, name calling, or deliberately excluding others. *Covert bullying* includes subtle acts of aggression or intimidation, which may take many forms, such as nonverbal gestures, threatening looks, gossiping, divulging secrets or private information, furtive attempts to exclude or isolate, and microaggressions (Lloyd-Hazlett, Pow, & Duffey, 2016). *Direct bullying* consists of intimidation that occurs directly between the aggressor and the target, whereas *indirect bullying* involves multiple people, usually to harm another person's reputation, exclude him or her from social groups, and damage his or her sense of self-worth. *On-ground bullying* involves subtle or overt acts that occur in person. *Cyberbullying* (or *online bullying*) involves the use of electronic devices to harm others and can take many forms. Some common experiences, according to the U.S. Department of Health and Human Services (2018, para. 1), include the following:

1. Posting comments or rumors about someone online that are mean, hurtful, or embarrassing
2. Threatening to hurt someone or telling them to kill themselves
3. Posting a mean or hurtful picture or video
4. Pretending to be someone else online to solicit or post personal or false information about someone else
5. Posting mean or hateful names, comments, or content about any race, religion, ethnicity, or other personal characteristics online
6. Creating a mean or hurtful webpage about someone
7. *Doxing,* an abbreviated form of the word *documents,* is a form of online harassment used to exact revenge and to threaten and destroy the privacy of individuals by making their personal information public, including addresses; social security, credit card, and phone numbers; links to social media accounts; and other private data

Sidebar 14.1 • Bullying in Higher Education

Have you ever thought about the bullying experience in higher education? There are several power dynamics at work within a university setting. This chapter talks about some of them (e.g., professor vs. student, department chair vs. professor, supervisor vs. supervisee). Most individuals in universities or community colleges are striving for academic success; however, bullying behaviors occur. How do you navigate the system? Are there times when you have seen (or experienced) bullying in higher education?

Physical bullying involves acts of violence toward another person, such as pushing, punching, or kicking. *Psychological bullying*, also called *verbal bullying*, includes name calling and using threatening remarks. *Relational bullying* (or *social bullying*) includes attempts to sully individuals' reputations, rupture their relationships, exclude them from social situations, and isolate them (Chester, Spencer, Whiting, & Brooks, 2017).

Frequency and Consequences of Bullying

Limited studies have provided some insight into the frequency of bullying in higher education settings. Chappell et al. (2004) sampled 1,025 undergraduate students and reported that 25% witnessed on occasion a student bullying another student, 5% had occasionally been bullied by a fellow student, 13% witnessed an instructor bully a student, and 4% reported that they had been bullied by an instructor. Although cyberbullying was occurring when the aforementioned study was published, access to and use of electronic devices to communicate have proliferated greatly since 2004. Exploring bullying in online settings, MacDonald and Roberts-Pittman (2010) surveyed 439 college students and found that 38% knew someone who was cyberbullied, 22% were targets of cyberbullying, and 8.6% engaged in cyberbullying themselves. The most prevalent media forms used to bully online were social media networks, followed by text messages, email, instant messaging, chat rooms, and websites.

Consequences of bullying for students on college campuses may include low academic motivation and success, feelings of anxiety and depression, relational difficulties (e.g., inhibition, shyness in intimate relationships), alcohol and drug abuse, aggressiveness, nonsuicidal self-injury, and suicidal thoughts and behaviors (Young-Jones, Fursa, Byrket, & Sly, 2015). Bullied university employees experience lower productivity, psychological pain, loneliness, and job resignation (Hollis, 2015). Employees of color and sexual minorities may be particularly vulnerable to persistent acts of harassment, intimidation, and threats. These may be overt acts, such as disrespectful hand gestures and racial epithets, or covert acts, such as microaggressions. It is important to note as well that bullying on college campuses is not always a unidirectional process from individuals with more power bullying those with less power. Bullying also may occur in the other direction, particularly with faculty of color, such as when students group together to harass or intimidate the professor.

Bullying on college campuses, although similar in many respects to bullying in other settings, may have some important differences to consider. First, in contrast to elementary and secondary school settings, college instructors may be less attuned to classroom management issues, particularly interpersonal dynamics between and among students. Moreover, for some students, it is the first time they have been away from home for an extended period of time. They may have fewer supports and opportunities to nurture their relational resilience (Jordan, 2018) as they face overt and subtle forms of bullying in a new and unfamiliar context. Additionally, when bullied by a roommate, people may feel trapped in an abusive relational living situation.

Sexual Harassment

Sexual harassment permeates the social context on many higher education campuses (Wood, Hoefer, Kammer-Kerwick, Parra-Cardona, & Busch-Armendariz, 2018). Although it has been prevalent for years, it has received heightened attention in the last few years because of the Me Too Movement. The toxicity of sexual harassment can sap relational and cognitive reserves and lead to impaired academic performance, isolation, and increases in the use of alcohol and other substances (Wood et al., 2018). College faculty, staff, and administrators also can be targets of sexual harassment, which can create an unsafe and hostile work environment, resulting in lower work satisfaction, decreased productivity, increased distress, and higher employee turnover. Inappropriate or negligent responses by institutions relative to sexual harassment claims also may have legal and accreditation ramifications.

The most common form of sexual harassment is sexual remarks, such as sexually implicit or explicit comments about a person's appearance or vulgar sexual jokes (Yoon, Stiller Funk, & Kropf, 2010). Excessive, unsolicited touching, such as the touching or rubbing of a person's shoulders, also is a commonly reported form of sexual harassment. Another form of sexual harassment on college campuses is *quid pro quo* harassment (Smith, 2015). In *quid pro quo* sexual harassment, harassed individuals receive pressure from an individual with evaluative powers over them to engage in sexual behaviors in exchange for some benefit. A common example is a professor giving a student a desired grade on an assignment or in a class in exchange for a sexual activity. For staff and faculty members, supervisors may provide the opportunity for promotion or advancement in exchange for sexual favors.

Up-to-date information is sparse regarding the prevalence of sexual harassment on college campus. However, in 2005, Hill and Silva conducted a study with male and female undergraduates. Results revealed that 62% of female undergraduates and 61% of male undergraduates experienced one or more forms of sexual harassment during college. Moreover, 41% of women and 36% of men experienced sexual harassment in their first year of college. College students are more likely to be harassed by their peers (Cantor et al., 2015), although faculty to student sexual harassment also occurs, as well as work supervisor to student harassment (Wolff, Rospenda, & Colaneri, 2017). In addition, women, sexual minorities, individuals working in low-paying and entry-level jobs, and younger students are more likely to be sexually harassed than men, heterosexual people, individuals employed in professional positions, and older students (Wolff et al., 2017). See Sidebar 14.2 for information on sexual harassment on campus.

Sidebar 14.2 • Sexual Harassment on Campus

For some students, living in on-campus housing is their first experience in being away from home. Sexual harassment may be the last thing they expect to happen to them. However, sexual harassment can happen anywhere and anytime. How would you support students in these instances?

The backdrop of the college experience may contribute to undergraduate students' susceptibility to sexual harassment. People newly graduated from high school come together and interact, largely without supervision. Many may consume alcohol during social interactions, which may increase the "opportunity for and occurrence of sexual harassment and assault" (Wolff et al., 2017, p. 362). Working college students may be particularly susceptible to sexual harassment because they often work in entry-level, low-paying jobs in which they have little influence or power. The hierarchical nature of higher education also may create an environment in which sexual harassment can thrive (Wolff et al., 2017).

Sexual Assault

Sexual assault is also pervasive on college campuses and, like sexual harassment, has received a great deal of recent attention. Sexual assault is defined by a range of nonconsensual behaviors, from touch to rape (Neilson et al., 2018). Recent statistics of sexual assault on college campuses indicate that 11.2% of undergraduate and graduate students experience sexual assault. For undergraduate students specifically, 23.1% of female students and 5.4% of male students are raped or sexually assaulted. Female and male college-age students (ages 18–24) are 78% and 20%, respectively, more likely to be the victims of sexual assault compared with nonstudents of the same age. In addition, 21% of college students who identify as transgender, genderqueer, and nonconforming have experienced sexual assault (Rape, Abuse, and Incest National Network [RAINN], 2019).

Sexual violence is more prevalent on college campuses than other types of crime, such as robberies. In fact, for every robbery on college campuses, there are two sexual assaults. College student survivors of sexual violence often do not report the offense to law enforcement. Approximately 20% of female students, compared with 32% of nonstudent females who are the same age, report sexual violence to law enforcement. Reasons given for not reporting sexual violence, in order of most frequent, include undisclosed reasons, the belief that the event was a personal matter, fear of retaliation, the belief that the event was not sufficiently significant as to warrant a report, not wanting the perpetrator to get in trouble, the belief that police are unwilling or unable to be helpful, and the report was given but not to law enforcement (RAINN, 2019).

People who were sexually assaulted may experience anxiety, depression, dissociation, eating disorders, sleep disorders, posttraumatic stress disorder (PTSD), or other mental health issues. People also may experience relationship difficulties as well as an increased likelihood of engaging in risky behaviors, such as excessive alcohol consumption, drug use, self-harm behaviors, and suicide. Survivors of sexual assault also may struggle academically. Although the effects of sexual assault can be serious and debilitating, it is important to note the strengths of survivors, encourage relational resiliency, and understand that not all survivors of sexual assault experience PTSD or other mental health disorders (Bryant-Davis, Ullman, Tsong, & Gobin, 2011).

Title IX, established as part of the Education Amendments of 1972, requires that all educational institutions that receive federal funding respond to and correct all forms of discrimination in educational settings, which includes sexual offenses. This means that institutions are responsible for stopping the discrimination, including sexually inappropriate behavior, putting into place mechanisms to prevent the behavior from reoccurring and addressing the negative effects of the discrimination. Title IX protects students, staff, faculty, and administrators against sexual harassment, gender-based discrimination, discrimination against pregnant women and parenting students, and sexual assault (Wood et al., 2018).

Other laws that protect students against sexual assault on college campuses include the Clery Act of 1990, the Campus Sexual Violence Elimination Act of 2013 (Campus SaVE), and campus climate surveys (Richards, 2016; Wood et al., 2018). The Clery Act is a federal law that overlaps with Title IX. It was named after Jeanne Clery, a student who was raped and murdered on a university campus in 1986. Following their daughter's murder, Jeanne Clery's parents lobbied the government to require schools to provide vital information about campus safety to students and employees. The act is aimed at promoting awareness of campus crimes by requiring higher education settings to report crime statistics on campus, alert members of the campus community about potential dangers, and publish annually a campus security report that is to be shared with current and prospective students as well as employees of the university (Wood et al., 2018).

Campus SaVE is a 2013 provision of the Clery Act. It states that domestic violence and stalking must also be incorporated into campus security reports. Like Title IX and the Clery Act, Campus SaVE applies to all educational institutions that receive financial aid. Under this act, higher education institutions must keep records of dating violence, sexual assault, domestic violence, and stalking on campus. Colleges and universities also must ensure that victims of violence receive appropriate protections and accommodations. These accommodations and protections must be granted even when a survivor does not report the offense to law enforcement. Examples of accommodations may include helping survivors find a new place of residence, different transportation options, a new academic class schedule, and different work situations. Institutions must also ensure that victims are aware of and know how to access supportive services on campus, such as health care, mental health counseling, and legal assistance.

Campus climate surveys, along with providing information about students' general beliefs and attitudes of campus, provide information about sexual assault and campus violence. These surveys are important because they allow colleges and universities to understand the unique factors that contribute to safety or sexual violence on their campuses. The U.S. Department of Justice, Office on Violence Against Women (2016) has provided recommendations for best practices to improve the utility of these surveys. These practices include ensuring confidentiality, developing action plans with long-term goals, making the surveys accessible to electronic devices such as tablets and smartphones, providing incentives for participating in the survey, and developing questions in the survey that allow for the collection of specific data related to sexual violence on campus.

Violence in Higher Education Settings

Violent acts such as mass shootings or intimate partner violence (IPV) occur on college campuses and can cause significant emotional, physical, and psychological distress. These events also can greatly affect individuals' sense of and actual safety, security, and connection to others. In this section, I discuss IPV, also called dating violence or domestic violence, as well as indiscriminate mass shootings.

Interpersonal Violence

People who inflict IPV may threaten, demean, or control their partners. They may also engage in physical or sexual harm. It is more common among college couples than it is with any other group (Karakurt, Keiley, & Posada, 2013), with the prevalence of IPV on college campuses being between 21% and 32% (National Coalition Against Domestic Violence, 2016). The physical effects of IPV can range greatly and may include such injuries as bumps, bruises, headaches, broken bones, chronic pain, and death (Anasuri, 2016). Psychological effects of IPV may include depression, anxiety, PTSD, and attachment issues (Sutherland, Fantasia, & Hutchinson, 2016). In addition, IPV victims may engage in self-injury, withdraw from others, and experience suicidal thoughts. They may also engage in smoking, risky alcohol behavior, using drugs, and risky sexual behaviors (Anasuri, 2016; Hays, Michel, Bayne, Neuer Colburn, & Smith Myers, 2015). People with few peer supports are more likely to remain in unhealthy relationships. Reasons why people engage in IPV against their partners are multilayered and complex. However, alcohol and drug intoxication are correlated with IPV, although not necessarily the causes of it. Moreover, unhealthy attachments in childhood, as well as fear of abandonment, may contribute to IPV behaviors (Anasuri, 2016).

Mass Shootings

The term *mass shooting* has been defined in various ways by different organizations. The Federal Bureau of Investigation defined it as an incident in which four or more people are killed during one event or in multiple places that are in close proximity of each other (Krouse & Richardson, 2015). In 1966, at the University of Texas, a gunman shot at individuals indiscriminately for 96 minutes from the observation deck of a tower, killing 14 people on campus and wounding 31 others (Neuberger, 2016). This shooter had shot and killed his wife and mother the night before. Forty years later, at Virginia Tech University, a gunman killed 32 students and faculty members and injured another 17 individuals in a classroom and dorms (Hong, Cho, & Lee, 2010). *Rampage shootings*, which may also be classified as mass shootings, take place on school premises or at functions connected with a school. They are carried out by a current or former student or employee. In these events, the shooters target specific students, staff, or faculty members because of some type of symbolic significance these individuals have to the shooters (Newman & Fox, 2009). Between 2002 and 2008, there were five rampage shootings that occurred on college campuses in the United States (Newman & Fox, 2009).

Prevention and Intervention Strategies

Strategies that institutions of higher education can use to prevent and intervene in crisis situations will vary on the basis of the crisis under consideration. However, what is important is that colleges and universities develop strategic and comprehensive initiatives that focus on both prevention and treatment. In this section, I discuss preventative approaches and interventions that universities may consider related to bullying, sexual harassment, sexual assault, IPV, and other forms of physical violence.

Bullying Prevention

Bullying is underemphasized on university and college campuses. Bullying on university campuses, compared with elementary and secondary school campuses, is frequently complex, indirect, and subtle, making it more difficult to observe and treat compared with bullying occurring in elementary and secondary school settings. Given that bullying on campuses involves adult-to-adult interactions, these power-over dynamics can threaten academic achievement and career progressions and can profoundly undermine the learning process. Many schools lack clear policies, definition, and sources for support to help people find relief from this form of abuse (American Educational Research Association, 2013).

Individual and organizational preventative measures can be used to curtail bullying on college campuses. On the individual level, students, staff, and faculty may consider the following recommendations:

1. Talk with a trusted friend, family member, or mentor about the threatening, intimidating, or coercive behavior.
2. If the threatening behavior is from a roommate, consider discussing concerns with a resident adviser or a residence life official.
3. Consult a Title IX officer if the behavior is discriminatory or may be considered sexual harassment.
4. If the behavior is cyberbullying, consider ways to reduce exposure to the behavior, such as temporarily suspending social media sites, increasing privacy settings on these sites, or reporting the offensive and inappropriate behavior to the social media sites. If the cyberbullying is occurring via cell phone, consider blocking the phone number.
5. Consult a counselor to process the emotional and psychological effects of the bullying as well as to discuss and possibly role play helpful methods of responding to the bullying.
6. If the behavior is illegal, consider reporting it to law enforcement.
7. If the behavior is between employees at the university, the target of the bullying should consider contacting human resources for support.

On the organizational level, the following recommendations may be helpful:

1. Consider the hierarchical structure and power imbalances of the institution as a whole and of individual programs and departments. Discuss ways to reduce institutional injustices that may advantage some individuals or groups over others.
2. Ensure that intimidating, threatening, and coercive behavior is clearly addressed in policies and procedures at the university and that violations of such conduct will not be tolerated.
3. Develop safe and simple strategies for students and employees to reach out for assistance should they experience bullying.
4. Provide periodic trainings on bullying for students, faculty, staff, and administrators that explicitly address diverse forms of bullying and ways to intervene should it be observed.
5. Initiate an antibullying campaign on campus that sheds light on its diverse forms and provides recommendations for creating a culture in which bullying is not supported (Everfi, 2019).

Prevention and Intervention Strategies for Sexual Harassment and Sexual Assault

Prevention and intervention strategies for sexual harassment and sexual assault share some commonalities with those of bullying. However, there are additional campus resources available for bullying that takes the form of sexual harassment or sexual assault. First, the Title IX office is available to students, staff, and faculty who experience gender-based discrimination, of which sexual harassment and sexual assault are an important part. The Title IX coordinator can help the individual determine whether the behavior constitutes sexual harassment and help the individual connect to helpful resources, such as the counseling center or human resources. The Title IX coordinator will also help survivors of sexual assault reach out to and connect with campus and community resources, such as law enforcement, legal representation, health care workers, and mental health counselors. The Clery Act also requires that colleges and universities report crime statistics, including sexual assaults, annually to prospective and future students as well as campus employees. These reports not only help individuals know what crimes are being committed on or around campus but also give campus leaders important information on which policies and procedures to develop to make campuses safer. The following recommendations can help institutional leaders reduce sexual harassment and sexual assaults on university campuses:

1. Raise awareness of the problem and provide education on what constitutes consent. The Me Too Movement has greatly increased the collective awareness of sexual harassment and sexual assault, but the education needs to continue. Awareness campaigns tied to Sexual Assault Awareness Month can help, but it is important to raise awareness throughout the year. In fact, the peak times for sexual assault on college campuses is between August and November of each year (RAINN, 2019), whereas Sexual Assault Awareness Month occurs in April.
2. Know the resources available to survivors of sexual harassment and sexual assault as well as to allies and supporters. A few helpful resources include the following:
   a. Culture of Respect (https://cultureofrespect.org/)—this organization is dedicated to reducing sexual violence in higher education settings.
   b. It's On Us (https://www.itsonus.org/)—this national movement is dedicated to eliminating sexual violence.
   c. National Sexual Violence Resource Center (https://www.nsvrc.org/)—this center provides resources and education to help survivors of sexual assault.
   d. RAINN (https://www.rainn.org/)—among other things, this website provides a 24/7 online hotline, safety and prevention tips, as well as warning signs for students and loved ones.
   e. SAFER (http://safercampus.org/)—this group is dedicated to helping student organizations combat sexual violence on university campuses.
3. Consider a comprehensive approach to preventing sexual violence on campus, such as the Centers for Disease Control and Prevention's Comprehensive Campus-Based Prevention Strategy (Dills, Fowler, & Payne, 2016).

In this model, preventative approaches are considered from all levels of a social-ecological model, including the individual, relationship, community, and societal levels. For example, on the individual level, approaches include helping students develop healthy interpersonal and relationship skills and educating them on appropriate attitudes and beliefs about gender, sex, and violence. On this level, a multisession intervention for incoming students also is recommended. On the community level, campus leaders are engaged to promote a culture of respect and safety. At this level, hot spot mapping occurs to identify areas on campus that may be unsafe (Dills et al., 2016).

Strategies Addressing IPV

Much of the information related to sexual violence provided earlier can be translated to physical violence. It is important that a comprehensive approach that includes preventative measures and interventions be implemented at all social and ecological levels. Title IX coordinators are important resources on IPV because they can help survivors tap into resources to keep them safe as well as to help them deal with the potential psychological and social effects of the violence.

Preventing and Responding to Mass Shootings on Campus

The recent shooting at the University of North Carolina at Charlotte where two people were murdered is another stark reminder that university settings are not immune to senseless acts of violence. Because of that shooting and others, campus leaders on many college campuses worked to develop strategies for dealing with rampage shootings and mass shootings. Regarding prevention, it is important that university faculty and staff be trained in recognizing signs that people are in crisis and ways to compassionately respond to them. In the event of an active shooting, it is important that individuals consider safety options, such as knowing where exits are in their classrooms or buildings as well as determining appropriate steps such as fleeing, hiding, or fighting. See Sidebar 14.3 for information on campus safety.

Emergency Operations in Higher Education

In 2013, the U.S. Department of Education, Office of Elementary and Secondary Education, Office of Safe and Healthy Students published guidelines for developing emergency and crisis response protocols and systems for institutes of higher education. The first step to prepare for emergencies and crises on campuses

Sidebar 14.3 • Campus Safety

Mass shootings may be debilitating for students, staff, professors, and college counselors. Just as college students may not think about violence or other traumatic events happening on their campus, college counselors may not either. However, it is important that college counselors remain knowledgeable about the campus safety plan, examine their campuses and learn the most effective method for escape, identify the safety annexes on campus, and provide psychological first aid when needed.

is to develop a threat assessment team composed of representatives from various departments and programs within the institution. Given that the scope of a campus emergency may include destabilization related to academic, legal, psychosocial, public health, infrastructure, transportation, and housing sections, this team provides buy-in and representation from individuals representing these areas.

Once assembled, this team develops a comprehensive plan to assess potential threats, risks, and annexes for campus community members to shelter in place or receive care; the team then develops lockdown protocols and plans to maintain communications and operations and to account for community members. Next, the collaborative planning team develops training protocols to disseminate this information to relevant stakeholders. Once implemented, the campus safety and emergency response team follows up and modifies the campus safety plans as new hazards emerge or become prioritized. The team also reviews processes used during drills and actual crisis and emergency situations (U.S. Department of Education, Office of Elementary and Secondary Education, Office of Safe and Healthy Students, 2013).

Conducting Threat Assessments

To learn of a campus community member or other person who threatens violence to themselves or others can be a frightening situation. In that moment, you will need to conduct a threat assessment, involve other entities as needed, and determine immediate and short-term safety issues. Van Brunt (2015) described the various methods in which threats are made on campuses. For example, *leakage* can occur during an intake session or counseling session with a client. The client may share plans to hurt others. In other instances of leakage, students may become concerned about a peer's text messages or social media content. Van Brunt has contended that many violent acts toward others are often premeditated, and when this information leaks to others, a potentially dangerous situation can be prevented from occurring.

Determining the lethality and potential of a threatening comment, or indirect behavior, can seem elusive in some instances. Some people may use threatening language as a form of catharsis or emotional processing but will not actually follow through with their thoughts and feelings (Van Brunt, 2015). Others, however, do initiate their attacks and may follow a process in which they justify to themselves the need for violence following a perceived grievance. Van Brunt (2015) has outlined the pathway to violence that perpetrators often take, beginning with a perceived grievance and ideation, as noted earlier. After a person has convinced themselves of the need to act out, they begin to plan their retribution and seek out the means to do so. In the actual act of violence, these perpetrators may attempt to circumvent procedures and physical contexts that keep people safe. They then attack in these vulnerable spaces (Van Brunt, 2015). When working with students and others expressing violent ideation, we can work with the behavioral and crisis response teams on campus to assess the severity of an individual's threats to others and the campus community. We then work with people in counseling who have been targeted and hurt by those with malintent and violent actions using strategies discussed in Chapters 5 and 6.

Counseling Approaches for Students Experiencing Crisis or Trauma

Several counseling approaches may help students or campus employees who experienced crises and abuse. Using a biopsychosocial framework may be particularly helpful because it allows counselors to consider clients' presentation from multiple perspectives. With many of these crises, biological, psychological, and sociocultural effects are operative. Cognitive-behavioral approaches also may be helpful for individuals whose experiences have caused behavioral excesses or deficits as well as cognitive distortions associated with themselves and others. Trauma-focused cognitive-behavioral therapy may be indicated for individuals who exhibit symptoms of PTSD (Cohen, Deblinger, & Mannarino, 2018). Narrative therapy, which focuses on clients' strengths and resources as well as a constructivist approach to understanding situations, also may be helpful because it empowers individuals to rewrite their narrative, or their way of viewing and responding to situations (Denborough, 2014). Humanistic-existential approaches also could be valuable because they can help individuals consider ways to increase their internal locus of control as well as process existential meanings that they have derived from their situations (Schneider, 2016). Most important, when working with college students or college employees who are experiencing or have experienced crises, it is important that counselors work diligently to develop a strong therapeutic alliance that is built on trust, nonjudgment, authenticity, and mutual empathy. The therapeutic relationship will be essential to the healing process, especially for individuals who were hurt by trusted peers, mentors, or supervisors.

According to RCT, relational connections enhance resilience, which can facilitate healing and growth. Discussing relational and controlling images can help people process how they view themselves in relationship with others and within a sociocultural context. An authentic and mutually empathic relationship can be a grounding, orienting, and corrective experience for clients. Many people enter the counseling space with controlling and negative relational images associated with the traumas they have experienced. Our emphasis on empowerment brings truth and connection in disempowering relationships with peers, roommates, intimate partners, mentors, or individuals in positions of authority and trust.

Case Example and Applications for Hope and Healing

Maria is in her sophomore year of college and is hoping to be accepted into the engineering program. Maria identifies as Hispanic and heterosexual. Her parents are first-generation U.S. citizens, having immigrated to the United States as adults from Chile.

Six months ago, Maria began seeing a counselor at the college counseling center. Her initial presenting concern was roommate and friendship difficulties. However, after a few months of meeting, Maria disclosed that she was in an unhealthy, intimate relationship with a fellow student. After some gentle probing questions from the counselor, Maria shared that her boyfriend, Martin, would yell at her when he perceived that she was "overly friendly" or "flirtatious" with other men. She also shared that Martin pushed her and threatened to hit her recently. After Maria expressed her thoughts and feelings about the relationship, the counselor gently asked Maria how she would like to proceed in the relationship. She answered that she would like to end the relationship but that she was too afraid. She said she cares about Martin and worries that, if she breaks up with him, he will hurt himself or try to hurt her.

The counselor expressed empathy for Maria's situation and provided her with resources, including helplines she can call and online information related to IPV.

The counselor also shared with her legal recourses she could take, such as getting a restraining order against him. The counselor also introduced Maria to the Title IX office on campus and noted that the office was available to help students navigate situations similar to hers.

After a few additional weeks, Maria reported that she was still dating Martin and that he again pushed her, this time knocking her to the ground. She also shared that, on a different occasion, he had not stopped touching her and trying to kiss her, although she told him she was not in the mood for physical contact. She said that it had not been the first time that he had pressured her to engage in sexual activities after she had said no. Maria also reported that her grades were slipping and that she was feeling more and more isolated, depressed, and anxious.

In the following session, Maria presented as agitated and fatigued, and she reported that she had broken off the relationship with Martin. She reported feeling a wide variety of emotions, ranging from sadness, depression, and anxiety to relief, embarrassment, shame, and exhaustion. The counselor asked Maria whether she felt safe, to which she answered that she did. She said that she had blocked Martin's phone number so that she would not receive any more harassing text messages and that she had unfriended him on her social media sites. She also said that she had talked with the Title IX coordinator, as suggested by the counselor, but did not want to file a report of sexual assault because she did not want to harm Martin.

The principal concern in Maria's situation was the abuse she experienced in relationship to her boyfriend, Martin, in which he verbally, physically, and sexually assaulted her. Although Maria's desire was to end the relationship, she struggled with fear that Martin would hurt himself or exact reprisal on her. As the relationship continued, Maria's sense of self-worth, mood, and academic performance dwindled. Moreover, because of the abuse, Maria was unable to be fully authentic in her relationship with Martin, or with others, for fear that she might upset him.

I also sensed this pulling away at times, as Maria appeared guarded and selective at times with the feelings and information she would share in session. As Maria's relationship with Martin became increasingly abusive, she struggled with the idea that she was to blame for his anger and violent behavior. She grappled with controlling images she had learned about women's roles in relationships. Moreover, as her support network became smaller, she began to feel increased isolation.

In counseling, we cultivated a relationship of trust, mutual empathy, empowerment, and authenticity. This relationship contrasted the painful relationship she experienced with Martin. Through our relationship, we explored the relational images she had about herself. She considered ending the relationship with Martin. We discussed resources related to IPV, which helped her consider new perspectives. Following the breakup, Maria began to reconnect with friendships she had neglected and developed new friendships that would empower and strengthen her. I also periodically checked in with Maria to assess her sense of safety, and we brainstormed strategies she could use to remain safe.

Future Directions and Emerging Research

Many crises and traumatic events occur on college and university campuses, including bullying, sexual harassment, sexual assault, IPV, and other acts of violence. For each of these concerns, a comprehensive response, reflective of work proposed by

Dills et al. (2016) for sexual violence, is needed. In that model, specific preventions and interventions associated with social and ecological levels, including the individual, relationship, community, and societal levels, are listed and addressed in counseling.

Much of the research and resources on bullying focus on elementary and secondary school settings or work settings. Research on bullying at colleges and universities is sparse, notwithstanding the unique aspects of bullying in higher education settings. More research exists related to sexual harassment on campus, but much of that research combines sexual harassment with sexual assault. Although a correlation exists between the two concepts, clear differences also exist. A vast amount of research and resources are available related to sexual violence, including sexual assaults and rape on college campuses. However, because of the high prevalence of sexual violence on campuses, more research needs to be done that will facilitate the development of more effective preventative approaches and intervention models. Research regarding interpersonal violence on college campuses is strong, but more information is needed to counteract the high prevalence of IPV for couples in higher education settings. Lastly, in the age of mass shootings and rampage shootings, research is sorely needed to better understand how to identify individuals in crisis who may be susceptible to acts of violence. Moreover, additional knowledge needs to be developed and trainings done on how individuals can protect themselves and others in active-shooter events.

References

American Educational Research Association. (2013). *Prevention of bullying in schools, colleges, and universities: Research report and recommendations.* Retrieved from https://www.aera.net/Portals/38/docs/News%20Release/Prevention%20 of%20Bullying%20in%20Schools,%20Colleges%20and%20Universities.pdf

Anasuri, S. (2016). Intimate partner violence on college campuses: An appraisal of emerging perspectives. *Journal of Education and Human Development, 5,* 74–86. https://doi.org/0.15640/jehd.v5n2a9

Bryant-Davis, T., Ullman, S. E., Tsong, Y., & Gobin, R. (2011). Surviving the storm: The role of social support and religious coping in sexual assault recovery of African American women. *Violence Against Women, 17,* 1601–1618.

Campus Sexual Violence Elimination Act of 2013, S. 834 (112th).

Cantor, D., Fisher, B., Chibnall, S., Townsend, R., Lee, H., Bruce, C., & Thomas, G. (2015). *Methodology report on the AAU Campus Climate Survey on Sexual Assault and Sexual Misconduct.* Retrieved from https://www.aau.edu/sites/default/ files/%40%20Files/Climate%20Survey/Methodology_Report_for_AAU_Climate_ Survey_4-12-16.pdf

Chappell, M., Casey, D., De la Cruz, C., Ferrell, J., Forman, J., Lipkin, R., . . . Whittaker, S. (2004). Bullying in college by students and teachers. *Adolescence, 39,* 53–64.

Chester, K. L., Spencer, N. H., Whiting, L., & Brooks, F. M. (2017). Association between experiencing relational bullying and adolescent health-related quality of life. *Journal of School Health, 87,* 865–872.

Clery Act, 20 U.S.C. § 1092 (1990).

Cohen, J., Deblinger, E., & Mannarino, A. (2018). Trauma-focused cognitive behavioral therapy for children and families. *Psychotherapy Research, 28,* 47–57. https://doi.org/10.1080/10503307.2016.1208375

Denborough, D. (2014). *Retelling the stories of our lives: Everyday narrative therapy to draw inspiration and transform experience.* New York, NY: Norton.

Dills, J., Fowler, D., & Payne, G. (2016, November). *Sexual violence on campus: Strategies for prevention.* Retrieved from https://www.cdc.gov/violenceprevention/pdf/campussvprevention.pdf

Education Amendments, 20 U.S.C. § 1681 (1972).

Everfi. (2019, October 29). *Bullying in college: What are 5 campus prevention methods?* Retrieved from https://everfi.com/insights/blog/5-ways-to-prevent-bullying-on-college-campus/

Hays, D., Michel, R., Bayne, H., Neuer Colburn, A., & Smith Myers, J. (2015). Counseling with HEART: A relationship violence prevention program for college students. *Journal of College Counseling, 18,* 49–65. https://doi.org/10.1002/j.2161-1882.2015.00068.x

Hill, C., & Silva, E. (2005). *Drawing the line: Sexual harassment on campus.* Retrieved from https://www.aauw.org/files/2013/02/drawing-the-line-sexual-harassment-on-campus.pdf

Hollis, L. (2015). Bully university? The cost of workplace bullying and employee disengagement in American higher education. *SAGE Open, 5*(2). https://doi.org/10.1177/2158244015589997

Hong, J. S., Cho, H., & Lee, A. S. (2010). Revisiting the Virginia Tech shootings: An ecological systems analysis. *Journal of Loss and Trauma, 15,* 561–575.

Jordan, J. V. (2018). *Relational–cultural therapy* (2nd ed.). Washington, DC: American Psychological Association.

Kalkbrenner, M. T., Brown, E. M., Carlisle, K. L., & Carlisle, R. M. (2019). Utility of the REDFLAGS model for supporting community college students' mental health: Implications for counselors. *Journal of Counseling & Development, 97,* 417–426.

Karakurt, G., Keiley, M., & Posada, G. (2013). Intimate relationship aggression in college couples: Family-of-origin violence, egalitarian attitude, attachment security. *Journal of Family Violence, 28,* 561–575.

Katz, D., & Davison, K. (2014). Community college student mental health: A comparative analysis. *Community College Review, 42,* 307–326.

Krouse, W. J., & Richardson, D. J. (2015, July 30). Mass murder with firearms: Incidents and victims, 1999–2013. *Congressional Research Service,* R44126. Retrieved from https://fas.org/sgp/crs/misc/R44126.pdf

Lloyd-Hazlett, J., Pow, A., & Duffey, T. (2016). The Impact Project: A relational cultural approach to combating bullying and interpersonal violence. *Journal of Creativity in Mental Health, 11,* 236–253. https://doi.org/10.1080/15401383.2016.1206842

MacDonald, C. D., & Roberts-Pittman, B. (2010). Cyberbullying among college students: Prevalence and demographic differences. *Procedia Social and Behavioral Sciences, 9,* 2003–2009. https://doi.org/10.1016/j.sbspro.2010.12.436

National Center for Education Statistics. (2019). *Back to school statistics.* Retrieved from https://nces.ed.gov/fastfacts/display.asp?id=372

National Coalition Against Domestic Violence. (2016). *National statistics.* Retrieved from http://www.ncadv.org/learn/statistics

Neilson, E. C., Gilmore, A. K., Pinsky, H. T., Shepard, M. E., Lewis, M. A., & George, W. H. (2018). The use of drinking and sexual assault protective behavioral strategies: Associations with sexual victimization and revictimization among college women. *Journal of Interpersonal Violence, 33,* 137–158. https://doi.org/10.1177/0886260515603977

Neuberger, J. (2016, June). *Behind the tower: New histories of the UT tower shootings.* Retrieved from http://behindthetower.org

Newman, K., & Fox, C. (2009). Repeat tragedy: Rampage shootings in American high school and college settings, 2002–2008. *American Behavioral Scientist, 52,* 1286–1308. https://doi.org/10.1177/0002764209332547

Pérez-Rojas, A. E., Lockard, A. J., Bartholomew, T. T., Janis, R. A., Carney, D. M., Xiao, H., . . . Hayes, J. A. (2017). Presenting concerns in counseling centers: The view from clinicians on the ground. *Psychological Services, 14,* 416–427. https://doi.org/10.1037/ser0000122

Rape, Abuse, and Incest National Network. (2019). *Campus sexual violence: Statistics.* Retrieved from https://www.rainn.org/statistics/campus-sexual-violence

Richards, T. (2016). An updated review of institutions of higher education's responses to sexual assault: Results from a nationally representative sample. *Journal of Interpersonal Violence, 34,* 1983–2012. https://doi.org/10.1177/0886260516658757

Schneider, K. J. (2016). Existential–humanistic psychotherapy. In I. Marini & M. A. Stebnicki (Eds.), *The professional counselor's desk reference* (2nd ed., pp. 201–206). New York, NY: Springer.

Smith, K. (2015). Title IX and sexual violence on college campuses: The need for uniform on-campus reporting, investigation, and disciplinary procedures. *Saint Louis University Public Law Review, 35*(1), 8.

Sutherland, M. A., Fantasia, H. C., & Hutchinson, M. K. (2016). Screening for intimate partner and sexual violence in college women: Missed opportunities. *Journal of Women's Health Issues, 26,* 217–224. https://doi.org/10.1016/j.whi.2015.07.008

U.S. Department of Education, Office of Elementary and Secondary Education, Office of Safe and Healthy Students. (2013). *Guide for developing high-quality emergency operations plans for institutions of higher education.* Retrieved from https://rems.ed.gov/docs/REMS_IHE_Guide_508.pdf

U.S. Department of Health and Human Services. (2018, May 10). *Cyberbullying tactics.* Retrieved from https://www.stopbullying.gov/cyberbullying/cyberbullying-tactics/index.html

U.S. Department of Justice, Office on Violence Against Women. (2016, October 14). *Best practices: Campus climate surveys.* Retrieved from https://www.justice.gov/archives/ovw/blog/best-practices-campus-climate-surveys

Van Brunt, B. (2015). *Harm to others: The assessment and treatment of dangerousness.* New York, NY: Wiley.

Wolff, J. M., Rospenda, K. M., & Colaneri, A. S. (2017). Sexual harassment, psychological distress, and problematic drinking behavior among college students: An examination of reciprocal causal relations. *Journal of Sex Research, 54,* 362–373. https://doi.org/10.1080/00224499.2016.1143439

Wood, L., Hoefer, S., Kammer-Kerwick, M., Parra-Cardona, J., & Busch-Armendariz, N. (2018, August 3). Sexual harassment at institutions of higher education: Prevalence, risk, and extent. *Journal of Interpersonal Violence.* Advance online publication. https://doi.org/10.1177/0886260518791228

Yoon, E., Stiller Funk, R., & Kropf, N. P. (2010). Sexual harassment experiences and their psychological correlates among a diverse sample of college women. *Affilia, 25*(1), 8–18.

Young-Jones, A., Fursa, S., Byrket, J., & Sly, J. (2015). Bullying affects more than feelings: The long-term implications of victimization on academic motivation in higher education. *Social Psychology of Education, 18*(1), 185–200. https://doi.org/10.1007/s11218-014-9287-1

Multiple-Choice Questions

1. Bullying occurs with
   a. K–12 students.
   b. Staff and administers.
   c. Faculty members.
   d. All of the above

2. Covert bullying can be
   a. Nonverbal gestures.
   b. Gossiping.
   c. Excluding people.
   d. All of the above

3. According to the U.S. Department of Health and Human Services (2018), cyberbullying does not include
   a. Posting rumors about someone.
   b. Posting mean pictures of someone.
   c. Asking others to join in a group.
   d. Posting a mean comment on a webpage about someone.

4. What type of bullying focuses on excluding others from social situations?
   a. Relational bullying
   b. Physical bullying
   c. Violence
   d. Excluding bullying

5. Chappell et al. (2004) reported that _____ of 1,025 undergraduate students witnessed bullying.
   a. 10%
   b. 80%
   c. 25%
   d. 2%

6. What is the most common form of sexual harassment?
   a. Sexual assault
   b. Sexual remarks
   c. Small talk
   d. Quid pro quo

7. _____ female and _____ male undergraduate students experience one or more forms of sexual harassment during college.
   a. 50%, 50%
   b. 62%, 61%
   c. 30%, 20%
   d. 85%, 5%

8. Female undergraduate students are _____ more likely to experience sexual assault when compared with nonstudents.
   a. 20%
   b. 50%
   c. 3%
   d. 78%

9. What is a reason, according to the Rape, Abuse, and Incest National Network (RAINN), for a student to not report sexual assault?
   a. Belief that the event was a personal matter
   b. Memory loss
   c. Grades
   d. Society

10. The Clery Act requires schools to
    a. Provide students and employees with classes.
    b. Provide students and employees with information about campus safety.
    c. Accept all students.
    d. Provide grants to students.

11. A 2013 provision of the Clery Act is known as the
    a. Campus Sexual Violence Elimination Act.
    b. Campus Awareness Project.
    c. Violence Elimination Project.
    d. None of the above

12. The prevalence of IPV on college campuses is
    a. Highly reported.
    b. Underreported.
    c. Unfairly reported.
    d. Never reported.

13. What is correlated with IPV, although not necessarily the cause of it?
    a. Anxiety
    b. Alcohol and drug intoxication
    c. Depression
    d. All of the above

14. Which office on a college campus can help a student determine whether a behavior is sexual harassment?
    a. Title IX
    b. Title X
    c. Office of Violence
    d. Campus Title IV

15. What is/are courses of action that a university can take to reduce sexual assault?
    a. Raise awareness about the problem.
    b. Know the resources available to survivors of sexual assault.
    c. Visit www.itsonus.org.
    d. All of the above

Essay Questions

1. If you were a counselor on a campus, how would you work with a student that confided in you about sexual harassment?

2. In this chapter, you learned about Title IX, the Clery Act, and Campus SaVE. Were you aware of these responses to sexual harassment? How do you feel your university does at educating students about their rights?

3. Creating a supportive and inclusive university setting is no easy feat. Students, staff, and professors all come from different backgrounds and worldviews. If you were a university president, how might you create change and promote a safe environment for the university community?

4. After reading this chapter, what are your thoughts or feelings about the violence and harassment that can take place in higher education settings? Do you know of peers who experienced bullying or harassment of some kind? If so, how did the university respond?

5. Many students do not report sexual harassment. The chapter gives some reasons as to why this is. What other factors do you think can lead to a student deciding not to report?

CHAPTER 15

Raising Our Resilience in Times of Risk

Linda Hartling, Evelin Lindner, Thelma Duffey, and Shane Haberstroh

As this is the final chapter in this book on crisis and trauma, we felt it fitting to discuss the important concept of resilience and the hope we have for one another following a critical or traumatic life experience. We live in a world in which countless stressors, crises, and traumatic experiences are becoming commonplace—where national and international news permeate our psyches with information on murders, hurricanes, floods, and violent acts. We are flooded almost daily with the kind of news that can threaten our sense of safety and comfort, and there are times when these experiences hit closer to home.

In a recent survey, the American Psychological Association (2017a, 2017b) reported that two thirds of Americans say they are stressed about the future of the United States. Americans noted multiple sources of stress that are "very or somewhat" significant, including the current political climate (57%) and concerns about personal safety (34%). In 2016, 71% of Americans in this survey reported at least one symptom of stress. This rose to 80% by January of 2017 and included symptoms such as headache (34%), feeling overwhelmed (33%), feeling nervous or anxious (33%), or feeling depressed or sad (32%). The economy (44%), terrorism (34%), and mass shootings and gun violence (31%) were cited as concerns that have added to American's stress levels in the past decade. Feeling it the most are women, younger generations, and lower income Americans.

In this chapter, we use a relational frame to explore how people can strengthen their resilience and transform their experience through creative change cultivated through mutually supportive relationships. We discuss some traditional modes of thought on emotional strength and what it means to be resilient. We distinguish these concepts from perspectives that carry a nuanced relational context. We ask you to explore your own understanding of resilience and consider the ways in which connected creativity can support the resilience of all who suffer from adversities and trauma. We look at the lived experiences of people enduring serious conditions of stress, crises, trauma, and loss, and we discuss the complexity of resilience. Through this discussion, we also consider those situations in which people are able to transform pain into purpose and consider the relational conditions that support this transformation.

For example, the organization Mothers Against Drunk Driving (MADD) was born out of tragedy. A mother who lost her 13-year-old daughter to a drunk driver launched MADD to improve laws against drunk driving and to keep more people safe on the roads (MADD, 2019). Undeniably, there are people who experience tragedy and are able to move forward with their lives—changed, of course, and with purpose. At the same time, there are people who, in spite of the best efforts of all involved, including their own, do not survive their traumatic experiences (Chapter 7 addresses the trauma of suicide). In these cases, words like "resilience" can sound insubstantial. Using relational-cultural theory as a foundation, and the principles of the Human Dignity and Humiliation Studies (HumanDHS) organization as context, we view resilience as fostered relationally and experienced collectively.

The Relational Foundation for Fostering Resilience After Crisis and Trauma

As counselors, we speak of resilience in ways that hold hope for a light at the end of the tunnel—for meaning in life after adversity or loss. As counselors, we question why it is that some people find their way through trauma, whereas others do not. We consider the protective factors that support a person's resilience and the relational dynamics that support resilience. We wonder, "How do we identify resilience?" and "How is it garnered?" See Sidebar 15.1 for more information on resilience.

Traditional Resilience Models

Resilience is traditionally viewed as a function of some innate, internal quality or constellation of qualities that will somehow see people through the darkness (Volk, 2014). Biological, environmental, and personal factors—such as temperament, intelligence, self-esteem, internal locus of control, mastery, and social support—are common characteristics cited as important in the resilience literature (Hartling, 2008). In fact, popular culture often depicts the image of a stoic, self-contained, and self-sufficient person who overcomes tragedies and seemingly unsurmountable losses independently (Sehgal, 2015). Western culture is replete with images of a person "bouncing back," as would a rubber ball, after great tragedies. These images support a general expectation across U.S. culture that life will return

Sidebar 15.1 • Resilience

Some theorists contend that resilience is an inner trait that people possess. A person is either resilient or they are not. In this chapter, the authors contended that resilience is relational and social in nature. Just as people can move in and out of connections, people can move in and out of resiliency. How do you see resilience changing?

to "normal," or at least to a close-enough semblance of normalcy, after the horror of a significant loss or catastrophe. In this respect, people are often encouraged to build their "emotional muscle" and to develop individual internal qualities that can support them during times of loss and struggle. However, this limited perspective about resilience is not enough. Moreover, we believe it can and does obstruct progress toward crucial social change.

As *New York Times* writer Parul Sehgal (2015) has suggested, the popular notion of resilience is a convenient catchword, placing the focus on a person's individual character while distracting them from critically examining social conditions that isolate and oppress. Without an awareness of the social conditions that impede human resilience, it is all too easy to assume that one's failure to be resilient is a failure of one's character. This is akin to assuming that alcoholism is an individual problem stemming from a lack of will power, which ignores the interrelated biopsychosocial conditions that contribute to this disease.

Furthermore, Sehgal (2015) observed that "demands for resilience have become a cleverly coded way to shame those speaking out against injustices" (para. 10). She reminds us that idealizing individual resilience can be a subtle, but effective, way to silence those whom society might deem insufficiently resilient because they protest hardships induced by social injustice, inequality, and discrimination.

Relational Resilience

Counselors working with people experiencing crises, stress, and trauma have an opportunity to compassionately offer a wider perspective on resilience by acknowledging and strengthening the crucial social and relational conditions that contribute to their client's capacity to be resilient. Moving beyond an individualistic approach, relational-cultural theory offers a new way of thinking about resilience (Jordan, 2018). Jordan (2018) proposed that resilience develops and is strengthened through relationships; specifically, relationships that cultivate the mutual growth and development of all involved.

The Native American indigenous people's metaphor of the sick forest (White Bison, 2002) we discussed in Chapter 3 speaks to the power of shared resilience and the ways that systems can poison or nourish the roots of people's growth and resilience. With this in mind, individualistic views of resilience seek to strengthen a tree removed from a sick forest and then expect that tree will thrive once placed back in its diseased ecological system. Sure, it may survive a while longer than others, but the tendrils of a sickness will eventually seep in, constricting the life and vibrancy of the individual tree, eventually suffocating all hope and growth. Counselors attuned to the systemic and shared nature of dysfunction and healing see how resilience makes sense in context and the ways that helping professionals have collective power to enact social change. We work to heal the forest. See Sidebar 15.2 for more information on counselor advocacy.

Sidebar 15.2 • Counselor Advocacy

The structures of social systems are embedded in communities and cultures. Counselors can use their power and voice for those with less power to create systemic changes. What are some ways counselors can advocate for others?

Relationally framed, people strengthen their resilience when they have opportunities to connect with others in a mutually beneficial way (Hartling, 2005; Jordan, 2018). This framework is in contrast to traditional models on resilience that speak to social supports but do not often describe specific relational processes that nurture resilience. These models typically view social support as one-directional, rather than a two-way, growth-promoting experience (Jordan, 2004, 2018). In contrast to these individualistic views of resilience, Jordan (2018) defined a *relational view of resilience* as "the capacity to move back into connection after disconnection, and the capacity to reach out for help" (p. 37). In other words, when people reach out in times of distress and are supported, they nourish and build their capacity for resilience.

Courage and Relational Resilience

Throughout this text, we explored the many kinds of stressors, crises, and traumas that profoundly disrupt people's lives, including systemic injustices that exert the full weight of oppression and disenfranchisement, interpersonal and sexual violence that shatters the heart of connection, and invalidations that alienate those deemed different. Not only do these experiences disconnect people from helpful relationships but they also disconnect people from their core sense of dignity as a human being. With an appreciation for the strategies people use to survive traumatic disconnection, we walk with them throughout the chaotic and disheartening journey to reconnect with themselves and others.

Courage in the face of such losses is hard won. Experiences of humiliation, betrayal, and attacks on our dignity—individually, within families, socially, and globally—cause damage to our psyches and hearts and threaten our potential to positively contribute to the world. In addition, these experiences profoundly disrupt our ability to be resilient. However, our potential for healing and resilience can be strengthened through the connections we form and through the support and care we offer one another during times of crisis and loss. We respect the courage it takes for a person to reach out from within traumatic and isolating contexts.

As counselors, we are in the ideal position to help our clients discover and cultivate the interpersonal lifelines that make their lives begin to work for them again. Working together, we can help our clients generate a relational refuge during times of hardship. However, what happens when abuse persists and people face insidious forms of discrimination, humiliation, and debasement that characterize too much of modern living? The many faces of mistreatment, financial hardship, discrimination and persecution, workplace harassment and exploitation, unaffordable housing, food insecurity, and manipulation and abuse in relationships profoundly disrupt people's lives.

Cara was a beautiful young woman who fought with all her heart to transcend experiences of trauma from abuse and her addiction to drugs. Cara's tenacity and courage in forging meaningful connections, her wit and keen intelligence, and her efforts to practice authenticity and genuineness contributed to several years of growth in connection to loved ones following years of trauma, drug abuse, and loss. However, in addition to her history of substance abuse, she had an especially heartbreaking Achilles' heel: unrequited love. Cara fought for a special relationship and did her best to gain perspective when it did not work out. Throughout her work in therapy, and during those times when life would throw her one more brutal blow, Cara appeared to face these circumstances with all the guts, connectedness, vulnerability, and raw honesty she could muster.

It had been several months since Cara had attended counseling when news spread about her death. How could this be? In spite of her sadness over that relationship, she was engaged in life and relaunching her career, and she appeared hopeful. Beloved by so many people, and deeply supported by her own parents and loved ones, her death came as a complete shock. Was it suicide? Did she relapse? We do not know. Rather, what we know is this beautiful person fought the hard fight against countless adversities. She fought with the kind of courage few are able to carry, and she did so authentically and in connection with those she trusted. We can't know what happened at the end of Cara's life. What we do know is the amazingly powerful way in which she lived beyond many, many hardships. Cara's life is a reminder to all of us that resilience can be fragile.

Roots of Resilience: Dignity

There may be many relational roots that foster resilience, yet one of the most promising paths is actively and consistently recognizing the dignity of all people. This is the quest of the global network HumanDHS, which strives to fully understand the dynamics of dignity as well as its violation through many forms of humiliation. HumanDHS is a transdisciplinary community committed to stimulating "systemic change, globally and locally, and to open space for dignity, mutual respect and esteem to take root and grow" (HumanDHS, 2019b, para. 1). HumanDHS brings together the work of scholars, researchers, lawyers, policy makers, artists, practitioners, and others from all backgrounds. These collective efforts emphasize the creation of tangible changes across varied social arenas, including art, architecture, business, microfinancing, politics, and global conflict, bringing the concepts and practices of dignity to fruition (HumanDHS, 2019b). Evelin Lindner, the founding director of HumanDHS, received nominations for the Nobel Peace Prize in 2015, 2016, and 2017, recognizing the impact of this network to bring about peace and dignity across the globe.

Humiliation

Humiliation is one of the most powerful forces that can damage dignity by breaking down the systemic relational conditions that allow people to be more resilient. On the basis of more than 40 years of global living and scholarship, Lindner (2006) has observed that humiliation may be "the strongest force that creates rifts between people and breaks down relationships" (p. 171). HumanDHS (2019b, para. 2) defined *humiliation* as the experience of being deeply devalued, demeaned, denigrated, or dehumanized, a sense of violation involving being cruelly or brutally "put down." Many dominance-based hierarchical systems are designed to keep people in their place, consigning them to subservience, stigmatization, and compliance through covert and overt forms of humiliation that can include violence. Arrogance, privilege, and the quest for power and dominance over others fuel presumptions of supremacy, creating boundaries, walls, and social structures to obstruct *relational equality in dignity*, thus perpetuating the privilege of a few while maintaining abusive status quos (Hartling & Lindner, 2016). Because relational resilience thrives in mutuality, dignity, authenticity, and respect, HumanDHS scholars and practitioners challenge these systems of indignity.

Linda M. Hartling, the Director of HumanDHS, articulated a course of action for all of us to take as we navigate these contentious times that can damage the dignity each of us needs to be resilient (Hartling & Lindner, 2017). She joins Lindner in suggesting that it is profoundly helpful to move from a language and identifiers of division that separate us from each other and separate us from our planet. Instead, we can think in terms of *relational ecology*, putting the quality of our relationships—with people and the planet—at the center of our concern. This is in contrast to the "me-versus-you" language and thinking that generate ruthless competitive achievement and distinct separate entities vying for limited power and resources. We especially need to decentralize the supremacy of economism (Norgaard, 2011) and strive to decouple our sense of worth and dignity from material forms of wealth, status, and power.

Relational Dialogue

Taking a relational approach, the HumanDHS community has learned to approach contentious and divisiveness issues with a methodology derived from appreciative inquiry (Hartling, 2010; Klein, 2004; Srivastva & Cooperrider, 1990). This method mobilizes the energy of curiosity and the skill of engaging in mutually dignifying dialogue—dialogue that resists verdict thinking or snap judgments (S. M. Miller, 2012). HumanDHS strives to access the strength of shared wisdom, collective intellect, and lived experience to thoughtfully examine and discuss the diverse global issues that require systemic change. Finally, HumanDHS efforts exemplify the enormous benefits of effectively "waging good conflict," a concept and practice introduced to us by relational psychiatrist, Jean Baker Miller (1976/1986, 1983). J. B. Miller observed that conflict is inherent to change, recognizing that all of us can differ in opinions without devolving into aggression. These relational skills act as guideposts that set the stage for creative exchanges. These exchanges lead to practical ideas, plans, and actions that emerge from a spirit of mutually, honesty, advocacy, and care for the dignity of all involved. Dignity is at the root of resilience. It is the social fabric we need to support resilience as a shared responsibility. Dignity is the seed that generates the creativity needed for positive change—the creativity needed in counseling.

Resilience Is Necessary for Creativity in Counseling

The second law of thermodynamics posits that closed systems will always naturally devolve into chaos rather than order (National Aeronautics and Space Administration, n.d.). The odds are minute that a deck of cards thrown into the air will reorder itself back into its original stack. Known as *entropy*, this process explains the seemingly chaotic nature of reality, the degradation of systems over time, and the courses of aging and death. Human creativity is the opposing process to entropy. From this perspective, counseling is clearly a creative endeavor. Indeed, it is a co-creative endeavor between the counselor and the client. Together, this sometimes lifesaving relational engagement seeks to make sense of disorder, chart new ways to live, offer dignity to our experiences and each other, and create light in the darkness of chaos. Although creativity in counseling draws on our innate ingenuity, imagination, and resourcefulness, it differs in some ways from other practices of creativity.

Creativity in Counseling Defined

Creativity in counseling is defined as "a shared counseling process involving growth-promoting shifts that occur from an intentional focus on the therapeutic relationship and the inherent human creative capacity to affect change" (Duffey, Haberstroh, & Trepal, 2016, p. 449). As a characteristic human experience, the creative process can serve to express or process deep pain, isolation, and the darker aspects of human experience. It is also true that human creativity can be mobilized in destructive ways. For example, people can find ways to seek revenge, take actions that use weapons of mass destruction, develop self-serving and other-oppressive financial schemes, and concoct ingenious ways to inflict pain and suffering on others. In complete contrast, creativity in counseling is antithetical to these dehumanizing forms of ingenuity. Counselors express creativity by creating safe spaces to strengthen the dignity and resilience of clients, supporting their psychological growth and their increasingly healthy sense of belonging, which, ideally, leads to positive action in their lives and in the world (Hartling & Lindner, 2016).

Creativity in Action

So how does creativity in counseling look in practice, and how can it help in times of stress, crises, and trauma? Creativity in counseling makes use of the full range of human expression, resourcefulness, and imagination to facilitate growth. It helps clients see issues and problems in a new light so they can engage in creative restorative social actions that increase their sense of dignity and ability to be resilient in the face of past experiences and going forward in their lives. Although creative counselors use a wide variety of media and techniques within their scope of training and ethical practices, many engage in creativity when we offer reframes, have brainstorming sessions, and seek novel solutions to seemingly intractable problems and complex difficulties. Professionally, creativity also drives the creation of *best practices* in counseling, including revisions to ethical codes, client care, and systemic change. I (Shane) was reminded of the power of creativity to address dire situations when a guest speaker from the Department of Child Safety (DCS) presented on their procedures for reporting child abuse. I expected to hear about the legalities, processes, and stories of a failing society and the stresses of casework, and I did learn about many of these topics. However, it was also inspiring to see how the presenter shared his creativity and resourcefulness.

Resourcefulness and Divergent Thinking

Imagine a loving family living in abject poverty—no running water, no heat or air conditioning, persistent food anxiety, children with a set or two of old worn and dirty clothes. The middle school children attend the school in the nearby town and are subjected to routine bullying, ostracization, and humiliation. Without access to basic necessities, the children appear unkempt, dirty, and neglected. At some point, the DCS intervenes, prompted by a call from the school. Rather than tearing

319

the children from their parents, as is often the response, the DCS staff used their creativity to find a more helpful solution to the problem that addressed the situation while preserving the relationships in this family. The DCS staff realized the children in this family could use the school showers early in the mornings before school in privacy. With DCS and school-coordinated support, this creative idea allowed the children to dramatically improve their self-care. Additionally, the DCS staff connected the family with social services to provide food and other basic necessities. Clearly, those with the power to make a change could have turned away from the real needs of this family; they could have inflicted a humiliating intervention or offered meager resources.

By thinking creatively, the DCS staff was able to repurpose and use the available resources beyond their conventional use for the benefit of a struggling family, not only improving the well-being and dignity of all involved but also cultivating the relational health of the entire system, the family, the school, and the service providers. Their creativity changed a system, strengthened the resilience and dignity of the family, and reduced the risk of further isolation and dehumanization of these children. See Sidebar 15.3 for more information on finding creative solutions.

Factors, Approaches, and Interventions That Foster Healing and Resilience

Societal expectations and perspectives on coping can skew our sense of how things need to be, distorting our trajectory for healing. In that respect, understanding the dynamics of resilience, the contexts in which our capacity for resilience grows, and the relevance of self-compassion (Neff, 2003) can be a source of comfort and support and bridge our understanding of how human beings survive critical losses and heartbreaks. It is important to consider the social and relational factors that can support a person's genuine strength and resilience (Hartling, 2005; Jordan, 2018) and the ways that people can appear strong and resilient while hurting inside, devastated, and alone. By breaking the bonds of isolation, stigma, and rejection, we can invite life back into a bleak existence.

Loss and trauma can bring what is truly important into sharp focus. We can never return to the comforts of what was lost. We cannot undue horrible truths. The bitter facts of loss can still leave us breathless, and the hope for posttraumatic growth seems rarely worth its price. Despite the pain that crises and traumas can bring, there is hope for the future for many people. van der Kolk (2014) wrote that recovery from traumatic experiences is more than just learning tools to deal with reactions and memories. It is engaging in the true possibility for living life fully again, or perhaps for the first time. There is the prospect of *posttraumatic growth*. Tedeschi and Calhoun (2016) found that posttraumatic growth leads to greater ap-

Sidebar 15.3 • Finding Creative Solutions

At times, it may feel (and possibly is) easier to go "by the book" and follow set plans. Think about the Department of Child Safety (DCS) story. Instead of the DCS staff taking the children away instantly from their parents, they used their creative thinking to come up with a plan that honored the family's dignity and met their need for basic necessities.

preciation of personal strength through vulnerability, greater valuation of relationships, spirituality, and embarking on new life courses.

Relational Resilience:
From Planting Seeds of Dignity to
Cultivating Global Creativity

To address the crises humanity is facing today, we need everyone's help! We need to become *a world of relational bridge builders*, composed of people, communities, and organizations that have the resilience to persevere through the daunting obstacles that undermine human dignity, inflict humiliation, and poison the planet in ways that obstruct our immediate and long-term social-global solidarity (Lindner, in press). We need everyone's creativity to find new solutions to surmount not only problems threatening our communities but also problems that threaten all life on earth. Counselors are among the most skilled relational bridge builders. We are in one of the best positions to help people find dignifying ways to contribute their creativity!

HumanDHS is one example of a community that strives to build relational bridges that strengthen resilience while planting seeds of dignity that lead to courageous creativity. HumanDHS is unique as a transdisciplinary community of concerned scholars, researchers, educators, practitioners, creative artists, and others who all collaborate in a spirit of mutual support to understand the complex dynamics of dignity and humiliation (http://www.humiliationstudies.org/). We (Linda and Evelin) feel privileged to share an introduction to this work with you.

For more than 15 years, HumanDHS's efforts have focused on stimulating systemic change, globally and locally, to open space for dignity, mutual respect, and esteem to take root and grow. From the start, HumanDHS emphasized a radical notion: putting the quality of our relationships first. The work is the outgrowth of HumanDHS's energy through the quality of these relationships. Our goal is ending systemic humiliation and humiliating practices, preventing new ones from arising, and opening space for feelings of humiliation to nurture constructive social change so that we all can join in healing the cycles of humiliation throughout the world. We do our best to cultivate a relational climate characterized by dignity, by walking our talk, and by encouraging mutual personal growth.

Relational Bridge Building

To address the crises humanity faces today, we propose becoming advocates for our communities and each other. We propose moving from language and division that separate us from each other and from our planet. In contrast, we propose movement toward relational ecology, putting the quality of our relationships—with people and the planet—at the center of our concern. This is opposed to the "me-versus-you" language and thinking that generate ruthless competitive achievement and separate entities vying for limited power and resources (Hartling & Lindner, 2017). We support decentralizing the supremacy of economism (Norgaard, 2011), which emphasizes our fundamental worth and dignity as tied to wealth, status, and power.

For more than a decade, our relational approach has been sustainable. It has offered a new model of collaborative action, a replenishing relational-organizational climate that is constantly evolving and growing with, rather than at the expense of, the people involved. Our work is a labor of love and maintained entirely by volunteers who give their time and energy as a gift. All our efforts are pro bono and not-for-profit endeavors, and Evelin Lindner's 2015, 2016, and 2017 Nobel Peace Prize nominations for the work of HumanDHS gave all our members great courage. It has been lifesaving for many who risk their lives and livelihoods to advance dignity in the world.

The HumanDHS currently includes approximately 1,000 personally invited members from all continents, more than 7,000 friends on our address list. Through the creativity and support of so many HumanDHS friends, we launched our World Dignity University Initiative (http://www.worlddignityuniversity.org/) in 2011 and our not-for-profit publishing house Dignity Press in (http://dignitypress.org/) in 2012. We organize two conferences per year: We gather for one global conference at a different location each year, which has led us since 2003 to Europe (Paris, Berlin, Oslo, and Dubrovnik), Costa Rica, China, Hawai'i, Turkey, Egypt, New Zealand, South Africa, Rwanda, Chiang Mai in Northern Thailand, and Indore in Central India. Then we come together a second time each December for our Workshop on Transforming Humiliation and Violent Conflict at Columbia University in New York City, with the late Morton Deutsch as our honorary convener since 2003. We have brought people throughout world together to join us for more than 30 conferences since 2003 (HumanDHS, 2019a). Furthermore, individual members of our community have countless books, articles, and projects supporting this effort.

Global Creativity in Counseling

Our work might be thought of as a type of global creativity in counseling in the ways we encourage relational resilience as we turn ideas into action for the benefit of people and the planet. Our creative work challenges us to ask the following questions: How do we as a human species sustainably arrange our affairs on our planet? Will we be able to offer our children a dignified future? Where do we stand? Is it possible to manifest relationships imbued with dignifying mutuality among all people on our planet? Is it feasible to believe that we can cooperate globally to solve our global challenges? Through our work, we counsel the global *Zeitgeist* so to speak, and we affect the global social-cultural climate. Even though individual counseling is not the focus, our members and the participants in our conferences often experience a profound consolidation of their ability to be resilient in facing the world.

The global scope of this work provides a deep sense of meaningfulness to people who feel dejected in the face of saddening news about social and ecological degradation at a global scale, and the experience of meeting people from all continents united in dignifying mutuality nourishes everybody's soul. Michael Britton, HumanDHS member since 2006, wrote on July 18, 2015: "I feel fortunate to have found a home in HumanDHS where the labours of inquiry, honesty, integrity, dignity, trust and trustworthiness, humility are at the heart of who we are and what we do."

Future Directions and Emerging Research

None of us are exempt from the crises and trauma situations that arise in life. Tragedy and wounds to our humanity can strike at a moment's notice, upending our worlds. Resilience is often offered during times of adversity and great loss, yet the pathways to resilience are often unclear. Recognizing our pain; acknowledging our right to grieve; and understanding the systemic, societal, and cultural influences that either support us in our healing or heighten our pain and feelings of humiliation are important variables.

As you work with people living in a world saturated with injustice, we invite you to consider Evelin Lindner's pledge (HumanDHS, 2019b, para. 4):

1. I am committed, to the best of my abilities, to realizing the values enshrined in the first sentence of Article 1 of the Universal Declaration of Human Rights: "All human beings are born free and equal in dignity and rights." Furthermore, the HumanDHS invites us to pledge the following:
2. I am committed, to the best of my abilities, to striving for self-reflection and alliance with like-minded friends to detect where I might be blind to my own shortcomings.
3. I am committed, to the best of my abilities, to encouraging and supporting the dignity of all people, and to counteracting and transforming practices of humiliation at all levels, from personal to systemic levels.

No doubt, crises and traumatic experiences can be catastrophic. However, when we recognize the impact of others on our resilience and our impact on theirs, we are supported in our loss, ultimately increasing our capacity for resilience with and through one another. We (Thelma and Shane) feel deeply privileged to collaborate with our esteemed colleagues and global bridge builders, Linda Hartling and Evelin Lindner, on this chapter. Together, we bring you expanded perspectives on resilience and invite you to partner with us in creating and expanding spaces and places where dignity and resilience thrive.

References

American Psychological Association. (2017a). *Many Americans stressed about future of our nation, new APA Stress in America™ survey reveals* [Press release]. Retrieved from https://www.apa.org/news/press/releases/2017/02/stressed-nation

American Psychological Association. (2017b). *Stress in America: The state of our nation.* Retrieved from https://www.apa.org/news/press/releases/stress/2017/state-nation.pdf

Duffey, T., Haberstroh, S., & Trepal, H. (2016). Creative approaches in counseling and psychotherapy. In D. Capuzzi & M. D. Stauffer (Eds.), *Counseling and psychotherapy: Theories and interventions* (pp. 445–468). Alexandria, VA: American Counseling Association.

Hartling, L. M. (2005). Fostering resilience throughout our lives: New relational possibilities. In D. Comstock (Ed.), *Diversity and development: Critical contexts that shape our lives and relationships* (pp. 337–354). Belmont, CA: Brooks/Cole Cengage Learning.

Hartling, L. M. (2008). Strengthening resilience in a risky world: It's all about relationships. *Women and Therapy, 31*(2–4), 51–70. https://doi.org/10.1080/02703140802145870

Hartling, L. M. (2010, April). *A frame of appreciative enquiry: Beginning a dialogue on human dignity and humiliation.* Paper presented at the 15th Annual Conference of Human Dignity and Humiliation Studies, Istanbul, Turkey.

Hartling, L. M., & Lindner, E. G. (2016). Healing humiliation: From reaction to creative action. *Journal of Counseling & Development, 94,* 383–390. https://doi.org/10.1002/jcad.12096

Hartling, L. M., & Lindner, E. G. (2017). Toward a globally informed psychology of humiliation: Comment on McCauley (2017). *American Psychologist, 72,* 705–706. https://doi.org/10.1037/amp0000188

Human Dignity and Humiliation Studies. (2019a). *Global dignity conferences.* Retrieved from http://www.humiliationstudies.org/whoweare/annualmeetings.php

Human Dignity and Humiliation Studies. (2019b). *A very warm welcome, dear newcomer, to the HumanDHS Network!* Retrieved from http://www.humiliation-studies.org/whoweare/newcomer.php

Jordan, J. V. (2004). Relational resilience. In J. V. Jordan, M. Walker, & L. M. Hartling (Eds.), *The complexity of connection: Writings from the Stone Center's Jean Baker Miller Training Institute* (pp. 29–46). New York, NY: Guilford Press.

Jordan, J. V. (2018). *Relational–cultural therapy* (2nd ed.). Washington, DC: American Psychological Association.

Klein, D. C. (2004, November). *Appreciative psychology: An antidote to humiliation.* Paper presented at the First Workshop on Humiliation and Violent Conflict, Columbia University, New York, NY. Retrieved from http://www.humiliation-studies.org/documents/KleinAppreciativePsychology.pdf

Lindner, E. G. (2006). *Making enemies: Humiliation and international conflict.* Westport, CT: Praeger Security International.

Lindner, E. G. (in press). *From humiliation to dignity: For a future of global solidarity.* Lake Oswego, OR: Dignity University Press.

Miller, J. B. (1983). The necessity of conflict. *Women and Therapy, 2*(2), 3–9. https://doi.org/10.1300/j015v02n2_02

Miller, J. B. (1986). *Toward a new psychology of women* (2nd ed.). Boston, MA: Beacon Press. (Original work published 1976)

Miller, S. M. (2012). *How to dialogue and why* [Online presentation]. Retrieved from https://www.youtube.com/watch?v=COnuz9mubnY

Mothers Against Drunk Driving. (2019). *Saving lives, serving people.* Retrieved from https://www.madd.org/history/

National Aeronautics and Space Administration. (n.d.). *Second law of thermodynamics.* Retrieved from https://www.grc.nasa.gov/WWW/k-12/airplane/thermo2.html

Neff, C. (2003). The development and validation of a scale to measure self-compassion. *Self and Identity, 2,* 223–250. https://doi.org/10.1080/15298860309027

Norgaard, R. B. (2011, January). *Economism and the night sky.* Retrieved from http://www.centerforneweconomics.org/publications/economism-and-night-sky

Sehgal, P. (2015, December). The profound emptiness of 'resilience.' *New York Times.* Retrieved from https://www.nytimes.com/2015/12/06/magazine/the-profound-emptiness-of-resilience.html?

Srivastva, S., & Cooperrider, D. L. (1990). *Appreciative management and leadership: The power of positive thought and action in organizations.* San Francisco, CA: Jossey-Bass.

Tedeschi, R. G., & Calhoun, L. G. (2016). Posttraumatic growth. In H. S. Friedman (Ed.), *Encyclopedia of mental health* (2nd ed., pp. 305–307). Waltham, MA: Academic Press.

van der Kolk, B. (2014). *The body keeps the score: Brain, mind, and body in the healing of trauma.* New York, NY: Viking.

Volk, K. (2014). *Childhood resilience.* Retrieved from https://www.samhsa.gov/homelessness-programs-resources/hpr-resources/childhood-resilience

White Bison, I. (2002). *The red road to wellbriety in the Native American way.* Colorado Springs, CO: White Bison.

Multiple-Choice Questions

1. According to Hartling (2005) and Jordan (2004), some individual traits of resiliency include
   a. Social support and intelligence.
   b. A collectivistic mind-set.
   c. Diagnosis and pathology.
   d. None of the above

2. Using a relational-cultural theory (RCT) viewpoint, resiliency would include
   a. Cognitive dissociation.
   b. Coping skills.
   c. The ability to connect and reconnect after disconnections.
   d. Setting boundaries.

3. What is a vital aspect of relational counseling, like RCT, that fosters healing?
   a. Dogmatism
   b. Individuation
   c. A focus on pathology
   d. Creativity

4. The viewpoint of the individualistic approach to resilience as of "bouncing back" after a crisis can be
   a. An inadequate image and feel unreachable.
   b. The best coping skill.
   c. Unique to the U.S. culture.
   d. None of the above

5. According to Jordan (2018), relational resilience includes
   a. Never developing PTSD.
   b. The ability to never let stressful events bother you.
   c. The ability to move back into connection after disconnection.
   d. The strength to never give up.

6. According to the chapter, which is a global network of people committed to stimulating systemic change and creating a space open for mutual respect?
   a. The Humane Society
   b. The Human Dignity and Humiliation Studies (HumanDHS)
   c. The Peace Corps
   d. The Human Rights Project

7. Which is a course of action of Linda Hartling and the HumanDHS?
   a. Setting strict laws
   b. Recognizing our independence
   c. Decoupling our worth from status
   d. Exerting our power over others when needed

8. Cognitive processing therapy is best delivered by _____ therapists.
   a. New
   b. Regimented
   c. Stoic
   d. Creative

9. Which is an evidence-based suggestion for incorporating creativity into sessions?
   a. Be open to your creativity
   b. Embody metaphors
   c. Meditate
   d. All of the above

10. Tedeschi and Calhoun (2016) discovered that _____ leads to greater appreciation of life.
    a. Posttraumatic growth
    b. Trauma
    c. Family
    d. The workplace

11. Whole body approaches may help integrate sensory and fragmented memories.
    a. True, if the trauma is not too intense
    b. False, because every person only needs cognitive therapy
    c. True
    d. False, integration comes with time only

12. Creativity always leads to positive outcomes that benefit society.
    a. False, it tends to lead to destructive ideas
    b. False, it can sometimes lead to oppression
    c. True, it is always a benefit
    d. True, if the society is financially stable

13. What is one commitment of the Evelyn Lindner's pledge?
    a. Always being on time
    b. Striving for self-reflection
    c. Striving for research on CBT
    d. None of the above

14. It is not correct to be present and connected with someone during their disconnection.
    a. True, because a person needs space
    b. True, because a person has lost all hope
    c. False, if we stay by their side, hopefully reconnection can occur
    d. None of the above

15. People may be _____ if they do not recover fully from a traumatic event.
    a. Weak
    b. Fragile
    c. Resilient
    d. Inadequate

Essay Questions

1. This chapter explores resilience as developing in relation to others. Do you feel your relationships contribute to your resilience? Why or why not?

2. The authors talk about how the U.S. culture values people who can "bounce back" after a traumatic event. What are your thoughts about this viewpoint? Think about your professional and personal life. Have you ever felt pressure to bounce back? How did this mind-set help or hurt you?

3. Think about the case of Cara. What feelings or thoughts did this bring up for you?

4. The chapter explores creativity and divergent thinking. The Department of Child Safety used creative thinking when solving a problem with children having their basic needs. Have you ever used your power or creative thinking to create a policy change?

5. Relational courage is reaching out for help, even when a person feels isolated or altered by a traumatic experience. Can you think of a time you displayed relational courage? Or when a client reached out for help?

ANSWER KEY

Chapter 1

1. a   2. c   3. d   4. a   5. d   6. a   7. c   8. a   9. b
10. a   11. c   12. c   13. b   14. c   15. c

Chapter 2

1. c   2. d   3. b   4. a   5. b   6. a   7. b   8. a   9. c
10. b   11. a   12. b   13. c   14. c   15. b

Chapter 3

1. a   2. d   3. b   4. b   5. b   6. b   7. b   8. a   9. b
10. a   11. b   12. c   13. c   14. b   15. a

Chapter 4

1. b   2. c   3. c   4. a   5. a   6. c   7. b   8. d   9. a
10. b   11. c   12. b   13. b   14. c   15. b

Chapter 5

1. c   2. a   3. d   4. a   5. d   6. b   7. c   8. d   9. a
10. b   11. c   12. d   13. b   14. d   15. a

Chapter 6

1. b   2. d   3. a   4. a   5. b   6. b   7. c   8. d   9. a
10. b   11. c   12. d   13. b   14. d   15. a

Chapter 7

1. b	2. a	3. c	4. d	5. b	6. b	7. c	8. c	9. d
10. a	11. d	12. c	13. a	14. b	15. c			

Chapter 8

1. a	2. c	3. c	4. a	5. d	6. c	7. b	8. a	9. c
10. b	11. c	12. c	13. a	14. d	15. d			

Chapter 9

1. b	2. b	3. b	4. d	5. d	6. b	7. c	8. d	9. a
10. b	11. a	12. d	13. b	14. d	15. d			

Chapter 10

1. a	2. c	3. b	4. c	5. d	6. c	7. d	8. c	9. a
10. d	11. b	12. b	13. a	14. b	15. c			

Chapter 11

1. c	2. a	3. d	4. a	5. d	6. d	7. c	8. d	9. a
10. d	11. c	12. b	13. b	14. d	15. a			

Chapter 12

1. b	2. c	3. a	4. d	5. c	6. c	7. d	8. a	9. c
10. b	11. d	12. a	13. c	14. c	15. c			

Chapter 13

1. d	2. a	3. d	4. a	5. c	6. a	7. a	8. c	9. a
10. d	11. c	12. a	13. b	14. d	15. a			

Chapter 14

1. d	2. d	3. c	4. a	5. c	6. b	7. b	8. d	9. a
10. b	11. a	12. b	13. b	14. a	15. d			

Chapter 15

1. a	2. c	3. d	4. a	5. c	6. b	7. c	8. d	9. d
10. a	11. c	12. b	13. b	14. c	15. c			

INDEX

References to figures and tables are indicated by "f" and "t" following the page numbers.

A

AAS (American Association of Suicidology), 139, 142, 152

Abuse. *See* Violence, abuse, and neglect

ACA Code of Ethics, 11, 279–280

Accelerated response therapy (ART), 15

Acupuncture, 15

Acculturation, 232

Action planning, 103

Active listening, 102–103

Acupuncture, 15

Acute stress disorder (ASD), 115

Addiction. *See* Substance use and addiction

Adolescents, 179. *See also* School counseling

Adverse childhood experiences (ACEs), 117, 167–168, 191, 274

Adverse Childhood Experiences questionnaire, 117

Advocacy
community, 51, 321
culturally centered, 51–52
domestic violence and, 210, 258, 261
grief models and processes, 97
for older adults, 176–177
online, 62
relational resilience and, 315
self-assessment for, 49
suicide prevention and, 12–13, 142, 151, 283

African Americans. *See* Black people

AFSP (American Foundation for Suicide Prevention), 142

Age, effect of crises and, 95–96

Agency, 105, 125, 174

Ainsworth, Mary, 72

Alaskan Natives, 50

Alcohol. *See* Substance use and addiction

Alesch, D. J., 229

Alexander, J., 54

Allen, Misty Vaughan, 107

Alvarado, V. I., 48

Ambiguous losses, 97

American Association of Suicidology (AAS), 139, 142, 152

American Counseling Association (ACA), 34, 283. *See also ACA Code of Ethics*

American Foundation for Suicide Prevention (AFSP), 142

American Indians, 50, 58–59, 142, 315

American Medical Association, 218

American Psychiatric Association, 147, 168

American Psychological Association, 313

American Red Cross, 99–100, 105, 229–230

American School Counselor Association (ASCA), 280

Amygdala, 74–75, 77

Amygdala authenticity, 35

Anderson, M., 62

Animal therapies, 264–265

ANS. *See* Autonomic nervous system

Anti-Bullying and Interpersonal Violence Presidential Initiative 2015–2016, 283

Anticipatory empathy, 9–10, 40, 275

Anticipatory grief, 216

Antidepressants, 122

Antonak, R. F., 198

Arendt, L. A., 229

ART (accelerated response therapy), 15

Art therapy, 119, 130

Asbill, L., 52

ASCA (American School Counselor Association), 280

ASD (acute stress disorder), 115

ASD (autism spectrum disorder), 192–193

Q

R

(Continued)

(Continued)